2016 Crosby Ave, Pittsburgh, PA 15216
(740) 963-9565 // rehumanizeintl.org

Philosophy of the Law of Nations

Philosophy of the Law of Nations

by

Ingrid Detter

D.Phil.(Oxon); Jur.Dr.(Stockholm),
Lic. en Droit (Paris); Dipl. Eur.Law, CHEE (Turin);
sometime Fellow of Lady Margaret Hall and of St. Antony's College Oxford;
Barrister-at-Law of the Middle Temple and Lincoln's Inn;
Adviser on International Law to the Holy See;
Honorary Professor at Åbo Academy in Finland;
Lindhagen Professor Emeritus of International Law in the University of Stockholm.

MONTESA JAGELLONICA
&
ORDO IURIS
2018

*To my five children and
my fifteen grandchildren*

MONTESA JAGELLONICA
&
ORDO IURIS
London, 2018

All rights reserved. No part of this publication may be reproduced, stored in a retrieval system, or transmitted in any form or by any means, electronic, mechanical, photocopying, recording, or otherwise without the prior permission of Montesa Jagellonica & Ordo Iuris Institute.

ISBN 978-1-9998820-4-4 (hardback)
ISBN 978-1-9998820-9-9 (paperback)

© Ingrid Detter de Lupis Frankopan 2018

SIR ROGER VERNON SCRUTON, FBA, FRSL.: Ingrid Detter de Frankopan's study of the Law of Nations and the philosophical principles on which it should be founded is a ground-breaking treatise, covering problems and conceptions that are of the first importance in the world today. We lack a proper definition of the extent of international law, who and what are subject to it, and how to use it both to avoid conflict and to resolve conflict when it comes. Dr Detter's learned survey, and her search for a proper philosophical foundation, will be of great utility both to practitioners and to those who wish to lean on international law in the practice of diplomacy and conflict resolution. The clarity with which she expounds the existing problems and her subtle responses to them will be appreciated by all her readers. Her proposals are often radical, but the air of common-sense pervades the book from start to finish.

PROFESSOR JAMES MAYALL, FBA, Sir Patrick Sheehy Professor Emeritus of International Relations at the University of Cambridge: International lawyers and scholars of International Relations should work closely together but often engage in a dialogue of the deaf based on mutual incomprehension. The distinguished international lawyer, Ingrid Detter has written a marvellous book challenging the conventional understanding of international law as stemming from what she calls 'the nebulous flow of behaviour and custom'; and implicitly also the tendency of International Relations scholars to focus solely on power politics, ignoring the intrinsic rules that allow international society both to accommodate change and survive. It deserves to be read by all those with a serious interest in the future of mankind and the international order we have created.

PROFESSOR STIG STRÖMHOLM, Professor Emeritus of Private International Law and Jurisprudence, and former *Rector Magnificus* of Uppsala University: Ingrid Detter Doimi de Lupis Frankopan is not only a learned and experienced member of the community of international law experts. She is also a prolific writer on broad areas of that increasingly important field of law. In this book, she develops an independent and critical view of both traditional ideas and modern trends of development in international law. She insists eloquently on the fundamental importance of intrinsic rules and on the clear consent of relevant actors to international rules in the making. She opposes the traditional belief in the vague creation of an equally vague customary law. It is well worth listening to her arguments.'

Table of Contents

Abbreviations	15
Acknowledgments	17
Preface	19

PART ONE:
THE SCENARIO OF INTERNATIONAL SOCIETY

I. The Core Problem of International Law	27
i. Competing Assertions	27
a) The 'Monists' *versus* the 'Dualists'	27
b) The School of New Haven *versus* the 'Normativists'	29
c) The 'Positivists' *versus* the 'Naturalists'	34
1. Natural Law	35
2. Positivism	42
ii. A New Theory	53
a) Law as a Framework	53
b) The 'Hypothetical Goal'	54
c) The Intrinsic Law	55
1. Essential Maxims and General Principles	57
2. The Reserved Domain and Prohibition of Harm	57

3. The Rule of Reciprocity	62
d) A Great Number of Subjects	66
e) Formation of Rules	70
1. Dominance of Anglo-Saxon Ideas on Judge-Made Law	71
2. Identification of Relevant Law	73
f) *Interactivism*	76
iii. The Drift Away from the Exclusive State Paradigm	77
a) A General Trend	77
b) International Legal Personality	77
c) International Personality and Imputation	79
d) Entitled Persons	80
1. States	81
2. Inter-Governmental Organisations	86
3. Non-governmental Organisations	87
4. Nations	91
5. Social 'Classes'	98
6. Minorities	101
7. Majorities	102
8. Liberation Movements	103
9. International Orders	105
10. Institutes and Universities	107
11. National Public Bodies	108
12. National Private Bodies	109
13. International Companies	112
14. Multinationals	114
15. Joint Ventures	121
16. Private Companies	123
17. Individuals	125
18. Belligerents and Insurgents	133

19. Terrorists and Pirates	134
iv. A Society or a Community?	135
v. The Existence of a Legal System	136
vi. A Primitive Law?	137
vii. Universality of the System	138
viii. The Fallacy of the Subjectivity Test	141
a) The Criteria of a National Law	142
b) The Criteria of International Law	143
II. Methods of Classifying International Rules	145
i. The Notion of 'Regimes'	145
ii. The Sources of International Law	148
a) Ambiguities of Meaning for a 'Source' of Law	149
b) Systematic Induction	151

PART TWO:
CLASSIFICATION OF RULES

A. The Doctrine of International Relevance and Comity	153
i. The Questionable Division of Law into Public and Private Law	153
ii. One Legal System: Public and Private International Law	155
iii. International Rules and the Internal Law Systems of States	165
a) The Effect of International Law Inside States	165
b) The Adoption of National Rules in the International Legal Order	169
iv. The Notion of Comity	170
a) The Importance and Definition of Comity	170
b) Comity, Sovereignty and Jurisdictional Issues	172

c) Comity, Acts of State and Public Policy	175
d) Comity as a Link Between Public and Private International Law	177
B. Intrinsic Rules	180
i. 'Rules', 'Principles', 'Norms' and 'Decisions'	182
ii. Diversity of Material Rules According to Their Function	183
iii. Protection of the Hypothetical Goal	184
I. Inherent Maxims	185
i. Initial Maxims	185
ii. Conditional Maxims	187
iii. Contingent Maxims	188
iv. Stabilising Maxims	189
v. Consequential Maxims	190
vi. The Origin of Compulsory Maxims	195
II. General Principles	196
i. The Nature of General Principles	196
ii. Maxims and General Principles	200
iii. Substantive General Principles?	201
iv. Compulsory Formal General Principles	202
III. Prophylactic Rules	210
i. Ethics and Intrinsic Law	212
ii. Compulsory Rules: *jus cogens*	224
iii. Prohibition of Harm to Groups: Use of Force	234
iv. Prohibition of Harm to the Environment	239
a) Use of Resources, Climate Change and Pollution	239
1. Use of Resources	239
2. Climate Change	241
3. Pollution	241

b) Prophylactic Rules for Threats to the Environment: Duty to Warn	244
v. Prohibition of Harm to Individuals	245
a) Human Rights	245
b) Humanitarian Rules	249
c) Protection of Aliens	249
d) Protection of Diplomats: Rules on Immunity	250
IV. Effect of Violation of Intrinsic Rules	251
C. Extrinsic Rules	253
I. Stabilising Rules	253
i. Distributive Rules	254
a) Allocation of National Space	254
1. General Divisional Rules	254
2. The Notion of Prescription	256
b) Jurisdiction and Nationality	257
c) Sovereignty and Democracy	258
ii. Rules on Mutual Contacts	259
a) Objective Regimes	260
b) Communications: Right of Transit, Duty to Warn and Right of Contact	262
c) Formal Rules on Treaties	265
II. Supplementing Rules	266
i. Promotional Rules	266
a) Duty to Cooperate?	266
b) Duty to Share?	267
c) Programmatic Rules	270
ii. Unifying Rules	271
a) Integration	271
b) Institutionalisation of Functions	272

	c) Further Regimes	274
	d) Law Making Rules, Recommendations, Standards and Pre-Standards	275
iii.	Substantive Rules for All Contacts: *lex mercatoria*	277
	a) 'Filling in' Rules	280
	b) The Quest for a *lex mercatoria*	285

III. Consequential Rules — 288
  i. Correctional Rules — 289
    a) Sanctions — 289
      1. General Nature — 289
      2. The Two-Fold Nature of Sanctions — 291
      3. The Subjects and Objects of Sanctions — 291
      4. Sanctions and the Use of Force — 292
    b) Institutionalised Correction — 293
  ii. Settlement Rules — 294
    a) Institutional Judicial Rules — 295
    b) Rules on Penalties — 296

PART THREE:
OPERATION OF RULES

I. Theory of Acts — 297
  i. The Notion of a 'Legal Act' — 297
  ii. The Doctrine of Legal Relevance — 299
  iii. Graduated Scale of Presumption of Consent — 304

II. Typology of Acts — 305
A. Types According to Substance — 306
  i. Types According to the Envisaged Goal — 306
    a) Structural Acts — 306
    b) Operative Acts — 307

ii. Types According to Immediacy	307
a) Programmatic Declarations for Later Action	307
b) Responsive Acts	308
iii. Types According to Normativity	310
a) Individual Acts	310
b) General Acts	310
c) Exhortations	311
d) Programmatic Declarations for Vague Action	311
B. Types According to Mode of Consent	312
i. Types According to Degree of Participation	312
a) Basic Participation	312
1. Passive Participation	312
2. Active Participation	313
b) Enhanced Participation	314
ii. Types According to Degree of State Control	314
a) Permissive Acts	314
b) Acts of Delegation	315
iii. Types According To Form of Expressed Consent: Statement Acts	315
a) Contractual Acts	316
b) Promissory Acts	317
c) Parallel Acts	321
d) Acts of Adoption	323
e) Acts of Recognition	324
f) Authoritative Acts	324
C. Types According to Form	326
i. Types According to the Number of Authors	326
a) Unilateral Acts	326
b) Bilateral Acts	328
c) Multilateral Acts	329

ii. Types According to Solemnity	329
a) Functional Acts	330
b) Verbal Acts	330
c) Written Acts	330
d) Elaborate Acts	331
iii. Types According to Durability	331
a) Framework Acts	331
b) Transient Acts	332
iv. Types According to Frequency	332
a) Extraordinary Acts	332
b) Current Acts	333
III. The Mechanisms of *Interactivism*	333
IV. Another Way of Making Rules: Customary Law	334
i. The Traditional Definition of Customary Law	334
ii. Emerging Dissatisfaction with Traditional Customary Law	335
iii. The Absurd Views of Customary Law	340
a) Whose 'General Practice'?	340
1. Practice of *All* States?	342
2. Only Practice of *'Civilised States'*?	343
3. Practice of 'Numerous States'?	345
b) Also Negative Practice?	346
c) Practice for a 'Long Time'?	347
d) Whose *opinio juris*?	348
iv. The Fallacies of 'Customary' Law	349
v. 'True' Customary Law	354
a) A Territorial or Maritime Bond	355
b) Regional Rules	356
c) Diplomatic Rules	356
d) The Law of War	357

vi. The 'Allergy' to Natural Law	358
vii. The Correct Concept of Intrinsic Law	363
V. Assessment of the Legal Effect of Acts	366
i. Intersecting Patterns	366
ii. 'Actors', 'Persons' and 'Creators'	368
iii. A Model of Formation of Rules	369
iv. The Need for Accurate Terminology	372
VI. The Obligation of Activated Rules	373
i. Activation of Rules	373
a) Intrinsic Rules	374
b) Rules Triggered by Acts	374
ii. Traditional Solution of the Obligation	374
iii. A New Theory of Obligation	376
a) Variability of the Basis of Obligation	376
1. Logical Necessity	377
2. Social Necessity	377
3. Consent	378
4. Reciprocity	379
5. Solidarity Rules	380
b) Consequences of Violation of the Most Basic Intrinsic Rules	383
Conclusions	387
Selective Bibliography	399
Index	455

Abbreviations

AFDI	*Annuaire français de droit international*
AJIL	*American Journal of International Law*
ASIL	American Society of International Law
ASDI/SJIR	*Annuaire suisse de droit international/ Schweizerisches Jahrbuch für internationales Recht*
AVR	*Archiv des Völkerrechts*
BYIL	*British Yearbook of International Law*
CLJ	*Cambridge Law Journal*
ColLR	*Columbia Law Review*
GYIL	*German Yearbook of International Law*
ICJ	International Court of Justice
ICLQ	*International and Comparative Law Quarterly*
ILC	International Law Commission
ILR	*International Law Reports*
ITU	International Telecommunications Union
JDI	*Journal du droit international*
JIR	*Jahrbuch für internationales Recht*
LNTS	*League of Nations Treaty Series*
LQR	*Law Quarterly Review*
MLR	*Modern Law Review*
NedTIR	*Nederlands Tijdschrift voor Internationales Recht*
NordTIR	*Nordisk Tidskrift for International Ret*
PCIJ	Permanent Court of International Justice
RCADI	*Recueil des Cours de l'Académie de droit international de la Haye*
RDI	*Revue de droit international*
RDILC	*Revue de droit international et du droit comparé*
REDI	*Revista espagnola de derecho internacional*
RGDIP	*Revue générale de droit international public*
RBDI	*Revue belge de droit international*
RivDI	*Rivista di diritto internazionale*
SFDI	Société française pour le droit international
TIAS	United States Treaties and Other International Acts
UNTS	*United Nations Treaty Series*
UPU	Universal Postal Union
ZaöRVR	*Zeitschrift für ausländisches öffentliches Recht und Völkerrecht*
ZVR	*Zeitschrift für Völkerrecht*

Acknowledgments

On a page for acknowledgments, writers normally thank their research assistants and/or their long suffering spouse and others who have assisted in the production of their work.

I have not had any assistants for this work, so no one but me can be blamed for what I say and how I say it.

So whom do I thank? Even if I struggled alone without assistants working out my theories in my ivory tower, I could not have done this work without the inspiration given to me by my five children, Paola, Peter, Christina, Nicholas and Lawrence. Therefore, I dedicate this book to them, and to my – so far – fifteen grandchildren, who represent my best legacy.

St. Antony's College, Oxford,
Easter Sunday,
1st April 2018

Ingrid Detter Doimi de Lupis Frankopan

Preface

This work, in a sense, represents my *opus vitae*: this work is certainly my most ambitious venture. It is the result of my inability to accept what I was taught about *rules* in all the Universities I attended. Rules are obviously essential in any society. Still, the rules I heard about did not seem to emerge in the way my professors taught. My colleagues happily accepted what was presented as solid theories and practice. But I did not.

Since I was a student I have been suspicious about what I was taught in international law. States and others did not seem to behave at all as they were supposed to according to the textbooks. Few of my professors ever spoke about the self-interest of States, about *Staatsraison* or about and other notions more familiar to scholars of international relations. On the other hand, I did not quite approve of the 'IR terminology' either as, to them, a recurrent adjective appears to be 'realist', a word that I often associate with imminent death or generally bad news.

For many years I tried to work out a new theory that would be compatible with how actors in international society actually behave. I have tried to construct a viable theory that would be acceptable to international lawyers, to international relations scholars, to courts, to arbitration tribunals and to statesmen.

It has been of particular importance to find common ground with international relations scholars and suggest a theory that would also be acceptable to that discipline. Those who study international relations often seem to be a step ahead of international lawyers who still do not seem to have noticed that there are other important actors than States.

In this work a new theory of international law is presented as an alternative to views which have been perpetuated in textbook after textbook but which lack foundation in reality. In particular, the notion of 'customary law' is dismissed, at least in its traditional form, as a nebulous fiction: it is suggested that the notion is often used to denote any general rules of international law that have their origin in other sources than 'custom', often in what we call in this work, '*intrinsic law*'.

The substantial contents of norms called 'customary rules' does exist in international society but these rules have a completely different origin, different nature and a different function from that normally ascribed to them in traditional textbooks.

The new theory of this work may be called *interactivism*: it seeks to explain how rules emerge in international society by the mechanisms of intersecting legal acts.

Identifiable 'legal acts' by States and by numerous other 'actors' and 'subjects' on the international scene operate, in conjunction with what can be called 'norm-pools' from where rules are fetched for specific situations. The 'legal acts' thus 'activate' various rules that are latently pre-existing in 'norm-pools', a 'latent' or 'dormant' complex set of numerous prescriptions.

Virtually all traditional textbooks claim that *only* States and inter-governmental organisations are endowed with 'international personality', that is to say, most writers on international law suggest that only these bodies have the right to *directly assume rights and obligations under the international legal system*. This is not correct. An analysis of practice in international society shows that there are numerous actors apart from States and inter-governmental organisations that also have direct rights and duties under international law. Those who are endowed with 'international personality', and enjoy the capacity to assume direct rights and obligations under the international legal system are thus not only States and inter-governmental organisations but a host of innumerable subjects, entities and individuals.

Practice and behaviour on the international scene readily confirm that war criminals and terrorists also have 'international personality' – how else would we be able to try them in international courts? It is clear that they have *direct obligations* under the international legal system. Conversely, how can we claim that the victims of genocide have human rights unless they have these *direct rights* under the international legal system? Indeed, we can observe that, in practice in international society, individuals are often endowed with 'international personality'.

Multinationals and research institutes, towns and private organisations can also assume direct duties and enjoy specific rights under international law. Let us only mention the Red Cross, a *non-governmental organisation*, and its rights and duties in war situations. Or let us refer to INMARSAT, an inter-governmental, organisation, founded by an inter-State Treaty, but that was *privatised*: does that mean that *it did have* international rights and duties and full international personality and the following week that was all gone?

It is also clear that numerous direct rights and duties are enjoyed by individuals and by numerous entities, irrespective of international treaties and conventions and irrespective of any authorisation by States. Furthermore, some direct rights and obligations emerge without any anterior 'custom' or previous practice: the international system often expands with new rules in a dynamic way to cater for new needs.

It seems that writers, statesmen and students have too long accepted what traditional textbooks say, although the practice of States and Courts do not confirm these traditional views. New ideas of the nature of the law of nations are long overdue.

My theories in this field have attracted considerable attention, in the United States, in communist and post-communist countries. It seemed that I had achieved my task of presenting a theory which was acceptable to different political systems. I was invited to lecture on my new theory at Åbo Academy in Finland, at the London School of Economics, at University College London and at the Institute for Law and State in Moscow as well as at the Academy of Science in Beijing and to the Institutes for International Law in Nanjing and Shanghai.

I do not think that the bulk of rules of international law emerge though custom in the way the traditional textbooks pretend. I do not think that States and other subjects of international law consciously 'adopt' or 'approve' every rule in the international legal system. Nor do I think that the only subjects entitled to assume rights and obligations under the international legal system are States and inter-governmental organisations.

I have sought to observe how States and other actors actually behave in practice rather than accept the sterile theories of the current textbooks that do not take into account '*real*' practice and '*real*' behaviour of international actors. States even behave, at times, to present themselves as 'generous' to developing countries, 'courageous', 'strong' and 'reliable' to military allies, '*avant-garde*' and 'responsible', to environmentalists.

Some such behaviour is due to human nature. But international lawyers should not impute legal 'customary' rules from such actions, even if repeated over and over again, over a long time. On the whole, behaviour of States form but a small part of international law; and most of that conduct is only relevant if States *wish* and *intend* to assume new or further obligations. The bulk of international law is already 'there', in the form of *intrinsic* law, as we will explain in this work. The 'rest' of rules are predominantly forged by pressure of individuals, the main subjects and bearers of rights and duties in international society, when individuals perceive new social needs for new rules.

It is not true that governments consider how may other States follow a rule before they act: States and other subjects *know* beforehand, thus *a* priori, what is *right or wrong* in international society. All subjects are somewhat influenced by self-interest, and certainly by the impact their actions will have on the behaviour of others.

In the case of States there will also be certain attention to the danger of giving up a position that could lead to others assuming that no defence will be put up against in a similar situation: not to defend the territorial interests of the United Kingdom in the Falklands Islands might lead to a loss of Gibraltar. Thus, the consideration of a *projection of ensuing consequences* is relevant to actual and political decisions by States and also by other subjects of international society.

This work sets out to examine and analyse how subjects of the international legal order actually behave in reality. The focus will be on the behaviour of States, entities and individuals to see how rules are brought into being to control the behaviour of the various subjects. It will also attempt to demonstrate why certain rules gain immediate force and validity and become respected in international society.

In this way it becomes possible to deduce certain principles to suggest a new *optique* for analysis of international rules. By observing and analysing factual political and judicial behaviour patterns this book may be useful not only to international lawyers but to scholars of international relations and to statesmen.

My new theory relies on three fundamental ideas:

1. In the first place, this theory assumes that numerous 'principles' and 'rules' are '*intrinsic*' or '*inherent*' in the international legal system and operate without 'authorisation', 'custom' or 'acceptance', as prescriptions that constitute basic rules without which the international system cannot function. I suggest that numerous further rules enter into effect by *specific acts* that *mobilise or activate* more or less *latent rules* in a vast '*norm-pools*' to enter into effect for general or specific application.

Numerous *intrinsic rules* are *formal maxims* that automatically enter into function in the international legal system and without which no legal order can function.

Other *intrinsic rules* are not merely formal but have compelling contents. The most important *substantive* rules of the *intrinsic law* is the rule on *prohibition of harm*. This rule operates to prohibit harm to all other subjects of the international legal order and is binding on all subjects in international society. An intrinsic rule that prevents harm is, in this sense, what we call, in this work, a *prophylactic rule*. This fundamental rule, the *prophylactic rule* that prohibits harm, operates in international society in conjunction with and the Rule of Reciprocity, sometimes called with *The Golden Rule*, that is to say the rule that one should treat others as one prefers to be treated oneself, thus the forceful and basic rule of reciprocity.

Together, the essential formal maxims, the formal general principles and the material *prophylactic rules*, form an operating network of *intrinsic law* in international society.

2. Secondly, I suggest that the 'subjects' of international law are innumerable: it is not only States and inter-governmental organisations that may assume rights and that have obligations under international law, but individuals and other entities may also have direct rights and duties under the international legal system. But, again, this 'personality' is only activated when these entities take acts that are internationally *relevant*. That means that, for example, the personality of individuals and of other private bodies is *latent* or *dormant* since most acts of individuals have only national relevance. On the other hand, most acts of a State are *presumed* to be relevant on the international scene.

3. In the third place, this new theory presupposes *a hypothetical goal* for international society, *a postulate of finality that is the survival of mankind*. Rules of international law strive to secure this survival. Every rule of international law must also be interpreted in the light of this *hypothetical goal* of international society. This

postulated objective of international relations and of international law implies that most rules of international law will, above all, purport to *eliminate or prevent harm* to other subjects of the international system or to the environment. Respecting the rules of *intrinsic* law will ensure and protect the *hypothetical goal*.

In this work, I suggest a novel approach to understand how rules emerge in international society and how these rules function to promote this *hypothetical goal*.

St. Antony's College, Oxford,
Easter Sunday,
1st April 2018

Ingrid Detter Doimi de Lupis Frankopan

PART ONE:
THE SCENARIO OF INTERNATIONAL SOCIETY

I. The Core Problem of International Law

i. Competing Assertions

a) The 'Monists' *versus* the 'Dualists'

The traditional dispute between international lawyers used to concern the merits or the 'monist'[1] or the

---

[1] Monists claim that international law and municipal law form part of the same legal system, normally with prevalence of international law, see, Kelsen, H., *Das Problem der Souveränität und die Theorie des Völkerrechts*, Berlin: Mohr Siebeck, 1928; *idem*, *Reine Rechtslehre*, Berlin: Mohr Siebeck, 1934 and 2008; *idem*, *General Theory of Law and State*, Cambridge Mass.: Harvard University Press, 1945, 363 *et seq.*; *idem*, 'Les rapports de système entre le droit interne et le droit international', 14 *RCADI* 1926 iv 227; *idem*, 'La transformation du droit international en droit interne', 43 *RGDIP* 1936 5; Verdross, A.v., *Die Einheit des rechtlichen Weltbildes und Grundlage der Völkerrechtsverfassung*, Tübingen: J. C. B. Mohr, 1923; *idem*, 'Zur Konstruktion des Völkerrechts', 8 *ZVR* 1914 329; *idem*, *Die völkerrechtliche Kriegshandlung und der Strafanspruch der Staaten*, Berlin: H.R. Engelmann, 1920; *idem*, 'Droit international et droit interne', *RDI*, 1954, 219; *idem*, *Abendländisches Rechtsphilosophie*, Vienne: Springer, 1963; *idem* and Simma, B., *Universelles Völkerrecht*, Vienne: Springer, 1974 and 2010; Kunz, J., 'La primauté du droit des gens', 52 *RDILC*, 1925 556; *idem*, 'Völkerrecht und der Diplomatie', in Strupp, K., (ed.), 1 *Wörterbuch des Völkerrechts*, Berlin, Leipzig:

'dualist'² approach, *i.e.* whether international and municipal law are one or two legal 'systems'. But, in any event, international law was assumed to be a body of normative rules.

Among those who still look upon international law as a normative system³ there is nowadays little discussion whether

---

W. de Gruyter & Co, 1924, 1 787; *idem*, *Changing Law of Nations*, Columbus: Ohio University Press, 1968; Lauterpacht, H., 'Is international law part of the law of England?', 25 *Transactions of the Grotius Society*, 1940, 51; Scelle, G., *Droit international public*, Paris: Domat-Montchrestien, 1948, *passim*. On the rarer form of monism with prevalence of national law, see Jellinek, G., *System der subjektive öffentlichen Rechte*, Tübingen: Mohr P. Siebeck, 1905; *idem*, *Die rechtliche Natur der Staatenverträge*, Vienna: Hölder, 1880.

² Dualists regard the international legal system and municipal law as conceptually and functionally distinct, see, Triepel, H., *Völkerrecht und Landesrecht*, Leipzig: C.L. Hirschfeld, 1899; *idem*, 'Les rapports entre le droit interne et le droit international', *RCADI* 1923 77; v Liszt, F., *Völkerrecht*, 11ᵗʰ ed., Vienna: Springer, 1918; Walz, G.A., *Völkerrecht und Staatliches Recht*, Stuttgart: Kohlhammer, 1933; *idem*, 'Les rapports du droit international et du droit interne', 61 *RCADI* 1937 iii 375; Anzilotti, D., *Il diritto internazionale nei giudizi interni*, Bologna: Ditta N. Zanichelli, 1905; Cavaglieri, A., *Lezioni di diritto internazionale*, 3ʳᵈ ed., Naples: G. Maio, 1924; Quadri, R., *Diritto internazionale pubblico*, Palermo: Priulla, 1960; Balladori Pallieri, G., *Diritto internazionale pubblico*, 8ᵗʰ ed., Milan: Giuffrè, 1962; Ross, A., *Theorie der Rechtsquellen*, Leipzig & Vienna: Franz Deuticke, 1929; Drost, H., *Grundlagen des Völkerrechts*, Munich & Leipzig: Duncker & Humblot, 1936; the dualist theory was also adopted as the Soviet view, much influenced by exaggerated importance attached to the notion of sovereignty, see Krylov, S., 'Les notions principales du droit des gens', 70 *RCADI*, 1947, i 445 and my *Concept of International Law*, 1ˢᵗ ed., Stockholm: Norstedts, 1992, Ch. 2, on 'classes' as subjects of international law and *infra*, in this Part, ii 7.

³ We refer here to a 'normative system', meaning a stable framework for future action and not in the sense that Hans Kelsen uses the term 'normativism' implying a pyramidical system of rules, ranged according to their hierarchy above a 'base' rule, the '*Grundnorm*', see, Kelsen, H., *Reine Rechtslehre*, Leipzig & Vienna: J. Springer, 1934 & and his other works cited in note 48 and in this section i c) 2. Even authors who adhere to the New Haven School use the term 'normative but

the monist or dualist approach is of greater merit. Textbooks set out discussions and arguments only as part of the historical development of international law.

b) The School of New Haven *versus* the 'Normativists'

It may be useful to reserve the term 'normativists' for those who claim that international law is a set of rules among States (and perhaps, inter-governmental organisations).

An international legal system does exist, according to the traditionalists of the normative school, but its frontiers are extremely hazy as is also its archaic contents and field of application. The claim that international law is a system between States and inter-governmental organisations is difficult to uphold as persistent questions recur concerning situations involving other actors where international law appears to apply. There is an increasing number of paradoxes in the traditional normativist theories, that claim that States (and inter-governmental organisations) are the only 'subjects' (*i.e.* that can have rights and duties) in the legal system. This claim cannot be reconciled with the advent of liberation movements, multinationals and other actors in international society.

On the other hand, not everyone agrees today that international law is a 'normative' system. The 'normativists – as we can call them – find themselves increasingly opposed by those who adopt the 'social process theories'.

---

not in the sense of a stable framework but as part of the 'continuous process' of law production. Note that Bos, in his *Methodology of International Law*, Amsterdam: North Holland, 1984, uses a narrow 'normative concept' related to a larger notion of 'general concept of law'.

Some writers, especially in the United States, prefer, as a result, to consider that international law is not a set of rules at all but rather a 'process', or a 'tool for political action', where 'perspectives and goals' and 'expectations' play a prominent part.[4] Thus, some say that,

> 'International law will be explicitly conceived as a comprehensive process of authoritative decision, transcending the boundaries of particular territorial communities, which the peoples of the world establish and maintain for the purpose of clarifying and implementing their common interests'.[5]

This view is often referred to as the *social process theory*, or the *New Haven School*. Their adherents state that:

> 'the New Haven School of jurisprudence is an entirely secular theory of law but it takes the perspective long associated with natural law, that of the decision maker. For New Haven, the notion of decision extends across the range of social organisation and throughout the hierarchy of power; it includes the making of law or legislation as well as its application through courts or other institutions, and it conceives of both these activities as operating at the constitutive or structural level and in all of the various value processes of a community, including the

---

[4] Some of this terminology and language is now to be found in some judgments in the United States: Thus, it is said that the cross-border movement of legal rights and judgments depends largely upon a 'spirit of co-operation' among States, which in the end is guided by 'many values' beyond substantive justice, 'among them predictability, . . . ease of commercial interactions, and *stability through satisfaction of mutual expectations.*' (emphasis added), see *Société Nationale Industrielle Aérospatiale v United States Dist.*, 482 U.S. 522, 543 n.27 (1987).

[5] Reisman, W.M., 'The view from the New Haven School of international law', 86 *American Society of International Law Proceedings* 118 (1992).

> production of wealth, of enlightenment, of skill, of health and well-being, of affection, of respect and rectitude.'[6]

This language is not easily understood by lawyers from civil law systems or even by those who have knowledge of jurisprudence as taught in England. Its claim to be linked to 'natural law' does not seem warranted, at least as 'natural law' is understood in civil law countries, or, indeed, in English law.

According to the theory of the New Haven School, the actors in international society are innumerable, from States to pressure groups and individuals, and emphasis is placed on the claim that the *law* is itself a *process*; however, the question of legal personality is largely avoided as is the question of the need for stability and the need of foreseeability of rules of a legal system.[7]

The main rift between the New Haven school and what we might call the '*normativists*', is that the normativists claim that the legal system is stable with a high element of foreseeability whereas the New Haven adherents assume that law is a 'process' and in ever on-going development. Another main difference is that the New Haven adherents assume that law in all countries is made by 'decision makers', essentially by judges but also by a myriad of 'decision makers' that 'participate' in a law making process. But

---

[6] *Idem*, Abstract, *Faculty Scholarship Series*, 1992, Paper 867, http://digital.commons.law.yale.edu/fss_papers/867.

[7] McDougal, M.S., Laswell, H.D., & Reisman, W.M.,'Theories about international law: 'Prologue to a configurative jurisprudence', *Virginia Law Journal*, 1967, 202; Cf. McDougal and Reisman, *International Law in Contemporary Perspective, The Public Order of the World Community*, 1981, 7; for earlier ideas that law is 'what lawyers do in law jobs' Llewellyn, K.N., 'The normative, the legal and the law jobs, The problem of juristic method', *YLJ*, 1940, 1355.

this is not so in most other legal systems. In the United States, England and in other systems that follow the Anglo-Saxon model, the judge exercises an important law making function.[8] This role is strengthened by a tradition of binding precedents in that thus lower courts and judges in subsequent cases are bound to respect such 'leading' judgments.

However, this is not at all the case in civil law countries. There, the judge merely 'applies' the law that comes from elsewhere, from the 'legislature', *i.e.* the law making authorities, the government in conjunction with the Parliament or other 'Assembly', representing the citizens. In discussions between adherents of the New Haven school it becomes apparent that it is almost questionable whether the adherents of the 'social process' theory are aware of this basic divide.

The rivalry between the two present main schools of international law, the 'normativist school' according to which law is a stable and fixed normative set of rules, and the 'social process school' or variations thereof, that regard the law as being in a constant flux, has resulted in numerous studies mutually critical of the opposing side's approach.[9] However, discussions have not been fruitful. They have not resulted in any clear consolidation of previous standpoints, at least not on the normativist side.[10] It is almost as if the two sides proceeded in isolation from each

---

[8] See, *infra*, in this Part, I ii e) 1, Dominance of Anglo-Saxon Ideas on Judge-Made Law.

[9] See, McDougal & Al., 'Theories', *op. cit.; cf.* Schachter, O., 'Towards a theory of international obligation', 8 *Virginia Law Journal*, 1968, 300; Fitzmaurice, G., 'Foundations of authority of international law', 19 *MLR*, 1956; Allott, P. 'Language, method and the nature of international law', *BYIL*, 1971 79.

[10] With the notable exception of the innovating views of Bos, *op. cit. supra.*

other, both entrenching their positions, rather than analysing the merits, similarities or advantages and disadvantages of the views from opposing sides. As a result, there has been a great deal of confusion among many international lawyers unwilling to take sides, unconvinced of the merits of either theory.

There are clear problems with the 'social process' theory at least for those who work in the civil law system where law is made by a legislature and not by judges. Legal *foreseeability* is part of the essence of law in the civil law systems as it is held indispensable to know *beforehand* the consequences of one's actions, both in criminal and civil law situations. Another essential principle in the civil law systems is the general and *absolute prohibition of retrospective legislation*, a matter where Anglo-Saxon attitudes are more relaxed.

Most normativists retain many of the traditional standpoints. The position is now that the social process school provides little guidance on the normative value of the international legal system; and the normativists, because of their uncertainty about their legal persons and nature of their system, provide few guidelines on non-State behaviour. The social process school now appears to lack normativity and the normative school to lack universality.[11]

There may be hopes, as in other disciplines[12] that, from the present welter of competing terminologies, there will eventually emerge a common language. However, at present there is some uncertainty as to the present state of international law and it has

---

[11] *Cf.* O'Connell, *op. cit., loc. cit.*

[12] See, for example, Bull, H., 'The case for a classical approach', in Knorr, K. and Rosenau, J.N., (eds.), *Contending Approaches to International Politics*, Princeton: Princeton University Press, 1969.

become increasingly noticed that the theory itself of international law is in a state of anarchy.[13]

We claim, in this work, that international law is a *normative set of rules between States and numerous other subjects of international law*. It might be useful to do what we try to achieve in this work: to provide suggestions for an entirely new theory of international law, a theory founded on how States and other actors actually behave in the world, rather than on how they should act according to out-dated textbooks.

c) The 'Positivists' *versus* the 'Naturalists'

Neither the contemporary normative theorists nor the adherents of the 'social process' school explain in any satisfactory manner how rules emerge, develop and function in international society. Adherents of both schools have problems referring to *natural law*, a concept so long treated with contempt although it remains an essential part of the international legal system. The New Haven school insists that they its adherents 'takes the perspective long associated with natural law', but there is little sign of the modalities of that in their various writings. They also attach the 'perspective' of which they speak to 'the decision maker', which obscures the link they claim with 'natural law' as this link is rarely further explained. The normativist school largely disregard natural law and rejects it, often assuming its essence to be some expression of religious fanaticism.

---

[13] O'Connell, D., 'The role of international law', in Hoffman, S., (ed.), *Conditions of World Order*, Boston: Houghton & Mifflin, 1968, 52.

What is clear with regard to virtually all contemporary lawyers is that the vast majority wildly exaggerate the importance of customary law. Yet, the term *'customary law'* has often become a *euphemism of 'natural law'*. But it has become politically more correct to speak of 'customary rules' – however nebulous – than about 'natural law.'

1. Natural Law

Discussions about natural law go back to Antiquity.[14] Antigone, in Sophocles' tragedy, knows she has to bury her brother whatever the laws of the State say: it is her innate feeling that this is the 'right' thing to do.[15] Which law is greater: the one of the gods or the one made by men? The conflict between natural instincts as to what is honourable and important and the forbidding laws and rules issued by authorities, becomes a veritable dilemma. This dichotomy is still the focus of numerous works by legal philosophers.

Plato speaks of a *demiurge*, an organising god, external to the world, who, according to a preconceived plan, creates the world and organisms. At the basis of this orderly universe or nature are the forms, most fundamentally the Form of Good which Plato describes as 'the brightest region of Being'. The Form of the Good is the cause of all things and when it is seen it leads a person to act wisely.[16] Plato's demiurge is external to the world and his views

---

[14] But see below, in this section, on even earlier thoughts on natural of, for example, the philosophy of Confucius.

[15] Alford, C.F., 'Antigone and the natural law', in *idem, Psychology and the Natural Law of Reparation*, Univ. of Maryland: CUP, 2011, 1.

[16] Plato, *The Republic*, 540a, 517b–d. *idem, Timeus*, 118, 29d; 124, 35a-d, 145, 48b. For teleologic interpretation of Timeus, see, Lloyd, G.E.R., 'Plato as a natural scientist', in 88 *Journal of Hellenic Studies*, 1968, 78.

reflect thus an extrinsic teleological vision. Plato speaks of the need to work towards the Good with mathematical order *and* with the perspective of the intervention of a *telos*, (Τέλος), a 'purpose' or a 'goal'.¹⁷ Natural law is conducive to such a purpose.

Aristotle adheres to ideas of natural law and also speaks of a *telos*, (Τέλος) a 'purpose' or a 'goal' of mankind. In his philosophy, the *telos* is a principle of intrinsic development, internal to all living beings. To Aristotle the *final cause* or the *final goal* is one of the four 'causes' that give rise to matters.¹⁸

The Romans adopted most of what the Greek philosophers had taught and incorporated the rules of natural law in their legal system. State law is *jus civile* whereas 'the law that natural reason establishes among all mankind is followed by all peoples alike, and is called *ius gentium* as being the law observed by all mankind.'¹⁹

---

17 Lloyd, G.E.R., 'Plato on mathematics and nature, myth and science', in *Methods and Problems in Greek Science*, CUP, 1991, 335: *Cf.*, L. Brisson, 'Le rôle des mathématiques dans le Timée selon les interprétations contemporaines', in *Le Timée de Platon: contribution à l'histoire de sa réception*, ed. Neschke-Hentschke, A., 2000, 302.

18 Aristotle, *Metaphysics*, A, 3, 983a; the other three causes are the material cause, (the matter of the thing), the formal cause (the essence of the thing, *eidos*) and the efficient cause (the moving force, *kinèsis*) The fourth cause (*telos*) is thus 'the final cause', probably the most important cause. On Aristotle's ideas on telos, (Τέλος), the final goal, see also, Aristotle, *Nicomachean Ethics*, fragments 6 and 11 and on law of nature, Aristotle, *Rhetoric*, Book I – Chapter 13, The notion of finality is an essential concept in Aristotle's philosophy, also with regard to animals, *On the Parts of Animals*, or in art in the form of *tékhnê*, *Physics*, 199a, 9-10 et II, 8, 199b27-9: it would be absurd to think that actions are undertaken without a goal. Further, in *Nicomachean Ethics*, Book I, 1094a, he underlines that every activity has a final cause, the good at which it aims.

19 *Institutes of Roman Law by Gaius*, *Gai Institutiones*, Trans. Poste, E., ed: Whittuck, E.A., Oxford: OUP, 1904; A certain confusion has been caused by the reference to the *jus naturale* applying to animals and the *jus gentium* to people: Justinian, *Institutes*, trans. Birks, P. & Macleod, G., New York: Cornell Univ. Press, I, 2.

In the modern era, Christian writers held that the Scriptures should be interpreted according to a theory of 'four senses', that is to say in the historical (literal) sense, allegoric (with hidden meanings), tropological (moral) sense or anagogic sense (concerning the final aim). All rules should be interpreted as conducive to a final goal. Such rules would form part of a body of natural law.

St. Augustine proposed the ultimate goal was the establishment of the City of God, that is to say the Kingdom of God.[20] The idea of a final goal of 'good' was followed by writers during the XII and XIII century by a convergence of the philosophy of Aristotle, St. Augustine and St. Thomas Aquinas.

Aquinas divided rules into 'divine' and 'non-divine' norms, while expanding and clarifying the meaning of natural law. St. Thomas also adopted a very clear version of Aristotle's final goal saying that an act is good or bad depending on whether it contributes to or deters us from our proper human end – the *telos* or final goal at which all human actions tend to aim. That specific *telos* is *eudemonia*, or happiness, understood in terms of completion, perfection, or well-being.[21] To Aquinas, *jus gentium*, is derived from natural law and was applicable to *all*. Its legal force was based on its origin in natural law as applied by human *reason*.[22]

In the 15th century we also note renewed discussion in Chinese philosophy, resuming thoughts of Confucius from 4th century BC.

---

[20] St. Augustine, *De Civitate Dei contra* Paganos, *City of God Against the Pagans*, Book I-X, ed. P. Schaff, Buffalo, 1887; idem, *De Libero Arbitrio, On Grace and Free Will*, ed. P. King, Toronto: CUP, 2005.

[21] *Summa Theologiae*, Ia 5.1.: Goodness and being are really the same; *cf. Confessions* VII.12.

[22] See, St.Thomas Aquinas, *Summa theologica*, Rome, 1266-1273, Indianapolis: Benzinger Bros., 1947; Lander, Wyoming: The Aquinas Institute, 2012, I-II, q. 95, a 2, 4.

Even before the Greek philosophers we note that the *Analects* of Confucius, known as the *LunYu*, set out the ethical teaching of Confucius[23] in lectures with his disciples.[24] One major tenet of this teaching is to emphasise that, subduing oneself and returning to propriety, represents *'perfect virtue'*.

The ethics and harmony theory of Kong Zi gave clear emphasis to the goodness of the human heart expressed in the *discharge of duties*. These teachings had considerable influence in the Middle Kingdom and beyond.[25] The concept of '*li*' is particularly suitable to explain an intrinsic or innate feeling of honour. The '*li*' in Chinese thought also corresponds to an intrinsic notion of what is right.[26] It is also this concept that implies honour and fairness. Some claim that the reason why China did not abrogate treaties but considered, especially written agreements, as '*clad in iron*' is because of the impact of *li*: it would be 'dishonourable' to violate a treaty freely entered into.[27]

The teachings of Confucius are similar to later thoughts on natural law in the West. In the Middle Ages, the philosopher Wang-

---

[23] BC 551-479. Hu Shih, 'Natural law in the Chines tradition', Natural Law Institute, *Proceedings*, 1953.

[24] The *Analects* represent the official teachings of Confucius were probably compiled in the early 4th century B.C., supplemented by other sayings of his disciple Zhen Seng.

[25] Dionisio, G., 'Natural law tradition and Confucian culture: Beyond East-West divide', *Filocracia*,1:1, 2014, 62, at 63.

[26] Needham, J., *Science and Civilization in China*, vol. II, London: CUP, 1972, 533. idem, 'Human law and law of nature in China and the West' (II), *Nature Journal of the History of Ideas*, 194.

[27] See, my article on 'The problem of unequal Treaties', *ICLQ* 1966.

Yang Ming[28] developed further the thoughts of Confucius during the Ming period. Wang-Yang Ming said that there is in every man the 'innate and intuitive knowledge (*liang-chih*) that is the moral conscience of man', that knows 'right to be right and wrong to be wrong'. This was a new and clearer perception of natural law (*li*) as man's innate and intuitive conscience to perceive the truth and the 'law' that then became his duty to 'extend and apply to all things and all events'.[29] Such considerations assisted those who were persecuted during the fierce reign of this period.[30]

In the West, a century later, Suárez held that the *jus gentium* consisted in rules to which there had been no formal consent at any particular time. These unwritten rules were so close to nature that they naturally emerged among members of the human race. These rules applied to *all*, citizens and foreigners alike, as well as to any members of any nation.[31]

Pufendorf largely followed the ideas of Hobbes[32] and held that there is a set of rules for the '*law of man*' and another '*law of States*', the '*jus gentium*'. Hobbes claimed that the 'state of nature' of States was one of war; but Pufendorf, accepting other ideas of Hobbes, distanced himself from that suggestion.[33] Grotius, on the other hand, suggested that one system of law regulates the behaviour between States, grounded in the law of nature, and

---

[28] 1472–1528. See, Hu Shih, 'The Chinese natural law tradition', in Natural Law Institute, 5 *Proceedings*, 1953, 119.
[29] *Ibid.*, 152.
[30] *Ibid.*, loc.cit.
[31] Suárez, F., *De legibus, ac deo legislatore*, 1612, 11.17-20, New York: Hein, 1995.
[32] Hobbes, T., *De Cive*, ed. Warrender, H., Oxford: OUP, 1983, 28.
[33] Pufendorf, S., *De jure naturae egentium*, ed. Böhling, F., Berlin: Akademie Verlag, II, III, 23.

another rule set governs internal situations of States in their civil laws.³⁴

Other later philosophers took again great interest in the ideas of a final goal and that consideration became very wide spread. Men of the Church interpreted the aim of humanity in the similar light.³⁵ Leibniz considered as a final goal some necessary principles for all laws of nature, *fundamentum naturæ legum*.³⁶ Also for Kant, such a teleological approach was useful as a regulating idea.³⁷

Although Brierly, the eminent Chichele Professor of International Law at Oxford University for 25 years from 1922 to 1947, also emphasised the role of the State as a principal subject of international law, it is remarkable to find that he also seeks a social purpose for the legal system and fiercely defends the notion of *natural law*.³⁸ He was considerably irritated that 'natural law' had been ridiculed, especially in England, and regarded as

---

[34] Grotius, H., *De jure bellie ac pacis*, ed. Barbeyrac, J., Indianapolis: Liberty, 2005, i, 17 *et seq.* & 39 *et seq.*

[35] Bossuet. J.B., *Discours sur l'histoire universelle*, Dijon: Le Cerf, 1681.

[36] Leibniz, G.W., *Opera Philosophica* (ed. Erdmann, J. E.), *De Ipsa Natura*, Berlin: Eicher, 1839-*1840*, *155*; *idem*, *Leibnitii opera omnia*, Geneva: L. Dutens, 1768; *Philosophical Essays*, Indianapolis: Hackett Publishing Company, 1989; *idem*, *Philosophical Papers and Letters*, Dordrecht: Kluwer, 1989.

[37] On the transcendantal ideas of Immanuel Kant, see his *Critik der reinen Vernunft*. Riga: Hartneck, 1781; *Kritik der reinen Vernunft*, Hamburg: Meiner Verlag, Hamburg 1998; (§10, 220) & Ginsborg, H., 'Kant's biological teleology and its philosophical significance' in *Blackwell Companion to Kant*, ed. Bird, G., Oxford: Blackwell Publishing, 2006, p. 4: 'the object of a concept in so far as the latter is regarded as the cause of the former'.

[38] Brierly, J.L., *The Law of Nations*, Oxford; OUP, 1928, 1st ed., 9 *et seq.*; 6th ed. by Waldock, H., 16 *et seq. Cf.* 7th ed. by Clapham, A., 2012.

a 'superstition' when, in fact, it stands for something that 'no progressive system of law does or can discard'.[39]

Brierly goes on to explain that the notion in Roman law of *jus gentium* claimed to be of universal importance because its rules were so simple they were held to be recognised by everyone everywhere. In due course, this form of law was held to be synonymous with the *jus naturale*, as 'the ideal law conforming to reason'.[40] The identification of natural law became easier as Roman law was recognised as *ratio scripta*, or 'written reason': this law was respected everywhere and 'revered everywhere as the supreme triumph of human reason'. Moreover, this law had a further claim to respect from its close association with the Canon law of the Church'.[41]

What Brierly suggests, and what is compatible with some of the theories of the present work, is that natural law cannot receive any 'final definition' as 'it is always, and above all in the sphere of human conduct, relative to conditions of times and place' and it is thus a law of nature '*with a variable content*'.[42] But Brierly did not differentiate, as we do in this work, between *imperative maxims*, other binding rules and dispositive rules; he rejected the idea that natural law can displace positive law although even Blackstone held such a view, inherited from the medieval scholars.[43] But if a

---

[39] *Ibid., loc. cit.*

[40] *Ibid.*, 11 and 18 respectively.

[41] *Ibid.*, 13 and 19.

[42] *Ibid.*, 14-15 and 20-21.

[43] Blackstone, W., *Commentaries on the Laws of England*, Oxford: OUP, 1765-1769, Introduction § 2, On the Nature of Law in General, where he states that the 'law of nature, being co-equal with mankind and dictated by God himself, is of course superior in obligation to any other. It is binding over all the globe, in all countries,

distinction is made, as we do in this work, between various levels of norms, even this proposition appears valid.

2. Positivism

After the Reformation we notice a fierce and hostile reaction to natural law and to any ideas about an ultimate goal for humanity. Teleological attitudes are rejected by philosophers, from any epistemological point of view, after the Reformation. We then notice a ferociously hostile reaction to ideas of natural law and of finality.

Teleological ideas are rejected by Francis Bacon in 1620 as he insists on the necessity to distance us from such perspectives:

> 'For new discoveries must be sought from the light of nature, not fetched back out of the darkness of antiquity'[44]

But by 'light of nature' he does not mean 'natural law' but rather according to the 'light' of science and humanism. During the 19th century, the attacks against natural law theories continue. The very term 'positivism' indicates a host of different trends of thought according to which the certainty of facts can only be ascertained by scientific experience. Therefore, any natural law theory must be rejected as 'unscientific'. This extreme version of positivism is adopted by, for example, Auguste Comte, who rejects any metaphysical approach to understanding the concept of 'law'.[45] The ideas of 'positivism' gradually became diffused in

---

and at all times: no human laws are of any validity, if contrary to this; and such of them as are valid derive all their force, and all their authority, mediately or immediately, from this original.'.

[44] Bacon, F., *Novum Organum*, 1620, Livre I, CXXII; *The New Organon*, Cambridge Texts, Cambridge: CUP, 2000.

[45] Comte, A., *Cours de philosophie positive*, 6 vols., Paris: Bachelier, 1830-1842; Paris: Herman, 1978; *Cf.* criticism by Aron, R., *Introduction à la philosophie de l'histoire*, (1938), Paris: Gallimard, 1986.

various areas: in science,[46] in philosophy,[47] in jurisprudence[48] and in politics, where Comte's ideas had a marked influence on the development of Marxist theory.

A new anti-metaphysical version of positivism developed in legal thought in the 20th century. The main representative of this form of 'legal positivism' is Hans Kelsen. His theses are expressed in *Theory of Pure Law*, inspired by the positive political system of Auguste Comte. Kelsen constructed a theory of a pyramid of norms .[49] But the definitions and distinctions of various forms

---

[46] Darwin, C., *On the Origin of Species by Means of Natural Selection, or the Preservation of Favoured Races in the Struggle for Life*, London: John Murray, 1859, who does not include any *telos* in this theory, but who however shows some teleologic and axiologic bias with regard to the concept of 'function'. Nietzsche remarks that a natural selection indicates direction in evolution by progressive improvement in teleologic perspective, towards a finality, see, Nietzsche, F., *Sämtliche Werke: Kritische Studienausgabe*, ed. Giorgio Colli and Mazzino Montinari, Berlin: de Gruyter, 1980.

[47] Bentham, J., *Plan for a Universal and Perpetual Peace*, London: Sweet & Maxwell, 1927; *The Works of Jeremy Bentham*, ed. Bowring, J., London, 1838-1843, Russell & Russell, New York, 1962;

[48] Austin, J., *Province of Jurisprudence Determined*, London: John Murray,1832; idem, *Lectures on Jurisprudence or the Philosophy of Positive Law*, London: R. Campbell, 1874; 5th ed., London: Murray, 1885;

[49] Kelsen, H., *Hauptprobleme der Staatsrechtslehre entwickelt aus der Lehre vom Rechtssätze*, Tübingen: Mohr Siebeck, 1911; idem, *Das Problem der Souveränität und die Theorie des Völkerrechts, Beitrag zu einer reinen Rechtslehre*, Tübingen: Mohr Siebeck, 1920; *Allgemeine Staatslehre*, Berlin, J. Springer, 1925; idem, *Grundriss einer allgemeinen Theorie des Staates*, Vienne: R.M. Rohner, 1926; idem, & Faure, V., *Théorie générale du droit et de l'Etat, suivi de La doctrine du droit naturel et le positivisme juridique*, Brussels: Bruylant, 1997; idem, *Der soziologische und der juristische Staatsbegriff*, Tübingen: Mohr Siebeck, 1927; idem, *Rechtsgeschichte gegen Rechtsphilosopie: Eine Erwiderung*, Vienna: Springer, 1928; idem, *Reine Rechtslehre*, Leipzig & Vienna: Springer, 1934; idem, *Principles of International Law*, New York: Rinehart, 1952; idem, *Pure Theory of Law*, Berkeley: University of California Press, 1967; idem, *What is Justice?: Justice, Law, and Politics in the Mirror of Science: Collected Essays*, Berkeley:

of positivism are confused: Kelsen, thus considered by many to be the founder of modern 'legal positivism', was, according to some actually 'anti-positivist' and rather more orientated towards natural law.[50] However, there is little sign of support for these latter arguments.[51] Kelsen is certainly a relativist who, in his earlier writings, even rejects the legal concept of the 'State'.[52]

Some attribute the 'originality' of ideas on 'legal positivism' to Jellinek[53] who, with his theory of 'auto-limitation' gives less importance to the idea of absolute sovereignty than those who follow the Hegelian tradition of unlimited sovereignty of the State.

It is important to emphasise that 'positive' law need not mean much else than *jus positum*, that is to say *jus quia jussum*, in other words 'law' promulgated by an authority.

In this context we may note again the precipice that exists between Anglo-Saxon ideas of law and those of the so called 'civil

---

University of California Press, 1971; *idem*, *Essays in Legal and Moral Philosophy*, Dordrecht: Reidel, 1973; *idem*, 'Théorie du droit international coutumier', 1 *RITD*, 1939, 253; *idem*, *Law and Peace in International Relations*, Cambridge, Mass., Harvard University Press, 1942; *idem*, *Peace through Law*, Chapel Hill: The University of North Carolina Press, 1944; *idem*, *La paz por medio del derecho*, Buenos Aires: Losada S.A., 1946; *idem*, *Allgemeine Theorie der Normen*, Vienna & Mainz, 1979; *idem*, *Auseinandersetzungen zur reinen Rechtslehre: kritische Bemerkungen zu Georges Scelle und Michel Virally*, Vienna & New York: Springer, 1987.

[50] Marmor, A., 'The nature of law', *Stanford Encyclopaedia of Philosophy*, 2013.

[51] Rigaux, F., 'Hans Kelsen on international law', 9 *EJIL* 1998, 325.

[52] Kelsen, H., *Das Problem der Souveränität und die Theorie des Völkerrechts, Beitrag zu einer reinen Rechtslehre*, Tübingen: Mohr Siebeck, 1920; *cf. Reine Rechtslehre*, Leipzig & Vienna: Springer, 1934; few writers have commented on the fact that he merely repeats Austin's idea that law is the 'command of the sovereign' when Kelsen adopts his '*Ursprungsnorm*': '*Verhalte dich so, wie der Monarch befielt*' ('behave as the Monarch orders'), the command he then translates as the '*Grundnorm*' *pacta sunt servanda* for international law.

[53] Bernsdorff, J.v., 'Georg Jellink and the origins of liberal constitutionalism in international law, 4 *Göttingen Journal of International Law*, 2012, 659.

law systems', adopted by the whole of the rest of Europe and by many overseas countries. In the Anglo-Saxon system adopted by, Great Britain and its vast Commonwealth (Canada, India, Australia, New Zealand etc.) as well as the United States, all perceive 'law' as something in principle announced by *the judges in their countries.* The concept of law in the Anglo-Saxon world is thus fundamentally different from that in continental Europe and its ex-colonies and a vast number of other countries, like China and Japan that have followed the civil law tradition.[54]

In contrast to the judge-made law in the Anglo-Saxon world, 'law' in the European and other systems, is made by its legislators, normally their parliaments in cooperation with their governments. The role of a judge in these countries is this to find the legal rules in promulgated texts and apply those to the facts in a case before the court.

Some define 'positivism' as a legal doctrine according to which all law can be reduced to *rules that are enacted in written form.* But this formulation had, had, for some time, a different meaning in continental Europe and in the Anglo-Saxon legal systems: in the civil law countries such written rules will mean the rules *that* are issued by the legislature as written *legislation*; but since Anglo-Saxon countries consider law as largely 'judge-made', such 'written law' will also include judgments.[55] Positivists in the Anglo-Saxon tradition thus include judgments of courts in what is properly laid down as 'written law'. In recent times, as a result of the considerable influence of Anglo-Saxon lawyers on

---

[54] Holmes, O.W., 'The path of the law', 10 *Harvard Law Review*, 1897, 457: *'The prophecies of what the courts will do in fact, and nothing more pretentious, are what I mean by the law'.*

[55] See, *supra*, under I ii e) 1.

international law,[56] jurists of the civil law countries now *also accept court judgments as part of 'positive law'*.

We shall note later the disastrous effect this attitude has on deciding what is the *lex lata*: in the context of 'customary law', some thus claim that a handful of judgments of arbitrarily chosen countries reflect the law – but the judgments are virtually all in English, or possibly in French or German. But where is the balance involving Japanese, Brazilian or Russian judgments? All this research to establish the 'law' is hampered by the limited language knowledge of scholars to seriously misrepresent what is 'international law'.[57]

It is not easy to discern the actual situation in the conflict between the contemporary 'positivists' and the 'natural law' adherents as positions of their followers continuously change, at least on the positivist side. There are innumerable definitions of 'legal positivism'. There are those who insist that this positivism depends on social factors and that it should not be judged on its own isolated merits but in the context of its social function.[58]

'Legal positivism', to most commentators,[59] excludes any reference to any 'natural law' and any metaphysical arguments. The great majority of jurists, specialists in international law now consider themselves as 'positivists' and only a small minority adhere to any school of 'natural law'.[60] But the 'positivists' are

---

[56] See, *infra*, in this section, on the dominance of literature on international law in English.

[57] See, *infra*, in further detail, Part Three, III iii a) 1-3.

[58] Green, L., 'Legal positivism' in *Stanford Encyclopedia of Philosophy*, ed. 2003.

[59] There are exceptions: see the efforts to allow the use of moral elements in Marmor, *infra*, note 37.

[60] *Cf.* Wild, J., *Plato's Modern Enemies and the Theory of Natural Law*. Chicago: Univ. of Chicago Press, 1953, 136.

divided in innumerable factions, and have as *their only common denominator a rejection of 'natural law'*.[61] An analysis of arguments from the two camps, the positivists and the natural law scholars, shows that on both sides there is a great deal of misunderstanding.

Theories of natural law are becoming more fashionable, especially after efforts of various writers to clarify the actual contents of natural law.[62] The basis of the international legal system is certainly natural law and we should view positive law as supplementing the basic natural rules.

As mentioned above, most positivists think, without much reason, that 'natural law' has 'religious' overtones. Some positivists appear to be vaguely 'relativist', or adopting other 'fluid' 'modernist' ideas as to what law represents. Some combine their views with clear spiritual values and idealistic attitudes. But we may also note that among 'positivists' there are some prominent nihilists.[63]

As we have seen, one cannot generalise as to what 'positivists' hold as their belief: there are too many factions of international lawyers who all call themselves 'positivists' but who do not agree much with each other about the substantive contents of their theories. What they all have in common though is that they all

---

[61] Finnis, J., 'Natural law theories', in *Stanford Encyclopedia of Philosophy*, 2011.

[62] Finnis explains that the 'positivists' have formulated their ideas in opposition to natural law, whereas the jurists who adhere to the natural law theory do not have any severe criticism against the theses of the positivists except in so far as these reject natural law as erroneous. Finnis, J., 'Natural law theories', in *Stanford Encyclopedia of Philosophy*, 2011. *Cf.*, his other works *Natural Law and Natural Rights*, Oxford: OUP, 1980, 2nd ed. Oxford: OUP, 2011; *cf.* his *Fundamentals of Ethics*, Oxford: OUP, 1983;

[63] See, *infra*, note 72 on Hägerström, Lundstedt, Olivecrona and on the works of the Swedish nihilists.

reject any merits of 'natural law'. It is important to stress that the over-whelming majority of writers on international law definitely declare themselves as 'positivists'.

Some 'positivists' find faults in the international legal system that negate its character as 'law'. There are also those, who misrepresent what *other* positivists have said, possibly by not having consulted the original text. There are thus some who erroneously claim that Austin considered that international law is not a 'real legal system', as a legal system cannot exist without sanctions. And, as there is no coercive system nor any organised sanctions in international society, the pretended 'legal' system is defective and, hence, international law is nothing but 'positive morality'. But Austin never said this.[64] Austin held that 1) international law is not 'positive law' but 'positive morality' but 2) 'positive morality' is divisible into those items which can be treated as 'law properly so called' and those which, cannot and that 3) *international law is 'law properly so called'*.[65]

To those who negate that international is 'law' because it lacks sanctions, this argument can be countered: there are actually sanctions in international society, if we bear in mind the pressure of public opinion in the world, that may work as a 'sanction'.[66] In this sense, there are clearly sanctions in the international legal

---

[64] Austin, J., *Province of Jurisprudence Determined*, London: John Murray, 1832; *idem*, *Lectures on Jurisprudence or the Philosophy of Positive Law*, London: R. Campbell, 1874; 5th ed, London: Murray, 1885;

[65] Manning, C.A.W., *The Nature of International Society*, London: Macmillan, LSE reissue, 1975 & *idem*, 'The legal framework in a world of change' in Porter, B., ed., *The Aberystwyth Papers, International Politics 1919-1969*, London: OUP, 1972, 301-335 at 305.

[66] See further *infra* in Part Two, C III i a) on sanctions.

system. Let us not forget that South Africa abandoned its *apartheid* system because of the pressure of such world-wide public opinion,[67] and France ceased it nuclear tests because of the hostile reaction to such tests in other countries.[68] There can thus be a coalescence of countries and of individuals to force a country into a certain behaviour or to refrain from certain actions.

Another form of criticism in Austin's theory – and in that of many other jurists – is that a 'real' legal system consists of the commands of a 'sovereign' and as there is no 'sovereign' in international society, international 'law' cannot be true 'law'.

Others consider international law as defective for other reasons and reduce it to a system of 'morality'[69] and thus, for such reasons deny that it is a true system of legal rules. The adherents of 'positivism' sometimes accuse those who prefer the school of natural law that they only accept law with the qualification that the law is 'just', thus the *jus quia justum*. In other words, many positivists *assume* that the 'naturalists' only accept the law that corresponds to certain moral requirements. But this is a false assumption and is not correct. Those who support the natural law school accept willingly that 'positive' law has a role to play in the international legal order. After all, it was St. Thomas Aquinas, the

---

[67] See, my *International Legal Order*, London: Gower, 1986, 557 *et seq.*

[68] See, my *Law of War*, 2nd ed., Cambridge: CUP; 3rd ed. London: Ashgate, 2000, 249 *et seq.*

[69] Hart, H.L.A., *The Concept of Law*, Oxford: OUP, 1961; 2nd ed. with a Postscript by Raz, J., & Bulloch, P., (eds.), Oxford: OUP, 1994; 3rd ed.by Green, L., Raz, J., & Bulloch, P., Oxford: OUP, 2012; idem, 'Positivism and the separation of law and morals', 71 *Harvard Law Review*, 1958, 593 and, Dworkin, R., (ed.), *The Philosophy of Law*, Oxford: OUP, 1979; idem, *Essays in Jurisprudence and Philosophy*, Oxford: OUP, 1983.

principal founder of the school of natural law, who was the first to use the term 'positive law' as form of law that supplements other rules. But many arguments in these discussions depend on definitions.

One principal preoccupation in identifying the 'law' should not be its source but its contents. Social facts are only a *cause* of how positive law develops. Rules are enacted to fill certain social needs. The validity of the rules cannot depend on its contents, but only on its origin as enacted by a competent authority. As in the Bible, one should render to Caesar what belongs to Caesar; one has to obey laws properly enacted whatever their contents may be, even law that offends our moral perceptions and ideas. If one does not like the laws one cannot so easily 'fly away' as Aristophanes suggests in *The Birds*. But, anyway, it may be better to stay to bring about a legislative change of unwelcome laws. Finally, it may be that one is morally excused for not obeying legal rules but one is not legally excused and sanctions may follow under the same legal system.

On the other hand, we should remember that authorities in the *Third Reich* did obey national legislation and local rules, rules that often were in conflict with the conscience of people and their moral beliefs. The consequences of refusing to obey were severe and show that an immoral positive law can be effective and considered valid in a national system. Modern examples of this dichotomy may be practices in the few communist States still in existence, for example in North Korea.

In international society, there is no central system to promulgate positive law. All we can find of such law on the international level is what we find in treaties and conventions, and even such agreements have only legal force between the contracting parties. The only exception to this is when a treaty or a convention reflects a norm that is *binding because of another source of validity*, namely in the existence of a norm of 'natural law'.[70] Then the treaty will *appear* to be binding *erga omnes* – but that is naturally an illusion: the content of the treaty is binding because it *also* forms part of another binding set of rules.

The 'positivists' are divided in numerous sub-factions. There are those that include a portion of morality in what they call 'inclusive positivism', and there are those who refuse to include such elements so that they can construct a system of 'exclusive positivism'; the difference is thus whether or not one accepts certain moral aspects to validate the 'law'.[71]

Numerous conflicts of opinion result from misunderstandings and may be explained by the adoption of arbitrary definitions and erroneous presumptions. The situation is not made easier by some positivists, who resort to complicated expressions and often incomprehensible arguments. As mentioned above, even the term 'positivism' is defined in numerous ways. This term and others, *e.g.* 'normativism', are thus understood in several contradictory manners.

---

[70] See, *infra*, Part Three IV vi on 'Allergy' to natural law and on such law 'disguised' as 'customary law'; *cf.* the Variability of the Basis of Obligation in Part Three VI iii a).

[71] Marmor, A., 'The nature of law', *Stanford Encyclopedia of Philosophy*, ed. 2013; *idem, Interpretation and Legal Theory*, Oxford: OUP, 1992; 2nd ed., Oxford: Hart Publishing, 2005; *idem, Positive Law & Objective Values*, Oxford: Clarendon Press, 2001; *idem, Philosophy of Law*, Princeton: Princeton University Press, 2011; *idem*, 'Farewell to conceptual analysis (in jurisprudence)', in Waluchow & Sciaraffa (eds.), *Philosophical Foundations of the Nature of Law*, Oxford: OUP, 2013, 209.

We can note that at the present stage, the 'positivists' are in a large majority, often having rejected 'natural law' because of its alleged religious overtones. In Sweden and in Denmark, natural law has long been rejected as an illusory and erroneous doctrine.[72] On the other hand, in Norway,[73] as in Finland,[74] there have been far more welcoming attitudes to natural law.

To the present writer, international law is a normative system, laying down rules and obligations. But this normative system may be continuously revised by a process prompted by various

---

[72] Certain nihilistic writers influenced for over half a century the teaching of law in Scandinavia and forcefully discouraged researchers to publish any works inspired in any way by natural law. These writere are, above all, in Sweden: Hägerström, A., *Aristoteles etiska grundtankar och deras teoretiska förutsättningar*, Uppsala: Akademiska boktryckeriet, E. Berling, 1893; *idem, Till frågan om den objektiva rättens begrepp*, Uppsala: Almqvist & Wiksell, 1917; *idem, Inquiries into the Nature of Law and Morals*, Stockholm: Almqvist & Wiksell, ed. Karl Olivecrona, trad. C.D. Broad, 1953; Lundstedt, A. V., *Die Unwissenschaftlichkeit der Rechtswissenschaft*, Berlin: W. Rothschild, 1932; *idem, Le droit des gens: danger de mort pour les peuples*, Brussels: de la Phalange, 1937; Olivecrona, K., *Law as Facts*, Copenhagen, Munksgaard, 1939; *idem, Rättsordningen*, Lund: Gleerup, 1966; 2nd ed. 1976; in Denmark, Ross, A., *Teorie der Rechtsquellen. Ein Beitrag zur Teorie des positiven Rechts auf Grundlagen dogmenhistorischer Untersuchungen*, Uppsala & Leipzig: Franz Deuticke, 1929; *idem, Kritik der sogenannten praktischen Erkenntnis. Zugleich Prolegomena zu einer Kritik der Rechtswissenschaft*, Copenhagen, 1933; *idem, Virkelighed og gyldighed i retslaeren. En kritik af den teoretiske retsvidenskabs grundbegreper*, Copenhagen: Levin & Munksgaard, 1934; *idem, Lehrbuch des Völkerrechts*, Stuttgart: W. Kohlhammer, 1951; *idem, On Law and Justice*, London: Stevens, 1958.

[73] See, Castberg, F., *Naturrett og menneskerettigheter*, Oslo: Universitetsforlaget, 1967; *idem, La Philosophie du droit*, Paris, 1970: Pedone, 1970.

[74] See, Koskenniemi, M., *From Apology to Utopia, The Structure of International Legal Argument*, 1989; with an epilogue of the author, Cambridge: CUP, 2005; *idem, The Gentle Civilizer of Nations: The Rise and Fall of International Law (1870-1960)*, Cambridge/New York: CUP, 2005.

subjects of the international legal order. This normative system as presented in this work, may be more dynamic than traditional normativists contend: whenever there is a need for a legal rule to be amended, abolished or modified, the legislative bodies take action – normally relatively rapidly – often prompted by democratic pressure, sometimes expressed in the media.

ii. A New Theory

The new theory developed in this work will seek to reflect what actually happens in international society. According to this theory the international rights and obligations of both States and non-State entities will be clarified and apportioned to fit into a pattern of behaviour in the contemporary world. This work will attempt to analyse the vast field of certain entities whose actions, in practice, do have an impact on international relations and that contribute to the formation of rules of international law.

In this work a new theory is presented: a theory that will cater for new legal needs of actors in today's international society. Traditional writers have problems explaining the role of the 'non-State actors' in their textbooks: here such actors will be given special attention, given their obvious importance in the new legal world system.

a) Law as a Framework

There are, among lawyers, fundamentally divergent ideas on the meaning of 'law'. In this work, '*law*' is understood to be a mere *framework* designed for the subjects and the actors of a legal order.

These subjects and actors have to behave in a way that can be inserted within this framework.

b) The 'Hypothetical Goal'

The *function of law* thus presupposes that subjects and actors limit their freedom by respecting the freedom of others. The free interdependence of these units, subjects and actors, is only possible if everyone agrees to limit their freedom.[75]

But the will of subjects and actors to limit their freedom in order to respect the freedom of others is more readily understood if we accept some *intrinsic rules* that visualise a common goal for international society. In this sense, we refer to a *hypothetical goal* of international society, that we postulate to be the 'survival of mankind'.

In order to systematise international rules, we shall adopt, for functional purposes, a *hypothetical goal* of international society.

One may suggest that 'preservation of international society'[76] or of 'mankind' is a viable goal of international society.[77] But such 'preservation' indicates a static element which would not demand any action; mere freezing of an undesirable situation would satisfy compliance with such a target. Therefore, to explain and

---

[75] Fichte, J. G., *Grundlage des Naturrechts nach Prinzipien der Wissenschaftslehre* (1796), ed. Berlin: W. de Gruyter, 1971, § 8, following Kant's ideas: '*Das Beisammenstehen der Freiheit mehrerer sei nur dadurch möglich, daß jedes freie Wesen es sich zum Gesetz mache, seine Freiheit durch den Begriff der Freiheit aller übrigen einzuschränken*'. *Cf.* Zippelius, R., *Rechtsphilosophie*, 6th ed., Munich: Beck, 2011, § 26 I, II 2, 3 & *Das Wesen des Rechts. Eine Einführung in die Rechtstheorie*, 6th ed., Stuttgart: Kohlhammer, 2012.

[76] *Cf. supra*, in this Part, under I iv, A Society or a Community?

[77] *Cf.* 1 Hyde, 23; Bull, H., *Anarchical Society*, *op. cit.*, 1619; Holsti, *op. cit.*, 129; Modelski mentions 'survival', *Principles of World Politics*, New York: Free Press, 1972, 288.

classify positive action by the actors in the society, it appears that 'promotion of the welfare of international society' or of 'mankind' is a more acceptable notion to cover activities that, by pragmatic analysis, we observe in the contemporary society.

The hypothetical goal of international society can be construed to have existed historically. However, certain rules, designed to assist in reaching that goal[78] have only developed recently. Attitudes have undergone great changes in international society and, correspondingly, there have been great changes in the modalities of rules for the implementation of the set goal.

Positive law is, according to this writer, a host of rules included in rules in written legislation emanating from the legislators in States and the texts in treaties, conventions and other agreements between States. One should exercise a certain prudence to accept the Anglo-Saxon idea that decisions of judges contribute to positive law, unless such effect is limited to the Anglo-Saxon countries. Even for such effect it is required that the decision is final and has acquired legal force and even then it is not certain that a decision forms part of the relevant positive law.[79]

c) The Intrinsic Law

A set of rules that we prefer to call '*intrinsic law*' – to avoid misunderstandings about its contents as it is not identical to 'natural law' – is nothing else but a set of rules of common sense, as we

---

[78] For example, 'effective' Prophylactic Rules, see, *infra*, in Part Two, B III, Prophylactic Rules; *cf.* C I, Stabilising Rules.

[79] See, the *Tadić Case*, with numerous errors in law but followed by several judges in subsequent Cases as they considered this decision to be 'binding'; see my criticism in my *Law of War*, 3rd ed., *op.cit.*, 200-202 and *infra*.

express it, rules that are *socially necessary* to limit the effects of positive law.

Most writers of international law claim that rules in international society have largely developed through 'custom'. It must be admitted that suggestions that most international legal rules are created by the customary behaviour of States is pure *fiction*. On the contrary, most rules do not emerge through custom but through response to social needs, sometimes of an immediate character.

It is the *individuals*, the human beings, that are the main bearers of rights and obligations in the international system and thus the main *subjects* of international law. Individuals play a primordial role in international society and their rights and obligations are not derived from custom but from rules necessary to ensure the survival of international society, rules that are even easily identifiable. The tendency in the contemporary world is actually to return to rules that are *necessary* in a society.[80] It is clear that what some often call 'customary law' is nothing but a euphemism for 'natural' or what we prefer to call '*intrinsic law*'.[81]

A main component of *intrinsic law* is, in our opinion, '*sociologically necessary norms*'[82] that is to say rules that enable

---

[80] *Cf.* Finnis, J., *Natural Law and Natural Rights*, Oxford: OUP, 1980 and *idem*, *Fundamentals of Ethics*, Oxford: OUP, 1983. See also *infra*, Part Three, IV vi, on 'Allergy' to Natural Law.'

[81] See, *infra*, Part Three, IV vii.

[82] My expression, '*sociologically necessary norms*' was accepted even by members the Soviet *Institut gosodarstvo i pravo* when I gave a lecture there in February 1989; although my formulation comes near to the thoughts of St. Thomas Aquinas, the Institut considered this formula compatible with Marxism. *Cf. infra*, I ii c) 3, on acceptability to Chinese scholars, finding similarities with teachings of Confucius.

States and individuals to live side by side in international society. Such co-habitation requires the freedom of one person or entity to be limited by the freedom enjoyed by another.

1. Essential Maxims and General Principles

As we will demonstrate in Part Two of this work, there are some essential maxims and some essential general principles without which no legal system can function. These maxims and principles must clearly be respected in international society. However, since these rules are so essential and so engrained in any legal order, it is rarely necessary to remind actors in international society of their existence: *anyone* who acts on the international scene is immediately made aware of these intrinsic rules.[83]

The maxims and general principles have a *formal* character and largely concern the framework, rather than the substance, of international action. But there are also two essential substantive principles that guide international behaviour of the subjects and actors on the international scene.

The *Rule Prohibiting Harm* is possibly the most important rule in international society. The *Rule of Reciprocity* plays a similarly important role and furthermore strengthens the effectiveness of the international legal system.

2. The Reserved Domain and Prohibition of Harm

An essential ingredient in the *intrinsic law* is the fundamental rule of *prohibition of harm*. That rule covers prohibition of harm to

---

[83] See, *infra*, Part Two, B I and II.

States and/or individuals and/or the environment. Only such a rule can contain the ambition of some to profit at the expense of another. But each subject[84] of international law enjoys his own 'freedom' unless and until it infringes on the freedom of another subject.[85]

The rule concerning the prohibition of harm covers all forms of use of force and it forbids attacks on other subjects save in the case of self-defence. Military interventions in other States as well as harm to individuals that is to say violations of fundamental human rights and of humanitarian rules, infringement of immunity of diplomats as well as harm to the environment by deliberate or negligent pollution or misuse or overuse of natural resources to the detriment of the common good.

---

[84] See, *infra*, on the myriad of subjects of international law, in this Part, under I ii c); note that the personality of these subjects is only '*activated*' in certain situations.

[85] This view is clearly related to the conception one may have of 'international society' in general. It may be useful to refer to Hedley Bull's survey of Martin Wight's analysis of various trends of thought: Wight refers to what he calls 'sacred history or divine providence'. Wight suggested that there are three, or possibly four, conceptions, if not paradigms, of international relations. The 'Machiavellians' who would include figures like, Hobbes, Hegel; Frederick the Great, Clemenceau, Carr and Mongenthau, that, in principle, reject the notion of an international society and claim that each State or ruler merely pursues his own interests. Secondly, the 'Grotians' in which group Wight includes Locke, Burke, Castlereagh, Gladstone, Franklin Roosevelt and Churchill, to whom there is an international society where States may be in conflict at times but also cooperate. The third group are the 'Kantians' who consider relations between States only as a transient form before the actual relationship between individuals is realised on the basis of morality and imperatives to behave in accordance with such ethical rules. There is possibly a fourth 'pacifist' stream, represented by people like Tolstoy and Ghandi. See, Bull, H., 'Martin Wight and the Theory of international relations, The Second Martin Wight Memorial Lecture', *British Journal of International Studies*, Vol. 2, No. 2, July 1976, 101-114.

The greatest harm in international society is clearly full scale war and war-like activities. There is a reasonable debate as to whether harm may be inflicted on others in the process of self-defence. The Charter of the United Nation sets out certain conditions as the League of Nations had failed to denounce war: in other words, as demonstrated in treatises,[86] war was not 'illegal' under positive international law until 1945. But war is clearly a tragic situation brought about by failures of politics. As Clausewitz formulated this: war is continuing politics by other means.[87]

But are there situations when 'war' and use of military force can be justified? Clearly, there are situations of legitimate self-defence[88] even though it remains questionable whether 'pre-emptive' self-defence is legitimate.[89]

Are there other situations when use of military force is warranted or does the prohibition of harm cover other eventualities? The theories of *just war* may illustrate this dilemma.[90] Recent events,

---

[86] See, in great detail, my *Law of War*, 3rd ed., London: Ashgate, 2013, *passim.*

[87] Clausewitz, C.v., *Vom Krieg, Hinterlassenes Werk*, Berlin: Dümmler, 1832; English ed., Howard, M. & Paret, P., eds., *On War*, New Jersey: Princeton University Press, 87.

[88] See, in great detail, my *Law of War*, *op.cit.*, Chapter One.

[89] *Ibid., loc. cit.* A prime example of such pre-emptive 'self-defence' that led to massive loss of lives and great suffering, is the invasion of Iraq in 2003. Here, it emerged that the 'fears' of an attack by Saddam Hussein were groundless. So was the claim that his country had the capability to strike against the United Kingdom 'within 45 minutes'. His alleged arsenal of 'weapons of mass destruction' also turned out to be non-existing. It had all been a figment of Prime Minister Blair's imagination that caused this disastrous venture for which not even an exit strategy had been planned.

[90] The *Catechism of the Catholic Church* sets out in para. 2309 in its 1992 edition, conditions for self-defence. Thus, the damage inflicted by an aggressor on the nation or community of nations must be *lasting, grave, and certain*; all other means

when terrorist attacks virtually amount to war-like situations, have resulted in renewed interest as to whether war can ever be justified, in other words whether there can be any '*just wars*'. [91] In the Middle Ages there had been many fruitful debates about this theme and St. Thomas Aquinas had suggested some conditions: even today some of these criteria might be useful to assess the morality or the legality of a 'war'. St. Thomas sets out his efforts to restrain the resort to war in one passage where he also refers to St. Augustine's views on war:

> 'There are three conditions for a war to be just.
>
> The first thing is the authority of the prince by whose command the war is to be waged. It does not belong to a private person to start a war, for he can prosecute his claim in the court of his superior. In like manner the mustering of the people, that has to be done in wars, does not belong to a private person. But since the care of the commonwealth is entrusted to princes, to them belongs the protection of the common weal of the city, kingdom, or province subject to them. And as they lawfully defend it with the material sword against inward disturbances by punishing male-factors, so it belongs to them also to protect the commonwealth from enemies without by the sword of war.
>
> The second requisite is a just cause, so that they who are assailed should deserve to be assailed for some fault that they have committed. Hence Augustine says: 'Just wars are usually

---

of putting an end to it must have been shown to be *impractical or ineffective*; there must be serious *prospects of success*; the use of arms must *not produce evils and disorders graver than the evil to be eliminated.*

[91] See, for examples, Guthrie, C. & Quinlan, M., *Just War: The Just War Tradition: Ethics in Modern Warfare.* London: Bloomsbury, 2007.

defined as those which avenge injuries, in cases where a nation or city has to be chastised for having either neglected to punish the wicked doings of its people, or neglected to restore what has been wrongfully taken away.

The third thing requisite is a right intention of promoting good or avoiding evil. For Augustine says: 'Eagerness to hurt, bloodthirsty desire of revenge, an untamed and unforgiving temper, ferocity in renewing the struggle, dust of empire, – these and the like excesses are justly blamed in war'.

These conditions can perhaps be summarised in the following way:

> 'A just war must be waged by a properly instituted authority such as the State; war must occur for a good and just purpose rather than for self-gain or as an exercise of power; peace must be a central motive'.[92]

Judged against these criteria it is clear that the 'war' presently waged by Islamist terrorist organisations like ISIS or Al-Qaeda, cannot be 'just' even if the perpetrators claim that the *jihad* is justified. On the contrary, the *jihad* may demonstrate the very antithesis of what is 'just'.

But it is not only the wars waged by the Islamist fundamentalists and their cruel terrorist attacks that are 'wrong' in contemporary international society. Ill-judged interventions[93] in the last two decades demonstrate that States should not seek, by war or other

---

[92] St. Thomas, *Summa Theologiae*, Secunda Secundae Partis, Q. 40.
[93] See, my *Law of War*, 1st & 2nd ed., 1989 & 2000, Cambridge: CUP; 3rd ed., 2013, London: Ashgate, Ch., 2 III, 80 *et seq.* on various forms of Intervention.

force, to 'correct' or 'replace' policies in the internal sphere of other States.

States do enjoy their own *reserved domain*[94] where other States or entities should not intervene *unless* there is some serious violation of *jus cogens*. This fair rule has repeatedly been broken when 'Western' States have considered themselves more 'competent' to decide what is good for other States. Things have often gone dramatically wrong. Civilians and particularly Christians were safer under the rule of Saddam Hussein in Iraq, under Colonel Gaddafi in Libya, and even under Assad in Syria, than after the various military interventions in recent years.[95]

The devastation and suffering brought about by war may amply show that war is something that, at all cost, must be avoided. There is nothing that endangers the *hypothetical goal* to a greater extent than an outright war. The fundamental *prophylactic*[96] rule not to cause harm is essential to ensure and protect the attaintment of the *hypothetical goal*.[97]

3. The Rule of Reciprocity

The *intrinsic law* of international society includes, as a main component, the *Rule of Reciprocity*: that is the moral exhortation of *reciprocity* to treat others as you wish to be treated yourself.

---

[94] *Cf. infra*, in this Part, I ii c) 2 and Part Two C I i a) on Allocation of National Space. See, further, my *International Law and the Independent State*, 1994, London: Gower, *passim* and conclusions at 232.

[95] See, *ibid.*, *loc.cit.*

[96] See, *infra*, Part Two, B III.

[97] See, *supra*, in this Part, I ii b).

This simple but forceful rule has been the core of 'legal morals' since Antiquity, and forms the core of any legal system. The rule has been expressed in vaguely similar form since Plato's Socrates,[98] Pittacus,[99] Thales,[100] Sextus Pythagorean,[101] Isocrates,[102] Epictetus,[103] Seneca;[104] there is a long list.

The idea of the Rule of Reciprocity is clearly absorbed in Christianity as an essential pillar of morals and of Christian behaviour. Christ even insisted that this rule, together with the commandment to love God with all your heart, soul and mind, is *the foundation of the whole 'law'*.[105]

The impact of Christianity has obviously exerted considerable influence on thinkers – and statesmen – as there is an obvious advantageous result in the stability of international society if this rule is respected.

The use of Princes to send messengers, a practice crystallised and stengthened by the force of the Rule of Reciprocity, developed

---

[98] Crito, 49c, c. 469 BC–399 BC: 'May I do to others as I would that they should do unto me.' and 'Do not do to others that which would anger you if others did it to you.'

[99] c. 640–568 BC: 'Do not do to your neighbour what you would take ill from him.'

[100] c. 624 BC – c. 546 BC: 'Avoid doing what you would blame others for doing.'

[101] 3rd Century BC:'What you do not want to happen to you, do not do it yourself either.'

[102] 436–338 BC: 'Do not do to others what would anger you if done to you by others.'

[103] AD 50–135: 'What thou avoidest suffering thyself seek not to impose on others.'

[104] BC 4-AD 65: 'Treat your inferiors as you would be treated by your superiors,' Epistle to Lucilius 47:11.

[105] Matthew, 22:34-40: 'You shall love the Lord your God with all your heart, and with all your soul, and with all your mind. This is the great and foremost commandment. The second is like it, 'You shall love your neighbour as yourself.' On these two commandments depend the whole Law and the Prophets.'

into the law of diplomacy: probably the most striking example of the importance of reciprocity. Since ancient times rulers have needed to send an envoy to another ruler and this mutual practice is entirely founded on the strength of reciprocity, knowing that the exchange of messengers depended on the certitude that they would be treated well and safely sent back. With the rise of the nation-States in the 16th Century this practice developed into keeping permanent embassies in other countries. Diplomatic law[106] represents a most important part of international law although some privileges are being reduced in cases of, for example, traffic offences, or the duty to pay congestion charges, not immediately related to the official functions of envoys. Privileges and immunities of diplomats are, as the International Court of Justice emphasised in the *Hostage Case*,[107] a fundamental rule of international society, a peremptory norm of international law, and as such – although the Court did not use the term – a part of *jus cogens*.

Islam also has recourse to natural law[108] and claims to apply the Rule of Reciprocity.[109] But in Islam there appears to be so many exceptions to the basic structure of ethics that some have

---

[106] See, for a leading textbook, Denza, E., *Diplomatic Law: Commentary on the Vienna Convention on Diplomatic Relations*, Oxford: OUP, 4th ed., 2016; Satow, E.M., *Guide to Diplomatic Practice*, London: Longmans, 1917; 6th ed. Sir Ivor Roberts, Oxford: OUP, 2009; *cf. International Law and the Independent State*, London: Gower, 2nd ed.1994, Ch. Two.

[107] *Hostages in Teheran Case (United States v Iran)*, 1980, ICJ, *Reports*, 1980, 1. Here diplomatic personnel at the US Embassy in Teheran had been taken hostage for some time and were only released when the blocked Iranian assets in US banks in London were released, *Iran v Seven American Banks*, High Court in London, 1980 (settled).

[108] Emon, A.M., *Islamic Natural Law Theories*, Oxford: OUP, 2010.

[109] 'As you would have people do to you, do to them; and what you dislike to be done to you, do not do to them', *Kitab al-Kafi, Al-Kafi*, London: Islamic Texts

questioned[110] whether the Rule of Reciprocity should be considered as having been adopted in Islam.[111]

Gratian, the Christian lawyer who compiled what gradually becomes the Canon Law, considers that *the Rule of Reciprocity, sometimes called 'the Golden Rule' summarises the whole natural law.*[112]

The list of philosophers that rely on the essential Rule of Reciprocity continues and we note that even those who have no enthusiasm for natural law, or even totally rejects it, or understands it to be the produce of religious thoughts, still accept the Rule of Reciprocity: Thomas Hobbes,[113] Immanuel Kant[114] and John Stuart

---

Institute, vol. 2, 2012, 146. *Cf.* Donaldson, D.M., *Studies in Muslim Ethics*, London: S.P.C.K., 1963, 82.

[110] Pokorski, J., 'Islam and natural law', Commentary, CNSnews.com, 2nd June 2017.

[111] *Ibid.* Pokorski gives examples of practices and rules that deviate from basic ethics in other religious or philosophical systems: for example, *Taqiyya* is a form of lying specifically permitted to advance the cause of Islam; *Dawa* is the Islamic doctrine of imposing *sharia* governing Muslims and the entire legal order; *capital punishment for apostasy* from the Islamic faith, and *taharrush* which is the practice of permitting the sexual abuse of infidel women in public, justified in the Koran: 'And forbidden [sexual intercourse] to you are wedded wives of other people except those who have fallen in your hands [as prisoners of war] … (The Koran in Surah 4:24; c). (See also Surahs 4:3 and 33:50). *Cf.*, Maududi, S.A., *Towards Understanding the Qur'an:* Delhi: Islamic Publishing, 2007.

[112] 1140: 'By natural law, each person is commanded to do to others what he wants done to himself and is prohibited from inflicting on others what he does not want done to himself.'

[113] 1588-1679: 'Do not do that to another which thou wouldst not have done to thyself.' and 'When any one questions whether what he plans to do to another will be done in accordance with the law of nature or not, let him imagine himself in the other man's place.

[114] 1724-1804: 'Act as if the maxim of thy action were to become by thy will a universal law of nature.'

Mill.[115] In contemporary philosophy the Rule of Reciprocity, then often called *'The Golden Rule'*, has been revived in numerous new studies.[116]

We prefer to speak about *intrinsic law* and *intrinsic rules*, rather than 'natural law', in order to avoid any arguments by those who reject 'natural law' or those do not accept any of the various multiple definitions of this elusive concept. To us, *'intrinsic law' is limited to 'sociologically necessary norms'*, a formulation that ought to be acceptable to all scholars that observe actual behaviour of actors in international society.[117]

d) A Great Number of Subjects

The *intrinsic law* of international society is thus based on the fundamental *prohibition of harm* and on the *Rule of Reciprocity*.

---

[115] 1808-1873: 'To do as you would be done by, and to love your neighbour as yourself, constitute the ideal perfection of utilitarian morality.'

[116] For example, Wattles, J., *The Golden Rule*, Oxford: OUP, 1996, 35. Gensler, H.J., *Ethics and the Golden Rule*, New York: Routledge, 2013. But note a critical review by Simkulet, W., 'Review of Ethics and the Golden Rule by Henry Gensler, *Philosophy in Review*, Vol. 34, No. 5, 2014, 225, emphasising that the Golden Rule must always be understood to imply the condition 'treat others as you would wish to be treated *in their situation* – to avoid situations when 'a monkey saves a fish from a pond and the fish dies'.

[117] It was this formulation of *intrinsic law* as *'sociologically necessary norms'* that was found acceptable when I lectured in the then communist controlled *Institut gosodarstvo i pravo* in Moscow in February 1989: the Soviet lawyers surprisingly found this expression compatible with Marxism. The *Foreign College of Law* in Beijing in May the same year, welcomed my lecture and noticed the similarities with thoughts of St. Thomas and emphasised the compatibility of my views with statements of Confucius, still acceptable in communist China. *Cf. supra*, I ii c 1.

These two fundamental concepts touch on a number of 'subjects' of the international legal order.

Innumerable actors enjoy *potential international personality*, that is to say, *from time to time* they have direct rights and duties under the international legal system. But that is only the case when their activity is *internationally relevant*: then their personality, with their rights and duties, is *activated*.

According to traditional theory, both in civil law and Anglo-Saxon systems, there are 'subjects', *i.e.* 'bearers of international rights and duties' in international society, but those subjects are, according to the vast majority of writers, *only* 'States' and 'inter-governmental' organisations.

Such a limited view of those who have direct rights and duties under the international legal system is not adequate in today's world, where the actions of multinationals, other non-State entities, and the actions of individuals become more and more prominent. Although there is intense attention on the actions and status of 'non-State actors', in numerous conferences and seminars on this subject, current academics have not produced any coherent theory of their status in international law. Present theories of international law do not reflect what happens in reality in today's international society: present prevailing attitudes can only lead to confusion and loss of legal security. Are we saying that NGOs, multinationals, war criminals, pirates and terrorists have no international rights and duties? It is no longer possible to ignore all these entities and we must recognise that, in practice, these and individuals in general, have direct rights and obligations under international law.

Our extension of the traditional number of 'subjects' of the international legal order is due to a pragmatic analysis of how actors actually behave on the international stage. It is erroneous to claim that only States and inter-governmental organisations have the right to assume rights and to be subjected to duties by international law. To give only one example why this must be wrong, let us observe how statesmen as well as the general public urge that war criminals should be tried and punished for their crimes and, conversely, that their victims had legal *rights* not to have their human rights curtailed by such crimes. How is it possible to contend this unless we acknowledge that *individuals* have direct rights and obligations under international law?

The 'subjects' of the international legal system are innumerable: to be a 'subject' merely implies the capacity to assume rights and to subject to obligations. But the various 'subjects' of international law do not always act as such. Their international personality is only *activated* when they take acts that are internationally *relevant*. When they do not act in such a way their personality is merely *dormant* or *latent*.

Some international lawyers[118] have also adopted views that there are numerous subjects in the international legal order but they have then failed to accurately explain what holds the legal system together in international society; it has also been left unclear by what criteria one may draw a line between organisations which may have rights and duties under the international legal system and those which may not do so. The traditional but rudimentary distinction between so called 'inter-governmental' and 'non-governmental' entities (NGOs) does not adequately explain the roles of certain actors in international society.

---

[118] *E.g.*, Jessup, P., *Transnational Law*, New Haven: Yale University Press, 1956, 1.

INMARSAT[119] is a good example of where the absurd theories lead in practice. INMARSAT was founded in 1979 by a Treaty between States and the International Maritime Organisation, one of the Specialised Agencies of the United Nations. INMARSAT was thus a *typical inter-governmental organisation and a full subject under all the traditional theories of international law* as bearer of international rights and duties.

And what happened? On 15 April 1999 INMARSAT was *privatised.* Not only was it transformed into a limited UK Company but it was even the first inter-governmental organisation to be transformed into a private company and even later floated on the London Stock Exchange (LSE: ISAT.L) in 2005.

The question arises whether INMARSAT acquired a substantially different position in international society after it was privatised? And, when it was an inter-governmental, but small, organisation did it have an essentially different position in international society from, say, the Red Cross, another non-governmental organisation, but one of considerable size and importance?[120]

As we have indicated, the social process school allows anyone to be 'actor' or, as some prefer, 'participant' in what is going

---

[119] INMARSAT was founded in 1979 by an international Treaty between States but was 'privatised' in 1999 and converted into a limited UK Company, as stipulated by a UK law promulgated 15 April 1999. The same day the UK signed an agreement with the International Organisation for Mobile Phones, ISMO and a service agreement was concluded between INMARSAT Ltd and ISMO.

[120] The International Committee of the Red Cross is the over-reaching authority. See, on the international personality of the Red Cross, Reuter, P., 'La personalité juridique internationale du Comité international de la Croix Rouge,' in *Hommages Pictet*, 1984, 783.

on in the 'theatre' of the world society. The law is said to be the process of 'authoritative transnational decisions'[121] but the problem of 'subjects' or 'persons' is avoided.

But normativists, who have insisted for considerable time that international law is essentially a system between States, do not appear to have been able to influence the social process school but, unable to disregard what appears to have changed in international society, they have begun to accept that there are also other 'persons' than States. But they cannot explain how this reality fits in with the main contention that only States and inter-governmental organisations are endowed with international personality.

A few normativists have adopted a progressive outlook and emphasised that, although international law has an important function in regulating the behaviour of States, it has changed character and has drifted away from being a purely inter-State system. It is, they say, on its way of becoming a supranational system where the development of rules is no longer subject only to the will of individual states. Rather than emphasising more the role of individuals, they go the other way, towards collective solutions. International law, according to these writers, has thus become a system where issues like security, trade and social development can only be solved on a collective basis, often by the assistance of international and supranational organisations.[122]

e) Formation of Rules

We propose in this work a new theory of the *formation of legal rules* in international society: the analysis of actual behaviour of subjects

---

[121] McDougal & Al., Theories, *op. cit.* 254.
[122] Dahm, G., *Völkerrecht*, Stuttgart: de Gruyter, 1958, i, p.2.

and actors on the world stage appear to confirm our ideas on the creation and the essence of law rather than those of the current and traditional text books. We must thus have the courage to refute the ideas of the majority of writers and of judicial decisions.

It must be conceded by all scholars and statesmen that the traditional theories on the nature of international law, maintained by the vast majority of writers and courts, grieveously mislead us. The time has come for a new fresh theory which reflects what is actually happening on the international scene.

1. Dominance of Anglo-Saxon Ideas on Judge-Made Law

The respect for judicial decisions among international lawyers is furthermore due to the overwhelming predominance of Anglo-Saxon *literature* in every field of international law. Virtually all textbooks on international law in universities all over the world are in the English language. There are exceptions: in France, Germany and Italy there are numerous authoritative textbooks but even so, at the doctoral level, there is normally recourse to further works in English.

Secondly, Anglo-Saxon works on international law invariably refers to important and binding *precedents*, judgments and decisions that, in the opinion of Anglo-Saxon lawyers are binding or at least 'guiding' in subsequent cases. But the authors of these books have persistently failed to take in account that numerous other countries do not accept the concept 'judge-made law', neither in theory nor in practice.

In contrast to the judge-made law in the Anglo-Saxon world, 'law' in the European and other systems, is made by its legislators, normally their parliaments in co-operation with their governments.

The role of a judge in these countries is thus to find the legal rules in promulgated texts and apply those to the facts in a case before the court.

In this context we may stress again the precipice that exists between Anglo-Saxon ideas of law and those of the so called 'civil law systems', adopted by the whole of the rest of Europe and of many over-seas countries. In the Anglo-Saxon system adopted by Great Britain and its vast Commonwealth (Canada, India, Australia, New Zealand etc.) as well as the United States, all perceive 'law' as something in principle announced by *the judges in their countries*. The concept of law in the Anglo-Saxon world is thus fundamentally different from that in continental Europe and its ex-colonies and a vast number of other countries, like China and Japan that have followed the civil law tradition.[123]

As stressed above, the judge plays an important role in the Anglo-Saxon systems as a veritable *legislator*. But *this is not at all the case in the numerous other countries* in the world: there the judge merely *applies* rules enacted by institutions that have the power to do so in respective countries, such as the parliaments, with or without the participation of the governments.

But once a judge strays from clear texts and seeks to 'develop' international law by examining the 'customary' behaviour of States *or* if he relies heavily on the judgment of other judges, he behaves in a way that is only considered legitimate in the Anglo-Saxon world. In other jurisdictions – in well over a hundred States – the

---

[123] Holmes, O.W., 'The path of the law', 10 *Harvard Law Review*, 1897, 457: *'The prophecies of what the courts will do in fact, and nothing more pretentious, are what I mean by the law'*. Note that one third of the ICJ Judges follow the Anglo-Saxon tradition.

judge is held to act *ultra vires* if he acts in this way as he is devoid of competence to legislate but only entitled to *apply* the existing law.

Although Lord Phillimore represented the United Kingdom in the Advisory Committee that drafted the Statute of the Permanent Court of International Justice, the PCIJ, in 1920 – almost exactly copied in the Statute of the International Court of Justice, the ICJ, in 1947 – he was adamant that the Court should not have any *legislative* function. After lengthy discussions, his colleagues agreed with him.[124] It is of utmost importance to resist any suggestion that judgments of the International Court of Justice have any legal binding effect, except *inter partes*. If some judgments *appear* to have wider effect and to apply as general rules, it is because of *another* underlying ground of obligation, for example, because the judgments *reflect* other already binding rules.[125]

2. Identification of Relevant Law

How can we identify what is the *real* international law? Which rules are *really* reflecting what is needed in international society? We must first rid ourselves of fictitious ideas that the bulk of

---

[124] PCIJ, *Procès-verbaux des séances du Comité consultatif des juristes 16 juin – 24 juillet 1920*, 393 *et seq.*

[125] See, in detail, *infra*, in Part Two, B III ii under *jus cogens. Cf.* See, my *International Legal Order, op. cit.*, 244 *et seq;* 'apparently' binding Resolutions of the United Nations General Assembly. *Cf.* my article on 'The legal value of recommendations of international organisations', *Anglo-Soviet Symposium*, London, 1986, 10 and my article 'The effect of Resolutions of international organisations' in *Theory of International Law at the Threshold of the 21*st *Century, Essays in honour of Krzysztof Skubiszewski*, ed. Makarczyk, J., The Hague: Kluwer, 1996.

international rules stem from the actual 'behaviour of States', usually presented as 'customary law'.[126]

We must thus finally admit that the ideas according to which international law is the result of the behaviour and custom of States is pure *fiction,* and we must watch out for the illusory and fallacious arguments adopted by the majority of international jurists.[127] The individuals, the human beings, the 'people', play a primordial role in international society and their rights and duties do not follow from any customary behaviour but from rules that are necessary for the survival of international society, and these are rules that are even easily identifiable.

In the mind of civil law lawyers, a judge should, on the international level, apply, as 'legislative material' in a specific Case, the basic texts of a treaty or a convention. In the case of a treaty setting up an organisation, the role of a judge can then go further and assess what later rules issued by the organisation could be relevant in the Case. The entity involved in the Case might have implied powers to emit further rules accepted by the Member States by implicit or '*abstract consent*'.[128]

But beyond such pedestrian efforts to find relevant texts – only possible when there are relevant treaties or rules of organisations – thus in other cases, what does the Judge do? The contemporary

---

[126] See, *infra*, for criticism of the traditional notion of 'customary law', Part Three, IV iii.

[127] See, *infra, loc. cit.*

[128] See, for my theory on *abstract consent*, my *Law Making*, *op.cit.*, Chapter One: the founders of an organisation give their authorisation, in advance and in *abstracto*, to enable this entity to take necessary measures to obtain the objectives for which is was founded. *Cf.*, *infra*, Part Two, I iii and Part Three B i-iii, on the mechanisms to provide such consent.

international judge, from any background, Anglo-Saxon or civil law systems, refers to *precedents*. Why? Sometimes judges do not seem to realise that this is only expedient *in the Anglo-Saxon world*.[129] Elsewhere, why would a judge seek precedents when he seeks to find the contents of the law? The result has been that numerous international cases follow others that might have been wrongly decided.[130] It may be noted that article 38 of the ICJ Statutes refers to the law that the Court will apply, and ranges 'judicial decisions' only as a 'supplementary' source of law for the Court and specifically as the first few words of that reference only bearing in mind that such references to 'judicial decisions' can only be 'subject to the provisions of Article 59' that, in turn, reminds us that cases have only binding force between the parties to the dispute in question.[131]

Worse still, the international judge pretends to decide according to such precedents, claiming that they represent 'customary law. Why? How? How can a court case in another action possibly provide evidence of the substance of the law especially as that other judgment only has force between the parties to that earlier dispute.

Furthermore, judges in international cases do not even seem to realise that local, municipal cases, should not carry much weight as to the contents of a rule of international law. This irregular procedure endangers the Rule of Law in international society. It is, above, noticeable when international judges, especially in the International Court of Justice, in the International Criminal Court

---

[129] *Cf.* Jain, N., 'Judicial Law making and general principles of law in international criminal law, 57 *Harvard International Law Journal*, 2016, 111.

[130] See, *infra*, Part Three, IV iii 3 on, for example, the *Tadić Case*.

[131] See, further on the impact of this article on 'Sources', *infra*, in Part Two, B II.

or in the War Crime Tribunals, seek to prove what customary law says on a particular subject. This problem is aggravated by political elements that have been allowed to influence such Tribunals. It appears furthermore that apologies due to those who have been wrongly accused are sorely missing.[132]

So what should the international judge ideally do to find out the contents needed for the relevant rules to be applied in a specific case? Rather than relying on vague and arbitrary findings of customary rules, he could perhaps assess whether the case in question has a bearing on the *prophylactic* rules set out in this work or on any other rules of the *intrinsic law*, or indeed, on any of the *extrinsic supplementary* or facultative rules. Such an approach might be far more in line with successful attempts to achieve justice between parties.

f) *Interactivism*

Numerous subjects of the international legal system contribute to amplify and supplement the '*intrinsic law*' by various measures that will activate other *latent* rules of the international legal order.

In the majority of States in the world the *intrinsic law* is thus supplemented by the acts of various subjects of the international legal order. Some of these subjects have their personality *activated* when they take action that is internationally 'relevant'. Thus, individuals are not always acting in a way that has this relevance.[133]

---

[132] Note, for example, spectacular deviations from normal court proceedings in the *Gotovina Case*, ICTY, IT-06-90, acquitted on appeal in 2012. See, for my forceful criticism of this state of affairs, *infra*, in Part Three, IV iii 3.

[133] See, *infra*, in Part Two, A, The Doctrine of International Relevance.

Other entities also contribute to the development of further rules by a mechanism we have called *interactivism*: a system by which *an international subject takes a decision that activates a set of rules from a pool of norms.*[134]

iii. The Drift Away from the Exclusive State Paradigm

a) A General Trend

It has, for a considerable time, been accepted that not only States are *actors* in international society. To writers on international relations the drift away from the exclusive State paradigm has been particularly prominent.[135]

b) International Legal Personality

Some argue forcefully that it is not 'useful' to analyse who is endowed with 'international personality' under the international legal system.[136] Those who adhere to the American process school prefer to speak of 'participants' in the process; but we do not learn much from that. Yet, personality is an essential concept in any legal

---

[134] See, *infra*, in Part Three, III, The Theory and Mechanisms of Interactivism.
[135] *E.g.*, Burton, J.W., *Systems, States, Diplomacy and Rules*, London: CUP, 1968, *passim;* Aron, R., *Paix et guerre entre les nations*, Paris: Calman Lévy, 1962, 133.
[136] Millon, D., *The Ambiguous Significance of Corporate Personhood*, Stanford Agora, 2001, *available at* http://papers.ssrn.com/paper.taf? abstract_id=264141. *Cf.*, Alvarez, J. E., 'Are corporations 'subjects' of international law?' in 9 *Santa Clara Journal of International Law*, 2011, 1.

system as it is that enables us to assess responsibility and liability by the process of imputation.[137]

States are certainly the most important 'legal persons' acting on the international stage. However, apart from States also other entities are subjects of the international legal order, individuals, groups, institutes etc., but these units are merely *potential subjects* of international law as they are not always active, or in other words, their actions are not always relevant on the international stage. We therefore suggest that the personality of any non-State entity of individuals is *activated* in certain situations by certain acts.[138]

We may also note that even States do not always act in their capacity of international subjects when they devote themselves to internal matters, specific to their own *reserved domain*.[139] It is only when States acts in their external capacity *or* when they violate certain peremptory norms[140] of international law in their own internal affairs, that their actions become relevant to international law.

Our expansion of the subjects that enjoy international personality represents a dramatic area of change in international law that will have considerable impact on the theory of international law. This must be seen in the light of the *function* of international personality that merely implies that an entity is entitled to *assume*

---

[137] See, on Imputation, *infra*, in this Part.

[138] See, for the mechanism of such *activation*, *infra*.

[139] *Cf. supra*, in this Part, I ii c) 2 and Part Two, B I I a) 1 on Allocation of National Space. See, further, my *International Law and the Independent State*, 1994, London: Gower, *passim* and conclusions at 232.

[140] See, *infra*, Part Two, A III ii, on *jus cogens*.

certain rights in the international legal order and may be *imposed certain duties* under the same legal system.

c) International Personality and Imputation

In this work, we strive to embrace an extended comprehension of *international personality*, that is to say the capacity to assume *rights and obligations* under international law. This implies indeed a dramatic change of theory: but we only adjust what the textbooks already should have done to make the theory comply with what is actually going on in the world. Individuals and hosts of other 'subjects' act to show they do have such direct rights and obligations under international law. We even consider individuals to be the main subjects of international law; individuals are much neglected by the traditional textbooks who relegate them to the arbitrary enjoyment of human rights, limited to what States afford them.

Legal personality is, of course, mainly a formal concept which does not confer, by itself, any specific rights of duties. Once we link a specific act to an international 'subject' or 'person', we use a mechanism normally referred to as 'imputation'. Thus, legal personality serves as a *focus* of imputation.[141] This notion is essential in order to trace the 'actor' and above all to apportion the responsibility for an act if such an act violated a binding rule. Imputation is also necessary if an act is derived back to an actor

---

[141] Sereni, 2 *Diritto internazionale*, 1956, 258; Kasme, B., *La capacité de l'Organisation des Nations Unies de conclure des traités internationaux*, 1960, 30.

who enjoys immunity for his behaviour, such as a diplomat or a statesman.[142]

Some have sought to dispense with the notion of imputation,[143] but it is hardly possible to identify who are the true authors of acts, nor is it possible to assess the value of consent, unless the notion of imputation is retained as a main tool. An act may be imputed[144] to a State, to a non-State or any other actor in international society.

d) Entitled Persons

To the present writer, who considers *law* to be *a normative system between legal subjects*, it is important to *identify the subjects* of the international legal order. In some national systems a distinction is made between '*subjects*' and '*persons*'; this is not so in international law. A subject, or a legal 'person' in the international system, is defined by having direct international rights and obligations and being bound by the international legal system.

Thus, any entity or person capable of exercising international rights or capable of being under international duties must be a subject – legal person – of the international legal order.

The principal subjects of international law are, without any doubt, the individuals. But as will explained later, their behaviour is not always *relevant* in international society. It is normally the States that are the strongest entities and whose actions are most

---

[142] But note that this immunity is being gradually reduced, see, *infra*, in Part Two, B v d).
[143] Brownlie, *Responsibility*, op. cit., 367.
[144] See, *supra*, I, i, d and *infra*, I, ii, b.

visible on the international scene. But contrary to what traditional textbooks claim, States are not the only entities that are 'subjects': a pragmatic analysis reveals that a great number of entities appear to be 'subjects' and have international 'personality', that is to say the right to assume rights and obligations under the international legal order.

We must remember that until recently 'international law' was called in France, where the leading jurists published their works during the 17th and 18th century, *le droit des gens* or the '*law of peoples*'. In Germany a similar expression has been retained, *Völkerrecht* as in the Scandinavian languages *folkrätt* and *folkeret*. These expressions reflect the importance of the *individual* and the *nations* in this legal system.

In England Brierly's famous treatise on international law was called *The Law of Nations* which shows that well into the 20th century legal thought in England was also open to recognising the importance of *individuals* grouped in various *nations*.[145]

1. States

There is little variation in the traditional definition of international law by those who consider it as a normative system. Most textbooks of the normative school refrain from going into any elaborate definition of and, in a cursory manner, refer to international law as

---

[145] *E.g.* Brierly, J.L., *The Law of Nations*, 1st ed., Oxford: Clarendon Press, 1928, & 6th ed. by Waldock, Oxford: Clarendon Press, 1963, p. 41. But see below that the ICJ considered the term 'law of nations' as inappropriate.

a 'system of law between States'.[146] States are said to be the main subjects of the international legal order.[147]

The Permanent Court of International Justice entrenched the common view that international law regulates only relationship between 'independent' States.[148] 'International' in the sense of a law between 'peoples' as indicated in German (*Völkerrecht*),[149] would even be a misnomer.[150] It would at least be a system 'primarily'

---

[146] Gihl, T., *The Legal Character and Sources of International Law*, Stockholm: Almqvist & Wiksell, 1957, 53; idem, *International Legislation,* Oxford: OUP, 1937; Parry, C., 'The Function of Law in the International Community', in Sørensen M., (ed.), *Manual of International Law*, London: Macmillan, 1968, 1; idem, *Les sources du droit international*, Copenhagen: E. Munksgaard, 1946; Hall, W.E., *A Treatise on International Law*, 8th ed. par Pearce Higgins, A., Oxford: Clarendon Press, 1924, 1. Some authors have called international law 'external constitutional law', (*äusseres Staatsrecht*), Heffter, A.W. & Geffcken, F.H., *Das europäische Völkerrecht der Gegenwart*, Berlin: E.H. Schröder, 1888.

[147] Kelsen, H., 'La naissance de l'état et la formation de sa nationalité,' *RDI*, 1929, 613; Mouskhely, M., 'La naissance des états en droit international public', *RGDIP*, 1962, 469; Bluntschli, J.K., *Deutsche Staatslehre für Gebildeten*, Nördlingen: Beck and idem, *The Theory of State*, Oxford: OUP, 1895; Guggenheim, P., 'Les états comme sujets de droit des gens', in 'Les principes de droit international public', 80 *RCADI* 1952 80; Marek, K., *Identity and Continuity of States in Public International Law*, Paris: Droz, 1954; Arangio-Ruiz, G., *L'Etat dans le sens du droit des gens et la notion du droit international*, Bologna: Coop. Libreria Universitaria, 1975; Münch, F., 'Staat und Völkerrecht', *Festschrift Doehring*, Berlin: Springer, 1989, 625; Uibopuu, H.J., 'Gedanken zu einem völkerrechtlichen Staatsbegriff' in Schreuer, C., ed., *Autorität und internationale Ordnung*, 1979, 87.

[148] *The Lotus Case*, (1927), PCIJ, Series A., No. 10, 18.

[149] In Scandinavian languages, '*folkrätt*' or '*folkeret*'.

[150] '*...ein falscher Name*': Sauer, E., *Grundlehre des Völkerrechts*, 1948, 17. *Cf.* 'le droit des gens' in French.

between States[151] or between States and entities which, from a formal point of view, were 'equal' to States.[152]

What are the 'hallmarks' of States? One usually demands three standard criteria to be fulfilled before an entity is considered to be a State: it must have a territory, a population and organs to exercise effective control over both.[153] Once such an entity is formed, it has emerged as a State. Many claim that recognition, that is to say acknowledgment by other States that the new State 'there',[154] has only 'declarative', but not 'constitutive', effect: that is to say, it is not the recognition by itself that will bring about the creation of a new State.[155] Consequently, it is held by most writers that an entity may come into existence as a State, regardless of whether other States recognise this existence.

However, State practice shows that it is only through recognition that a new entity can obtain the right to take part in, for example, diplomatic relations, or become member of certain

---

[151] '...vorwiegend': Seidl-Hohenveldern, *Völkerrecht*, 3rd ed., 1975.

[152] Sauer, *op. cit.*, 23. We are, in this context, not concerned with the essential criteria of what constitutes 'a State'. For a discussion on this, see, in this Part, I iii d) 1 and 4; *cf.* the following note.

[153] See, Crawford, J., *Creation of States*, 1979; Mouskhely, M., 'La naissance des états en droit international public', *RGDIP*, 1962 469; Touscoz, J., *Le principe d'efficacité dans l'ordre international*, Paris: LGDJ, 1964.

[154] See, *cf. infra* in Part Two, C I ii a) and II ii c) on Objective Regimes.

[155] In detail for various theories, see Blix, H., 'Contemporary aspects of recognition', *RCADI* 1970 ii 587; Chen, C., *The International Law of Recognition*, New York: Praeger, 1951; Lauterpacht, H., *Recognition in International Law*, Cambridge: CUP, 1947; Charpentier, J., *La reconnaissance internationale et l'évolution du droit des gens*, Paris: Pedone, 1956; Salmon, J.J.A., *La reconnaissance d'état*, Paris: Colin, 1971.

technical organisations, vital to the survival of the new State.[156] Recognition has thus both declaratory and constitutive elements.

Once a unit possesses the hallmarks of a State it is questionable whether any distinction should be made between those which depend on a treaty and the ordinary type of State. The Holy See is included among States, not only after the Lateran Treaty of 1929[157] but also earlier in history.[158] Danzig, established as a free City under the Treaty of Versailles, and Trieste, given a similar status under the Italian Peace Treaty, were normally held to be subjects '*sui generis*', although it is not clear what the difference would be between their status and 'States'[159]

Cyprus, also set up as a new subject of international law by international agreements, was not allowed to alter its own Constitution under the treaties of 1960 granting it independence.[160]

---

[156] See in detail my *International Law*, 1993, Ch. II and my *International Legal Order*, *op. cit.*,Ch. II; note that Manchukuo, the Japanese puppet State was forced out of existence in the 'thirties by not belonging to the Universal Postal Union (UPU) and the International Telecommunications Union (ITU) without which a State cannot send letters or communicate by telephone and telegram. The Republic of Northern Cyprus has suffered a similar fate as only Turkey has recognised this entity, that possesses all hallmarks of a State but had failed to be recognised by other States, see above the text accompanying note 160.

[157] 1 Whiteman 587, this note and text on the following page.

[158] Phillimore, W., *Droits*, *op. cit.*, 32; *cf.* Phillimore R., *2 Commentaries* and *cf.* Bluntschli, J.E., *Le droit international codifié*, Paris: Guillaume, 1870, 137; Heffter, W.A., *Das europäisches Recht der Gegenwart*, Geffcken, 1848; Cruchaga Tocomal, M., *Nociones de derecho internacional*, 3rd ed., 1870; de Pierredon, T.M., *Histoire politique de l'Ordre souverain de Saint Jean de Jérusalem, (Ordre de Malte) de 1799-1955*, Paris: Wetteren Cultura, 1956, 3056.

[159] *Cf.* 2 Rousseau 413.

[160] See my *Independence*, *op. cit.*, 211 *et seq.*

This, in a sense, produced an anomalous situation, as Cyprus was thus deprived of one of the *main sovereign functions*: that to amend its own Constitution. However, it is unquestionably a 'State', taking part in the United Nations and in numerous other international organisations as a full member. It is possibly even two States, after the unilateral declaration of independence of the Northern part of the country on 15 November 1983, now the Republic of Northern Cyprus, which also seems to possess the hallmarks of a State, although subject to forbidding Security Council Resolutions and merely recognised by Turkey.[161]

Not so long ago it was acceptable to reduce international law to the system between 'civilised' States and some authors emphasised this in their definition of States as subjects of international law.[162] It should be noted that the Statute of the International Court of Justice *still* refers to 'civilised' States in its article 38 which deals with the sources of law that the Court applies in its judicary function.[163] But few now protest against this fairly offensive adjective although it necessarily provokes the question as to whether there are also States that are *not* 'civilised' in contemporary international society?

---

[161] See, Ertekün, N.M., *The Cyprus Question*, Lefkosa: Rustem, 1984; Necatgil, Z.M., *The Cyprus Question and the Turkish Position in International* Law, Oxford: OUP, 1989; see also *e.g.* SC Resolution 365 1974; *Cf.* GA Resolutions 3212 (XXIX) 1974 and 37/253 1983.

[162] See, Bluntschli, J.C., *Das moderne Völkerrecht der civilisierten Staaten* 3rd ed., 1878; Hall, W.E., *A Treatise on International Law*, 8th ed. by Pearce Higgins, A., 1924, 1. See, *infra*, Part Three IV iii A 2 on 'Only Practice of Civilised States?', for formation of customary law.

[163] Article 38 refers to 'general principles recognised by civilised nations'. *Cf. infra*, in this Part under ii II on Sources and in Part Two, B II on General Principles.

2. Inter-Governmental Organisations

The International Court itself set the trend in 1949 towards a expansion of the subjects by its Advisory Opinion in the *Reparations for Injuries Case*.[164] This set off a spark among international lawyers to rethink their categories for, with few exceptions,[165] there had not been, in their quarter, much argument for a deviation from the pattern of sole States. But writers swiftly changed and now all accept that international inter-governmental organisations are legal persons in international society.

Yet, before confirming the international personality of inter-governmental organisations, it was initially suggested that certain criteria must be fulfilled. One would, it was claimed in the 1950s, have to investigate whether the organisation had concluded treaties or not,[166] whether it had the capacity to sue and being sued at law[167] or whether all actions are taken through the organisation in the international field.[168]

---

[164] ICJ *Reports* 1949 174.

[165] *E.g.* Jenks, 'The legal personality of international organisations', *BYIL*, 1945, 267.

[166] But not even NATO had been a party to its Headquarters Agreement, and has surprisingly been held *not* to have international personality, see the aforementioned *Mazzani Case, loc. cit.*

[167] See, *e.g. Germany v Reparations Commission*, 1 RIAA 429; *Germany v Reparations Commission.* 2 *ibid.* 745 and 873; *Germany v Commissaire aux revenus gagés*, 2 *ibid.* 777; *cf.* Institut de Droit international, 44 *Annuaire*, 1952, ii, Recours judiciaire à instituer contre les décisions des organes internationaux, Report by Wengler, W., and observations by *e.g.* Hambro, E., at 325; *cf.* Jenks, C.W., 'Status of international organisations in relation to the International Court of Justice', 32 *Transactions of the Grotius Society*, 1946, 19; cf. 24.

[168] Pescatore, P., 'Les aspects fonctionnels de la Communauté Economique Européenne, notemment les sources de droit', in Universite de Liège, *Aspects juridiques du Marché Commun*, Liege, 1958, 82.

But all these caveats disappeared with time and today even what we call the 'traditionalists' – who, for example, do not widen the circle of international subjects to include individuals – all unanimously agree that international inter-governmental organisations enjoy legal personality in international society.[169]

3. Non-Governmental Organisations

Non-governmental organisations (or the NGOs) are important actors in international society. Such organisations are referred to in article 71 of the Charter of the United Nations where it is provided that the Economic and Social Council of the United Nations

---

[169] See my own work on *Law Making by International Organisations*, Stockholm: Norstedt, 1965; Reuter, P., *Institutions internationales*, Paris: Thémis, 1975; Abi-Saab G., ed., *The Concept of International Organisations*, Paris: Unesco, 1981; Colliard, C-A., *Institutions des relations internationales*, 6th ed., 1990; Valticos, N., International Organisations and International Law, *JAIL* 1986 1; Dehousse, J.M., *Les organisations internationales*, Essai de théorie générale, Liège: Gotier, 1968; Virally, M., *Définition et classifications des organisations internationales*, 1951; Seidl-Hohenveldern, I., *Das Recht der internationalen Organisationen einschliesslich der supranationalen Gemeinschaften*, Cologne: Heymann, 4th ed., 1984; Carillo Salcedo, J-A., *El derecho internacional en un mondo de cambio*, Madrid: Tecnos, 1984; Merle, M., *Les acteurs dans les relations internationales*, Paris: Economica, 1986: Monaco, R., *Scritti di diritto delle organizzazioni internationale*, Milan: Giuffré, 1981; Diez de Velasco, V., *Instituciones de derecho internacional publico*, Madrid: Tecnos, 1986; Dupuy, R.J., ed., *A Handbook of International Organisations*, Dordrecht: Nijhoff, 1988; Schermers, H.G., *International Institutional Law*, 2nd ed., 2005; Bowett, D.W., *International Institutions*, London: Stevens, 4th ed., 1982; Panebianco, M., *Introduzione al diritto della organizzazione internazionale*, Salerno: Edisud, 1987; Ribbelink, O.M., *Opvolging van internationale organisaties*, The Hague: Asser, 1988; Taylor, P. & Groom, A.J.R., eds., *International Institutions at Work*, London: Pinter, 1988.

(ECOSOC) may consult such organisations. These organisations, which may be registered as legal persons under municipal systems but which have activities in the international field, have been a focus of attention of the *Institut de Droit international*.[170] But few attempts have been made later to suggest rules common for such entities or to identify their role in international society. The growth in importance of NGOs has been considerable; some claim that the recent expansion and reinforcement of the respect for human rights has been due to activities by NGOs.[171]

What is clear so far about the position of NGOs in international law, is that they should obviously possess certain *consolidated features to enable them to be distinguished from their members or founders* so that they can *act in their own name*.[172] To be an international legal person, an organisation must be of a certain consolidated type: a mere association is not sufficient for the enjoyment of international personality.[173]

Furthermore, in order to be perceived as 'true' NGOs, they must not pursue lucrative aims.[174] In any event, they cannot be

---

[170] See, Report by Mme Suzanne Bastid, 43 *Annuaire de l'Institut*, 1950 i 547 *et seq.* and ii 335 *et seq;* on earlier work, see 30 Annuaire 1923 i 385.

[171] Feld, W.J. and Jordan, R.S., *International Organisation*, New York: Praeger, 1983, 250.

[172] *Cf. supra*, under Organisations in the previous sections.

[173] *Cf. Mazzani v HAFSE and the Ministry of Defence*, Court of Florence, *ILR* 1955 759 and my doctoral thesis at Oxford University, *Treaty Making Power of International Organisations*, 1962, Chapter One.

[174] 43 *Annuaire de l'Institut*, 1950 i, Resolution, 384. In this respect the price fixing policies of IATA for its own members makes it an uneasy member of the NGO group. It may be more readily associated with the international companies, see *infra* under 13. International Companies.

registered with the ECOSOC of the United Nations unless they have this non-commercial character.

To act as international persons, NGOs, like other associations, must have some coherence. Some NGOs may even be incorporated under municipal law but still enjoy international personality. For example, the International Red Cross consists of the League of Red Cross Societies incorporated under French law and the International Committee of the Red Cross which is incorporated under Swiss law.[175]

However, when the Red Cross acts in an international situation, the organisation certainly possesses international personality, having rights and duties under the international legal system.

On the other hand, if you consult any textbook on international law you will probably not find the Red Cross among the 'subjects' of this legal system. The majority of writers consider the Red Cross to be 'an organisation under private law' which means that the entity has no rights – or duties – in the international field. It is obvious to the present writer who has specialised in the Law of War[176] that the Red Cross has played a most important role in wars and in international armed conflicts and its work in the

---

[175] See, Ruegger, R., 'The Juridical Aspect of the Organisation of the International Red Cross', *RCADI* 1953 i 481; Pictet, J., 'La Croix Rouge et les Conventions de Genève', *RCADI*, 1950, I, pp. 27 et seq.; Guggenheim, P. & Bindschedler-Robert, D., 2 *Traité du droit international public; Avec mention de la pratique international et suisse*, 1953, Geneva, 337.

[176] See my *Law of War*, 1st and 2nd ed., Cambridge: CUP, 1997 and 2000; 3rd ed., London: Ashgate, 2013.

humanitarian field has been more important than that of many inter-governmental organisations.[177]

The NGOs have a very important role to play as *pressure groups* to bring about changes in the law which is important for the development of international law. It is the NGOs that have brought about change in the rules concerning the protection of the environment, the reduction of nuclear armaments and the abolishment of racial discrimination like *apartheid*. The importance of these organisations cannot be ignored as they perform vital activities in the international field.

Many of the non-governmental organisations are not only governed by the international system but also *contribute* to its development: there is an important inter-change with these agencies. The view that international law is a wide system applicable to numerous international relationships is gaining an increasing foothold in modern doctrine. Only if such a comprehensive notion forms the basis of our studies is it possible to understand the network of international rules. The practice of States and other actors in

---

[177] This does not mean that the Red Cross has always acted faultlessly: the Red Cross had its offices very near the hospital in Vukovar where the attacking Serbs took out 297 wounded Croatian soldiers to be shot, see my *Law of War*, cited in the previous note, 3rd ed., 119, 172, 448. The explanation of the Red Cross for not intervening was that their offices in Vukovar in Croatia 'had to await instructions from their Headquarters in Belgrade' in Serbia, the country of the aggressors. At other times it appears that the Red Cross has been ill advised by its ambitious legal experts with little or no experience in the Law of War and who provided the Red Cross with dangerously erroneous advice, for example insisting that terrorists have the right to be treated as Prisoners-of-War, see my article, 'Illegal combatants and the Law of War', *Law Journal of George Washington University*, 2007, 1050, and my *Law of War*, op.cit., 368.

international society provides much material which enables us to establish certain types of rules.

Non-governmental organisations certainly possess international personality in the sense that they can assume rights and be subject to duties.[178] But, as we shall see in the case of individuals, this personality is only *activated* when the NGOs act on the international scene.

4. Nations

The original grouping of a number of individuals who share the same history, culture and perhaps the same religion, can crystallise into a 'nation'. Nations, of ethnic or other coherent type, which form homogeneous entities inside States may have a claim to their own independence by virtue of the rule of self-determination. This principle, much voiced in recent years,[179] entitles a unit to break loose from a mother State, from colonial regimes[180] or from a larger existing unit. Even if such 'nations' decide not to break loose from a State, they often play a role as actors in international society.

Some 'nations' are 'minorities' protected by treaties. Individuals may have been given the right of complaint before international or national tribunals to protect their specific rights under such treaties.[181] But even if there is no treaty, by 'lifting up' groups or minorities, they may acquire a position in international

---

[178] Seyersted, F., 'International personality of inter-governmental organisations: Do their capacities really depend on their Constitutions?' 4 *AJIL*, 1964, 1-74.
[179] See *e.g.* GA Resolutions 1514 (XV) 1960 and 2526 (XXV) 1970.
[180] This was the original ambit of the rule, see GA Resolution 1514 (XV) of 1960.
[181] See *e.g. Polish Nationals in Danzig* (1931), PCIJ, Series A/B, No.44, 24.

society and capacity to act. In the case of South Africa it was a question of a 'majority' that did not have its voice reflected in the ruling of the country. There, too, nations took decisions of importance to international society.[182]

A nation, in the strict sense of the word, is a group of people bound together by historical, ethnic, linguistic, religious or other clear bonds. It is convenient to draw parallels between such units, which, in a sense, represent natural entities, as products of history, and other components of federal structures, for example the States in Australia, or in Canada,[183] which may be conceived as artificial units, but which yet, because of local ties, gradually developed very similar features to 'natural' nations.

The novel rules of 'democracy'[184] safeguard a general right of 'majorities', substantial 'minorities', natural nations, or components of federal or central structures, to achieve their own self-determination, *if there is a concerted and democratic will to obtain such independence.*[185]

A useful example of peaceful and democratic secession from the mother country is the 'Commonwealth of Dominica', a small State with a population of about 76.000, in the Caribbean. Dominica is an English (and Patois) speaking country not to be confused with the much larger Spanish speaking Dominican Republic. Dominica decided to become independent, remaining within the British

---

[182] For example, Prince/Chief Butulezi of the Zulu nations played an important role in international society in the campaign to abolish *apartheid*. *Cf. infra*, in this Part, I iii d) and in Part Two, B II iv.

[183] Quebec has a special position as a clearly distinguishable 'nation', especially because of its language.

[184] See, *infra*, under Part Two, C II c).

[185] See my *International Law*, Stockholm: Jagellonica, 1993, Chapter Two.

Commonwealth. Yet, Guadelope, a French (and Patois) speaking nation, ten minutes away by air from Dominica, preferred to stay with France, their mother country; they even adopted the Euro as their national currency, and is totally integrated in French society as a 'département'.

The difference in the preferred political stance in these two neighbouring countries, Dominica and Guadeloupe, may illustrate the importance and the effectiveness of the concerted *'national democratic will.'* The individuals, the citizens, of these two nations, decided to go different ways.

Many nations in Africa and elsewhere have come to regret leaving a mother country under whose reign the economy and especially the agriculture was flourishing. It may be politically correct to encourage independence of former colonial countries but not all were properly prepared to take on that role. Furthermore, to allow the principle of self-determination without restriction would lead to unacceptable fragmentation of international society. This might, in turn, lead to instablity in specific regions.[186]

The difference between insurgency which, in a sense, represents an illegitimate effort to rebel against central government, and self-determination, which ensures the right of a 'nation', for example, to leave a federation, lies thus in the notion of a *concerted democratic will.* Thus, many nations are content and see themselves as fortunate to remain within viable and strong federations or with a mother country. This is advantageous from many points of view: from the point of view of common defence, of common political

---

[186] See my *International Law and the Independent State*, London: Gower, 2nd ed., 1986, 17.

strength and, not least, from the point of view of reduced costs for representation at embassies and consulates.[187]

As mentioned, it is only a nation with *a consolidated democratic will* that may wish to leave a federation, and often because it attaches importance to its own independence. To produce such a will to go against the federal government, one may expect there to have been a lack in the balance of rights or some other oppression of a constituent nation. In a sense, *it is on the central government that blame falls if there are movements for secession*. This can clearly be seen in the development in Eastern Europe. When the oppressive communist rule was dismantled, nations were content to become independent. In some cases the loosening process was swift and violent, especially in federations where Western powers had earlier contributed to establish a central government by artificial means.[188]

Thus, the principle of democracy operates restrictively to allow secession in the sense that only a nation with a *determined will* to secede can succeed, if this will is anchored in a democratic basis. But the principle of democracy operates also with great force in its other aspect to ensure that the elected government of a State represents the majority of the nation. The idea of

---

[187] But there are some healthy examples of limiting such expenses in the case of the above-mentioned small State, Dominica, who after independence has three Ambassadors, one High Commissioner, one Ambassador in Washington and one with the United Nations in Geneva. The last appointment gave rise to a case in the International Court of Justice when Switzerland delayed granting diplomatic privileges to the newly appointed Ambassador, a Russian. See *Dominica v Switzerland*, 2002, (settled) ICJ, *Reports*, 2002.

[188] The Federation of Yugoslavia was such a construction, assembling peoples with different heritage and different religions, after the First World War. Czechoslovakia was another artifical federation, combining two nations that had different history and often different religions.

democracy, a 'collective human right',[189] which is at the root of self-determination, is a new trend in international law: gone are the days when a State had unlimited power to do anything within its territory, with or without majority support.[190]

The rule of democracy[191] leads to increased international safeguards of individuals and is indicative of the fact that specific groups of individuals, associated into 'nations', may act in international society in their own name. In other words, even nations that have decided not to secede from, for example, a federal State, may in numerous instances act in their own name in international society. In these cases, we notice a duplication of a legitimate international subject, on the one hand the federal or central State, and on the other hand, a nation which forms part of that State. That they both may act as international subjects is clear from the mere fact that treaties can be concluded by such nations.

It has recently been argued that a referendum in a nation that considers becoming independent, would be 'illegal'.[192] In the dramatic events on 1st October 2017 in Catalonia, a nation in the north of Spain, it became clear that the quest and the right of self-determination, entrenched in the Charter of the United Nations, has lesser force in practice, than the right of the central government to

---

[189] See, my *International Legal Order*, *op. cit.*, Ch. V, 284 *et seq.*

[190] This also affects the rules on Human Rights, see, *infra*, Under Part Two, B III v a).

[191] On democratisation of international society, see my *Law of War*, *op.cit.*, Part I iii a.

[192] So, Javier Solano, former Foreign Minister of the European Union and former Head of NATO, *New York Times*, 30 September 2017, claimed that the planned Referendum for Catalonia on 1st October 2017 would be 'illegal'. It may be questioned whether Mr. Solana's allegiance to Spain, as a Spanish citizen, and to the EU as a former Eurocrat, played a major role in this argument.

prohibit a constituent nation from sounding out the opinion of its citizens concerning independence by organising a referendum. In this case, such efforts were quelled by considerable police force.

Here, there is a clear conflict between the right of self-determination – and the right of freedom of expression – and the right of the central government to preserve the *status quo* of a unified State. But the forceful reaction of the central government may well backfire and, instead of quelling what the central government sees as a 'rebellion', the effect may be an even more strengthened aspiration for independence. This could presumably have been averted had the central government arranged talks and negotiations to accommodate various demands of the Catalonians well ahead of any move to arrange the referendum. Force is never a useful solution when there is a quest for secession, as demonstrated in the case of Croatia demanding to leave the Serb-dominated Yugoslav Federation.[193]

The right to independence and the right to organise a referendum about the views of citizens of a nation, has also become topical with regard to the Kurds. Questions about the appropriate balance between the desire for self-determination and the wish for a State to remain intact, may be asked in the context of the planned referendum of the Kurds in Iraq to become an independent State,

---

[193] Croatia had the right under the Federal Constitution to demand independence but when it did present such a demand in 1990 the response of the Federal Government to invade Croatia with the 4th strongest army in Europe. But, as the Croats were fighting for their independence, they were more motivated than the soldiers of the invading army, largely conscripted soldiers, who lacked similar motivation, and the Croats won this conflict with ensuing independence; but with the cost of many lives, see my *Law of War*, *op.cit.*,

given the complications here with numerous of their co-citizens living not only in Iraq but also in Turkey and Syria. Iraq is arguing here too, that a referendum would be 'illegal.'[194] President Erdõgan of Turkey threatened on 1st October 2017 that the Kurds would 'have to pay the price' if they go ahead with a referendum for independence.[195]

By all accounts it would seem an important collective human right of citizens of a nation to go their own way, provided they have the required cultural coherence as well as the concerted *will* to become independent.

The term 'Nation-States' for the emerging units in the 16th and 17th century is increasingly a misnomer for many States in contemporary international society. There are few States where a 'nation' coincides with the 'State'; but there are many States, whether or not federations, that contain several nations. The United Kingdom is one State but there is clearly a Welsh and a Scottish nation[196] within that State structure. As the Referendum in Scotland in 2014 shows, there was no concerted democratic will among Scottish citizens to leave the United Kingdom.[197]

---

[194] Statement by President Erdõgan of Turkey at the National Security Council of Turkey, *New York Times*, 22nd September 2017.

[195] *New York Times*, 1st October 2017.

[196] There are limits to what a 'nation' may undertake in international negotiations without the authorisation of the central government. In 2016 Nicola Sturgeon, the Scottish Premier, sought to obtain a separate agreement to stay in the European Union although the central government was committed to 'Brexit', to leave the EU after a Referendum. The EU refused to accommodate her demands of an agreement with the Scottish nation; but this might also have been a political attempt of the EU to prevent the UK leaving the EU.

[197] The Referendum took place on 14th September 2014 with a considerable majority in favour of remaining with the United Kingdom.

5. Social 'Classes'

Before the collapse of communism, there was a whole school of thought pretending to distinguish the separate legal personality of *classes*. As communist thought was founded on the 'struggle' between classes, individuals could not enjoy such personality by themselves under Marxist legal doctrine, but only in the conglomerate of a 'class'. Now, such thoughts are obviously merely of historical interest. On the other hand, a short summary of Marxist ideas in this field may be helpful to understand other theories put forward by scholars of the ex-Soviet Union and its satellite States. It may particularly useful to clarify the exaggerated claims to State sovereignty presented by such scholars.

Soviet writers thus insisted early that international law involves actors other than States, primarily 'classes' rather than individuals as such; these 'classes' were said to be involved in a struggle between two systems.[198]

Korovin defined international law as the totality of legal norms in force which determine the rights and duties of the collectivities of governing classes that participate in international relations.[199] But when – as it was then thought possible – the universal socialist system prevails, this would inevitably imply the 'swan song' of international law: there would be no need for such law.[200]

---

[198] Pashukanis, E.B., *Ocerki po mezhdunarodnoe pravo*, Moscow: State Publishers,1935, 5.

[199] Korovin, E.A., *Sovremennoe Mezhdunarodnoe*, Moscow & Leningrad: State Press, 1926.

[200] Koshevnikov, F.I., *Sovetskoe Gosudarstvo Revoluciya Prava*, No.3, 1930, 148. Lenin abolished the Chair of International Law in Petrograd in 1918 but this post was re-established in 1922 when it became impossible to conduct international

Soviet writers later returned to the prevailing idea that international law is a system of legal rules between States.[201] However, they still claimed that States do not necessarily express *their own collective will* but only *the will of the dominant classes* in each society. In this way classes, or at least one type of class, would still be involved in the formation of international law albeit in a fairly indirect way. In line with traditional Marxist-Leninist thought, international law was thus held to form a superstructure above world economic relations which exist between States and in which dominant classes are antagonists.[202]

One reason for the return to the idea of the State as the central actor in international law was the reemphasis of the notion of sovereignty in Soviet legal writings. Sovereignty had always been emphasised as paramount to Marxist-Leninist theory and entrenched in basic constitutional rules,[203] although some noticed

---

communications and negotiations without recourse to advice on international law. The Communist Party also installed special tribunals for consular law. *Cf.*, Butler, W.E., 'The origins of international legal education in the Soviet Union: the Kravchenko syllabus', 43 *Revue d'Histoire du Droit*, 2014, 297. *Cf.*, Malia, M., *The Soviet Tragedy: a History of Socialism in Russia, 1917-1991*, New York: The Free Press, 1994.

[201] Vyshinski, A.Y., 'Mezhdunaronoe pravo i mezhdunarodnaya organizaciya', in *Sovetskoe Gosudarstvo i Pravo*, No.1., 1948, 32.

[202] Durdenevski, V.N., and Krylov, S.B., *Mezhdunarodnoe Pravo*, Soviet Academy of Sciences (ed.), 1947, 5. *Cf.* Tunkin/Toukine, G.I., *Droit international public*, Paris: Pedone, 1965, 244.

[203] See the Declaration of 2nd November 1917 on the Rights of Peoples of Russia as well as in the Soviet Constitution of 10th June 29 1918. *Cf.* the emphasis given to sovereignty in the new Constitution of the Soviet Union of 7th October 1977, article 29. *Cf.* views of writers such as Korovin, *Mezhdunarodnoe pravo pereshodnogo vremini*, 2nd ed., 1924, 37.

early that it ought, logically, to be subordinated to the socialist objectives and not form an end in itself.[204]

The concept of sovereignty soon demoted the influence 'classes' had been held to have on the development of international law.[205] Sovereignty to socialist theorists in the Eastern bloc was said to form the very basis of international law.[206] On the other hand, the concept of sovereignty was claimed to have different 'contents' in socialist countries than in other States.[207]

But Soviet writers possibly overlooked the simple fact that sovereignty is merely a convenient point of focus to explain the external expression of the will of peoples, (and, in Soviet terms, of 'classes'), in international affairs. Sovereignty is thus largely a formal concept which can be used to explain the convergence of wills of groups within one country in the apex of internal power and serve for subsequent imputation of acts.[208]

Later works by Soviet writers took a broader view of subjects of international law, acknowledging a number of actors in international society, beyond both States and 'classes'.[209] At the very end of communist rule in Russia, there was also a sudden

---

[204] See Koshevnikov, *Sovetskoe Gosudarstvo i Revoluziya Prava*, No.3., 149 and Ratner, Mezhdunarodoe pravo v Marksistkom osvecenii, in *Sovetskoe Gosudarstvo* No.6, 1935, 131.

[205] See *e.g.* Levine, I.D., *Suverenitet*, Moscow, 1948, 64.

[206] See also *Supra*, I i d) 2 on Legal Personality and Imputation.

[207] Bystricki, R., *Le droit de l'integration économique socialiste*, 1978, Leyden: Sijthoff, 13; Tunkin, *Teoria, op. cit., loc. cit.* and *supra*, I i d) 2 on Legal Personality and Imputation.

[208] *Supra*, I i d) 2 on Legal Personality and Imputation.

[209] Tunkin, G.I., *Law and Force in International Society*, Moscow: Progress Publishers, 1983, 25; *Pravda i sila v mezdunarodnogo sistema*, Moscow: Progress Publishers, 1981.

acknowledgment that not only is international law important – it even prevails over national law.²¹⁰

6. Minorities

Some minorities are protected by treaties. Individuals may have been given the right of complaint before international or national tribunals to protect their specific rights under such international agreements.²¹¹ Even outside treaties it appears that minorities may enjoy international personality and thus be entitled to protection.²¹² This protection may be enhanced if the State where they reside has bound itself by a specific unilateral declaration²¹³ to respect certain minorities in some particular way. Furthermore, general rules may also protect minorities as some relevant rules coincide with, or are subsumed under, general rules on human rights.²¹⁴ Rights of

---

²¹⁰ *Supra*, under I I d) 2 on statements by the then Soviet Foreign Minister in 1989.

²¹¹ See *e.g. Polish Nationals in Danzig* (1931), PCIJ, *Series* A/B, No. 44, 24. For specific treaties see Treaties of Versailles, Neuilly, Trianon, Lausanne and St. Germain after the First World War in 1919 and the Treaty of Dorpat of 1920, of Riga of 1920, of Brunna of 1920 and Upper Silesia of 1922. Cf. also the 1947 Peace Treaty which in parts deals with South Tirol/Alto Adige as well as the Austrian State Treaty of 1955.

²¹² See, Claude, I.L., *National Minorities*,Cambridge, Mass.: Harvard Univ. Press, 1955; Modéen, T., *International Protection of National Minorities in Europe*, Åbo: Åbo Akademi, 1961; Pietromarcho, L., (*i.e.*Sabelli, L.), *Nazioni e minoranze etniche*, Bologna: Zanichelli, 1928; Langenhove, F.V., 'Le problème de la protection des populations aborigènes aux Nations Unies', 89 *RCADI* 1956 321; Kunz, J.L., 'The present state of international law for the protection of minorities,' *AJIL* 1954, 282.

²¹³ For unilateral declarations see my *Concept, op. cit.*, 105-106.

²¹⁴ See my *Independent State, op. cit.*131 *et seq.*

minorities must be finely balanced against the rights of the State to decide in its own territory[215].

7. Majorities

In the case of South Africa, there was a question of a *majority* – not a minority – which did not have its voice reflected in the ruling of the country during the *apartheid* system.

The action of majority groups is important and relevant to international society. The novel rules of *democracy*[216] would appear to ensure that a majority group should always be guaranteed influence in the running of the country. But, as seen from ample practice around the world, this is not always so. From the 1970s onwards, South Africa is obviously the most flagrant example of disrespecting this rule. In due course, the aim of a 'one man – one vote' was ensured in South Africa.

This took some time to achieve: much was needed in terms of education and information before such policy could be effectively introduced so that every man and woman knew what they were voting for in open elections.

Majorities thus enjoy rights and duties, as coherent groups, under international law and accordingly, majorities are subjects of the international legal order. They are, for example, assured a general right of self-determination, even if this cannot always be immediately realised.

---

[215] On this power and its limitation see my *Independent State*, *op. cit.*, passim.
[216] See my *Law of War*, *op. cit.*, 24 and *supra*, in this Part I iii d) 1 under States, *infra*, d) 17; *cf.* Part Two, C I c) on Sovereignty and Democracy.

They also enjoy a right not to be subjected to *apartheid* or other degrading treatment. Any State which exposes them to such a system is immediately responsible for a serious violation of international law. This is clearly indicated by Article 19 of the Draft of the International Law Commission on State Responsibility. Offending States may be subjected to economic sanctions[217] or other forms of disapproval.

On the other hand, the black majority in South Africa is itself now under duty, when its political influence has increased, to respect the rights of white and other minorities.

As majorities tend to be naturally more powerful because of the numerical superiority, they have an important duty to, in turn, respect and safeguard the interests of minorities, particularly with regard to their safety under the law.

8. Liberation Movements

In the 1960s and '70s the 'liberation movements' were regarded as a 'new-comers' as actors on the international scene. Such movements were occasionally allowed to attend certain international meetings as 'observers' in international organisations, but without the right to vote. 'Liberation movements' properly so called were those that sought to rid themselves of colonial rule. That means that their number was vastly reduced after 1980 – most colonial regimes had been abolished during the 1960s and '70s. For some reason, however, the Palestinian Liberation Organisation – the PLO – has traditionally been considered as a 'liberation movement' in

---

[217] Sanctions are not necessarily the most effective way of dealing with an unwanted situation in international society, see, *infra*, Part Two, III i a) under Sanctions.

its attempts to establish its own 'State' although it is long after it was subjected to any 'colonial rule'.[218] But it appears to consider itself as 'subjugated' by Israel and therefore *mutatis mutandis* in a similar role as the previous 'liberation movements'.

Some 'liberation movements' were gradually admitted as voting delegates to some organisations, and even granted the ability to accede to proper State treaties.[219] But, as mentioned above, there are hardly any 'liberation movements' left – apart from the PLO. The PLO's own proclamation as a State – then without a specific territory – was largely ignored in the textbooks on international law. However, Israel's limited and ambiguous 'recognition', later contested as such by Israel itself, of the PLO in 1993 implied, in the opinion of some, a confirmation that the PLO 'exists' but this did not imply any admission that Palestine is a 'State'.

The border line between a 'State' and a 'liberation movement' is indeed difficult to discern in some situations. But a State is supposed to have a more or less fixed territory, an identifiable population, a government and organs to control the population and the territory.[220] It is difficult to claim that Palestine fulfils these criteria. On the other hand, had the PLO not been a 'subject' of international law at the time of negotiation with Israel, there could not have been any agreement, as even for contractual negotiation legal personality must be required.[221]

---

[218] Palestine was under British rule 1919 – 1948 according to a Mandate of the League of Nations and before then under the Ottoman Empire from 1516.
[219] See, in detail, my *Law of War*, op. cit., loc. cit.
[220] See, *supra*, under I iii d) 1 on States.
[221] But the United States cut all funds to UNESCO when Palestine was admitted as a full member in 2011. *Cf.* my *Essays on the Law of Treaties*, 1967, with respect to treaties concluded with the DDR.

What must be stressed, though, is that the quality of being a 'subject' of the international legal order does not mean that an 'entity' is a 'State'. International personality does not confer any automatic rights or obligations but rather serves as a point of imputation of specific acts.[222]

9. International Orders

Some textbooks refer to the Order of Malta as a subject of international law, usually without much discussion, apart from the traditional reference to its 'sovereign' character. The Order of St. John of Jerusalem, the Order of Malta, had earlier a territorial basis for its sovereignty, in modern times both in Rhodes,[223] and later, in Malta.[224]

When Malta was lost to the Order in 1798, administration was temporarily transferred to Trieste,[225] but the territorial basis of sovereignty was undoubtedly lost. The island of Gotland had been offered by the Swedish King Gustaf IV Adolphus in 1806 but the Order hesitated to accept while the offer was available.[226] The Treaty of Paris of 1814 made abundantly clear that Malta had

---

[222] Imputation is an essential notion in any legal system to allocate liability and responsibility for acts. See, *supra*, I i d) 2 on Legal Personality and Imputation.

[223] Wienand, A., 'Der Orden auf Rhodos' in Wienand, (ed.), *Der Johanniter Orden, der Malteser Orden*, Cologne: Wienand Verlag, 1970, 145.

[224] Heritte, L., *Essai sur l'Ordre des hospitaliers de St. Jean et son gouvernement civil et militaire a Malte*, Paris: Editions Documents d'Histoire, 1912.

[225] de Pierredon, M., *Histoire politique de l'ordre souverain des hospitaliers de St. Jean de Jérusalem, dit de Malte*, Geneva, Paris: s.p., 1925, 303.

[226] Engel, C-E., *Histoire de l'Ordre de Malte*, Geneva, Paris, Munich: Nagel, 1968, 311.

come under British sovereignty although Napoleon as late as 1802 had 'recognised' the sovereignty of the Order.[227]

When a new Grand Master was elected in 1879 the Order consolidated its international position by further international recognition.[228] The Order had, through its national associations,[229] provided valuable humanitarian aid to those wounded in the Dalmatian uprising in 1869 and during the wars of the 1870's. During the 1885 Balkan war it provided further assistance. In 1924 the Order was expressly recognised by France and the Order was allowed to wear and use their insignia in France. But the way the decision of recognition was phrased it is not entirely clear whether there was recognition of the use of insignia or recognition of sovereignty.[230]

Regardless of formal acts of recognition, which, in any event are not necessary for an entity to enjoy international personality, the Order has undoubtedly been an important actor in international society. It has been particularly active in the humanitarian field, and has sought to improve humanitarian protection in certain treaties bearing on armed conflicts.[231]

The Order of Malta has a number of accredited ambassadors and thus enjoys the right of both active and passive legation. It is, however, questionable whether other international orders are

---

[227] Wismes, A. de., *Les chevaliers de Malte*, Paris: France-Empire, 1972, 225.

[228] de Pierredon, *op. cit.*, *loc. cit.*

[229] See, Maschke, E., *Der deutsche Ordensstaat*, Hamburg: Hanseatische Verlagsanstalt 1935; Pflugk-Harttung, J. v., *Die Anfänge des Johanniter-Ordens in Deutschland*, Berlin: Spaeth, 1899; Bergstrand, Hj., *Johanniterordens historia*, Stockholm: Nya Tryckeribolaget, 1922.

[230] Engel, *op. cit.*, 317.

[231] See further my *Law of War*, *op. cit.*

similarly endowed with such sovereign rights, even though they may be endowed with international legal personality.

10. Institutes and Universities

Numerous international research institutes may act in international society and conclude agreements with various departments of the State where they are based or with which they cooperate. Here we may, for example, mention institutes cooperating under the *Eurospace* programme.[232] Such institutes have normally a non-profit aim in common with the NGOs, although some may, because of their research activities, be more introvert than many NGOs which often have their objective to bring about changes. Research institutes, on the other hand, have as their aim to enhance knowledge (which, in turn, may lead to changes later). When that knowledge becomes internationally relevant, institutes may become actors in international society, being consulted by States for their expertise.

To this category we may also refer standardising organisations that deal with technical matters. Some of these types have been established as international organisations, like the *International Standardisation Organisation (ISO)*[233] whereas others, carrying out very similar tasks, operate as standardising entities under the municipal law of a member State. This is the case of the *European Committee for Standardisation,* formed in 1961, incorporated under Belgian law. Both these bodies consist of 'members' that function

---

[232] *Infra*, I ii c) 16 under International Companies.
[233] Established in Geneva in 1946.

as national standardising bodies.[234] The *Bureau for Weight and Measures*, possibly an example of the present group, has been held to have personality in both international and national law.[235]

As mentioned repeatedly above, the vast majority of contemporary writers on international law insist that only States and inter-governmental organisations have international personality and that no one else[236] contributes to the 'law making' in international society. Yet, here we have an excellent proof that there are others in international society that contribute directly to the making of highly important rules. The 'standards' adopted by the aforementioned bodies clearly form part of some of the most important technical rules of the international legal order.

There are even sometimes important *'pre-standards'* that actors of international society respect *before* they formally enter into effect as it is often commercially expedient to conform with expected technical standards for industrial production.

11. National Public Bodies

Central banks perform important acts in international society. It is not always easy to ascertain whether or not such banks act

---

[234] For further details and for other examples, see my article 'The effect of Resolutions of international organisations' in Makarczyk, J., (ed.), *Theory of International Law at the Threshold of the 21st Century: Essays in Honour of Krzysztof Skubiszewski*, The Hague: Kluwer, 1996; see also my 'Legal value of recommendations of international organisations,' Anglo-Soviet Symposium, London, London School of Economics, 1986.

[235] *Supra*, sections 2 and 3 on inter- and non-governmental organisations.

[236] The 'social process school' does admit numerous 'participants' in the 'decision making process' but it is not clear in what precise way contributions are made, see, *supra*, I i b on the School of New Haven.

'on behalf' of a State.[237] Whether or not central banks act as such agencies, they often conclude agreements of considerable importance.

'Departments' or 'ministries', other than ministries of foreign affairs, often conclude agreement with their 'opposite numbers' in other States,[238] either within a framework laid down by States or by provisional agreements which are subsequently approved by States.

It has also become quite fashionable for cities and towns to 'twin' with other cities and towns in other countries. Such 'understandings' sometimes involve actions where it is clear they are acting on the international scene, assuming rights and obligations.

Other bodies which enter into such cooperation are universities or cities which establish ties with foreign counterparts.[239]

12. National Private Bodies

Some companies, close to their governments, have in the past represented their home States in such a way that they have effectively concluded international agreements on their home State's behalf. Such were the cases of the British, Dutch and French *East India Companies*, The British *North Borneo Company* and the *British South African Company*. Their actions were often imputed

---

[237] See, *The Trendtex Case* (1977) 1 QB 529 (CA).
[238] Blix, H., Statsmakternas förbindelser, Stockholm: Norstedt, 1967, *passim*.
[239] Carreau, D., *Droit international public*, Paris: Pedone, 1986, 28.

to their own States. The companies were even held to be 'mediate sovereigns'[240] or to enjoy 'delegated sovereignty'.[241]

These companies even had the right of legation and sent envoys to Asian States[242] and, as envoys, they concluded 'treaties' and enjoyed far-reaching privileges of immunity.[243] Nowadays the line between public bodies and private companies is hazy.[244] There are certainly still some companies where the State influence is such that the acts of the companies translate the will of its State.

Some of these companies conclude agreements with important consequences in international society. On the other hand, for commercial reasons and, occasionally, for security reasons, such agreements are not always available to the public. For example, companies concerned with development of fissile material have concluded international agreements but these are not readily available. The United Kingdom *Atomic Energy Authority* has been a partner to international agreements with *Studsvik Energiteknik AB*, formerly *AB Atomenergi*[245] and the Norwegian opposite number, *A/S Energiteknik*, formerly the *Institutt for Atomenergi*.

---

[240] Westlake, J., *Collected Papers on Public International Law*, Cambridge: CUP, 1914, 197.

[241] Alexandrowicz, Ch. H., *An Introduction to the History of the Law of Nations in the East Indies*, Oxford: OUP, 1967, 15.

[242] Vattel, E., *Droit des gens ou Principes du droit naturel*, Paris, 1758, 7, iv, vii, 103; Bynkershoek, C. van, *Quaestionum juris publici libri duo*, Lugd. Bat., 1737; ed., Oxford: OUP 1930, ii ch. iii.

[243] Alexandrowicz, *op. cit., loc. cit.; cf.*, Terway, V., *East India Company and Russia 1800 1857*, New Delhi: S. Chand, 1977.

[244] *Cf. infra*, under Part Two C I v on Substantive Rules for All Co-operation on public and private law.

[245] The earlier company was State owned but Studsvik is an independent company.

In the Dragon Agreements of 1957-1962 it was explicitly said that the UK Authority would be 'responsible' for the project to avoid creating a new 'international person'.[246] These agreements were elaborated and concluded under the auspices of the Nuclear Energy Agency of the OECD (then the OEEC), and were subsequently approved by the respective home States of the companies. But it is not always possible to avoid 'creating an international person' as once a body has rights and duties under the international legal system, it is irrelevant how it came into being. It is not States that decide on international personality but the factual functions of an entity that engages in acts in international society.

Similarly, national airline corporations have concluded important international agreements.[247] These are also agreements that are concluded between private bodies. Yet, it is clear that these agreements between airlines engender important effects in the 'international law of communications'. Given the nexus with national governments, often present in airline companies, some of these agreements are close to State agreements.

Private entities have concluded agreements most similar to treaties contracted between sovereign States as is shown in Fishing Agreements in Japan.[248] These agreements have much in common with State treaties. Other agreements between private associations

---

[246] *Cf.* the Halden Agreement of 1958 using a similar technique in favour of the Norwegian Institute.

[247] See, *e.g.* General Agreement of 25th September 1956 on Meteorological Services and Telecommunications; a national institute is charged with the administration and control. *Cf.* Interline Traffic Agreements concluded by national airlines within the framework of inter-State treaties 'registered' by each State, see *Multilateral Interline Traffic Agreements*, Manual, 13th ed., 1986.

[248] See, Lee, L.T., *China and International Agreements*, Leiden: Sijthoff, 1969, 65.

and groups are concluded by various trade unions, political parties, sporting associations and other clubs.[249]

13. International Companies

Another type of entity are 'international' companies, often created by a treaty between States, or in whose equity two or more States participate. These bodies have become important in practice and have clearly international personality to act, as a unit, in the international sphere to attain their purposes.[250]

However, when Fiore put forward the idea in 1915 that such companies enjoy international personality,[251] his suggestions met with disapproval and even scorn. In 1923 W. Phillimore dismissed Fiore's idea that such companies had any 'international position'.[252] Fiore would be the 'only' one to have such an idea, said Phillimore.[253]

Nowadays, it is clear that is Fiore who was the visionary and that it is Phillimore's ideas that must be refuted. Nowadays, it is clear that international companies are very important subjects of international law. There is a great variety of so called international 'enterprises'.[254] Some of these companies may be incorporated

---

[249] See, *e.g.* Agreement between World Lottery Association (WLA) and the International Sport Association (ISA) in 2016.

[250] *Supra*, under International Organisations. and note 29.

[251] Fiore, P., *Il diritto internazionale codificato e la sua sanzione internazionale*, 5th ed., Turin: Utet, 1915.

[252] Phillimore, W., 'Droits et devoirs fondamentaux des Etats', *RCADI*, 1923, 64.

[253] *Idem, op. cit., loc. cit.*

[254] See, *Report* by Seidl-Hohenveldern, I., 60 *Annuaire de l'Institut*, 1983 i, 1 *et seq.*, 97. Among the literature in general, see Adam, H.T., *Les établissements internationaux*, Paris: LGDJ 1957; *idem*, 4 *Les organismes internationaux*

under a national legal system. The EURATOM Treaty, for example, contains provisions on such common enterprises which, from the inception of the Treaty, were of major importance.[255] Under the EU rules, *European companies* for other purposes may now be created, and we can expect this form of entity to become prolific in the future of tightened European cooperation. One other type of entity incorporated under Swiss law but created by a treaty is the *Bank for International Settlements*.[256]

Some bodies of this type are charged with specific duties concerning the management of communication, such as the *European Central Inland Transport Organisation*.[257] Another example is the *Bâle-Mulhouse Airport* which is a company formed under French law.[258] As a further example one may mention the *International Mosel Company* formed by a treaty but incorporated under German law.[259]

An important entity charged with space development in Europe is *European Space Agency (ESA)*[260] that operated, originally, as a French *société anonyme* but under the control of participating

---

specialisés, Paris: R. Pichon et R. Durand-Auzias,1977; Liebbrecht, E., *Entreprises à caractère juridiquement international*, Geneva: IHEI, 1972.

[255] Article 45 *et seq.*

[256] Convention of 20th January 1930, 104 *LNTS* 441; 6 *UNTS*; concluded by France, Germany, Italy, Japan, Switzerland and the United Kingdom. Belgium is now a member but Japan ceased to be one under the 1951 Peace Treaty of 8 September 1951, 136 *UNTS* 45. See, further, Schloss, H.H., *The Bank of International Settlements*, Amsterdam: North-Holland, 1958.

[257] *Cmnd.* 6685, 1945.

[258] Created under a Treaty of 4th July 1949 between France and Switzerland.

[259] Council of Europe, (ed.) *International Public Enterprises in Industry and Commerce*, 1957.

[260] *UNTS* 1/2 15 241, 1962.

States. It was later converted into an international organisation.[261] Another example of such entities working on a regional basis in Europe is the *Eurofima*, a company formed in Switzerland but on the basis of a treaty[262] or *Eurochémie*, incorporated under Belgian law.[263]

14. Multinationals

Another type of company is the multinational company, distinct from the previous category in that it is founded without any basic international treaty. There might well be government participation, like in the case of *British Petroleum*, but multinationals (MNCs) are entities normally founded as companies, organised by private interests within a particular country and according to the private law of that State.[264] Such companies, which often spread their activities through subsidiaries and through their transactions to a number of States, have been analysed by scholars in various disciplines.[265] Some even suggest that such companies enjoy a

---

[261] Convention of 1975, entered into force in 1980, having been ratified by 11 nations.

[262] Convention relative à la constitution d'EUROFIMA, Société pour le financement de materiel ferrovière, see Sweden, Prop. 211/1955 and Prop. 59/1958 concerning the Convention of 20th December 1957 for compensation for chemical radiation of fissile material; cf. Prop. 58/1957 on Agreement of 22nd December 1957 on security control matters before the OEEC/OECD members, administered by Euratom States and, for non EC members, by OEEC/OECD organs; see Prop. 186/1959 on ratification.

[263] Sweden, Prop. 186/1959.

[264] *Cf.* Sereni, *op. cit.*, p. 133.

[265] The vast literature is mainly in the field of economics or international relations, but see, for international law aspects, Angelo, H.G., 'Multinational corporate

measure of what is analogous to sovereignty,[266] as their economic impact is such that they even surpass the scale of the economy of many smaller States.

Still, most international lawyers deny that MNCs have international personality and thus refuse to accept any possibility for MNCs to have direct rights and obligations under international law. Some deny this outright, claiming that States must 'grant'

---

enterprises', 125 *RCADI* 1968, 447; Goldman, B., in Institut de Droit international, 57 *Annuaire*, 1977 i, *Exposé préliminaire*, 266 & *Rapport definitif, ibid*, 318; *idem*, 'The law of international companies', 90 *JDI* 1963 321; Kopelmanas, L., 'L'application du droit international aux sociétés multi-nationales', 150 *RCADI* 1976, 114; Aramburu Menchaka, A.A., 'Multinational firms and regional processes of economic integration', 150 *RCADI* 1976 ii 394; Rubin, A., 'Development in the law and institutions of international economic relations: The multinational enterprise at bay', *AJIL* 1974 475; *Cf.* Vagts, D., 'The multinational enterprise: A new challenge for transnational Law', *Harvard LR*, 1970,739; Vernon, R., 'The multinational enterprise: power versus sovereignty', *Foreign Affairs*, 1971, 736; *Cf. Proceedings of ASIL*, 1972, 14; *Cf.* Dunning, J.H., & Pearce, R.D., *The World's Largest Industrial Enterprises 19621983*, New York: St. Martin's, 1985; Tugendhat, C.S., *The Multinationals*, London: Eyre & Spottiswoode, 1971; Kronstein, H.D., *The Law of International Cartels*, Ithaca: Cornell University. Press 1973; Rolfe, S. E., & Damm, W., & Al., (ed)., *The Multinational Corporation in World Economy*, New York: Praeger, 1970; Hadari, Y.,'Tax treaties and their role in the financing planning of multinational enterprises', *AJCompL*, 1972, 111. See also, for further details, Fayerweather, J., *International Business Government Affairs: Toward an Era of Accommodation*, Cambridge Mass.: Ballinger, 1973; *Cf.* Griffith-Jones, S., 'The growth of multinational banking: The Eurodollar markets and their effect on developing countries', 16 *Journal of Development Studies*, 1980.

[266] *Cf.* Timberg, S., 'International combines and national sovereignty', *Univ. Pennsylvania LR*, 1947, 578.

rights and/or obligations to such entities.²⁶⁷ Others find the whole discussion of international personality of MNCs 'unhelpful'.²⁶⁸

It is useful to remember that MNCs, like States,²⁶⁹ are merely groups of individuals, merged together in a legal structure. As such there is little difference between the acknowledgement that individuals have international personality and that corporations and MNCs do so as well.²⁷⁰

But multinationals often conclude agreements with States and organisations very much along the lines that States do themselves in matters *de jure gestionis*.²⁷¹ Because of their way of acting, particularly in the Third World, multinationals have attracted much negative attention from those who wish²⁷² to see regulating codes of

---

[267] Norwot suggests that '…participation is not equivalent to acting on the international scene in legally relevant ways, and thus does not convey the status of a subject of international law. Rather, international legal personality requires some form of community acceptance through the granting by states of rights and/or obligations under international law to the entity in question.' Nowrot, K., *'Reconceptualising international legal personality of influential non-State actors: Towards a rebuttable presumption of normative responsibilities'* at http://www.esil-sedi.eu/sites/default/files/Nowrot.PDF. *Cf.* Cassese, A., *International Law in a Divided World*, Oxford: OUP, 1986,103; Akehurst, M., *Modern Introduction to International Law*, 7th ed. by Malanczuk, P., London: Routledge 1997, 100.

[268] *Cf.* Statement by Crawford, J., in the context of individuals, in his edition of Browlie's *Principles*, *supra*, under Individuals in this section. For the situation of MNCs, see Higgins, R., *Problems and Process: International Law and How We Use It*, Oxford: OUP, 1994, 49; Clapham,A., *Human Rights Obligations of Non-State Actors*, Oxford: OUP, 2006, 199; Klabbers, J., *An Introduction to International Institutional Law*, 2nd ed. Cambridge: CUP 2009.

[269] See my comments about States and Imputation, *supra*, I iii c).

[270] *Citizens United v FEC*, — U.S. —, 130 S.Ct. 876 (2010).

[271] *Infra*, Part Two, A i-iv.

[272] See *Institut de droit international*, 57 *Annuaire* 1977 ii 338.

behaviour adopted. It seems that MNCs are bound by obligations of international law in the field of human rights.[273] But if they have obligations, that means that they do have international personality. Some Courts have also made it emphatically clear that rules of *jus cogens* certainly bind the MNCs.[274]

In spite of world-wide intense negotiations, numerous statements, promises about 'self-regulating' pledges, drafts and plans, there has not been much advance during the last two or three decades to regulate the behaviour of multinationals.

All these years there have been hopes of various 'codes'.[275] Since 1978 there have been plans for a *United Nations Code for Transnational Corporations*,[276] an ILO so called *Tripartite Declaration on Principles Concerning Multinational Enterprises and Social Policy* of 1978, marginally revised in 2008,[277] a set of OECD *Guidelines for Multinational Enterprises* of 1976, upgraded

---

[273] Dunhoff, J.L., Ratner, S.R., & Wippman, D., *International Law Norms, Actors, Process: A Problem Oriented Approach*, 3rd ed., Aspen: Aspen Publ., 2010.

[274] *Presbyterian Church of Sudan v Talisman Energy, Inc.*, 582 F. 3d 244 (2d Cir. 2009).

[275] Horn, N., 'International rules for multinational enterprises: The ICC, OECD and ILO initiatives', 30 *The American University Law Review*, 923; and Jackson, J. K., *Codes of Conduct for Multinational Corporations: An Overview*, Washington, DC: Congressional Research Service, 2013.

[276] E/C.10/AC.2/8 1978; 17 *ILM* 1978 453; there have been numerous revisions since then and there are recurrent new drafts. The term transnational was adopted to distinguish the Code from the ILO rules. After nearly forty years, there is still only a 'Draft' of the UN rules on this matter in spite of intense negotiations.

[277] The original rules were enacted in 1978, 17 *ILM* 1978 453 and the 2017 version is the 5th edition of these rules.

but not expanded in 2008,[278] a Council of Europe *Draft Code on Multinationals* of 1977,[279] the EU *Code of Conduct for Subsidiaries of Multinational Enterprises* is still the EEC documents of 1977 and 1986. To these may be added the *Principles of the International Chamber of Commerce Regarding Multinational Enterprises* of 1974[280] which had considerable influence *e.g.* on the substantive provisions of the OECD Code. The reason for failure to lay down binding rules may be largely due to the political influence of multinationals.

The abovementioned problems of 'behaviour' of multinationals have over-shadowed any question of applicable law of their transactions. Because of their power position, there is often similarity between their contracts and State contracts.[281]

It is often uncertain whether international law or the national law of the home or of the host State shall apply to transactions of multinationals. It appears that, in practice, at least initial agreements between multinationals and the host State are not always clearly subjected to laws of the host State or to any particular municipal law. Conflicts of jurisdiction (possibly implying primarily conflicts of law) are said to occur 'often'.[282] Such claims are possibly exaggerated: there is little evidence that there are ever many cases on this point before courts or arbitration tribunals. On the other hand,

---

[278] 15 ILM 1976 969; 17 *ILM* 1527; see Blainpain, *The Badger Case and the OECD Guidelines for Multinational Enterprises*, 1977, 1937; the *Guidelines* were revised in 2008.

[279] Doc. 3762 1976. There is no final code yet adopted.

[280] No. 191/83.

[281] *Cf. infra*, in Two, C II iii, Substantive Rules for All Contacts.

[282] Department of Economic and Social Affairs, The Impact of Multinationals in International Relations, New York, 1974, 4950.

it may be useful to suggest that there is a *presumption*, that actions of multinationals before 'arriving' in a host country are governed by their home State. This presumption is particularly obvious with regard to investments in countries affected by UN sanctions. Once the multinational has established a subsidiary company in another State, the laws of that host country should apply.[283] There is little new in this suggestion that merely re-affirms the presumption of the territorial competence of a State. Yet, multinationals are held to have *duties* under international law, especially in the field of human rights.[284] There is thus an area when international law could play an important part when there are violations by multinationals of human rights: legal actions seem to confirm that multinationals are subjects of international law.

An interesting question whether multinational 'corporations' can be liable for violations of international law has arisen in some Cases before Courts in the United States. The US *Alien Tort Statute* (ATS) of 1789 provides federal jurisdiction over lawsuits brought by non-U.S. nationals for torts 'committed in violation of the law of nations or a treaty of the United States.'[285] Until the 1980s this Statute was rarely invoked, but the rise in interest in human rights led to some 150 lawsuits being filed for violations in third countries during the last two decades. Cases have been filed concerning human rights breaches by *UNOCAL* in Burma,[286] by *Pfizer* in Nigeria,[287] by *Coca-Cola* in

---

[283] *Ibid., loc. cit.*

[284] See further *infra*, in Part Two under B III v a).

[285] 28 U.S.C. § 1350. But the Statute does not by itself provide a substantial cause of action: *Sosa v Alvarez-Machain*, 542 U.S. 692, 713–14 (2004).

[286] *Doe v Unocal*, 395 F.3d 932 (9th Cir. 2002).

[287] *Abdullahi v Pfizer, Inc.*, 562 F.3d 163 (2d Cir. 2009).

Colombia[288] and by *Yahoo* in China[289] and – the largest ATS Cases – *Ford*, *IBM* and another 50 companies, for violations of human rights in South Africa during the *apartheid* era.[290]

In 2013, the US Supreme Court ruled in *Kiobel v Royal Dutch Petroleum* that the ATS is limited by the legal presumption that U.S. laws do not extend beyond U.S. borders unless Congress says otherwise. However, the judgment can be understood to rule that the ATS may have extra-territorial application when some of the relevant conduct took place in the United States; but the Supreme Court decided *Kiobel* without reaching the question of corporate liability.[291] The judgment in *Kiobel may* indicate that the general rule is that there is no corporate liability for violations of human rights in another country. But another Case, *Flomo v Firestone,* concerning alleged child slave labour in Liberia, shows that corporations can be held liable in their own right for violations of international law.[292]

Even if lower courts are divided on the question whether corporations can be sued under the ATS,[293] it may be warranted to claim, as we do in this work, that multinational corporations

---

[288] *Sinaltrainal v Coca-Cola Co.*, 578 F.3d 1252 (11th Cir. 2009).

[289] *Xiaoning v Yahoo!, Inc.*, No. C07-02151 (N.D. Cal. July 30, 2007).

[290] *Balintulo v Daimler AG*, 727 F.3d 174 (2d Cir. 2013).

[291] *Kiobel v Royal Dutch Petroleum*, 133 S. Ct. 1659, 1669 (2013).

[292] *Flomo v Firestone Nat. Rubber Co., LLC*, 643 F.3d 1013, 1021 (7th Cir.), 2011.

[293] The 2nd Circuit held in *Kiobel* that ATS does not apply to corporations and the Supreme Court did not specifically pronounce on this: *Kiobel v Royal Dutch Petroleum*, 133 S. Ct. 1659, 1669 (2013). But the 7th Circuit has held that Corporations may be subject to ATS suits: *Flomo v Firestone Nat. Rubber Co.*, LLC,643F.3d1013,1021(7th Cir.2011); so has the 9th Circuit: *Sarei v Rio Tinto PLC*, 671 F.3d 736, 748 (9th Cir. 2011) and the 11th Circuit: *Romero v Drummond Co.*, 552 F.3d 1303, 1315 (11th Cir. 2008) as well as DC Circuit: *Doe v Exxon Mobil Corp.*, 654 F.3d 11, 57 (D.C. Cir. 2011).

may enjoy international personality and can have direct rights and duties under international law.[294] However, the prescriptions of international law may not be *activated* until there is a dispute and such a dispute reaches either a Court or any other instance, like an international organisation with competence in the area.[295] But the mere knowledge by international media of human rights abuses may trigger sanctions by the force of public opinion.[296]

15. Joint Ventures

Since the early 1960s there has been a trend to set up joint ventures for investments in the Third World where both the investor and the host government partake.[297] Normally, the form of cooperation is structured as a company.[298]

The reason for setting up such joint ventures was initially a fear of nationalisation: when a company had invested much capital in surveying, prospecting and on other R&D in a developing country, it seemed unfair if the territorial State then nationalised the company. There were views that full, adequate and prompt compensation had to be paid in the case of a manufacturing company[299] but there was less enthusiasm for this formula on the part of developing countries

---

[294] *Cf.*, Alvarez, J. E., 'Are corporations 'subjects' of international law?' in 9 *Santa Clara Journal of International Law*, 2011, 1.

[295] Beguin, J.P., *Les entreprises conjointes internationales*, Geneva: Droz, 1972.

[296] See, in detail, *infra*, Part Two, C III I a) on sanctions.

[297] See, Beguin, J.P., *Les entreprises conjointes internationales*, Geneva: Droz, 1972; cf. my *Finance and Protection of Investments in Developing Countries*, 2nd ed., 1986, 155 *et seq.*

[298] *Cf. supra*, I ii c) 13 on International Companies and 14 on Multinationals.

[299] See my *Finance and Protection of Investments in Developing Countries*, London: Gower, 2nd ed., 1987, Ch. 4.

if the investment had been in natural resources, such as in minerals or oil. To pay full, adequate and prompt compensation[300] would in such cases involve considerable sums that might risk bankrupting the economy of a developing country. It was often claimed that the right to nationalise would, however, always be justified in the case of natural resources on the basis of the 'eminent domain' and not always against full compensation.[301]

Investors then considered it expedient to reduce the risk of nationalisation by entering into an agreement with the host State. It was sometimes thought wise to even allow the host State to retain the majority of a joint venture, for example at 60/40 % in favour of the host State.[302] For some time the formula contributed to major investments, expecially in oil, even if history shows that the risk of nationalisation cannot always be avoided.[303]

The joint venture is different from other national and international companies: it has peculiarities of its own in so far as it is not designed to run or develop common services or other matters for the parties but rather acts as an umbrella for exploitation

---

[300] *Ibid., loc. cit.*

[301] A number of inter-State treaties contain a clause concerning so-called Investor-State Dispute Settlement (ISDS) procedures that enable private corporations to sue a sovereign State. The United States, for example, have concluded fifty agreements with ISDS clauses. However, according to UNCTAD only a quarter of ISDS cases have been won by investors and not one single case has been successful against the United States. Office of the US Trade Representative, Executive Office of the President, Fact Sheet, 2017. It is to be noted that governments cannot sue investors under the ISDS regime that often do not incorporate human rights: de Zayas, A., OHCHR, 2 February 2016.

[302] *Ibid., loc. cit.*

[303] See, my *International Legal Order*, London: Gower, 2nd ed. 1992.

by one party-expert in the territory of a party-host, for mutual benefit and profit.

Many joint ventures multinationals now have[304] as partners. The ventures, being formed and run by one State party and one private party, often a multinational, function as new entities in international society, even if their popularity has decreased during the last two decades.

16. Private Companies

Naturally, an entity must have some degree of consolidation if it is to act under any legal system. An organisation has international personality if its founders intended it to be such a unit in the international sphere.[305] But we suggest that even personality under municipal law, endowed by the founders of a company indicates that it has also, whenever necessary, personality in the international sphere.[306] In other words, a body, able to act as an entity under the national law of a State may, in certain cases, also act as a unit in the international legal system.

Cases show that even when the organisation is an entity 'merely' under municipal law, rules of the relevant national system are not always sufficient to settle a dispute but recourse has to be made to international rules.[307] Municipal personality is thus

---

[304] *Supra*, in the previous section.
[305] Zemanek, K., *Das Vertragsrecht der internationalen Organisationen*, Vienna: Springer, 1957, 12.
[306] See my *Treaty Making Power of International Organisations, op. cit.*, 47.
[307] *Chemidlin v International Bureau of Weights and Measures*, ILR 1943 5 281; *Maida v Administration for International Assistance*, ILR 1956 510, 515.

sufficient proof of consolidation of an entity also for action in the international sphere. Organisations will often use their municipal personality to act *de jure privatorum*[308] in which case their acts are normally subjected to some municipal law.[309] But if they act in the international sphere, which they clearly are entitled to do if this is necessary to attain the purposes for which they were founded,[310] they act as international persons.[311]

Two important examples may highlight our submission that even private companies may be subjects of international law. As mentioned above, INMARSAT *was* an inter-governmental organisation that was *privatised* and thus became a private company. The European Space Agency was a company registered under French national law that *became* an international inter-governmental organisation. Is it tenable to suggest that these two organisations had diametrically different status under international law during their different structural phases? All the time the two organisations worked on the international scene and their actions had the highest possible relevance to international society. The main activity of both entities concerned Outer Space, the geostationary orbit and beyond. Is it not obvious that they both, during their time as companies under national laws and during their time as international organisations had all the ncessary rights and duties

---

[308] *Branno v Ministry of War*, ILR 1955 757.

[309] *Infra*, under Substantive Rules for All Cooperation.

[310] On implied powers and the classification of what I call '*operative acts*', see my *Law Making by International Organisations*, 1965, 29-34.

[311] See, *infra*, in Part Two, A iv, on the Notion of Comity and C II iii on Substantive Rules for All Contacts: *lex mercatoria*.

under the international legal order to carry out the purposes for which they were founded?

17. Individuals

All the abovementioned categories are *collective entities*, entitled to be qualified as international 'persons', thus capable of assuming rights and obligations under international law. But all these collective bodies are made up by *individuals*. If we analyse actual practice in international society, it is clear that individuals are *also* direct bearers of international rights and duties. However, it is only when their situation or acts are *relevant* in international society that their personality is activated.

Most writers adopt the view that individuals are *not* subjects of the international law legal system. It is claimed that individuals may only act in the international sphere, if they are specifically empowered to have certain rights and duties under a treaty, or, in some cases, endowed with powers by States under internal legislation. Thus, suggestions in the 1920s that individuals are subjects of international law were ferociously dismissed. Thus, propositions by eminent scholars like Spiropoulos[312] or, later, Georges Scelle,[313] that individuals enjoy international personality and can assume rights and duties directly under the international order, were fiercely contested by the majority of international jurists.[314]

---

[312] *E.g.* Spiropoulous, J., *L'individu en droit international*, Paris: LGDJ,1928; Scelle, G., *Droit international public*, Paris: R. Pichon & R. Durand-Auzias), 1949.
[313] Scelle, G., *Droit international*, *op. cit.*
[314] Brownlie, I., *Principles*, *op.cit.*, and literature cited.

Yet, four hundred years earlier the eminent writer Francisco de Vitoria held that not only were individuals subjects of international law but they were even held to be *the main subjects*.[315] Later, around the turn of the century 1899-1900, several Russian theorists supported the idea that individuals were direct subjects of international law.[316] The eminent Russian writer Martens expressed himself in very similar language when he emphasised that the main function of the State is to protect its citizens and safeguard their human rights. The way he phrases this comes very near to holding that individuals are subjects of international law.[317]

Valiant efforts were made later during the 20th century to raise the question again whether individuals did not merit to be

---

[315] De Vitoria, F., In *De indis et iure belli relectiones*, ed. Nys, E., Washington: Carnegie, 1917, I III: '*Quod naturalis ratio inter omnes gentes constituit vocatur jus gentium*'.

[316] Mälksoo, L., *The Oxford Handbook of the Theory of International Law*, Oxford: OUP, 2016, on theories put forward, for example, by Kasanski and Komarovski.

[317] Although Martens did not fully suggests that individuals have international legal personality, his insistence that a main duty of the State is to protect the individuals in its territory, his theories come very close to accepting the international legal personality of individuals. There is now huge interest in the writings of Martens in Russia and his main treatise has been reprinted. Martens, F.F., *Sovermennoe mezhdunarodnoe pravo y sivilizovannykh narodov*, St. Petersburg: Benke, 1883; 5th ed., 1887-1888; reprinted Moscow: Yuridischeskii Kolledzh, 1996; *idem*, *Traité de droit international*, Paris: Librairie A. Maresco Ainé, 1887. *Cf.* German translation, von Martens, F.F., *Völkerrecht. Das internationale Recht civilisierten Nationen* (trans. Bergbohm, C.), Berlin: Weidmannsche Buchhandlung,1883, 2 vols. & Berlin: Weidmann,1887. *Cf.* French translation, de Martens, F.F., *Traité de droit international*, Paris: Librairie Maresco Ainé, 1887; *cf.* Martens, F. de, *La paix et la guerre*, Paris: A. Rousseau, 1901. The Christian name of Martens is Fedor with the patronymic Fedorovich. By commentators he is sometimes called 'Frédéric', 'Friedrich' or 'Fredrik'and his surname is either cited as 'de' or 'von' Martens, depending on the language setting, as is the habit with aristocratic families.

subjects of the international legal order.[318] Thus, one writer held in the 1940s, nearly 80 years ago, with insistence that individuals lack international personality should be dismissed by one as a 'legal fossil'.[319] Observing what was going on in international society in practical terms it would seem that it would make sense that individuals were under direct duties of that order – for how else could 'war criminals' be punished?

But the traditional viewpoint, maintained by the vast majority of contemporary writers,[320] is that individuals are certainly deprived of international personality: some even insist that it would be 'unhelpful' to seek to include individuals among international subjects.[321] Through some misunderstanding some fear that considering individuals to be international subjects would somehow conflict with the eminent importance of the concept of

---

[318] Scelle, G., *Cours de droit international public*, 1947-1949, *op.cit. Cf.*, Dahm, G., *Die Stellung der Menschen im Völkerrecht unserer Zeit*, Tübingen: Mohr Siebeck, 1961; Sperduti, G., 'L'individu et le droit international,' 90 *RCADI*, 1956 727; Korowicz, M.S., 'The problem of the international personality of individuals', *AJIL*, 1956, 533; LaPradelle, A., 'La place de l'homme dans la construction du droit international', *CLP*, 1948 140; Salvioli, G., 'L'individuo in diritto internazionale,' *RDI*, 1956, 5; Norgaard, C.A., *The Position of the Individual in International Law*, Copenhagen: Muncksgaard, 1962; Wengler, W., 'Die Stellung der Einzelpersonen im gegenwärtigen Völkerrecht', in *Festschrift Laun*, 1953, 431.

[319] Dunn, F.S., 'The international rights of individuals', *ASIL* 1941 14.

[320] But see, Walter, C., 'Subjects of international law', Max Planck Institute, Heidelberg: OUP, 2010. *Cf.* my *Concept of International Law*, Stockholm: Norstedt, 1st ed. 1989; 2nd ed. 1994, and my *International Legal Order*, 1st ed. Stockholm: Juristförlaget, 2nd ed. London: Gower, 1994.

[321] Crawford, J., in his edition of Brownlie's *Principles of International Law*, 8th ed., 2009.

sovereignty.[322] The promotion of the international legal personality of individuals, or rather the correction of the mistaken view that individuals are deprived of international personality, does not affect the important framework of the State, the sovereign entity where the individuals are citizens.

Sovereignty provides the essential point of imputation[323] of what the State does and sets the limits of its competence vis-à-vis other States. But, we emphasise again, it is the individuals that make up the State. It is the individuals that legitimise the power of the State. If the balance between the interests of individuals and the authorities that represent them is disturbed, the State will face decline in its social bonds with its citizens although its sovereignty may be preserved.[324] But a balanced orderly State will benefit from the allegiance due to it by its citizens, in return for the protection the State affords its citizens.[325]

In the present work we adopt the view that individuals are not only subjects of international law but even *the most important subjects* of this legal order. It is individuals that make up States and the whole of international society. But, again, as in the case of non-governmental organisations, we note that the international personality of individuals is only *activated* in certain situations and for certain purposes. But such 'activation' does not depend on the

---

[322] For example, in Russian contemporary theory on international law, Garadzhu, N., (ed.), *Suverenitet*, Moscow: Europe, 2006.

[323] See, *supra*, under I iii c) 13 on Legal Personality and Imputation.

[324] See on this point *infra*, in Part Two, C I i c) under Sovereignty and Democracy.

[325] To protect its citizens is, according to Martens, the main task of the State, see Martens, F.F., *Sovermennoe mezhdunarodnoe pravo*, *op.cit*. Note that he also stresses that international law is not built on absolute sovereignty but on the idea of an international society of which sovereign States form part, 178 *et seq.*

will of the State but rather on the specific situation and the acts by or towards an individual.

The fact that an international case is about an individual is not necessarily conclusive for international personality.[326] Thus, for example, there was an individual who was the party of substantial interest in the *Nottebohm Case*[327] or at the centre of the *Lotus Case*.[328] But the primordial importance of an individual, at the centre of a law case, does of course not prove, by itself, that the individual is endowed with international rights and duties.[329]

It became impossible in the 1980s to criticise, for example, South Africa for *apartheid* policies, unless it was admitted that international law had a direct effect inside States, granting individuals certain direct rights: South Africa was not bound by any treaty to grant such rights. Conversely, it becomes impossible to criticise any State's behaviour in war, unless it is admitted that international law has direct effect inside States, also imposing certain duties on individuals, for example with regard to human rights, giving other individuals corresponding rights. Hitler's Germany was only bound by the Geneva Convention of 1929 and yet numerous actions were thought punishable by international society.

If individuals have direct rights and duties under international law, this must mean that *certain rules* of the international legal

---

[326] *Cf.* McDougal, M.S., and Reisman, W.M., *Contemporary Perspective, op. cit.*, 83.

[327] *Nottebohm Case (Second Phase) (Liechtenstein v Guatemala)* (1955) ICJ *Reports* 4, 16.

[328] (1927), PCIJ, *Series* A. No. 10.

[329] *Cf.* also *La Grand (Germany v United States)*, 2001, ICJ, *Reports*, 2001, 466.

system enter the national legal sphere without any 'transformation' by the State organs.

Propositions that rules of international law must be transformed in order to gain validity in the national sphere must be rejected. One may make a distinction between detailed treaty rules that may benefit from such a conversion but rules that concern basic human rights cannot be subjected to such a procedure, as amply shown in practice. The idea of a necessary transposition of international rules to be operative in national law has become an obsession of the Nordic countries.[330] But, again, how can we, on the one hand, punish war criminals, and on the other hand recognise the rights of individuals that have been harmed by the actions of these (or other) war criminals, unless we recognise that international law is directly effective in the interior realm of a State?

Whatever the textbooks say, State practice does confirm that individuals, in numerous situations, are the direct bearers of rights and duties under international law. It is thus amply shown in many cases that individuals act as international subjects.

Among individuals we can also count Heads of State and the members of a Government who can no longer act with impunity in violation of international law. Immunity that was previously generously granted to Heads of State and Ministers have nowadays been reduced or withdrawn. [331]

---

[330] See, *infra*, Part Three, IV vi on 'Allergy' of natural law.

[331] For example, see the case law of the War Crimes Tribunals, for war crimes in former Yugoslavia, ICTY (*The Case of President Slobodan Milosović*, ICTY IT-02-54); the Tribunal for Sierra Leone, (*The Case of Charles Taylor*, SCSL-03-1-T); for details, see my *Law of War*, 3rd ed., London: Ashgate, 2013, 459 & 465 *et seq*.

Just before the fall of communism in 1989, we must note that the Soviet Foreign Minister Edward Shevardnadze – later President of Georgia – was one of the first, Western statesmen included, who in modern times recognised the clear primacy of international law over national legal systems, at least as far as 'fundamental rights' of individuals are concerned.[332]

Again, whatever the textbooks say, State practice thus clearly confirms that individuals, in numerous instances, are direct bearers of rights and duties under international law. There is ample evidence that individuals in many cases act as international persons. The Nuremberg Court ruled emphatically that individuals may have direct international duties[333] and that, conversely, individuals in many cases enjoy specific rights under international law. Subsequently, the whole development of the rules of human rights,[334] shows that individuals are endowed with important rights and duties, not only under treaties, but under general international law, or, as we shall see, under what we, in this work, more conveniently call, *'intrinsic law'*.

The claim that international law has to be transformed into national law before individuals can derive any rights or duties under that system can therefore be refuted as lacking any basis in contemporary State practice.

The behaviour of Hitler's Government was certainly against morals and the respect due to our neighbours. But the acts were not contrary to German internal law: on the contrary the acts purported

---

[332] See my *International Legal Order*, *op. cit.*, and *infra*.
[333] Judgment 1 October 1946, 1st Nuremberg Trials, 222; 41 *AJIL* 1947 220.
[334] *Infra*, under Part Two, B I ii c).

to follow and obey such laws. But the laws were in conflict with the norms a State is obliged to follow under international standards.[335]

Unless we recognise that there are rules that prevail over the authority of the State, it is impossible to explain how those who commit for example war crimes (that were *not* crimes under, for example, German national law) can be punished: if (as the majority of writers claim) they are not international subjects, they can have no *duties* under international law; nor can their victims have any *rights* under international law according to these writers.

We know this is wrong. We know this does not correspond to how things work in contemporary international society. It becomes impossible to criticise any country for its behaviour vis-à-vis individuals unless we admit that international law operates directly in the national sphere, giving rights and duties to individuals. In other words, the citizens and those who live in a country, are endowed with international rights and duties, making these individuals enjoy *international personality*. The main duty of the State is precisely to protect its citizens.[336] Even foreigners present in a State's territory have the right to be protected.[337]

Thus, in any situation where human rights or humanitarian rights become pertinent, it is clear that the rights and duties of these individuals are '*activated*'. However, it is not the acts of the States that produce this situation as the majority of writers pretend: it is

---

[335] *Cf. infra*, in Part Two, under B, Intrinsic Rules.

[336] *Cf. supra*, in this section, on the views of Martens.

[337] See, *Case Concerning Barcelona Traction, Light, and Power Company, Ltd. (Belgium v Spain)*, (1970), ICJ *Reports* 1970, 1, at para 33. 'When a State admits into its territory foreign investments or foreign nationals, whether natural or juristic persons, it is bound to extend to them the protection of the law and assumes obligations concerning the treatment to be afforded them.'

an *automatic activation* once the rights and duties of individuals become *internationally relevant*.

These rights and duties are thus not *indirect*, nor are they *granted by States* – as most textbooks claim. They are not brought into effect by State authorisation or by agreements between States. On the contrary, the rights and the obligations of individuals derive from *intrinsic law*, a system that is developed by the *collective conscience of individuals*. It must be underlined that no rule in any treaty or any convention at present in force at the time, explains why war criminals of the Second World War should be held as guilty of crimes. Nor were there any treaties or conventions concerning the treatment of minorities but it was recognised that individuals of a minority group derived their rights directly from the international legal system. On the other hand, it must be emphasised that it is only the most *fundamental* rights that come into effect in this way.[338]

Thus, not only are individuals subjects of international law but they are probably the most important subjects. They are the subjects that contribute to new law making, who 'prompt' new rules by new attitudes to military interventions, to human rights and to care of the environment that result in binding rules.

18. Belligerents and Insurgents

According to traditional rules of war insurgents may, at a certain stage, be recognised as belligerents. In such a case individuals have

---

[338] There are also what I have called 'luxury' human rights, the right to clean food or even the right to work, that do not belong to this group. Here, we are concerned with the *right to avoid* the most heinous crimes like genocide, torture, *apartheid*, and racial discrimination, *cf. infra*, in greater detail, Part Two, A III v.

then, as a special group, acquired personality in international law. They may conclude agreements with the other belligerent party/parties which are valid as treaties. Should, however, their attempts to achieve independence in a civil war fail, the personality of the group may dissolve.[339]

19. Terrorists and Pirates

A radical proposition that we make here is that terrorists should also be accepted as subjects of international law. Yet, such a suggestion would seem to make practical sense. How can we otherwise punish terrorists and hold them responsible for their crimes? The same conclusions applied to pirates who throughout history have, at an early stage been treated as *out-laws*, but later considered as common criminals.

To endow terrorists and pirates the status of having international personality, allows us to explain why we can punish them and, at the same time, how we can consider it correct to allow them a minimum of privileges to avoid certain forms of maltreatment or torture.[340]

---

[339] See, in detail, my work on *The Law of War*, 37 *et seq.*, also on the problems relating to the efforts of Biafra to achieve independence from Nigeria, 1967-1969.

[340] See, my *Law of War*, 3rd ed., *op.cit.*, 164-166 on the contemporary situation concerning threats and actions by pirates. See, *ibid.*, 368-39& on the treatment of captured terrorists; even if they, in our opinion, should not be treated as Prisoners-of-War, they have certain minimum of rights, see in detail my article 'Illegal combatants' cited *supra* in this section. For earlier contrary and erroneous views of the Red Cross, see *ibid., loc. cit.*

iv. A Society or a Community?

The theatre for our study is international society. The members of international society are the various States that exist in the world as well as organisations, other entities and individuals. States and organisations cannot be studied without immediate reference to individuals as the abstract entities are nothing but agglomerations of individuals assigning (explicitly or implicitly) various functions to a larger entity.

Many international relations scholars claim[341] that the very term 'community' denotes something more than 'society' and indicates a more closely knit group. Peaceful, friendly relations characteristic of a 'community' are lacking in many areas of the world and it may therefore be more appropriate to speak of an international 'society', saving the word 'community' for the unrealistic optimists who shut their eyes to reality. Such semantic arguments may be exaggerated[342] and in the common language of international lawyers the term 'society' and 'community' may be

---

[341] *E.g.* Bull, H., *The Anarchical Society*, London: Macmillan 1977, 10; Manning considers it to be a nascent society of mankind, see Manning, C.A.W., *The Nature of International Society*, London: G. Bell, 1962, 177; there was never a 'family of nations' says Gong, G.W., *The Standard of Civilisation in International Society*, Oxford: OUP, 1984, 40. *Cf.* Herczeg, I., 'Futurity research in international law', in Haraszati, G., *Questions of International Law*, Leiden: Sijthoff, 1977, 96. International relations scholars are at pains even to justify the word 'society': Aron, R., 'The anarchical order of power' in Hoffman, S., (ed.), *Conditions of World Order*, New York: Macmillan, 1968, 25; Bull, *op. cit.*, 10, 13, 249; Holsti, K.J., *International Politics*, 4th ed., Englewood Cliffs, N.J.: Prentice Hall, 1983, 27.

[342] Note that the distinction is impossible, or awkward, in many languages; *cf.* Finnis, J., *Natural Law and Natural Rights*, Oxford: OUP, 1980, 135.

synonymous. But since 'an international community', to many, conveys a pattern of an extremely closely knit unit, with identity of values and with a high degree of integration, it is expedient to avoid such a charged term, especially in view of trans-disciplinary dialogue which will always be enhanced by a common terminology.

v. The Existence of a Legal System

If we accept that there is an international society it follows that there must exist an international legal order, for *ubi societas ibi ius* – where there is a society there will also be a legal order. Not everyone accepts this obvious inference. It is often said that international law is not 'law' at all.[343] International law has even been said not to be 'necessary' to world order.[344] Not only would international law be insufficient to bring about world order but it would even actually hinder such order, for example, by prohibiting preventive war, or by imposing sanctions which upset the 'balance of power'.[345] But we shall attempt to show that international law can be a valuable tool precisely to bring about world order and secure peace.

---

[343] See further *supra*, under 'Positivism' and especially Austin, J., *Lectures on Jurisprudence or the Philosophy of Positive Law*, 5th ed., London: J. Murray, 1885; Lundstedt, A.V., *Le droit des gens, danger de mort pour les peuples*, Paris: éditions de la Phalange, 1937; *idem*, *Superstition or Rationality in Action for Peace*, London: Longman, 1925; *idem*, 'Den historiska rättspositivismen: med särskild hänsyn till Bergbohms lära', Uppsala, *Uppsala Universitets årsskrift*, 1929; Olivecrona, K., *Law as Fact*, Oxford: OUP, 1939; Ross, A., *On Law and Justice*, Berkeley & Los Angeles: Univ. of California Press, 1959. See, also further, in detail, *infra*, Part Three, IV iii vi on 'The 'Allergy' to Natural Law.

[344] Bull, *The Anarchical Society*, op. cit., 142.

[345] *Ibid.*, *loc. cit.*

Any contention that it is a hindrance to world order, is the result of confusing and inadequate statements by international lawyers themselves as to the substance of the rules as well as lacking a systematic presentation of international law. Some textbooks no longer make sense: alleged rules set out in these works do not match realities of international society. Furthermore, the increasing tendency to examine various subsets of rules as watertight compartments leads to an ever increasing lack of coherence of international law.

vi. A Primitive Law?

International law is certainly 'different' from 'municipal law' (the term normally used for 'internal' or 'national' State law'): international law deals with a wider range of subjects and has a more comprehensive range of topics on which it can regulate.

There are sociological factors which contribute to the special features of international law. It is often said[346] that one of the main reasons why international law differs from other contemporary legal systems is that it is 'primitive'. It is indeed surprising that the comprehensive bracket above the advance modern municipal systems of the world, *i.e.* the network which ties together such sophisticated legal orders, would itself be a 'primitive' system. If by 'primitive' legal order one understands a system devoid of a centralised legislature and centralised enforcement mechanisms, one may be tempted to agree. Yet, given the refined complexities of law making and law revising in international society, it may

---

[346] Kunz, J.L., 'The distinctiveness of the international legal system' in *idem.*, (ed.) *A Changing World of Nations*, Ohio: Ohio State Univ. Press, 1968, 30.

well be that the international legal order is more developed and sophisticated than many municipal laws which, by the rigour of entrenched procedure and unadaptable legislative instruments, have become inflexible and outmoded collections of detail.

vii. Universality of the System

The importance of ideologies have increased with the growing rift between the blocs in the world. But we no longer have the traditional split between East and West but, rather more pertinently these days, a North-South division between industrialised States and the developing world. A further very serious rift can also be perceived between Europe, the United States, and the Arab world.

In many States and among many groups, we find a different approach to international law as a result of respective ideologies in other fields such as politics and economics. In a sense it is not possible to adhere fully to any political or economic theory without some repercussions of the way international law is perceived.

International law should, by definition, comprise the whole of international society: its contents cannot differ to accommodate different political views. On the other hand, there are basic rules which must not be violated by anyone: thus, certain ideologies are forbidden in the sense if they, for example, violate fundamental human rights.

International law forbids ideologies which preach the superiority of one race so that another race will be extinguished or subjected to far-reaching inequalities. International law may even forbid ideologies which embrace war propaganda.[347]

---

[347] *Cf.* Tunkin, G.I., 'Conflit ideologique et droit international', in *Hommages Guggenheim*, Geneva: IHEI 1968, 895.

In this respect international law is a coherent system of legal rules and these rules are the same for everyone and do not differ according to the political and economic ideology held in individual States. The objective of national 'legal policy' of many States is sometimes to show the existence of a 'universal' system of international law.[348]

When it comes to socio-economic rights international law cannot prescribe any specific ideology. Here, it must leave room for States, groups and individuals to decide their own views on rights and corresponding duties. For example, there are certain rules which international society cannot prescribe because of diverging ideologies.

It was long thought that international law could not demand that a State always paid full compensation to a State's own nationals: a State would be unable to effectively change to a 'socialist' or 'communist' economy[349] as any compensation paid would be a substitute for the taken assets and the State would thus merely exchange value for value but without being able to reallocate resources. Most international lawyers consequently assumed that there was no universally applicable rule that compensation must be paid to a State's own nationals in the case of nationalised property; for if there had been such a rule, it would preclude a State from adopting a communist or socialist economy and the international legal system, it was thought, could not prescribe or prohibit any specific ideology.

---

[348] de La Charrière, G., *La politique juridique extérieure*, Paris: IFRI, 1983, 196.

[349] These are two ideologies with largely the same objective, possibly at a different 'speed'. The adjectives are often used as synonyms: the Soviet communists invariably called themselves 'socialists'.

Now, on the other hand, positions are reversed. After the demise of communism, revived ideas are put forward that there is indeed a rule under international law which protects *a minimum right of private property*. In this sense, then, the international legal system is *now* of universal application, although, during a period of some seventy years, the legal situation was probably that rules on property did not have universal reach or, at least, such rules were not fully implemented.

However, even then during this interlude of communism in international society, it was still possible that, on a regional basis, there were stronger rules that applied because of a common political and economic outlook. In Western Europe such rules preclude, for example, any nationalisation without compensation to a State's own nationals. Such common rules in Europe form no doubt a part of an advanced regional system of international law.[350]

It may be emphasised that it is now difficult to find rules of mere regional application. Most rules of international law are universal and, furthermore, of a nature superior to all national rules. The Permanent Court of International Justice (PCIJ) and its successor the International Court of Justice (ICJ) have thus confirmed that international law is superior to all national

---

[350] But such rules were invoked without success in the Nationalisation Cases before the European Court of Human Rights as of fundamental importance to the Western conception of international law within this region, see *Sir William Lithgow and Others v UK*, European Court of Human Rights, Reports, 1986, and further, *infra*, under Part Three, IV iii v b) under Regional Rules.

constitutions,³⁵¹ to national laws,³⁵² to administrative acts³⁵³ and to national judicial acts.³⁵⁴ There may, however, be new problems of claimed superiority of the judgments of the Court of the European Union. The EU claims that its judgments rank higher than judgments of national supreme courts of the Member States. But the EU itself is certainly unable to outrank *jus cogens* in any conflict.³⁵⁵

The universal system may also affirm its superiority to regional rules by specific provisions in treaties.³⁵⁶ But within this 'universal' system, there may be subsets or regimes on a regional or functional basis.

viii. The Fallacy of the Subjectivity Test

Among traditional normativists, international law is commonly identified as the legal system which applies 'between States'. Those who oppose this traditional definition merely insist that intergovernmental organisations³⁵⁷ and, occasionally, individuals, if

---

[351] *E.g. Polish Nationals in Danzig* (1932), PCIJ, *Series* A/B No 44, 24.

[352] *Advisory Opinion on Upper Silesia* (1926) PCIJ *Series* A., No. 7A, 19; *Greco-Bulgarian Communities* (1930), PCIJ, *Series* B., No. 17, 32; *Free Zones of Savoy* (1932) *Series* A/B No. 46, 167; *Peter Pazmany Case* (1933), PCIJ *Series* A/B No. 61 243.

[353] *The Boll Case*, (1958) ICJ Reports 65; *The Wimbledon*, (1923) PCIJ, *Series* A., No. 1, 30.

[354] *The Chorzow Factory Case* (1928), *Series* A. No. 17 33.

[355] See, *infra*, Part Two, B, especially B III ii.

[356] On compatibility, *cf.* article 103 of the UN Charter; cf. article 20 the Covenant of the League of Nations; article 82 of the ICAO Convention of 1944; article XXIV of GATT.

[357] *E.g.* Brownlie, Principles, *op. cit.*, 65, 677 *et seq.*

their home State 'agrees',[358] can be subjects alongside with States; others prefer the social process school which discards the notion of a normative system altogether and attaches little importance to the concept of 'subjects'.

Yet, it is impossible to ascertain the substantive contents of a legal system by identifying the subjects it controls. In other words international law cannot be said to be a system between any particular subjects.

Thus, by saying that 'the subjects of international law are States' or, possibly 'States, and, at times, inter-governmental organisations', we find out nothing further about the provisions of the law.

a) The Criteria of a National Law

One would not define, for example, French law as 'the law which applies between Frenchmen', for this is not true: French law may also govern activities of, for example, an American company in France, and will also, for example, punish a German who commits a crime in France. Is French law then the law which is applied in France? Is there a geographical criterion? This does not appear to be so either as French law may also be applied by, for example, a Swedish Court in a conflict of laws suit; and it may control the rights of French nationals in the United States inheriting property situated in Venezuela. French law is then perhaps better identified as the set of rules which controls matters where there is *a French connection or a connection with the interests of the French legislature.*

---

[358] *Ibid.*, 69.

French law emanates from the French legislative process: it is the legislature of France, with or without exercising delegation of its functions, that enacts, approves or identifies rules which will apply as French law. There is thus an *organic link* between French law and the French legislature. It is that legislature which has a prime interest in regulating situations with a connection to France.

Other legislators may also have an interest to regulate the relevant matters and there is then a conflict of competing legal systems. This is, for example, the case if one legal system attempts to operate in extraterritorial situations, like the United States anti-trust legislation. Certain links are normally established based on nationality or domicile, or on 'prevailing' nationality or domicile, which connect a situation relatively more to one national legal system than to another.

b) The Criteria of International Law

Applying similar methods to the identification of international law as we do in the case of a national legal system, it may be deduced that international law governs matters of prevailing international concern or of trans-frontier importance.

In the case of international law, it is obviously difficult to apply the second organic test, that of emanating from a specific legislator that was adopted in the case of identification of a national law. For in international law there may only be a question of collective and dissipated law making techniques. We cannot say that 'international law emanates from States' as a sole statement of the origin of the international legal system as distinct from other rules, for States also enact their municipal laws and there are difficulties in distinguishing which rules form part of international law and which are embodied in internal law. Besides, a certain amount of international law also emanates from international organisations.[359] But the term 'international' holds true and provides valuable guidance in one respect: international law concerns matters of *prevailing international concern.*

It may be possible to narrow down the field of international law by claiming that its rules reflect prevailing 'international concerns'. There must be a balance between the sovereign right of the 'reserved domain' and the interest of international society.

In the field of human rights, 'apartheid' was of considerable international concern; the system was abolished in South Africa after international pressure. Other human rights problems have also been solved after such pressure. The Stockholm Declaration in 1972 evoked environmental concerns deserving international regulation. 'Acid raid' appeared to be one such concern but on this, there was little international regulation.[360] 'Global warming' and 'climate change' later took the centre stage as environmental problems. The devastating effect of nuclear weapons may be another example of international concern.

Claims that there would be 'customary' rules in these fields are clearly preposterous.[361] But there may be other mechanisms that explain the emergence of binding rules. By coupling the criterion of 'international concern' with the actual execution of an 'international act', it may be possible to arrive at the identification of rules of international law.

---

[359] See my *Law Making, op. cit., passim.*

[360] See the vague provisions of the 1979 Long-Range Transboundary Pollution Convention, 18 *ILM* 1442.

[361] See further *infra*, in Part Three, IV iv on The Fallacies of 'Customary Law'.

II. Methods of Classifying International Rules

i. The Notion of 'Regimes'

It may be useful to comment briefly on a concept which is often used by international relations scholars to describe certain *sets of rules* in international society. Some claim that a 'regime' is a

> 'network of rules, norms and procedures that regularise behaviour and control its effects' [362]

or perhaps

> 'a set of principles, norms, rules and procedures around which actors' expectations converge'.[363]

Some perceive a 'power structure' within the 'regimes'[364] and insist that, if that power is exercised by States, the concept appears to reflect the traditional State-paradigm.[365] Some distinguish between 'formal' regimes which are

> 'legislated by international organisations, maintained by councils, congresses or other bodies and monitored by international bureaucracies'[366]

---

[362] Keohane, R.O., & Nye, J.S., *Power and Interdependence*, Boston: Little, Brown and Company, 1977, 19.

[363] Puchala, D.J., & Hopkins, J.F., 'International Regimes: Lessons from inductive analysis', 36 *International Organisation*, 1982, No.2 2456. *Cf.* Krasner, S.D., 'Structural causes and regimes consequences: Regimes as intervening variables', *ibid.*, 185.

[364] Puchala and Hopkins, International regimes, *op. cit.*, 250.

[365] Strange, S., '*Cave! hic dragones.* A critique of regime analysis,' *ibid.*, 491.

[366] Puchala and Hopkins, Regimes, *op. cit.*, 248.

whereas others would be mere 'gentlemen's agreements'.[367]

The role of States is often emphasised as States constitute the main components of any regime. It is also claimed that there would be something static about the concept of regimes in so far as it leaves little to dynamics and that

> 'the bias of regime analysis can be corrected by attention to the determining basic structures of the international political economy, the structure of security, money welfare, production, trade and knowledge. Each of these raises the question 'How to achieve change?' which is surely no less important than the question 'How to keep order?''[368]

There may be little merit in this notion, if there are alleged legal consequences which are not made precise but left in the air and if the question of modification is not even tentatively dealt with by the exponents. There are no 'natural' systems in international society for which we can devise proper regimes.[369] Thus it is difficult to speak of 'eco-systems' which require a 'whole management' regime as some suggest.[370] The notion used in this hazy way fills little function and appears to confuse rather than clarify.

However, in international law the term 'regime' has been used for long in a different way to loosely describe the mere collective

---

[367] *Ibid., loc. cit.*

[368] Strange, *Cave!, op. cit.*, 496.

[369] Haas, E.B., 'Is there a hole in the whole? Knowledge, technology, interdependence and the construction of international regimes', 29 *International Organisations*, 1975, No.3, p. 840. But see *supra*, I iii d) 4, under 'Nations' for my own comments on certain 'natural units' in international society.

[370] Wenk, E., *The Politics of the Ocean*, Washington: University of Washington Press, 1972, 437.

regulation of certain factual situations. One would thus often talk about the 'international regime of straits' or the 'regime of Trieste', in both cases implying a territorial application of certain rules whereby States would be granted rights and assume obligations. But one also speaks of 'the regime of treaties' and of other areas without territorial connections, such as 'the regime under a treaty'.

The term may serve some purpose if it is used to imply a consolidated subset of rules under a treaty or other forms of consent and such rules are to apply to situations and events of varying types in the future. In this work the term will be used in that sense. The establishment of a regime does thus not have any legal consequences *per se* but a regime indicates, for convenience, a coherent subset of rules, subordinated to the universal system. A regime forms so to speak a framework bracket,[371] susceptible to recurring future application.

'Regimes' is also used in international law for 'objective regimes'. The term, in that context, implies the logical duty to recognise that another subject exists, for example, a new State but also to accept an 'objectively existing situation', for example, a specific regulation of a water system.[372] We will revert to the notion of regimes in the context of cooperating with other subjects in international society.[373] It is clear that, in the sense of 'objectively existing situations', the term 'regime' is useful in international legal terminology. Here is also an area where international relations

---

[371] *Infra*, under Part Three, C iii a), Framework Acts.
[372] *Infra*, under Part Two, B I ii on Objective Regimes and also Part Two C I ii, Further Regimes.
[373] *Ibid., loc. cit.*

scholars might take interest in broadening their conception of 'regimes' to include the variations set out above.

ii. The Sources of International Law[374]

Although criticised and deficient, article 38 of the Statute of the International Court of Justice is a starting point in any initial study of the sources of international law.[375] The article refers to 'conventions, whether general or particular, establishing rules expressly recognised',[376] international custom, obscurely formulated as 'the evidence of a general principle accepted as law', 'general principles of law recognised by civilised nations' and as supplementary means, 'decisions of courts and the writings of publicists'. There is no mention of acts of international organisations

---

[374] See, in particular, Verdross, A. v., *Quellen des Universellen Völkerrechts*, Freiburg: Rombach, 1973; Parry, C., *The Sources and Evidences of International Law*, Manchester: Manchester University Press, 1965; Sørensen, M., *Les sources du droit international*, Copenhagen: E. Munksgaard, 1946; see also the relevant commentaries in the leading textbooks, in particular, Rousseau, Ch., *Droit international public*, i, Paris: Sirey, 1970, 55443; Reuter, P., *Droit international public*, Paris: Thémis, 1973; *cf.* Finch, G.A., *The Sources of Modern International Law*, Washington: Carnegie, 1937; Maschke, H., *Die Rangordnung der Rechtsquellen*, Berlin: Rothschild, 1932.

[375] Article 38 of the Statute of ICJ is specifically invoked in the Revised 1928 General Act for the Pacific Settlement of International Disputes of 28th April 1949, 71 *UNTS* 101, articles 18(2) and 28. It is a provision which is also adopted in many international arbitration treaties. Although not specifically invoked, the same article of the Permanent Court of International Justice was applied in numerous international arbitrations, *e.g.* in *The Naulilaa Case*, (1928), 2 *RIAA* 1011, in *The Cysne Case*, (1930), 2 *RIAA* 1035 and in *The Case Regarding the Interpretation of Article 11 of the London Protocol (1926)*, 2 *RIAA* 755.

[376] By the contesting States before the Court; *cf. infra*, under Part Two, C III, Consequential Rules.

which clearly contribute to law making[377] or to unilateral acts of States which can entail obligations.[378] The article is also unclear on whether the ranging of categories implies any hierarchy of sources. On the whole the article, in spite of its ambition, has been a fairly unhelpful guide as to what constitutes sources international law.

a) Ambiguities of Meaning of a 'Source' of Law

'Source' of law can have various meanings. It can mean the 'ultimate' source of a law and in this sense be used synonymously with the basis of obligation.[379] Secondly, we may distinguish between a 'formal' and a 'material' source of law.

By 'formal' source we then usually understand the mechanisms through which the law comes into being, *i.e.* in any State, the normal constitutional mechanism. Some claim that the category of formal sources serves little purpose in international law as this system lacks such constitutional machinery.[380] Yet, if the term 'source' of international law is used, as it often is, to denote the very ways that rules comes into being,[381] then it would seem to come very near the way we understand a formal source in municipal law.

However, 'source' can also be understood in the material sense of the word indicating where the legal rules come from, *i.e.*

---

[377] See my *Law Making, op. cit., passim.*
[378] Pfluger, F., *Die einseitige Rechtsgeschäfte im Völkerrecht*, Zürich: Schulthess, 1936, *passim* and *infra*, under Part Three II C I a), Unilateral Acts.
[379] *Cf.* Berber, F., *Lehrbuch des Völkerrechts*, Munich: Beck, 1975, i, pp. 37-40.
[380] Brownlie, *Principles, op. cit*, 1.
[381] So Briggs, H.W., *Law of Nations, Cases, Documens and Notes*, London: Stevens, 1953, 44.

the factual framework where the rules are located.[382] Some equate material sources and the material facts which influence the creation of rules,[383] the rules which provide evidence of the existing law,[384] the material facts which express the 'prevailing will', *i.e.* facts which themselves incorporate the rules,[385] or the material facts which imply a recognition of the law.[386] But distinction must be made between these categories.

A 'source' of international law can most conveniently be understood to mean the very material facts which state the law. Thus, the sources are the law; the sources comprise the whole material network of rules in international society. But the term 'source' can also be understood to mean the way the law is formed:[387] the concept of different sources may serve a useful purpose in distinguishing how different legal rules are formed. A 'source' then has a twofold meaning of both indicating the font where to look for a legal rule and designating the process by which rules are formed by different types of methods of creation of law.

Thus, a 'source' of the international legal system means, in this work, the pool of rules where we may search for relevant rules and, also, the way international law is formed, *i.e.* the mechanisms for its formation and for entry into these pools.

---

[382] *Cf.* Scelle, G., on '*...la source profonde*'. *Manuel de droit international public*, Paris: Domat-Montchrestien, 1948, 9.

[383] So *e.g.* Ross, A., *Theorie der Rechtsquellen*, Leipzig & Vienne: F. Deuticke, 1929, 83.

[384] So, *e.g.* Brownlie, *op. cit.* 12.

[385] So, Dahm, G., *Völkerrecht* vol. i, Stuttgart: Kohlhammer, 15.

[386] Duguit, L., *Traité de droit constitutionnel*, Paris: E. de Boccard 1921, 71: sources are, he says, '*modes de constatation du droit*'.

[387] *Cf.* Duguit, *Traité, op. cit., loc. cit.*

There is not only one source of international law but many. The law is thus found in different locations or in different pools. In these various places the law will be stated and it is to these that we look to find rules that are binding in international society. The mechanisms by which the rules are created and by which they enter into the various source material explain how a rule of *courtoisie*,[388] for example, which may concern no more than 'good manners' but which is not formally binding, may become obligatory in international society. These mechanisms will also explain how, for example, a non-binding Resolution of the General Assembly may gradually be incorporated among the compulsory rules of international law. As international law is not static, so will its sources be ever dynamic and changing.[389]

The study of sources in international law is therefore important for a two-fold reason: by isolating the sources from other material we actually identify the law itself; secondly, by analysing how material enters into the sources we establish how legal rules come about in international society and we thereby identify the law making processes in the international legal system.

b) Systematic Induction

We shall use the material sources of international law in this work to classify the rules of the system. By an inductive method[390] it

---

[388] For the distinction between such *courtoisie* and *international comity*, which in my view is binding, see my *International Legal Order, op. cit.*, Chapter I, section I ii on Comity.

[389] Monaco, R., R., 'Observations sur la hiérarchie des sources du droit international', *Festschrift Mosler*, Berlin: Springer, 1983, p. 599.

[390] *Cf.* attempts by Schwarzenberger, G., *An Inductive Approach to International Law*, London: Stevens, 1965, where, however, few conclusions emerge. *Cf.* criticism by

may be possible to clarify the nature of the rules. During this period of confusion as to the status of the rules and of the system of international law, a fresh attempt may prove worthwhile.

By postulating an ultimate goal in a functional rather than in any transcending way,[391] we shall have a starting point for a classification of rules and acts of international law. These fall into different classes and can be viewed as rules that, by their various propensities, ensure the hypothetical goal.

Jenks, W., *The Prospects of International Adjudication*, London & Dobbs Ferry: Stevens-Oceana, 1964, 623.

[391] *Cf.* Mitrany, D., 'The functional approach', in Mitrany, D., (ed.), *A Working Peace System*, London: RIAA, 1966; *idem*, *The Functional Theory in Politics*, London: LSE, 1975.

PART TWO:
CLASSIFICATION OF RULES

A. The Doctrine of International Relevance and Comity

i. The Questionable Division of Law into Public and Private Law

Many problems have been caused in academia and in practice before Courts by the artificial and questionable division between what is called 'public law' and 'private law'. Especially in France, Italy and Germany, there is a sharp division between public and private law.

Yet, as we will demonstrate here the division is highly contrived and unnecessary. Most teachers of public *or* private international law do not even realise how close their subjects are to each other. In this work it is suggested that international law should be defined as *a set of normative rules regulating matters of international relevance.*[1] This legal system includes rules of *both*

---

[1] See, in detail, *supra*, Part One, I ii a) – f). C. my *Concept of International Law*, *op. cit.* 88-91; *cf.* 41-43.

public and private international law. This is even more obvious in arbitrations than in ordinary, national or international cases.

By public law in a State, one commonly understands rules laid down to regulate the 'common good' to ensure the order of the country and its subjects. Such rules emanate from a public authority, from the executive or the legislature, and, as is common in the case of numerous public 'administrative' rules, also from inferior or local organs of the State to which the power to enact has been delegated. Individuals can derive rights and duties under this regulatory framework but the rules are essentially designed to provide the details for the structure and functioning of the community itself.

Conversely, private law signifies the law that regulates the legal relationships between individuals and other non-State bodies. Although public and private law falls in two broadly distinguishable categories, the exact distinction between 'public' and 'private' law has long been blurred and ceased to serve any real purpose. The same can be said about the distinction between 'public' and 'private' international law.

The public/private terminology has been transferred into the realm of international law. Here too, a distinction between *private* and *public* law in international society is not always easy to draw. On the international scene, 'public international law' is said to denote the relationship between States or international organisations or between such organisations themselves. In other words, 'public international law' concerns, according to the traditional textbooks, only the (traditional) 'subjects' of international law, that is, in their opinion, States and inter-governmental organisations. Conversely, 'private international law' is held to regulate relationships between individuals (or non-State entities, like, for example, companies) in different countries or in affairs that concern different national jurisdictions.

The term *private law* is thus designed to convey that we are concerned with rights and duties of individuals *as between themselves*, whereas *public law* concerns the organisation of the State, its organs and administration, as well as the relationship between the individual and the State, or, as in criminal law, with the sanctions imposed by the State for certain undesirable behaviour of individuals. However, as we have seen, individuals and numerous other subjects often have direct rights and duties under the international system. So in that sense 'public international law' would be a misnomer as the international legal system does not merely concern the relationship between States.

It can no longer be correct to claim that 'public international law' only regulates the behaviour of States (and inter-governmental organisations): it is, in essence, no longer an inter-State system. Nor can it be correct to claim that private international law only regulates the behaviour of individuals and that through the operation of 'national rules' of the various States of the world. It is absurd to claim that private international law is not truly 'international' as the 'national' conflict of law rules are virtually identical in all the major national systems. There is thus, in our opinion, a legal system called 'international law' that covers both public and private international law.

ii. One Legal System: Public and Private International Law

The system of international legal rules regulating situations of international relevance includes rules on both public and private international law, or, as the latter subject is usually called in the

English-speaking world, conflict of laws. These two disciplines are difficult to distinguish unless we adopt completely artificial and unrealistic criteria.

Public international law is thus traditionally said to concern *relationships between States* (and inter-governmental organisations) and is said to be an *international system*. We have shown above that the international system also provides individuals and a host of other legal subjects with direct rights and duties when their acts are internationally relevant. We have also demonstrated that a large part of 'public international law' governs relationships between individuals, especially in the field of human rights. Public international law also provides rules for the relationship of numerous other non-State subjects of the international legal order.

Private international law or conflict of laws is thus traditionally said to concern *relationships between individuals* and, at the same time, form part of the *national law*. That this distinction does not hold true is shown and also by the fact that rules of 'private international law' (or 'conflict of laws') have become increasingly *international* and *uniform* and are no longer merely national in character.

Private international law is usually known in England as *conflict of laws*. The separate name for private international law may have strengthened the assumption of some that this is an entirely different subject from public international law. But it is not.

Traditional textbooks in most countries thus insist that public international law is a truly *international* system whereas private international law (or conflict of laws) forms part of *national* law. Thus, private international law should be *different* in each of the world's nearly 200 States as it is claimed to form part of the various national legal systems. But this is not so. In many national systems we have been able to verify that principles and rules of private international law are *virtually identical*. After a careful analysis, it appears that private international law is also an *international* system, contrary to what the textbooks claim. The rules of private international law also form part of what we, in this work call, the international legal order.

Private international law is thus traditionally considered to be a part of a national system.[2] It is useful to underline that private international law is not *only* a specific branch of internal law, like, for example, the law of contract. It regards and touches every field of internal law and is concerned with solutions when there is a *conflict* with a foreign competing law. Private international law is commonly taken to mean the rules in every State that govern conflict situations with other national legal systems. Typical situations involve precisely rights and duties of individuals, often derived from actions within different jurisdictions. Borderline situations arise which concern the relationship of aliens and a foreign government, as, for example, in an investment dispute, or those that bear on immunity; these questions may appropriately be considered to belong to either public or private international, or to both areas of law.

Private international law normally addresses two main questions, that of jurisdiction (which court is competent?) and that of choice of law (which substantive law shall apply?).

This legal system consists of several types of rules: *jurisdictional rules* which will decide which national court, if

---

[2] But already in the 1990s it was thought reasonable to merge public international law and conflict of law rules into a coherent unified system, see my *International Legal Order, op. cit.*, 14-28.

any, is competent to hear a specific case; *procedural rules* which will determine the way the case is handled; *substantive rules* which will decide the merits of the actual case.

Rules of the forum State govern all aspects of procedure. To such *procedural* rules we may count those which select a specific national court to hear a case, *i.e.* certain types of *domestic jurisdictional* rules, concerning which specific national court is competent. All such rules thus tend to be entirely national.

However, certain other types of *international jurisdictional rules*, that claim jurisdiction for a specific national legal system in general terms, cannot be entirely national: here the national systems must yield to demands of international comity[3] to avoid overlapping claims of jurisdiction.[4]

Yet, there are many emerging rules of conflict of laws which have taken on an increasingly international stamp – such as, for example, the rule of habitual residence. The difference between such a rule, which is *internationalised* in the sense that it is *derived* from the substantive laws of numerous countries, and one which is *international* by itself, is indeed a fine one. Yet, the distinction, with regard to source of derivation, is of some importance as a matter of principle.

Public international law has, as a legal system, much in common with private international law, or conflict of laws, which also regulates situations with international connections. However, we can concede that conflict of law rules are *largely* rules belonging to national systems, albeit considerably unified, whereas rules of

---

[3] See, *infra*, in the subsequent section, iv. on 'The Notion of Comity'.
[4] See, my *International Legal Order*, *op. cit.*, Chapter VII on Distributive Rules: Object of Sovereign Functions: Jurisdiction and Conflict of Laws.

public international law are *essentially* international in character, albeit quite often concerning individuals or other private entities.

When presented with obligations to teach public *and* private international law, one may have a welcome opportunity to analyse what bridges these disciplines.[5] Should there be two textbooks for students? One textbook[6] could perhaps combine the basic notions of public and private international law? After a careful analysis, it does become clear that these two systems have so much in common that they should both be subsumed under the wider bracket 'international law'.

Most law faculties ignore the most international of all legal subjects, maritime law, especially matters like actions *in rem* and salvage, matters of great importance in modern international society.[7] Some courses may include some teaching of commercial aspects as part of transnational commercial law or law of contract, but global rules of admiralty and maritime law do not normally

---

[5] The Government of Sweden appointed the author of this work to the Lindhagen Chair of International Law at Stockholm University with the remit of teaching Public *and* Private International Law *and* EU law. In spite of the considerable burden of being charged with so much teaching and examination duties, this made it possible to reflect on similarities in the contents of these two disciplines, of public international law and conflict of laws, leaving aside the less exciting subject of EU-law, to be the subject of a separate book. See, my *International Legal Order*, Stockholm: Juristförlaget, 1991; 2nd ed. London: Gower, 1994, for Public International Law and Conflict of Laws and my *Ekonomisk Integrationsrätt*, Uppsala: Almqvist & Wiksell, 1976, for EU-law.

[6] *The International Legal Order*, Stockholm: Juristförlaget, 1991 and 2nd ed., London: Gower 1994.

[7] See, Mandaraka-Sheppard, A., *Modern Admiralty Law*, London: Cavendish Publishing 2006; Mandaraka-Sheppard, A., *Modern Maritime Law and Risk Management*, 2 vols., London: Routledge, 3rd ed., 2013; see, Brice, G., *The Maritime Law of Salvage*, 5th ed., by Reeder, J., London: Sweet & Maxwell, 2013.

form part of the syllabus for undergraduates, neither in public international law, nor as part of conflict of laws. Nor is the law of multinationals, also highly topical in the present world,[8] taught in many universities as part of public *or* private international law.

The traditional distinction between public and private international law is no longer tenable.[9] All we can say, at the moment, about the usefulness of private international law, or so called conflict of laws, is that a municipal court will normally apply the conflict rules of its own national system to decide which *forum* is appropriate and, secondly, decide which substantive *law* should be applied to a case with international connotations.

Rules of private international law can be harmonised in two ways: either by unification of the internal laws themselves and, secondly, unification of private international law rules.[10] Both these avenues will reduce the possibility of conflict between laws. In recent years much work along these lines have been made and it is now clear that private international law rules applied in most countries are strikingly similar.[11]

---

[8] See, Robé, J.-P., Lyon-Caen, A. & Vernac, S., *Multinationals and the Constitutionalization of the World Power System*, Oxford and New York: Routledge, 2016; Blumberg, P. , I., *The Corporate Challenge to Corporation Law*, New York & Oxford: OUP, 1993.

[9] For forceful arguments that 'public' and 'private' international law constitutes *one* coherent system, see my *International Legal Order*, op. cit., Ch. One.

[10] *Cf. e.g.*, Cheshire, G.C. & North, P.M., *Private International Law*, Oxford: OUP, 15th ed., 2017, 9 *et seq.*

[11] In the past an exception always had to be made for the former Soviet Union and its satellite States; on the Soviet system, see Bogoslavski, V.N., *Private International Law: the Soviet Approach*, Moscow: State Publishers, 1988. Exception must still be made for for China, for Cuba, Vietnam and North Korea, virtually the only socialist States that are left after the great reversal of communist/socialist policies

If two (of the many subjects of the international legal order),[12] in two different countries, regulate a matter of interest to them, the matter of agreement becomes one of *international relevance*.[13] The agreement between them so to speak lifts out the matter on to the international stage. This may be a matter of a treaty between States, or a marriage between two citizens, or an inheritance of one estate to heirs in another country. But a sweeping survey of the main national legal systems lead to the conclusion that the result, according to repective 'national' rules, will be largely the same whereever the case is heard.

There are, of course, some variations: American courts, and even English Courts, will be more likely to allow a more generous alimony in divorce cases. This has led to what had become known as '*forum shopping*' when a party seeks to have a case heard where the winnings might be more substantial. But the reaction to this has been that Courts increasingly look for a persuasive 'link' of some sort, before they agree to hear a case to avoid the most blatant 'forum shoppers'.

But if we look up national rules to find the conflict of law rules on which forum is competent and which law shall apply, we find that such guiding rules, thus the choice of law rules, are virtually identical in all the major legal systems.

An important difference between Anglo-Saxon and civil law systems is, of course, that 'the connecting link' that determines an

---

in the world 1988-1990. On the Chinese system *cf.* Chiu, 'Contemporary practice and judicial decisions of the Republic of China', *Chinese Yearbook of International Law*, 1987-1988, 225 *et seq.*

[12] *Supra*, in Part One, I iii 1-18.
[13] *Supra*, in Part One, I ii a).

individual's 'personal law' is, in all civil law systems, his *nationality* whereas in the Anglo-Saxon systems it is his *domicile*, as understood in those systems, thus not merely a 'habitual residence'. There is thus a divergence in the sense the 'the law of the domicile' has a different meaning in English law – where domicile is thought to be a more or less fixed long-term quality – than in French law – where 'domicile' means little more than vaguely permanent 'residence'. But the choice of law rule is thus similar albeit applied slightly differently.

Apart from these divergences, we may note,[14] that even substantive laws in many countries have now been extensively harmonised, a process which naturally limits the number of occasions when we find ourselves in conflict of laws situations. Yet, most disputes that come before investment tribunals or arbitration panels these days, concern disputes between 'Western' type companies and countries where the laws are 'different' in countries that do not share European legal traditions.[15]

We must distinguish between the formal rules of private international law and substantive law of various countries. The formal rules on jurisdiction and choice of law are virtually the same in all the major national law systems.

Minor difficulties are, however, sometimes caused by *varying internal rules* on other important formal issues, for example, on procedural matters like on *hearsay evidence*, a prohibition not known in many countries in Europe. National legal systems have

---

[14] See, my *International Legal Order*, op. cit., Chapter VI.

[15] *Cf.* Paulson, J., 'Unlawful laws and the authority of international tribunals', 23 ICSID, *Foreign Investment Law Review*, 2008, 215, and *infra*, in this Part, C II iii under Substantive Rules for All Contacts.

also adopted radically different rules on some substantive issues, such the rule of *good faith acquisitions* well known in Europe but not generally admitted in English law; or on *common property of spouses*, again a rule not automatically applied in English law.

But in the same way as compulsory maxims apply in all cases before Courts,[16] conversely, many conflict rules also form part of the common comity rules[17] that are not dependent on the rules of only one State. Furthermore, many other rules of public international law, for example on nationality or immunity are founded on parallel acceptance of rules in different jurisdictions. Consequently, public and private international law are two legal systems which may have more in common than what is usually accepted. In areas like nationality or immunity they are furthermore intimately interconnected.

There are indeed tendencies to regard public and private international law as one and the same system.[18] Those who teach both subjects find it increasingly difficult to draw sensible limits between the two allegedly separate disciplines although the aforementioned guidelines may be useful. It is also difficult, and not always necessary, to distinguish between the two systems and the increasingly intrusive law of the European Union, which, in a

---

[16] On the role, contents and types of maxims, see, *infra*, in this Part, B I i-vi and my *Concept, op. cit.*, 49-52.

[17] *Infra*, in this Part, A I iv a) – h).

[18] See, *supra*, in this Part under A ii, under 'One Legal System: Public and Private International Law. *Cf.*, Jessup, P., *Transnational Law*, New Haven: Yale University Press, 1956.

sense, represents a subsection of both public international law and of '*international private law*'.¹⁹

'*International private law*' is not the same as *private international law* or *conflict of laws*. The term *international private law* is used to indicate a system of private law, common to several States. This is, in the European Union, often achieved by EU legislation and, partly, by harmonisation of national rules.²⁰ Conflict of laws rules are clearly unable to provide rules for cases concerning commercial transactions between States and/or international organisations.²¹ Here, rules are fetched from the latent 'norm-pools' in the system of the international legal order to accommodate any new need for rules.²²

Private international law does not provide rules for prosecution of individuals committing acts which are not crimes by the law of their own State²³ or the commission of acts that is condoned by their home State or the State where the individuals are present. The trend towards universal jurisdiction in the last mentioned cases²⁴

---

[19] See, my *Law Making, op. cit.*, 271-274; for the notion of international private law in relation to operations of the World Bank see *ibid.*, 184-187; see, *infra*, in this Part my *Concept, op. cit.*, 75-79, for the notion *lex mercatoria* applying to commercial international transactions between, for example, States and private entities.

[20] See, further, my *International Legal Order, op. cit.*, Chapters II, III and IV.

[21] See, *infra*, on *lex mercatoria*, in this Part, *infra*, C II iii. *Cf. supra*, Part One, B II iii.

[22] See, on these mechanisms, *infra*, in this Part, C II iii.

[23] As assessed by nationality, domicile or residence according to various conflict rules in different States.

[24] *E.g.* under Conventions on terrorism and hijacking; See the Hague Convention of 1963, *UNTS* 105. *Cf.* the Montreal Convention 1971, 10 *ILM* 1151.

is, however, ample evidence that there are emerging 'international' rules on the matter, available in the above-mentioned norm-pools.[25]

iii. International Rules and the Internal Law Systems of States

The *jus gentium* initially regulated the internal spheres of various nations as well as their inter-relationships. From an early age, it was thus not only the relationships *between* States which were regulated by international law, but also some *internal* matters of States: thus, under the early *jus gentium* as elaborated, for example, *slavery* was forbidden, and this prohibition could only be effective if the relevant legal rules had immediate application inside States,[26] in what international lawyers now call the 'municipal' or 'internal' law of States.

a) The Effect of International Law Inside States

A most important area which essentially concerns *individuals*, but is more normally classified under public international law, is that of human rights. In this field, there is general consensus on the requirements necessary to protect interests of individuals by internal rules. But individuals are *also* protected by international

---

[25] See my *Law of War, op. cit*, on jurisdiction for war criminals and terrorists. *Cf* my articles 'Illegal combatants and the Law of War', *Law Journal of George Washington University*, 2007; and on 'Extraordinary rendition', *University of North Carolina Law Journal*, 2008.

[26] Isidore of Seville, *Etymologiae* V:6. See, further, *infra*, in this Part, B III v under prophylactic rules on human rights.

rules, often represented by an *international minimum standard*.²⁷ Public international law thus also includes rules regulating the relationship between individuals and the *system itself*. It is this *system* of international law which in international society replaces the laws of a State in so far as it is this system that lays down the exact level of norms for acceptable or undesirable behaviour.

There is an ever increasing application of public international law in States. Foreign ministries are daily *practising* international law. Whenever a State takes action that in some way might be considered to deviate from international law, announcements are made, usually by a foreign ministry, by a Prime Minister or by a Head of State, to the effect that the State *claims to have the right* under international law to take the *action* in question, or, that there has been action by others *justifying a reaction*.

Occasionally, it is said by States that there has been a 'misunderstanding', a 'provocation' or other circumstances that entitled certain action. If, at times, States unwillingly concede that there has been a breach of international law, it is often argued that the breach is 'deplorable' and that there are 'extenuating circumstances', which makes the action 'excusable' or, at least, 'understandable'. Such arguments are designed to pre-empt outright condemnation of the action by other States, by the United Nations, NGOs, the media or individuals. Incidences like the invasion of Grenada, 'assistance' to the government of Afghanistan or, conversely, 'assistance' to the groups which, in the opinion of the United States *ought* to have

---

[27] See, my *International Law and the Independent State*, op. cit., Ch. Two, and my *International Legal Order*, op. cit., Ch. V, 304 *et seq*. On the acceptance of fundamental human rights as forming part of general principles of EU-law, see Hartley, *The Foundations of European Community Law*, Oxford: OUP, 7th ed., 2010, 132 *et seq*.

formed the government of Nicaragua, show a pattern of behaviour of States, justifying their decisions under a clear set of international rules.

The recent, and recurring, unfortunate practice to intervene in the domestic sphere of other countries with military means has led to increasing chaos in some regions. The way this has been done is often been done by what we have called 'patronising' intervention,[28] when some powerful States consider they know what is 'best' for another State, often neglecting cultural differences that make some forms of 'democratic' systems unsuitable to other countries.

National courts apply international legal rules in numerous situations. The *Tin Council Cases* in England bear further proof of the importance of substantive international legal rules in domestic courts.[29] However, in certain increasingly isolated countries, like Sweden and Norway, judges are under the impression that nothing but enacted laws can be applied in domestic courts. Erroneously, they tend to rely on doctrines like that of *dualism* in their efforts to contend that not even international rules on human rights have effect unless incorporated by national laws. If that argument was correct, there could not have been any War Crimes Tribunals at Nuremberg or Tokyo. Some slight changes are apparent after the adaptation of attitudes under the European Union.[30]

A question regarding the specific relationship between international law and municipal law and the *efficacy* of international

---

[28] See, in detail, my *Law of War*, op. cit., Ch. Two.

[29] [1988] 3 All E.R. 257; [1989] 3 All E.R.

[30] Although Norway is not a member of the EU, certain rules of EU-law have had to be accepted in the internal legal system.

law in the internal law of States concerns the field of *jus cogens*, that is to say international rules that are so compelling, that States and others may not deviate from them by agreements, nor set them aside by their behaviour in their own territory.

In some countries, such rules are familiar from national rules on the law of contract, as *indispositive* rules. A State cannot, by referring to some theoretical system, avoid obligations under international law by referring to its national constitution or to its national laws.[31] A State can thus not avoid obligations as laid down in peremptory norms, that is to say compelling rules,[32] forming part of a body of rules called *jus cogens*, which we shall study in some detail later.[33]

The *efficacy* of international law inside States is an area which naturally is of the greatest practical importance. *Any internal matter otherwise within the reserved domain*[34] can become uplifted to be a question of international relevance. This can be done either by *specific undertaking* by treaty between States or a *special pledge* to international organisations or another outside body. Similar *uplifting* to the level of international law may occur by various types of *outrageous action* of States in their own territory, for example in the field of human rights, such as treating nationals in a manner deviating from the minimum accepted norm,[35] thus

---

[31] See, *The Alabama Arbitration*, (1872) Hudson 6.

[32] A useful term is *indispositive* rules, to signify compulsory rules with similar legal force.

[33] See, *infra*, in this Part, B III ii, under *jus cogens* The field of international compelling rules from which there is no contractual or treaty right of derogation can also better be studied in the context of the right of States to consent to international law rules.

[34] See, *supra*, Part One, I ii c) 2.

[35] See *infra* in this Part III v a) under Prophylactic Rules: Human Rights.

violating *fundamental* human rights, harbouring terrorists or permitting other activity violating the legitimate rights of other States,[36] or using resources in violation of acceptable behaviour in international society.[37] In any of these situations, other States and other actors in international society may, as amply demonstrated in practice, resort to forceful measures such as sanctions[38] to compel a deviating State to turn back to comply with accepted rules of international law.

b) The Adoption of National Rules in the International Legal Order

Conversely, there are numerous situations when international courts, and especially, investment and other arbitration tribunals, *appear* to apply *national legal rules*.

However, in most cases this is a mere *illusion*: in a very high proportion of cases these rules are not 'national' but form part of *intrinsic maxims* or *intrinsic general principles* that form part of any legal system.[39]

---

[36] See my *International Legal Order*, *op. cit.*, Chapter V under Terrorism.

[37] See my *International Legal Order*, *op. cit.*, Chapter V under Environmental Rules.

[38] See my *International Legal Order*, *op. cit.*, Chapter IX under Consequential Rules: Sanctions.

[39] On the law applied in arbitrations, see, Born, G., *International Commercial Arbitration*, The Hague: Kluwer, 2nd ed., 2004; Caron, D.D., Schille, S.W., Cohen Smutny, A., & Triantafilou, E.E., eds., *Practising Virtue: Inside International Arbitration*, Oxford: OUP, 2015; Redfern & Hunter on Arbitration, Oxford: OUP, 6th ed., 2015 ; Reed, L., Paulson, J., & Blackaby, N., *Guide to ICSID Arbitration*, The Hague: Kluwer, 2004. *Cf. infra*, in this Part, B I i-vi and II i-iv.

iv. The Notion of Comity

a) The Importance and Definition of Comity

As far as we have been able to find out, no other textbook on public international law speaks much about 'comity'. Yet, it seems that this is a most important concept to explain how some rules emerge and operate in international society.

The term *comity* is occasionally used to denote a rule which is not legally binding but only forming part of the courtesy (*courtoisie*) between nations. In this sense the term is often used to describe various non-binding rules with regard to the treatment of diplomats, for example rules on *protocol and etiquette* to be observed in practice. Such rules are respected in the daily life of States, not on the basis of any legal obligations and not as part of the important compulsory rules on diplomatic rights, such as immunity,[40] but as *courtesy*; sometimes the term *comity* is used to denote such courtesy.

Most often, however, the term *comity* is used by practising lawyers, especially in the Anglo-Saxon world, to mean something else: it is taken to mean *the mutual respect States show each other with regard to the application of their respective laws*. As such, comity can be a very useful term in this work on the basic precepts of the international legal system.

In *Hilton v Guyot* the term comity in this sense was succinctly defined as a form of *recognition*[41] of another legal system. The Court said that

---

[40] See, *infra*, in this Part, B III v d) under the section on Diplomatic Protection.

[41] *Recognition* is a term which can be used in numerous different ways: in this context we are speaking of *acknowledging the existence, viability and efficacy of*

> 'Comity', in the legal sense, is neither a matter of absolute obligation, on the one hand, nor of mere courtesy and good will, on the other. But it is the recognition which one nation allows within its own territory to the legislative, executive and judicial acts of another nation, having due regard both to international duty and convenience, and to the rights of its own citizens or of other persons who are under the protection of its laws'.[42]

Comity, in this sense, is a most important concept in international law. It explains both certain consequences of the sovereignty of States, such as that of equality and of mutual respect. It crystallises numerous aspects of the *interdependence* of nations. Comity also lies at the very root of conflict of laws solutions. The Supreme Court of the United States expressed this connection clearly in *Lorenzen v Lydden*[43] where the Court said that

> 'International or maritime law in such matters as this[44] ... aims at stability and order through usages which considerations of comity, reciprocity and long-range interest have developed to define the domain which each will claim as its own. Maritime law, like our municipal law, has attempted to avoid or resolve conflicts between competing laws by ascertaining and valuing points of contact between the transactions and the States or governments whose competing laws are involved'.

---

a specific legal order. Infra, see, for this term, in relation to the *acknowledgment of objective regimes*, in Part Three, C i a).

[42] (1985) 159 US 113 233 per Mr Justice Gray.
[43] (1953) 345 US 571.
[44] The case concerned claims for injuries sustained in Cuba by a Danish seaman who had boarded the ship in New York. (Footnote added).

The technique of applying principles of comity leads, *inter alia* to what in conflict of laws is called the search for the *proper law of the contract*.[45] The Court in *Lorenzen v Lydden* said that the criteria that the Court should use

> '... appear to be arrived at from weighing the significance of one or more connecting factors between the shipping transaction regulated and the national interest served by the assertion of authority'.[46]

The concept of comity is thus closely connected with notions like sovereignty, extraterritorial application of laws and party autonomy. The reference to such broad notions needs to be explained.

b) Comity, Sovereignty and Jurisdictional Issues

A State is, as a matter of principle, sovereign in its own territory and therefore decides what laws and rules apply to its citizens and other persons in its territory. This sweeping statement has, as we already indicated and which we shall investigate in greater detail, several serious limitations: it is certainly not true that a State can do what it pleases in its own territory. We have already referred to the '*reserved domain*' – a mentioned in the UN Charter as article 2(7).[47] It is this domain which is now gradually limited. The most important limitations of the power of the State are in the field of *human rights* and of *immunity* of certain agents of other States,

---

[45] It is this technique which, in Scandinavia, with a less adequate term, is called the 'individualising method'.
[46] (1953) 345 US 571.
[47] See, *supra*, Part One, I ii c 2.

like members of foreign government and diplomats. There are also other important limitations with regard to rights of *transit* and with regard to activities that may cause transboundary, or probably even national, *pollution*.[48]

A State's power may furthermore be severely limited in its own territory by virtue of *treaties and agreements* which extend the powers of others or limit the powers of the territorial State in certain respects. The treaties of the European Union may illustrate this point as here national legislative measures are demoted by EU legislation.[49]

These *limitations* of a State's sovereignty in its own territory can, in many situations, be construed to correspond to *rights* of other States and can, in a sense, represent a form of recognition of the legal system of other States.

However, when we speak of *comity* we are no longer thinking of the clear limitations of a State's power by general rules or by treaties, but we have in mind the *attitude* of one State to the legislative and judicial machinery of another State. This notion is thus of considerable importance when we speak of public and private international rules.

National Courts have certain attitudes to legislation and judicial decisions of other States when such matters become relevant in any one case. The term comity then tends to imply that a national Court gives effect, or refuses effect, to a *foreign*

---

[48] See, my *International Law and the Independent State, op. cit.* Ch. 4, on Human Rights, Immunity, Transit and Environmental Rules and on other limitations of a State's sovereignty in its own territory. This book was written from the perspective of *statesmen looking out from inside their State* to the international legal order, rather than, what is usually the case, of *observing the State from outside*.

[49] See, my *International Legal Order, op. cit.* Ch. 4.

law or accepts the facts underlying a *foreign judgment* on the basis of respect for another State. There is often a considerable element of reciprocity in handling certain matters and a Court may, for example, often consider how and to what extent it is important that its own legislation or judgments of similar type are accepted elsewhere. Comity thus implies reciprocal respect that a State has for another State's legislative, executive and judicial structure, and for measures and acts emanating from its organs, such as for its laws, decrees and judgments.[50]

We shall later[51] investigate the practical implications of the *respect* that States have for the legal systems of other States. However, it may here be mentioned that the root of that respect is based on comity and entrenched and secured by the safest basis of obligation of all, that of *reciprocity*.[52]

It is useful to place the practice of application of foreign jurisdictional rules, carried out by many courts and authorities of the world, in the context of *comity*. Since comity implies the respect for the existence of another State's laws, it could be said to be a term which is applied at 'the receiving end': a court, for example, asks itself whether or not it shall apply a foreign law out of this respect for another country. At the 'sending end', the other State thus asks itself whether its own laws will have *extraterritorial effect*.[53]

---

[50] See, further, *infra*, under Distributive Rules: Jurisdiction: Territoriality. There are rules that may enlarge such recognition, see, Cheshire & North, *op. cit. passim*.

[51] See *infra*, Part Three, VI, on The Obligation of Activated Rules.

[52] See, further on this, my *Concept, op. cit.*, 122-128.

[53] There are, of course, a number of *conventions and treaties* to enlarge such recognition, see, Cheshire & North, *op. cit. passim*.

Older textbooks on conflict of laws, especially in Scandinavia, tend to treat recognition of judgments as something which can only have practical importance if a State has ratified a treaty obliging it to give effect to judgments of foreign States. Yet, as clear expression of respect for the judicial power of other States, such judgments are often in practice enforceable in other ways in other jurisdictions.[54]

Devices like *blocking statutes*, adopted to accommodate the legitimate interests of other States, are sometimes used to ensure that a case, out of respect for comity, is taken to another more appropriate jurisdiction.[55] The power of a court to consider itself as inappropriate or as a *forum non conveniens* is also an expression for the respect of comity and that other courts, in other jurisdictions, are more apt to deal with a particular case.[56]

c) Comity, Acts of State and Public Policy

The question of extraterritorial application of the laws and decrees of one country in another, forms part of the problem concerning *division of competence* between States with regard to legal persons. The so called *Act of State doctrine*, previously limited the power of courts to pronounce on the incompatibility of national acts and international law, and was a much debated topic.[57] In the light of nationalisation of assets, that was held to be contrary to human

---

[54] See, my *International Legal Order, op. cit.*, Chapter VII.
[55] See, in detail, my *International Legal Order, op. cit.*, Chapter VII.
[56] See, on this doctrine, *ibid., loc. cit.* and *supra*, in this Part, under A ii, on 'forum shopping'.
[57] See, my *Finance and Protection of Investments in Developing Countries*, London: Gower, 2nd ed. 1976, and my *International Legal Order, op. cit.*, Chapter VII, on Extraterritorial Application of Laws, Decrees and Judgments.

rights, including the right to hold private property, Courts became less wary of stating their views on compatibility of certain Acts of State.[58] The debate of the Act of State doctrine in relation to nationalisations was largely over-shadowed by intense attempts to reverse previous nationalisations by re-privatisation in Eastern Europe.

The Act of State doctrine is intimately connected with the notion of the *'reserved domain'*[59]: it thus implies that a State must not sit in judgment of another State's actions within its own territory, on the basis of the rule *par inter pares non habet imperium*.[60] This doctrine was, for long, respected by Courts and it is still followed, especially in the United States. But the *Sabbatino Case*[61] led to changes in attitudes: that Case concerned the legitimacy of nationalisations without compensation and the effect of US

---

[58] See, the references in the previous note.

[59] On this important notion, see, my *International Law and the Independent State op. cit., passim:* in that work, international law is presented through the *optique* of a Government, thus as a Statesman perceives the international legal system, thus, in what fields is the State obliged to limit its sovereignty? The work sets out the various areas in which this has to be done, in the area of human rights, of the immunity of diplomats, of the right of innocent transit of others and other limitations of a State's territorial sovereignty.

[60] 'An equal among equals, does not rule'. *Cf. infra*, in this Part, B II I, on General Principles. The importance of the Acts of State doctrine was strictly respected in US Courts, from the time of *Underhill v Fernandez*, (1897), 168 US 250. *Cf. Banco Nacional de Cuba v Sabbatino*, (1964), 376 US 398; that Case concerned the legitimacy of foreign nationalisations without compensation. *Cf. Maltina Corp. v Cawy Bottling Co.*, 462 F.2d 1021, 1025 (5th Cir. 1972): 'our courts will not give 'extraterritorial effect' to a confiscatory decree of a foreign state, even where directed against its own nationals.' See further, my *Finance and Protection of Investments in Developing Countries*, London: Gower, 2nd ed., 1986, Ch. II.

[61] See, the previous note.

Courts applying the Act of State doctrine to allow such measures by a foreign Government. As many US investors suffered losses by the decision in the *Sabbatino Case*, the '*Second Hickenlooper Amendment*',[62] was enacted to rule that US Courts should not apply the Act of State doctrine in cases of nationalisations of foreign sovereigns. This case can thus also be viewed as one proving the international human right of property.[63] Sometimes a foreign law is not applied if, in the opinion of a Court, it is contrary to normal rules about morals or justice.[64]

A court may refrain from applying certain foreign public laws, on the basis of the argument that it is not for the courts of one State to enforce the public law of another, equal, State. However, in numerous cases, courts do apply foreign public laws except in the realm of collection of taxes or fines, where there is still some hesitation to assist other States at the cost of intrusion in human rights of citizens.[65]

d) Comity as a Link Between Public and Private International Law

It has been thought useful to set out the basic rules concerning comity for several reasons. In the first place, as mentioned above, textbooks on international law rarely even refer to the notion of *comity* which is undoubtedly of primordial importance in the

---

[62] 22 USC § 2370.
[63] See, *infra*, in this Part, B III v a).
[64] See, *infra*, in this Part, B I v on Consequential maxims and C II iii, Substantive Rules for All Contacts.
[65] See, in detail *ibid., loc. cit.*

relationship between States and other subjects of international society.

Secondly, the notion itself illuminates the intricate and overlapping relationship between public and private international law, the two major disciplines between which no rigid or sensible demarcation can be drawn.

Thirdly, the notion clarifies many attitudes of States and their courts and States are, as we shall see, the most important power bases in international society. There are also many other subjects and actors in the world that partake in the setting of norms in international society and that contribute to the development of international law. New terrorist movement may now have forceful armies and are often even – sometimes with the help of some governments! – equipped with highly advanced weapon systems. But, it is, so far, only States that have an airforce. And it is only States that have organised courts that face the question whether they should give effect to a law or to a decree – or other form of executive order – of another State.

A spectacular example of the effect of a foreign Decree in another State was when the British Prime Minister, Margaret Thatcher, allowed the extraterritorial application of a United States Decree, in the Hostages in Teheran Crisis in 1979-1980. President Carter froze Iranian assets in US Banks in 1979 as diplomatic and consular staff at the US Embassy in Teheran had been taken hostage by revolutionary forces after they had overthrown the Shah. A considerable amount of these assets were held by US Banks in London. The British Government *allowed the extraterritorial effect* of the United States Decree, whereupon the Iranian Government sued seven US Banks in the High Court in London to release the funds held in England. On behalf of the US Banks some forty

Barristers and over a hundred solicitors' firms were involved; as a specialist in international law, it seemed useful to advise the US Banks in London to offer the release of frozen assets against the release of the Hostages.

This affair led to an important Case in the International Court of Justice in the Hague.[66] But, in practical terms, by far the most important Case was the one in the High Court in London: the Iranians accepted to release the hostages once the assets held were unblocked. A historic *telex* message – as was the form of communication in those days – confirmed the unfreezing of the assets and a reply came immediately that the hostages had been released. The following day, the newspapers announced that President Reagan – who had just taken over the presidency of the United States – was praised for his 'diplomatic success' to have had the hostages released when, in fact, they had been bought free, ironically with Iran's own money.[67]

Because of the *comity* between nations,[68] one State may respect and give effect to rules of another national legal system, thus, to the internal law of another State. Along one avenue of development, there has for some time been attempts to harmonise provisions of substantive internal law, whereas along another avenue, attempts are made to unify also the more formal conflict rules.

On the other hand, it is *because* of public international law that the conflict rules are generally held and respected. The

---

[66] *Hostages in Teheran Case (Iran v United States)*, ICJ *Reports* 1980, 1.
[67] *The Freezing Assets Case, (Iran v US Banks in London)*, High Court, 1980, (settled); unreported.
[68] See, *infra*, in this Part, A iv, on Comity, and A ii on public and private international law; *cf.* my *International Legal Order, op. cit.*, 499-502, 549-551.

systems thus intertwine and are thoroughly inter-dependent. Without understanding of this relationship we cannot appreciate the operation of rules in international society.

B. Intrinsic Rules

We can observe that in international society some rules appear to be *intrinsic*, that is to say, such rules exist without any specific authorisation or consent by States, entities or individuals. These *intrinsic* rules exist in public as well as in private international law.

In this category, we find what can be called '*maxims*', '*general principles*' – as well as rules – often contested with regard to the actual and precise contents and meaning – of '*jus cogens*', 'compelling' law from which no derogations are allowed.

Certain *maxims* are essential in any legal order. These maxims can be conceived as a sub-category of general principles[69] but are more clearly understood as forming a special *distinct* category, as we do in this work. Maxims thus form an independent and precise sub-section, often with procedural or technical connotations.

Certain of the so called *general principles*, not always identified in the traditional textbooks, also form part of *intrinsic rules*, necessary in any legal system, that is, when they are of a *formal nature*. As explained above, it is useful to keep the two categories *distinct*, that of *maxims* and that of *general principles*, as we shall demonstrate that maxims are essentially *different* from formal general principles.[70]

---

[69] *Infra, cf.* the following chapter.
[70] *Infra*, under II, ii.

However, we note that the majority of formal *'general principles'* cited by writers are often what we in this work prefer to call *'maxims'*. In fact, we have found no other writer or court that speaks of *'maxims'* in international law although it appears convenient to do so in setting out a systematic overview of rules in international society, as we attempt to do in this work.

Some writers, and Courts, use 'general principles' to mean the whole material contents of international law: some authors call a whole book on international law *'General Principles'* and then treat the whole material body of international law under that title.[71]

Others jurists sometimes refer to 'general principles' to explain the material law that is occasionally applied in an arbitration. The consent of the parties to the arbitration is necessary for the application of such rules as 'the law' of the arbitration and the relevant consent is given *ad hoc*, and clearly limited to the mandate of the arbitration tribunal. But in that case, we are mainly speaking of *material* rules of law.

In this section on 'intrinsic' rules, we limit the definition of 'general principles' to entirely *formal rules* and we only deal with *material* or 'substantive' general principles to distinguish that type from the main 'formal' category; to other material rules we will come back later.[72]

Certain prohibitive rules that we, in this work, call *prophylactic* operate without specific authorisation in international society. Such prophylactic rules intervene, as it were, as the term suggests, *before* a harmful action and are designed to prevent the action in question.

---

[71] For example, Brownlie, I., *General Principles of International Law*, Oxford: OUP, 8th ed., 2010.

[72] See, *infra*, in this Part, C II iii, Substantive Rules for All Contacts: *lex mercatoria*.

Some intrinsic rules thus concern the prohibition of harm.[73] Seen from the other side, certain *prophylactic* rules are of an intrinsic character – that is to say they are indispensable for the functioning of international society and without these this society cannot survive. Among these prophylactic rules we note, as the most important group, the rules of *jus cogens* that function *erga omnes*, that is to say these rules are binding on all, irrespective of any specific consent.

i. 'Rules', 'Principles', 'Norms' and 'Decisions'

The concept of a *'rule'* is normally reserved for a material stipulation of general application. The term *'norm'* is often used as a synonym of a *'rule'*. A *'rule'* (or a *'norm'*) can be distinguished from a *'decision'* in the sense that is it formulated to address a general audience of more or less vast size. On the contrary, a *'decision'* is directed to specific and named addressees. Thus, a *'rule'* cannot be addressed to one single individual but only to a more or less vast number of people or to the general public. There cannot be a *'rule' ad personam* concerning one person as there can be in the case of a *'decision'*.

The criteria of generality of a commandment is thus what enables us to distinguish a *'rule'* from a *'decision'*. A *'rule'* has always an impersonal character. A rule is not designed to concern one or several concretely specified persons. It will apply to *all* who find themselves in a situation described by the rule without us being able to ascertain beforehand exactly whom will be caught by the rule, now or in the future.

---

[73] See, *supra*, Part One, I b ii c 2.

Naturally, a 'decision' can address a 'group' of persons, for example, 'the members of the medical profession', but it would be more normal to regulate such questions by a 'regulation' or a 'set of rules'.

ii. Diversity of Material Rules According to Their Function

The rules that we can observe being applied in international society concern diverse matters. We can distinguish some '*prophylactic*' rules, for example those that forbid harm or prejudice to others.[74] As mentioned above, prophylactic rules are intrinsic in the international legal order whereas a multitude of other rules do not have this character.

Further '*extrinsic*' rules – that can be adopted and followed at will and that do not form part of the basic compulsory fabric of law – are rules that might be called '*stabilising*' and others that are '*distributive*' with regard to the allocation of national space of different States. Further '*extrinsic rules*' may concern the jurisdictional competence of these States, or rules on '*communications*' and '*mutual contacts*'.

These bundles of rules are supplemented by even further facultative or optional rules on *cooperation* or on closer integration. '*Correlative*', '*sequential*' or '*consequential*' rules lay down the effects of violation of the compulsory rules. Section B of this Part of this work deals with *intrinsic rules*[75] and Section C will analyse

---

[74] In this Part, B III i-v.
[75] In this Part, B I-III.

and discuss the character of all the other material *extrinsic rules* that operate in international society.[76]

iii. Protection of the Hypothetical Goal

Certain rules that we can observe empirically in international society concern the prohibition of certain acts that would endanger the attainment of the '*hypothetical goal.*'[77] Thus, acts that would partially or totally eschew this goal are forbidden. Once there is a society, a legal order will automatically develop by the principle *ubi societas ibi jus*: 'forbidding' rules emerge at once and these rules do not have to await any sort of catastrophe to be put in place. In this sense, the 'forbidding' rules function to *pre-empt* acts susceptible to endanger the hypothetical goal. These 'forbidding' rules are thus those that we call '*prophylactic*' rules in this work.

As we will demonstrate, prophylactic rules can be classified according to the degree of harm that is forbidden and according to what subjects or matters are concerned. Some of these rules are of a merely formal nature but they are still vital to guarantee the good functioning of international society. The respect for all prophylactic rules is of primordial importance to the survival of international society and of its subjects.

---

[76] In this Part, C I-III.
[77] For a definition and explications, see *supra*, Part One, I ii b).

I. Inherent Maxims

Once there is a legal order certain *maxims* emerge *immediately* as indispensable rules: inherent maxims are thus purely formal and we can observe them in every single legal system. In every legal order we thus find maxims like, for example, *pacta sunt servanda* (agreements must be respected); *audiatur et altera pars* (both parties to a dispute must be heard); and *nemo judex in causa sua* (a person cannot be a judge in a matter in which he has a direct personal interest).

It is interesting to note that these maxims exist in all legal systems whether or not these are based on Roman law, on the Napoleonic code, or stem from totally different backgrounds, like the ancient Scandinavian systems, where there was no influence of Roman law, nor of the Napoleonic Code. This may reinforce our assumption that the maxims are inherently and immediately necessary in *any* legal system.

i. Initial Maxims

We may note a distinction with regard to the chronology in the functioning of a maxim: the rule according to which one must respect concluded agreements (*pacta sunt servanda*), is pertinent *ab initio* and constitutes thus an *initial maxim*. On the other hand, in its Latin gerund form, the rule is looking to the future and thus establishes a model for future action.

The lawyer and philosopher Hans Kelsen makes of this maxim the 'base rule', the *Grundnorm*, of the whole international legal system. However, he puts this 'base rule' at the summit of a pyramid of rules (against all ideas of geometry or of gravity), and furthermore, claims that it is a 'customary rule'.[78] Severe criticism has been directed against the idea that this particular maxim should be considered as the base rule, the *Grundnorm*, whence other rules derive their validity.[79] However, Kelsen has also some enthusiastic admirers and followers,[80] although it is difficult to find much merit in his theory about the *Grundnorm* which is not much more than an initial formal maxim: this maxim says little more about the contents of obligations or aspirations in international society other than that it is useful to keep one's word.

The maxim *pacta sunt servanda* is obviously of considerable and primordial importance, coming as it does near ethical rules of behaviour, rather than being part of material positive law. It is thus a logical maxim that does not explain, as Kelsen claims, from

---

[78] Kelsen, H., *Hauptprobleme der Staatsrechtslehre*, Tübingen: Mohr Siebeck, 1911, from where he later transposes his ideas about national constitutional law to international law, see his *Reine Rechtslehre*, Leipzig & Vienne, 1934, where he first adopts the *pacta sunt servanda* rule as the *Grundnorm*, that is to say the fundamental rule from which all other rules derive their legal validity. *Cf. supra* in Part One, note 1 for references and in detail, *supra*, Part One, I i c) 2, on Positivism and *infra*, Part Three, VI on the Obligation of Activated Rules.

[79] Cavaglieri, A., *Corso di diritto internazionale*, Naples: Rondinella; 1938, 50; Romano, S., *Corso di diritto internazionale*, Padua: Cedam, 1926, cit., 20 & *Corso di diritto internazionale*, Padua: Cedam 1939, 21 who considers the acceptance of such a rule as a return to 'natural law' arguments: '...*in una concezione del tutto naturalistica...*'. *Cf.* criticism by Hart, H.L.A., *The Concept of Law*, Oxford: OUP, 1961. In this work we adhere to some of the views of natural law but for totally different reasons (see *infra* Part Three) and we reject Kelsen's theories on the *Grundnorm* as untenable. We introduce in this work the notion of '*intrinsic law*' to cover some trains of thought of St. Thomas Aquinas.

[80] Kelsen's views are adopted and followed for example by the positivists who seek to transform the United Nations by revising the Charter to endow the organisation with considerable further powers, see Clerk, G. & Sohn, L.B., *World Peace Through World Law*, Boston: Harvard University Press, 1958; 3rd ed., 1965.

where other rules come – but rather sets out how and why we must keep our obligations.

In following Kelsen, and without necessarily accepting the function of his invented *Grundnorm*, a long row of writers accept, in a most uniform way, Kelsen's absurd idea that the logical and formal maxim *pacta sunt servanda* would be the product and result of a 'custom' and thus a 'customary rulc'.[81]

However, the rule *pacta sunt servanda* has little to do with 'custom' but is an *inherent* and *intrinsic* maxim present, for *logical* reasons, in every single legal system.[82] Above all, it does not explain the binding force of rules in the international system, except insofar as agreements are concerned.[83]

ii. Conditional Maxims

The rule *nullum crimen sine lege* (that no act can be considered to constitute a crime unless a legal rule so stipulates), is known by all legal systems. This rule is different from initial maxims, as it contains a condition: the obligation not to impose a punishment for an act unless such an act has been 'criminalised' by legal rules in force at the time the act was committed. No sanctions must follow an act unless there is an *antecedent* legal rule forbidding this act.

---

[81] For exemple, Morelli, G., *Nozioni di diritto internazionale*, Rome: Giuffré, 1943, *cf.* 7th ed., Padua, 1967, 32, who accepts the maxim as a 'customary rule' without considering it to be any 'base rule'. See, for criticism of pretended 'customary rules', *infra*, Part Three, VI I a) on the 'Fallacies of Customary Law' and on the 'Allergy to Natural Law'.

[82] See, *infra*, Part Three, on the compelling nature of maxims.

[83] See in detail, *infra*, Part Three, VI iii on The Obligation.

This rule is thus intimately linked to another rule that forbids legal rules to have retrospective effects.[84]

Maxims, like the rule *nemo dat quod non habet*, *i.e.* you cannot legally give away things to which you have no title, or *lex specialis derogat generali* – a specific law derogates from a general one – and *lex posterior derogat priori* – a later law derogates from an earlier one, are also conditional.

Another maxim is the rule *sic utere ut alienum non laedas*, thus the obligation, *not to use one's own property or territory to harm that of others*. This maxim is present in all legal systems[85] and in international law it is particularly important in times of intentionally or negligently caused pollution, [86] or in the case of diversion of water.[87]

All these maxims postulate a pre-existing situation and thus concerns a condition of *chronology* that determines when these maxims become applicable.

iii. Contingent Maxims

Writers sometimes speak of 'equality' as a general principle of international law.[88] It may be more appropriate to consider the

---

[84] For international cases, see , *e.g.* EC, 15/60, 32 ILR 356; 42 & 49/59, 32 *ILR* 390; 111/63 (1965), *ECR* 690. This rule is often controversial in the context of war crimes where we have explained apparent exceptions to this rule by recourse to natural law: there are for example rules prohibiting genocide that normal people should have realised existed even before formal criminalisation, see, my *Law of War*, *op. cit.*, Ch. 12.

[85] In Roman law expressed as '*Sic utere tuo ut alienum non laedas*'.

[86] *The Trail Smelter Arbitration*, (1938) (1941) 3 RIAA 1905.

[87] *The Lake Lanoux Case* (1957) 12 *RIAA* 281.

[88] See, *infra*, under General Principles in this Part, B II i-iv.

concept of *'equality'* to be a 'contingent maxim', that is to say when something is to be divided or shared, it has to be shared in equal parts. This does not necessarily mean that something has be divided in equal portions but rather that the result must be reasonable and 'equitable'. It would appear that States and Courts confirm the existence of such a maxim.[89]

This maxim should not be confused with the demand to a Court to take a decision *ex aequo et bono*, a request to apply extra-juridical rules of 'fairness' in a specific case.[90] This latter eventuality may involve applying material rules rather than the formal maxim concerning equality.

Another maxim relating to equality is the rule *par in parem non habet imperium* – an equal among equals does not rule. Here too, there is a contingency. When there is a dispute, one State cannot decide alone but must, because of comity and equality, also respect the legal system of other States. In other words, this a notion linked to the sovereignty of States and to the pre-eminence of States in the international legal system.[91]

iv. Stabilising Maxims

Pacta sunt servanda, the command that 'agreements must be kept', can also be presented as a 'stabilising' rule in international society as it subjects the will to revise agreements according to circumstances (under the *rebus sic stantibus* doctrine) to the paramount rule that *preceding agreements must first be preserved*

---

[89] McNair, A., (later President of the International Court of Justice), 'Equality in international law', 26 *Michigan Law Review*, 1927, 131 *et seq.*

[90] *Infra*, in this Part, under General Principles.

[91] *Cf. supra*, in this Part, A iv c) on Acts of State.

and properly executed. This is an essential rule in the international legal order, or, indeed, in any legal order.

As explained above, however important this rule may be, it most clearly is not the foundation of international law as some writers have suggested, propositions that we have discussed and dismissed above.[92]

v. Consequential Maxims

Other maxims, like the rule *audiatur et altera pars*[93] and *nemo judex in causa sua*,[94] only become pertinent once there is a dispute before a court or a tribunal and when a reprehensible act has been committed. These maxims are essential to a fair hearing.[95]

Once there is a court hearing, it becomes convenient that the *lex fori* regulates the procedure and other formalities. That is

---

[92] See for my criticism of Kelsen, *supra*, in this part, B II under Initial Maxims and, in detail, under Positivism, in Part One I i c) 2.

[93] See, for case law, for example, 17/74 (1974) ECR 1080; *cf.* 32/62 (1963) *ECR* 55 and 35/67, 1968, *ECR* 344. Default judgments are compatible with the maxim: Colliard, C.-A., 'La non-comparution', SFDI, *Colloque de Lyon, La juridiction internationale permanente*, Paris: Pedone, 1986; Thirlway, H., *Non-Appearance before the International Court of Justice*, New York & London: CUP, 1985; *cf. Nicaragua v Etats-Unis*, (1986), ICJ *Recueil* 1986 and *The Times* 28th June 1986.

[94] Note that the maxim *nemo judex* can be conceived as equally applicable to a prohibition for someone who has taken part in deliberations of a decision to obtain advantages or benefits. Together with the maxim *audiatur et altera pars*, the maxim prohibiting bias, form part of what in English law is called '*natural justice*'; in the United States part of what is called 'due process', see *infra*, in this section.

[95] See, for example, Wade, W. & Forsyth, C., *Administrative Law*, Oxford: OUP, 11th ed., 2014; Foulkes, D., *Administrative Law*, London: Butterworth, 8th ed., 1995.

particularly important in a criminal case.⁹⁶ But in dispositive cases, the parties are to some extent free to agree on other rules.

Rules on burden of proof are also virtually universal, as based on practicality and common sense: thus, the rule *Onus probandi actori incumbit* or the *Qui dixit* rule, imply that the part that makes a claim also has the burden to prove his allegations.⁹⁷

Other extremely important maxims that only become operative when parties to a dispute face a court hearing, are those that prohibit gain on the basis of wrongful act. The reason for such maxims is clearly the ethical need that all actions in courts and between parties must be untainted by immorality.

One such conditional maxim is thus *nullus commodum capere de sua injuria propria* – no one can be allowed to take advantage of his own wrong, differently expressed as *nemo auditor propriam turpitudinem allegans* – that no one may seek a remedy, relying on his own illegal act or, again, *ex turpi causa non oritur actio* – no legal case can be heard if based on an illegal act.

This maxim, or these differently phrased maxims, also explain that a party cannot rely his own irregularities in bidding or tender procedures to obtain a judgment or award in his favour as that would lead to his '*unjust enrichment*'. One tribunal thus stated that

---

⁹⁶ See, for example, concerning the arrest of a British citizen in Peru, *The Captain Melville White Case*, Arbitrage de la Commission désignée par le Sénat de la ville libre hanséatique de Hambourg, 1864, La Fontaine, H., *Pasicrisie internationale 1794-1900, Histoire dcomentaire des arbitrages internationaux*, The Hague: Nijhoff, 1997, 48.

⁹⁷ For example, *The Queen Case*, 1872, de la Pradelle, A., & Politis, N., eds., ii *Recueil des arbitrages internationaux*, Paris: Editions internationales, 708.

'When the cause of the increase in the assets of a certain person is illegal, such enrichment must be sanctioned by preventing its consummation.' [98]

In their application the maxim about the prohibition of about unjust enrichment come near the operation of the general principle that concerns ethics:[99] yet, it is more convenient to insert these rigorous and clear rules among the maxims.

Investment and arbitration tribunals have specifically resorted to this maxim in numerous cases concerning culturally distinct legal systems.[100] Courts and arbitration tribunals have also regularly found for the innocent party in disputes where another party has relied on a wrongful act. In one case one party thus sought to argue that 'bribery' was a 'local custom' implying 'normal donations'. In an ensuing arbitration the tribunal rightfully held that this would be contrary the rule that no one should benefit from a wrongful act; and bribery is criminalised in an overwhelming number of jurisdictions.[101]

---

[98] *Inceysa Vallisoletana v El Salvador*, ICSID Case No. ARB/03/26, 2006, Award, Aug. 2, 2006, available at http://www.italaw.com/sites/default/files/case-documents/ita0424_0.pdf.

[99] See, *infra*, B III on Ethics and Intrinsic Law.

[100] *World Duty Free Company Ltd. v The Republic of Kenya*, ICSID Case No. ARB/00/7, Award Oct. 4, 2006 (bribery); *Kuwait Airways Corp. v Iraqi Airways Co.*, [2002] AC 19, 12, (fraud), available at http://www.publications.parliament.uk/pa/ld200102/ldjudgmt/jd020516/kuwait-1.htm. *Inceysa Vallisoletana v El Salvador*, ICSID Case No. ARB/03/26, Award, Aug. 2, 2006, (fraud); available at http://www.italaw.com/sites/default/files/case-documents/ita0424_0.pdf. *First Nat'l City Bank v Banco Para el Comercio Exterior de Cuba (Bancec)*, 462 U.S. 611, 613 (1983) (fraud).

[101] *World Duty Free Company Ltd. v The Republic of Kenya*, ICSID Case, 2006, No. ARB/00/7, 2006, Award, Oct. 4, 2006.

The above-mentioned maxims *audiatur et altera pars* – the obligation to hear both parties – and *nemo judex in causa sua* – that concerns *bias*, are, in English law and in jurisdictions following that system, held to be the basic notions of *natural justice* (not to be confused with natural law). Any judgment or award that has not respected these maxims and that does nor respect *natural justice* (thus, procedures that have that not respected the main two maxims about *hearing both parties* and about *bias*) risk to be *void* and impossible to enforce.[102] In the United States the disrespect for natural justice is often referred to as lack of 'due process'.[103]

Further consequential maxims concern *res judicata* (meaning the final and effective legal force of a judgment after time limits of appeal have expired) or the rule *ne bis in idem*,[104] (that a Court cannot judge more than once on the same matter between the same parties) are also consequential in so far as they are designed to prevent a case from being heard twice.[105] Furthermore, the normal

---

[102] *Hollingsworth v Barbour*, 1830 29 U.S. 466, 475 (1830); *Boswell's Lessee v Otis*, 50 U.S. 336, 35051 (1850). Such judgments are not possible to enforce: *Osorio v Dole Food Co.*, 2009, 665 F. Supp. 2d 1307, 1316-18, S.D. Fla. 2009.

[103] *Bank Melli Iran v Pahlavi*, 1995, 58 F.3d 1406, 1410, 1412, 9th Cir. 1995; *cf. Society of Lloyd's v Ashenden*, 2000, 233 F.3d 473, 477, 7th Cir. 2000; *Cunard Steamship Co. v Salén Reefer Servs. AB*, 1985, 773 F.2d 452, 457, 2d Cir. 1985; *Wilson v Marchington*, 1997, 127 F.3d 805, 811, 9th Cir. 1997.

[104] See *e.g.*, 18/65 (1966) ECR 119; 35/65 (1967) ECR 66; 14/68 (1969) ECR 24.

[105] There may be exceptions to this rule in certain criminal cases when the accused has been acquitted and new evidence of guilt has been found. A procedural rule allows a defendant in many countries to enter a plea of *autrefois acquis* or *autrefois convict* (already acquitted or convicted for the same crime). This rule on 'double jeopardy was abolished in English law by the Criminal Justice Act of 2003 and entered into effect in 2005: see, of 'double jeopardy', article 4 of the European Convention on Human Rights; and see a number of constitutional provisions of States, for example the Fifth Amendment in the United States.

procedural maxims on the burden of proof, *onus probandi actori incumbit* or, differently expressed, *qui dixit* (meaning, the party that alleges something must also prove it), is not only used in ordinary courts in criminal, contractual or other cases, but it is also used to advance cases in arbitration proceedings.[106] Thus, all these rules are consequential maxims and will not have occasion to operate unless there is a prior wrongdoing or a prior dispute.

In this category we may also include the rule that interest is payable on a debt[107] and that such interest may not exceed the initial principal sum, according to the principle *alterum tantum*.[108]

---

[106] For example, *The Queen Case*, 1872, de la Pradelle, A., & Politis, N., eds., ii *Recueil des arbitrages internationaux*, Paris: Editions internationales, 708.

[107] *Russian Indemnity Case, (Russia v Turkey)*, 1912, Scott, J.B., *The Hague Court Reports*, New York: OUP, 1916, 297. The Tribunal held, that all the private legislation of the States forming the European concert, admits, as did formerly the Roman law, the obligation to pay at least interest for delayed payment as legal indemnity, when it is a question of non-fulfilment of an obligation, consisting the payment of a sum of money fixed by convention, clear and exigible, such interest to be paid at least from the date of the demand made to the debtor in due form of law,'*ibid.* at 317. Note, that although the Tribunal *appeared* to take this rule from a number of national system, the right to charge interest, was already a rule of Roman law, where we should allocate its origin, see, Buckland, W.W., *Textbook of Roman Law*, 3rd ed. by Stein, P., Cambridge: CUP 2007; Buckland, W.W., McNair, A.F., *Roman Law and Common Law: A Comparison in Outline*, Cambridge: CUP, 1936, 2010: in the Empire, interest on ordinary loans was fixed at 4%, business loans at 8%; no interest above 12% was allowed and compound interest was prohibited, *ibid*. See, further, *infra*, in the following section.

[108] For example, as shown in *The Yuille, Shortridge & Cie. Case, Arbitrage de la Commission désignée par le Sénat de la ville libre hanséatique de Hambourg*, 1861, de la Pradelle, A., & Politis, N., eds., ii *Recueil des arbitrages internationaux*, Paris: Editions internationales, 108.

vi. The Origin of Compulsory Maxims

Rules *similar* to the abovementioned maxims may be found in the internal law of many States.[109] Maxims may even appear to constitute the lowest common denominator of rules applied in various national legal systems. But such rules are not uplifted into the international sphere from municipal systems and copied into international law as some claim: as mentioned above, maxims appear to be intrinsic to *any* legal system and, therefore, immediately applicable in international society *ipso facto*.[110]

The Latin form of maxims, virtually all expressed in short, compressed statements, is an indication sometimes ignored by writers that they obviously have their origin with regard to their *language*, in Roman law. This does not mean that Roman law invented these maxims but only that the Roman law system *formulated* them succinctly. These maxims are present in *every legal system* in one form or another: they are clearly an *intrinsic* feature of the international legal order.

What is furthermore certain is that these maxims did not develop through any nebulous 'customary law' – as most writers pretend – but derive their existence from simple *logical necessity* in a legal system. In this sense, they form a necessary and *intrinsic* part of all legal systems.

---

[109] See, the previous note on constitutional provisions.

[110] See, *infra* on how maxims inter-act with general principles and with material rules of international law.

II. General Principles

i. The Nature of General Principles

The terms 'norms', 'rules' and 'principles' are often used as synonyms. A 'norm' extends like a bracket over both material and formal behavioural patterns. As indicated above,[111] a 'rule' is of general character and applies to any number of designated addressees. 'Principles' are often, as we shall demonstrate, of a formal and often of less authoritative character.

The notion of general principles of international law is obscure and its content is often uncertain. There is little agreement in doctrine and in the practice of courts as to what the concept of 'general principles' actually means.[112] Some well-known international

---

[111] See, *supra*, B i, under 'Rules', 'Principles', 'Norms' and 'Decisions'.

[112] In the vast litterature, see above all, Virally, M., 'Le rôle des principes dans le développement du droit international' in *Mélanges Guggenheim*, Geneva: UHEI, 1958; and Verdross, A. v., 'Les principes généraux du droit dans la jurisprudence internationale', 52 *RCADI* ii 195; 1935 McNair, A., 'The general principles recognised by civilised nations, *BYIL*, 1957, 1; Lauterpacht, H., *Private Law Sources and Analogies in International Law*, London: Longman, 1927; Cheng, Bin, *General Principles of Law as Applied by International Courts and Tribunals*, London: Stevens, 1953; Cambridge: CUP, 2006; Ripert, G., 'Les règles du droit civil applicables aux rapports internationaux', 44 *RCADI* ii 565; Favre, A., 'Les principes généraux du droit, fonds commun du droit des gens', in *Mélanges Guggenheim*, Geneva: IUHEI, 1968, 366; Blondel, A., 'Les principes généraux du droit devant la PCIJ and the ICJ' in *Mélanges Guggenheim, op. cit.*, 201; *cf.*, Tunkin, G.I.,'General principles of law', 95 *RCADI*, 1958 9. For a relatively recent work, see Raimondo, F.O., *General Principles of Law in The Decisions of International Courts and Tribunals*, Leiden: Nijhoff, 2008.

lawyers have written their doctoral thesis on the subject.¹¹³ Furthermore, it is not easy to draw a distinction between what we call '*maxims*' set out above and 'formal' '*general principles*' of which '*maxims*' might possibly be conceived as a sub-set.

Some writers claim that 'general principles' do not have any material contents and therefore, as purely formal, they cannot be a 'source' of international law.¹¹⁴ It is not clear why 'formal' rules cannot be a 'source' of international law. Even formal rules form part of the law to be applied.

However, as mentioned above, some writers use the expression 'general principles' to include the whole material contents of the complex international legal system.¹¹⁵ To some extent, the blame for certain conceptual confusion must be borne by international lawyers themselves who have used the category of *general principles* in numerous different ways. Thus, general principles are often used to indicate the substantive rules themselves,¹¹⁶ in which case there is clearly no place for them in this section on 'intrinsic rules'; for then they do no mean anything else than 'rules of international law'.

---

[113] Pellet, A., *Recherche sur les principes généraux du droit international*, Brussels: Bruylant, 1974;

[114] Cavaglieri, *RivDI*, 19211922, 504; 1 Guggenheim, *Manual*, *op. cit.*, ch. iii f; *cf.* Scheuner, 'L'influence du droit interne sur la formation du droit international', *RCADI*, 1939 ii 162.

[115] Brownlie, I., *Principles of Public International Law*, 6th ed., Oxford: OUP, 2003; Delbez, L., *Les principes généraux du droit international public*, 3rd ed., Paris: LGDJ, 1964.

[116] E.g. *The Genocide Case* (1953), ICJ *Reports*, 23; *Corfu Channel Case* (1949), ICJ *Reports*, 4, at 22 on duty to warn and *infra*, under B II e) in this Part; *cf.* as mentioned some textbooks on substantive law are entitled '*Principles of International Law*'; e.g. Brownlie, in the previous note.

But '*general principles of law*' is the one category that the International Court of Justice mentions as a specific '*source*' in article 38 of its Statute. The article provides:

> '1. The Court, whose function is to decide in accordance with international law such disputes as are submitted to it, shall apply:
>
>   a. international conventions, whether general or particular, establishing rules expressly recognised by the contesting states;
>
>   b. international custom, as evidence of a general practice accepted as law;
>
>   c. the general principles of law recognised by civilised nations;
>
>   d. subject to the provisions of Article 59, judicial decisions and the teachings of the most highly qualified publicists of the various nations, as subsidiary means for the determination of rules of law.
>
> 2. This provision shall not prejudice the power of the Court to decide a case *ex aequo et bono*, if the parties agree thereto.'

This article, thus especially the part, '*c. the general principles of law recognised by civilised nations*', must be read in conjunction with article 59 which states that:

> 'The decision of the Court has no binding force except between the parties and in respect of that particular case.'

In other words, a judgment by the ICJ has only legal effects between the Parties to the dispute in question; yet, there have been efforts to pretend that the ICJ decides on the substantial contents of rules of international law and that its judgments are binding for all. But the

ICJ is not a Court in the Anglo-Saxon sense, a system where Judges 'legislate'.[117] So if the International Court of Justice pronounces itself on 'general principles' in a specific case, even statements of the Court can only provide guidance for third parties. The same goes for any other case before the Court where judgments and decisions only take effect *inter partes*.

Yet, most international lawyers rely on judgments of the International Court of Justice as if such judgments were authoritative statements on international law, binding on all. This is not correct.

Some judgments do *appear* to have that effect when the Court has dealt with what the Court usually calls '*peremptory rules of international law*' as there seems to be some hesitation of the ICJ to refer to rules of *jus cogens*. In such cases, *the rules cited* may well carry authoritative weight for all and operate *erga omnes*.[118] It is not the judgments of the International Court that carry such weight but it is the *rules* that are cited in the judgments that have such effect.

The effect *erga omnes* of a judgment is thus only apparent when the judgment reflects what is binding on all *for another reason*:[119] the judgments of the Court cannot by themselves have

---

[117] See, further *supra* on the important point concerning the power of a judge to 'make law' where civil law systems differ from the Anglo-Saxon tradition, Part One, I i c.

[118] See, *infra*, in this Part, Prophylactic Rules, III ii, compulsory rules: *jus cogens*.

[119] See, my *International Legal Order*, *op. cit.*, 244 *et seq;* 'apparently' binding Resolutions of the United Natios General Assembly. *Cf.* my article on 'The legal value of recommendations of international organisations', *Anglo-Soviet Symposium*, London, 1986, 10 and my article 'The effect of Resolutions of international organisations' in *Theory of International Law at the Threshold of the 21st Century, Essays in honour of Krzysztof Skubiszewski*, ed. Makarczyk, J., The Hague: Kluwer, 1996.

the effect of imposing obligations on all. The judgments of the ICJ can only have binding effect between the parties to the dispute before the Court. The Court has no power to enact or even re-state positive law with any binding effect on third parties to a dispute before the Court.[120] If it *seems* that a judgment is binding *erga omnes*, this will be for *another* reason, for example, often because the rules stated form part of what we in this work call *intrinsic law*.

ii. Maxims and General Principles

We may notice that the general principles, mentioned in article 38 (1)(c), form a separate and independent source of international law: this source is distinct from conventional rules, that is to say rules laid down in treaties and agreements, as well as distinct from '*custom*'. But the '*formal*' general principles of law are to be used to guide the ICJ in handling cases: such rules are also respected by other international courts and tribunals, and, indeed, by national courts. There is support in the *travaux préparatoires* of article 38 in the Statute of ICJ's predecessor, the Permanent Court of International Justice, the PCIJ, for our submission that the Statute refers to 'formal' and not to material and substantive rules in article 38 (1)(c).[121]

---

[120] See, my *Essays on the Law of Treaties*, London: Sweet & Maxwell, 1964, Ch. IV, on effect of treaties on third parties, and my *International Legal Order*, London: Gower, 1994, 224 *et seq.* on the lack of legal effect of decisions and judgments on third parties unless such acts reflect the *lex lata*.

[121] The Representative of the United Kingdom Permanent Court of International Justice, on the Comité consultatif de juristes (Advisory Committee of Jurists) for the drafting of the initial article on general principles, Lord Phillimore, suggested that the paragraph covers matters like *res judicata* and rules like *nemo judex in causa sua* (on bias). These are matters that we have included above under maxims

A rapid analysis shows that rules that the majority of writers consider to be '*general principles*' are, in fact, the rules we qualify as '*maxims*' and that we have set out above. As we have just demonstrated, the Drafters of the initial article of the PCIJ also had such rules in mind. These maxims have, as pointed out above, a largely technical and procedural character.

These '*formal*' general principles are not as numerous as sometimes suggested. Most of them cannot be thought to be a sub-section of the rules set out above as '*maxims*'. If there is any hierarchy to be established it is rather the 'maxims' that might be construed to form a sub-set of the general principles. But better still may be to treat these two groups of rules as conceptually distinct.

However, bearing in mind the characteristics of what we call 'maxims', it is not always easy to distinguish maxims from 'general principles'. Yet, it is clear that general principles cover other and perhaps wider matters than maxims. Contrary to maxims, general principles are sometimes vague and/or controversial. Most of these formal rules have a large latitude and an ambit that covers a variety of situations. But both types of rules are of vital importance and have a general and global application.

iii. Substantive General Principles?

A word of warning: the term 'general principles' is used in two ways: to signify *formal rules*, that may amplify maxims but still

---

as well as under formal compulsory general principles, in this Part, B I and II. But the article in the Statute would not contain any material rules. The Representative of the United States, former Secretary of State, Elihu Root, agreed with Phillimore, PCIJ, *Procès-verbaux des séances du Comité consultatif des juristes 16 juin – 24 juillet 1920*, 393 *et seq.*

constitute a separate category; and as *substantive rules*. We shall set out examples of both these types. But it is only the 'formal' general principles that properly belong in this section on *'intrinsic'* rules of the international legal order. Let us also underline, again, that *most rules* that writers call general principles of a *formal* character are actually better called 'maxims'.

There are relatively few general principles of a *formal character* but, contrary to substantive general rules, they can at least be identified and enumerated; they are not innumerable.

Substantive general principles, on the other hand; cannot be identified *a priori*: such rules can concern *anything* in material national or international law. They will be dealt with in the section below on *extrinsic rules* as their place is not among the rules forming part of the *intrinsic law.*[122]

iv. Compulsory Formal General Principles

General principles of the formal type are not as difficult to identify as many writers and courts assume. It is quite possible to narrow down some general principles that do not coincide (but well might explain or amplify) the maxims set out above but that do not constitute *substantive rules* as those set out later in this work.

General principles are thus in this context of a *formal nature* and guide legislators and courts in what the international legal system demands beyond the essential maxims.

Some specific general principles explain why there are ensuing maxims to guarantee the functioning of the general rules. The maxim *nullum crimen sine lege* is another aspect of the *general*

---

[122] See, *infra*, in this Part, C II iii under Substantive Rules for all Contacts: *lex mercatoria*.

principle in international society of the *Rule of Law*, or what is sometimes better expressed in the civil law systems as 'legal security' (*sécurité de droit*; *sicurezza di diritto*; *Rechtsicherkeit*; *rättssäkerhet*; etc.). To ensure the proper functioning of the general rules on the Rule of Law, we thus identify an ensuing (or preceding) maxim: *nullum crimen sine lege* (no crime exists unless so laid down in law). In other words, this maxim presents another aspect of the *Rule of Law* or, better expressed, the maxim ensures the operation of the general principle.[123] The *Rule of Law* demands, among other things, that a person must know the relevant legal consequences of a decision *before* he acts.

The *Rule of Law* has a wide and fairly vague ambit and cannot be said to be a 'maxim' but perhaps a good example of what a 'formal general principle' implies. A further example of a general principle is the rule of *non-retroactivity*, that is to say the prohibition of the retrospective effect of any rules. This principle presents itself as another aspect of the *Rule of Law*, or what in civil law countries is known as *legal security*.[124] This principle *explains* the maxim *nullum crimen sine lege*.[125] A subject cannot foresee the effect of an action unless relevant rules are already in force when the act is committed.

Other rules that secure the operation of the *Rule of Law* concern equality before the law, sometimes called *'forensic equality'*, meaning that the parties to a dispute should have the *same arms* to argue the Case, or the ability to assume the same

---

[123] See, EC, 13/60 (1962 ECR 120; 13/61 (1962) ECR 2; 10/69 (1969) ECR 316; 48/72 (1973) ECR 86; 78/74 (1975) ECR 433; 43/75 (1976) ECR 481; and 97/76 (1977) ECR 1078.

[124] *Sécurité du droit*; *sicurezza di diritto*; *Rechtsicherkeit*; *rättssäkerhet*; *retssikkerhetetc. Cf. supra*, in this section.

[125] *Supra*, in this section.

rights or obligations. Another such general rule that has been particularly prominent in case law during the last 20-30 years, is the rule of *proportionality*.[126] The rule of *proportionality* has certainly become fashionable in the legal thinking of the Courts of the EU[127] and in the European Court of Human Rights.[128] The same can be said about the principle of *subsidiarity*, only recently introduced in international legal proceedings,[129] although its application in practice has sometimes appeared erratic.[130] Other formal general principles may concern *limited responsibility*,[131] or *subrogation*.[132]

---

[126] For example, *The Case Internationale Handelsgesellschaft*, CEU, 11-72, (1970), *Recueil*, 1970.

[127] See, the *Handelsgesellschaft Case*, cited in the previous note.

[128] For example, *The Lithgow Case* (1986), ECHR, *Reports*, 1986.

[129] Commentators on the principle of subsidiarity never mention that the origin of this rule is found in the teachings of the Catholic Church, in, for example, the ecclesiastic documents: *Encyclica Quadragesimo Anno* of Pope Pius XI (1931). The rule proposes that a solution of problems is normally found on the local level; this has been adopted, without indicating the origins of these concepts, as an idea introduced by the European Union, see Treaty article 5(3) & Protocole 2. By virtue of the subsidiarity principle, the EU intervenes only if the Member States do not reach the aims of the EU by themselves. *Cf.* in the abundant case law, see *Grand-Duchy of Luxembourg v European Parliament and the Council*, Case C-176/09, (2011), *Reports*, 2011.

[130] The principle has been adopted and developed in EU law but in this context with little success and often met with little approbation from national authorities, see Pålsson, A.M., 'EUs princip om subsidiaritet – ett tomt löfte', *Forum för EU-Debatt*, 2013. However, the principle of subsidiarity forms part of several philosophical and social systems. For example, it is the most important principle in Catholic social thought. This rule implies, simply explained, that nothing should be done by a larger and more complex organisation that could be done by a smaller entity, or on a more local level especially one nearer to the source of concern. See, previous the note for references.

[131] *Barcelona Traction Case* (1970), ICJ *Reports*, 1970.

[132] *The Mavrommatis Case* (1925), PCJI *Series* A No. 5.

In international law, we also find numerous other well-known general principles without which the system would not be able to function. A general principle of a wide ambit is the requirement to behave in accordance with *ethics*, or with what at any given time, is perceived as 'morally correct'. *Ethics* is clearly a concept of considerable ambit and should possibly be treated as a special category of notions.[133] But for systematic reasons it may be convenient to classify *ethics* in this context as a general principle, not that different from the concept of *ordre public*, used in most national systems. Independently of the notion of '*ethics*', the principle of *ordre public* also exists in international law. The concept of *ordre public* is not a material source of law but rather a principle of *mitigation* in the Case where a decision otherwise would appear 'unjust' or morally or logically 'incorrect' with regard to the sense of justice.[134]

For similar reasons

> 'a provision of foreign law will be disregarded when it would lead to a result wholly alien to fundamental requirements of justice ...violate some fundamental principle of justice, some prevalent conception of good morals, some deep-rooted tradition of the common weal.' [135]

Another example of a 'general principle' that can be distinguished from 'maxims', by not being a procedural rule but still devoid of

---

[133] See, *infra*, in his Part, under III on Ethics and Natural Law.

[134] *Ibid.* and on application of foreign law, this Part C II iii Rules for all Contacts.

[135] *Kuwait Airways Corp. v Iraqi Airways Co.*, [2002] HL 19, 12, at 16, available at http://www.publications.parliament.uk/pa/ld200102/ldjudgmt/jd020516/kuwait-1.htm.

material contents, is probably the rule of *good faith*. The principle of *good faith* is extremely vague, difficult to prove, and of little assistance as an argument in any litigation. It still deserves to be included in the category of 'general principles' of international law.[136]

The rule of *good faith*, may have different significance in different national legal systems. For example, in certain civil law countries, the rule of *good faith* functions largely to protect a proprietory title when for example goods that did not belong to the seller have been bought by a buyer in good faith. In other legal systems, for example under English law, such a buyer is not protected except in special circumstances such as having bought the goods at an auction.

The rule of *good faith* in some legal systems signifies that the parties respect some ethical rules when they conclude a contract. It is perhaps in this last-mentioned aspect that the rule of *good faith* could occasionally be used in the international legal system, in particular when it comes to the interpretation of a treaty.[137]

As Lord Asquith emphasised in the *Abu Dhabi Case*, that an arbitrator has to decide in a manner compatible with *good will,*

---

[136] Cheng, Bin, *General Principles as Applied by International Courts and Tribunals*, 1953, 105 *et seq.*

[137] Article 31 of the Vienna Convention on the Law of Treaties of 1969 & *e.g. The Case of Phares in Crete and Samos* (1937), PCIJ Series A/B 62, Individual Opinion of Seferiades, S.P.; *cf. Metger Co. Case* (1905) and the *Nationality Case (Germany v Lithuania,* (1937) 3 RIAA 1719; *The Venezuela Case, (Germany, United Kingdom and Italy v Venezuela,* (1904), *RIAA* vol. IX, 9 & commentary by Mallarmé, A., 'L'arbitrage vénézuéléen devant la Cour de la Haye 1903-1904', *RDI*, 1939, I, 713 *et seq. cf.* Cases before the Court of the EU, *e.g.* EC 30/71 (1972) CMLR 1.

good faith and with *reason*.[138] Such principles would, according to Lord Acquith, be a sort of '*modern natural law*';[139] that statement perhaps confirms our classification of the formal general principle of *good faith* as part of the *intrinsic* law of international society.[140]

Arbitration tribunals have also relied on the principle of good faith and accommodated a party that has suffered by another's lack of such good faith. It has thus been held that the 'supreme principle' of good faith, which, in the context of contractual relations, requires the absence of deceit and artifice in (the) negotiation(s).[141]

Close to the notion of *good faith* is a new candidate to be accepted as a general principle in international law[142]: the concept of *estoppel*, a notion known in the Anglo-Saxon legal systems but largely unknown elsewhere. *Estoppel* stabilises the behaviour of actors in the sense that if an actor does something that causes another subject to place reliance of what has been said and done, and acts himself on this reliance, the first actor is unable to deny what he has said or done.

But it is important not to deduce consent to a proposition by mere behaviour unless there is a clear act of acceptance.[143] In

---

[138] *ILR* 1951, 149.

[139] *Ibid., loc. cit.*: '*principles rooted in the good sense and common practice of the generality of civilised nations – a sort of 'modern law of nature.*'

[140] See, *supra*, in this Part, B, i.

[141] *Inceysa Vallisoletana v El Salvador*, (2006), ICSID Case No. ARB/03/26, Award Aug. 2, 2006, 218 available at: http://www.italaw.com/sites/default/files/case-documents/ita0424_0.pdf.

[142] Martin, A., *L'estoppel en droit international public*, Paris: Pedone, 1979; Bowett, D., 'Estoppel before international tribunals and its relation to acquiescence', 33 *BYIL*, 1957, 176.

[143] *Infra, cf.* Part Three, B II, Types According to Form of Expressed Consent.

international law, as in all national legal systems, actors are free to accept or refuse certain obligations. It is most important not to infer acceptance, for example, to a treaty by relying on pronouncements during negotiations: until the treaty is ratified or finalised in any other form, it is not legally binding.[144]

There is an important principle not to *deprive others by any form of appropriation of resources* to which they are entitled.[145] This comes near the moral commandment to behave in an ethically acceptable way, by actions that appear morally correct.

In the international legal system, an important general principle concerns the *obligation to make reparation* for harm caused.[146] A harmful act or a deprivation of rights engages the responsibility of a subject to provide reparation. This obligation is *either* to restore the situation to a *status quo ante*, or, if such *restitution* is not possible, to offer *financial compensation*.[147] Such pecuniary compensation must be *adequate, prompt and effective*.[148] In exceptional cases the compensation may consist and be expressed in *excuses*.[149] The *obligation to make reparation* for any damage caused is thus a general principle of the international legal system.[150]

A harm caused in international society may obviously concern a number of very different situations. The method of *imputation* to

---

[144] See my *Essays on the Law of Treaties*, London: Sweet & Maxwell, 1968, Ch. 3.
[145] *The Lake Lanoux Case* (1957) 12 *RIAA* 281.
[146] *The Chorzow Factory Case*, (1928) Series A., No. 17, 33.
[147] *The Temple Prehar Case* (1962) ICJ *Reports*, 6; *Texaco v Libya* (1977) 53, *ILR* 389.
[148] For example, *The Lithgow Case* (1986), ECHR, *Reports*, 1986.
[149] *The I'm Alone*, (1935) 3 *RIAA* 1609.
[150] *The Chorzow Factory Case* (1928) PCIJ *Series* A No. 17; *e.g. Amoco Case* (1987) 15 Iran US CTR; *Lusitania Claim* (1923) 7 *RIAA* 32.

allocate or to apportion the responsibility – and the ensuing duty to repair – for an act that caused harm is clearly an essential principle in international law.[151] As for its character, it also belongs to the category of general principles.

Another such general principle concerns the *non-appropriation* of *parts of common areas*, for example, Outer Space, the High Seas, or the Arctic and Antarctic areas, and other such *res communis*.[152]

We have set out some important and compulsory general principles that guide courts and arbitration tribunals that will use such principles in conjunction with the above-mentioned maxims.

In this work, it is suggested that the category of 'general principles of law recognised by civilised nations' mentioned as a 'source' of international law in article 38 1 c of the Statute of the International Court of Justice includes precisely the maxims and the 'formal' general principles set out as above. But the article does not necessarily cover any substantive or material rules in the vast area of international law that, because of its vastness of contents, would make the notion 'general principles' meaningless as a tool for any court. On the other hand, courts, investment and arbitration tribunals will always have the right to resort to 'filling in' rules from other sources.[153] That obvious right does not depend

---

[151] See, in detail, *infra*, in this Part, under B i c) 2 on the importance of the mechanism of imputation. Note, *contra*, Brownlie who claims that imputation is not an important or necessary principle: Brownlie, I., *Responsibility of States*, 1984, 14.

[152] *Cf.* Verdross, A. v., & Simma, B., *Universelles Völkerrecht*, 3rd ed., Vienna: Springer, 1984, 698. Note, in this context, the importance of rules on Outer Space; see, the 'Outer Space Treaty' of 1967, Treaty on Principles Governing the Activities of States in the Exploration and Use of Outer Space, including the Moon and Other Celestial Bodies, incorporated in UN General Assembly Resolution (XXII) 2222.

[153] *Infra*, in this Part, C II iii on 'Filling in Rules' and on '*lex mercatoria*'.

on any specific authorisation but is always available to all courts and tribunals in order to ensure that justice is made: it is thus an *implied power to supplement applicable law*, given to courts and tribunals in conjunction with their creation and establishment in international society.[154]

III. Prophylactic Rules

Before we embark on an analysis of material substantive rules of international law, it may be useful to briefly set out certain rules that prohibit *harm* in international society. In this work, such rules are called *prophylactic* in the sense that such prohibitive rules may *prevent* a harm being committed.

Certain rules on prohibition that we can empirically ascertain in international society, forbid action that would preclude the hypothetical goal. Thus, acts which obviate the hypothetical goal, totally, or partially, are governed by rules which outlaw them.

Forbidding rules have been established[155] and do not have to await a destructive act of any kind before they come into operation. In this sense, they operate to *prevent* acts which may infringe the hypothetical goal. In this sense the rules are 'prophylactic'. In this category we may classify rules which prohibit harm of varying degree to various subjects.

---

[154] See, *mutatis mutandis*, on the *theory of implied powers* of international organisations, always entitled to all necessary action for the purposes for which the organisations were created: my *Law Making, op. cit.*, Ch. 1.

[155] See, *supra*, in this Part, under B. Intrinsic Rules, III. Prophylactic Rules.

All rules of international law are clearly not compulsory. The bulk of rules of the international legal system are the intrinsic precepts but numerous further rules are optional or facultative. States and other subjects of international law have a large margin of liberty to accept or discard many rules. However, some material rules are compelling and in this sense *intrinsic* to the international legal system. But some important distinctions must be made.

On the whole, the international legal system is based on the prohibition of *harm*. Numerous rules concern this regulation of behaviour in international society. Such rules are furthermore of such importance that their protection is the concern of *all*, as the International Court of Justice emphasised in the *Barcelona Traction Case*.[156] The Court went on to say, with regard to such rules, that:

> 33. In view of the importance of the rights involved, all States can be held to have a legal interest in their protection; they are obligations *erga omnes*.
>
> 34. Such obligations derive, for example, in contemporary international law, from the outlawing of acts of aggression, and of genocide, as also from the principles and rules concerning the basic rights of the human person, including protection from slavery and racial discrimination.'

Then the Court referred to an important earlier case where the notion of rules *erga omnes* had already been discussed by the International Court in the context of *harm to individuals*. Here the Court had said that:

---

[156] *Barcelona Traction Case*, (1970), ICJ *Reports* 1970, at paras. 33 & 34.

> 'Some of the corresponding rights of protection have entered into the body of general international law'[157]

i. Ethics and Intrinsic Law

Some rules are neither logical maxims, nor general principles and nor the result of any international agreements but forming part of what may be called the *ethics* of the international legal system.

Above we have mentioned above, *ethics* may, for classification purposes be included among general principles. But clearly it is a notion that needs further explanation to the extent this is possible. What does *ethics* mean to most people? It is useful to adopt a simple definition but we may accept that the concept is, in itself, a little vague: it conveys largely an exhortation to do what is '*morally*' right. But we must be aware that many positivists claim that 'morals' has nothing to do with 'law'.[158] Of course, such claims cannot be warranted: the whole reason for the existence of a legal system is to ensure that certain moral rules are implemented and that certain moral values are protected. On the other hand, there is a divergence of opinion what in a given historical situation is 'morally right'. As examples below show, ethical standards of the majority of people and of the majority of other actors in international society may change. There were times when slavery was not considered morally 'wrong'.[159]

---

[157] *The Genocide Case, (Reservations to the Convention on the Prevention and Punishment of the Crime of Genocide), Advisory Opinion*, ICJ. Reports 1951, 23.

[158] Brownlie, I., *Principles of International Law*, op. cit.

[159] See, *infra*, in this Part, under III iv a) and *supra*, I I c) 1. Note also that what St. John Paul II referred to as the 'Culture of Death', is regarded by many as 'morally right', see, his Encyclica *Evangelium Vitae*, 25th March 1995.

Other obvious examples touching on ethics concern, for example, prohibition of harm in the context of aggression, or concerning humanitarian rules in armed conflict or violation of fundamental human rights. In these areas, the rules do not depend on the consent of States or other subjects but function by what we may called *conviction* that these are binding rules.[160] This *conviction* is not the same as the subjective element *opinio juris*, relevant in the pretended formation of customary rules.[161] *That* subjective approval is allegedly provided by States – and we question in this work how that can be done considering the myriad of persons that are involved in the administration of States. Whose *opinio juris*, we ask below, will decide the validity of claims as to how 'customary law' is supposed to be formed?[162] In the context of *ethics* we are no longer talking about States but about general opinions of normal people. It is in that sense that a German Court dismissed a claim that concerned the *morality* of some Nazi Statute that '*normal*' people would realise were unethical.[163]

In this group of prescriptions, we can also include rules that prohibit force and rules prohibiting aggression, rules that are derived from considerations of the inherent basis of the international legal order.[164] This reasoning is supported by the judgment in the *Nicaragua Case* where the Court declared that

---

[160] In German this effect is known as 'Rechtsüberzeugung'.
[161] See, *infra*, in Part Three, IV i-vii.
[162] *Ibid.* under III ii d, for a discussion of this important and obvious point.
[163] See, *infra*, under III iv a.
[164] *Cf.* Rijkkema, P.P., 'Customary rules in the Nicaragua case', 20 *NYIL* 1989, 91.

'... Far from having constituted a marked departure from a customary international law which still exists unmodified, the Charter gave expression in this field to principles already present in customary international law, and that law has in the subsequent four decades developed under the influence of the Charter, to such an extent that a number of rules contained in the Charter have acquired a status independent of it. The essential consideration is that both the Charter and the customary international law flow from a *common fundamental principle outlawing the use of force in international relations.*'(italics added)[165]

Similar views were put forward in the *Hostages in Teheran Case* where the Court underlined the duty to respect *fundamental rules* in international society even by third parties who are not directly involved in a dispute: the reason for this *solidarity*,[166] is due to the basic and fundamental nature of the rule and the gravity of any violation of this norm.[167] The fundamental rules concerned in this Case are the respect for immunity of diplomats and embassies, rules without which the international system cannot function.[168]

---

[165] ICJ, *Nicaragua v United States*, ICJ *Reports* 1986, para. 181. Note, that the Court did not really speak of 'customary' but of '*intrinsic*' law as defined in this work, see, *supra*, in this Part, B iii, Protection of the hypothetical goal and B III, Prophylactic Rules: Prohibition of Harm. The Courts speaks of 'customary law' but is clearly referring to what we call *the intrinsic law* in this work. See further *infra*, in Part Three, B III ii-vi.

[166] Note that 'solidarity' may also be a ground of obligation, see, Part Three, V iii e) 1 and 2.

[167] ICJ *Reports* 1980, 4.

[168] *Cf. supra*, in this Part, B II I, under General Principles.

Certain rules, in particular those on human rights, obtain their legal validity by a simple recognition by States and other subjects of international law, by what could be called a *collective convergence of convictions*. In this field, States and others accept the rules by formulating their contents in precise terms. It is simpler to speak of natural law in this context, – or, even better, refer to the concept we have adopted in this work, '*intrinsic law*', as it is clear that the conceptual recognition of these rules implies that they are, more or less, *inherent* in the international legal system. These intrinsic rules have nothing to do with so called 'customary law', a notion much abused by international lawyers to cover any rules they cannot otherwise explain.[169]

The fear that many lawyers seem to have of recognising the category of rules of natural law is inexplicable: if we recognise the existence of natural law, we find ourselves in the good company of Plato, Aristotle and Aquinas, as well as of Hugo Grotius and Emeric de Vattel, or with the nestor of contemporary international law, Alfred von Verdross, rather than with Marx or the largely discarded Swedish nihilists.[170]

---

[169] *Cf.* in detail, the *Nicaragua Case* and comments above in note 165; see, further, *infra*, Part Three, IV i-vii.

[170] The Swedish philosopher Hägerström influenced several generations of jurists in Sweden: he taught that no rule of that does not emanate from the State must be ignored: no rule international law can have legal effect in a country unless it has been *transformed* into national law. See, Hägerström, A., *Stat och rätt, en rättsfilosofisk undersökning*, Uppsala: 1904; *idem*, *Das Prinzip der Wissenschaft*, Uppsala: Humanistiska vetenskapssamfundets skrifter, 1908. *Cf.* Lundstedt, V., *Superstition or Rationality in Action for Peace*, London: Longman, 1925; *idem*, *Le droit des gens: danger de morts pour les peuples*, Paris: Phalanges, 1937; *cf.* Olivecrona, K., *Law as Fact*, London: OUP, 1939; *idem*, *De la loi et de l'État. Une contribution de l'école scandinave à la théorie réaliste du droit*, trad. Jonason,

Some question whether there can be any role for ethics in international politics.[171] Above all, there would, they say, be problems to suggest that diplomacy is subject to moral obligations and it is also questionable how ethical guidelines for individuals would apply to States.[172] But it is individuals who make up the State and it is individuals that conduct diplomacy.

Various types of rules of natural law are entrenched in the international legal system. These rules adapt in their application according to the needs of international society. Certain notions, like '*justice*' are clearly *immutable* in their essence, in the platonic sense, but *variable in their application*. Other rules, however, are highly flexible and dynamic, adjusting their function according to the real needs in international society at any given moment. But we are not talking about evasive and vague rules – as sometimes the adversaries of the natural law claim – but rules that are more succinct and precise than the nebulous '*customary rules*'.[173] In a sense, 'customary law' is often a mere euphemism for 'natural law' or what we call *intrinsic law*.

P. B.-G., Paris: Dalloz, 2011. These ideas are still widely present and taught in Swedish Universities where disagreements on this point are discouraged: see, for example, the notorious *jus docendi Affair*, CEDH, http://www.ioir.se/, "Det är för UHÄ väl känt", and the *Case I.D. v Sweden*, ECHR, 22255/93.

[171] See, for example, Frost, M., *Towards a Normative Theory of International Relations*, Cambridge: CUP, 1986; *Cf.* Kegley, C.W., 'Neo-idealism: A practical matter', *Ethics and International Affairs*, 19.

[172] Kegley, C.W.,'Neo-idealism', *op. cit., loc.cit.*

[173] For criticism of this notion, see *infra*, Part Three, IV vi, the 'Allergy to Natural Law'; *Cf. supra*, note 47 in this section and the comment cited above by Lord Asquith in *The Abu-Dhabi Case*.

Certain intrinsic law rules are binding because of *logical necessity*.[174] Other rules are compulsory because of *social needs* or *social necessity*[175] caused by the interdependence that results from the partnership between States and other subjects of international law, subjects that live together side by side in a society, ruled by the preeminence of law.

An important question is the definition of pertinent rules belonging to this category. In this context, we will construe in this work a *theory of acts* that will explain how States and other actors in international society acknowledge by *adoption*[176] or *recognition*[177], the existence of an ethical norm. This act of adoption or recognition is not necessary for the existence of intrinsic rules but highly relevant for their definition.

It is in the nature of ethical and moral rules that some of their contents can be widened in the case of need. But the essence of some rules is immutable.

Here we will first treat the allegedly immutable concept of *natural law*, the notions of *justice* and the *hypothetical goal*.[178] But, as mentioned above, there are other parts of natural law that are flexible and that can be adapted to new developments. 'Natural law' may be immutable in its essence when it comes to notions like *justice* and *truth*, but it is variable in its application depending on the needs at a specific time in history.

---

[174] See, Part Three, VI iii a) 1, on the Basis of Obligation.
[175] *Ibid.*, VI iii a) 2.
[176] See, in Part Three, II B iii d) VI iii.
[177] *Ibid.*, art Three, II B iii e).
[178] See, *supra*, Part One I ii on the Hypothetical Goal.

Thus, a century ago an aggressive war was not necessarily considered as contrary to ethics;[179] five hundred years ago it was considered acceptable to cut off the hand of a thief; three hundred years ago, slavery was not considered 'wrong'; merely fifty years ago it was not considered by all that *apartheid* was ethically 'wrong'. Certain norms of what ethics demands change thus according to flexible opinions.

Prohibition of genocide has probably existed for some time and this rule was obviously reinforced after the Second World War. The Convention codifying rules was adopted shortly after the Nuremberg trials. But the standards were certainly already in place to be able to condemn the genocide of the Armenians as early as the beginning of the 20th Century. During the collapse of the Ottoman Empire nearly two million Armenians were massacred.[180] The major genocide took place in 1915 but there had been earlier massacres of Armenians, for example, in 1894 and 1895. As some stated at the time, the Armenian Genocide in 1915 marked 'a policy directed at the extermination of Christians of Asia Minor'.[181]

The condemnation of slavery is made surprisingly late in international society in spite of early condemnation for Christians to

---

[179] The First World War 1914-1918 was thus not "illegal" according to the rules in force at the time; even the Second World War 1939-1945 was not 'illegal' under the rules of the League of Nations, see, in detail, my *The Law of War, op. cit.*, Ch. I.

[180] In 1914 there were 2,133,190 Armenians in the Ottoman Empire; in 1922, there were about 387,000.

[181] *New York Times*, 17 September 1915: 'Turkey is now in the act to murder Armenia and she has almost completed her work', *New York Times* published 135 articles about the Armenian Genocide in 1915 alone.

have other Christians as slaves.[182] Slavery was gradually abolished at different times in different countries during the Middle Ages and later but the wide-spread slave trade continues well into the 19th Century.

Slavery was forbidden in England in 1807. But by then Lord Mansfield had already condemned slavery in his famous judgment of 1772. There, he emphasised that that *chattel slavery*[183] is unsupported by the common law and represents an unacceptable practice. In his judgment Lord Mansfield stated in very clear terms and in very strong language that:

> 'The state of slavery is of such a nature that it is incapable of being introduced on any reasons, moral or political, but only by positive law [statute], which preserves its force long after the reasons, occasions, and time itself from whence it was created, is erased from memory. It is so odious, that nothing can be suffered to support it, but positive law. Whatever inconveniences, therefore, may follow from the decision, I cannot say this case is allowed or approved by the law of England;…'[184]

The international Anti-Slavery Convention was only concluded in 1926. It is now certainly a universally accepted rule that slavery is forbidden under international law, although it is often not respected in the new forms of white slavery and of trafficking persons.

---

[182] Pope John VIII condemned such practices in 873.

[183] Slavery was forbidden by Statute in England in 1807 and possession of slaves in 1833.Slave owners were paid compensation in England for their 'financial loss' when slavery was abolished; but the slaves were not.

[184] *Somerset v Stewart* (1772) 98 ER 499.

The *apartheid* system developed in the 1940s after the wave of decolonisation in Africa and elsewhere. The prohibition of *apartheid* is now a rule that is no longer controversial. Yet, not long ago it was contested by the white regime of South Africa.

On the other hand, torture still presents problems with regard to its definition. When does 'harsh treatment' of a person becomes torture?[185] It is obvious that *subjective* elements are highly relevant as persons have different thresholds of 'pain'. To qualify specific treatment as 'torture' it is also relevant to consider the severity, or intensity of the suffering inflicted. The severity can be gauged by reference to the factors like: the duration of the treatment; and the manner and method of its execution; the physical and mental effects caused as well as the sex, age and state of health of the victim.

The so called 'five techniques' has sometimes been used as a guide to what would constitute torture: wall standing, hooding, subjection to noise, deprivation of sleep, deprivation of food and drink.[186] But in the famous Case *Ireland v Great Britain*,[187] the treatment of 14 accused subjected to the 'five techniques' was held not to amount to 'torture' but to 'inhuman treatment', a lower level of maltreatment than torture.[188]

---

[185] See, in detail, my *Law of War, op. cit.*, Ch.

[186] 'Wall standing' may not sound difficult but it involves standing for periods of some hours in a 'stress position', described by those who have undergone it as very painful, being 'spreadeagled against the wall, with their fingers put high above the head against the wall, the legs spread apart and the feet back, causing them to stand on their toes with the weight of the body mainly on the fingers'.

[187] *Ireland v United Kingdom*, ECHR, (1978), *Reports*, 1978.

[188] The European Convention of Human Rights specifies in article 3 various levels of harsh treatment: torture, inhumane or degrading treatment or punishment. A certain intensity is required for the qualification under these headings.

However, what was earlier qualified as 'inhumane treatment' – but not amount to 'torture' – may nowadays be thought of as such as the relevant latitudes for inhumane treatment/torture have changed with regard to human rights.[189] Constant condemnation,[190] however, shows that the rule against torture is also developing to encompass practices that at times were considered acceptable in order to compel individuals to provide information.[191]

The rule of the right of peoples to self-determination was strongly criticised in the 1990s when Croatia's attempt to declare itself independent was followed by the invasion of Serbian forces and pronounced passivity of third States. These attacks even led the European Union to introduce an embargo against the Croats, prohibiting them from buying weapons to defend themselves against the invasion. This embargo was imposed in order to try to maintain the unity of the Yugoslav Federation within the meaning of Article 2 (4) of the Charter of the United Nations. This article states that:

> 'All Members shall refrain in their international relations from the threat or use of force against the *territorial integrity* or political independence of any state, or in any other manner inconsistent with the Purposes of the United Nations.'(italics added)

---

[189] There has been intense lobbying in Ireland to re-appraise the judgment in the *Irish Case* to concede that the treatment of the 14 accused did amount to 'torture', *The Guardian*, 2 December 2014.

[190] This condemnation is also reflected in the Torture Convention of 1984, the Convention against Torture and Other Cruel, Inhuman or Degrading Treatment or Punishment, that came into force in 1987.

[191] *Ibid., loc. cit.*

Obviously, there is a clear conflict between this article and the right of peoples to govern themselves. A 'nation' may be a constituent member of a Federation and problems arise if 'peoples' in such a 'nation' wish to govern themselves. On the one hand, a State, also a federal State, has the right to maintain its territorial coherence and to refuse the secession of part of its territory.

Serious criticism followed the forceful police intervention by the Madrid Government on 1st October 2017 when Catalonia sought to hold a referendum about independence. Such action appeared to be both a violation of the right of expression (as initially Catalonia only sought to find out the democratic support for independence), of the right to at least consider self-determination *and* the right of citizens of Spain not to be subjected to violence by the police when no crime or offence had been committed.[192] Similar considerations may be relevant for the attempts of Kurds to establish their own State.[193]

Problems have arisen particularly in federations (or complex States, consisting of obvious 'nations' but not formal 'federations') that were constructed, with much support from the Great Powers, like in the case of Czechoslovakia and, also, to some extent, in the case of Yugoslavia. Here constituent nations had their own different historical, religious, ethnic or linguistic ties, but not necessarily shared with the other nation(s) in the federation or in the complex State. Some such 'nations' would appear to have the

---

[192] The Catalan separatists were charged with sedition and rebellion and some were jailed. The Referendum was declared '*illegal*' but it is highly unlikely a Government has the power to criminalise such an expression of opinion in a democratic State. See further, *supra*, in Part One, I iii d) 4 under Nations.

[193] *Ibid., loc. cit.*

right to separate from a 'mother', provided this is supported by the democratic will.¹⁹⁴ But there have been continuing problems, from the struggle of Biafra 1967-1969 – that failed to separate from Nigeria – to Kosovo that, with considerable international support, seceded from Serbia in 2012. Kosovo has a large Muslim majority but it is also an important 'historical symbol' to Serbia after an important battle in 1389; Serbia has still not recognised the independence of Kosovo.

The rule of the prohibition of the use of military force, which we have distinguished as part of *jus cogens*, is even more difficult to apply in practice. Some statesmen may say that it is a rule that no one disputes – before a situation occurs that affects the interests of the State of which they are citizens. They then present reasons to 'justify' any use of military force, such as the authorisation or request for assistance from another State to 'explain' an invasion or an intervention.¹⁹⁵

Some rules concerning the prohibition of nuclear arms appear to be anchored in the human conscience, not only from a moral point of view but as a legal rule. Such use undermines the duty of States to protect their own citizens and endangers the aim towards the hypothetical goal, and thus menaces the survival of international society, and of humanity.¹⁹⁶

---

[194] See, *supra*, in Part One, I iii c) on international personality of 'nations'.

[195] See, in detail above in this section and on changing attitudes to war, specifcally my *Law of War*, *op. cit.*, Ch 2.

[196] *Ibid.* and *supra*, Part One II ii b) on the Hypothetical Goal. See my criticism of the ICJ for having failed to condemn the use of first use of nuclear weapons, see, the *Opinion on the Use of Nuclear Weapons in Armed Conflict*, (1996), ICJ *Reports*, 1996, 66, and *infra*, in this Part, note 216. Surprisingly, a UN Treaty on

The dynamic nature[197] of this category of rules suggests thus that these rules may develop further. However, it appears that any rules concerning human rights can only be improved and that a reduction of privileges and rights already granted and accepted can probably not be reduced or eliminated. For example, actors in international society cannot again legitimately start engaging in slavery: prohibitions in this respect have been entrenched in the international legal order.[198]

ii. Compulsory Rules: *jus cogens*

'Compulsory *jus cogens*' is clearly a tautology: *jus cogens* means 'compulsory law'. Yet, to emphasise the binding force it might be useful to add a pleonastic adjective.

The most important compelling rules in international law belong to a category known as *jus cogens* (obligatory law). This is a category of rules often debated in the doctrine and in courts and there is wide divergence of opinions as to the contents of such a category.[199] As in the case of general principles there is little agreement on the definition of *jus cogens*.

Prohibition of Nuclear Weapons was rapidly negotiated and immediately signed by 53 States in 2017, *UN Treaty Collection*, 20 Sept. 2017.

[197] Some adversaries of natural law often argue that the contents of this system cannot change, a claim that makes it difficult to accept the function of natural law rules that are out of date. On the contrary, natural law is a highly flexible system that provides rules for any actual need *at any given time.*

[198] This clearly does not mean that human rights would be effectively guaranteed, but only that the *position* taken by contemporary international society would not tolererate a *legalised reduction* of these established rights.

[199] There is an enormous literature on *jus cogens* but little agreement on what this concept actually means, see, for example, Hayim, D., *Le concept d'indérogeabilité*

Writers often present rules of this category as 'general principles'. Many pretend that these compelling rules are 'customary rules'. But then we face the problem that specific prohibitive rules would often be based on *negative custom*.[200] It is obvious that certain rules of the international legal order are compulsory and of exceptional importance: the majority of writers and courts recognise the imperative and exclusive nature of these rules even if there is disagreement as to exactly which rules are included in this category.

The maxims as well as the majority of the formal general principles set out above clearly form *jus cogens*. But these maxims and the formal general principles are of a *technical nature*. They are thus duplicated in the form of *formal rules of jus cogens*.

---

en droit international, Saarbrücken: Presses Académiques Francophones, 2014; Tomuschat, D., & Thouvenin, J.M., (eds), *The Fundamental Rules of the International Legal Order: jus cogens and Obligations erga omnes*, Leiden & Boston: Martinus Nijhoff, 2006; Orakhelashvili. A., *Peremptory Norms in International Law*, Oxford & New York: Oxford University Press, 2006; Kolb, R., *Théorie du jus cogens international: essai de relecture du concept*, Paris: Presses universitaires de France/Pedone, 2001; Kadelbach, S., *Zwingendes Völkerrecht*, Berlin: Duncker & Humbolt, 1992; Robledo, A.G., *El ius cogens internacional: estudio históric-crítico*, México: Universidad Nacional Autónoma de Mexico, 1982; Hannikainen, L., *Peremptory Norms, jus cogens, in International Law*, Helsinki: Lakimiesliit kustannus, 1988; *cf.*, Talalaev, A.N., *Pravo mezhdunarodnykh dogovorov: deistvie i primenenie dogovorov*, Moscow: *Mezhdunarodnye otnosheniia*, 1985; Rozakis C., *The Concept of jus cogens in the Law of Treaties*, Amsterdam: North-Holland, 1976; Zotiades, G.B., *International ius cogens: a Contribution to the Study of the Nature of International Law Norms*, Thessaloniki: P. Sakkoulas Brothers, 1968. See, ILC, *Report*, 1986, & ILC, Tladi, D., Special Rapporteur, 1st and 2nd *Reports*, 2016 & 2017, A/CN.4. 693 & 706.

[200] See, in detail on this problem, *infra*, Part Three, IV iii b) . *Cf.* my *Law of War*, *op. cit.*, and my article, 'Illegal combatants and the Law of War', *George Washington Law Journal*, 2006, *op. cit.*

But what are the material rules of *jus cogens*? Doctrinal debates – of courts and tribunals – accelerated after the negotiations and the conclusion of the Convention on the Law of Treaties in 1969. Article 53 of the Convention sets out the consequences of 'treaties in conflict with an imperative norm of international law'. The Convention mentions specifically '*jus cogens*', and 'peremptory norms of international law' although the International Court of Justice has generally preferred to refer to 'fundamental rules' as compelling.

The Convention sets out article 53, under a heading '*Treaties conflicting with a peremptory norm of general international law ('jus cogens')*' and, further, article 64 under the heading '*Emergence of a new peremptory norm of general international law ('jus cogens')*', that no action in international society may infringe these important rules. Article 53 thus stipulates that:

> 'A treaty is void if, at the time of its conclusion, it conflicts with a peremptory norm of general international law.'

The Convention defines thus a rule of *jus cogens* as:

> 'For the purposes of the present Convention, a peremptory norm of general international law is a norm accepted and recognised by the international community of States as a whole as a norm from which no derogation is permitted and which can be modified only by a subsequent norm of general international law having the same character'.

Article 64 of the Convention speaks of 'intervening' conflict with a new rule and stipulates that the consequences of such a conflict will be that:

'If a new peremptory norm of general international law emerges, any existing treaty which is in conflict with that norm becomes void and terminates.'

The Barcelona Traction Case clarified further the notion *jus cogens*: but the International Court avoids using the term *jus cogens* and prefers to speak of 'fundamental rules' or of rules that operate with an effect '*erga omnes*', that is to say the rules are applicable and compulsory for all.[201] The Court said that:

> '33. When a State admits into its territory foreign investments or foreign nationals, whether natural or juristic persons, it is bound to extend to them the protection of the law and assumes obligations concerning the treatment to be afforded them. These obligations, however, are neither absolute nor unqualified. In particular, an essential distinction should be drawn between the obligations of a State towards the international community as a whole, and those arising vis-à-vis another State in the field of diplomatic protection. By their very nature the former are the concern of *all* States. In view of the importance of the rights involved, *all* States can be held to have a legal interest in their protection; they are obligations *erga omnes*.
>
> 34. Such obligations derive, for example, in contemporary international law, from the outlawing of acts of aggression, and of genocide, as also from the principles and rules concerning the basic rights of the human person, including protection from slavery and racial discrimination. Some of the

---

[201] With the increasing decline of the teaching of Latin, some contemporary commentators appear to misunderstand the expression *erga omnes*, not realising the preposition, *erga*, signifying literally, 'for' or 'towards'.

corresponding rights of protection have entered into the body of general international law *(Reservations to the Convention on the Prevention and Punishment of the Crime of Genocide, Advisory Opinion, I.C.J. Reports 1951*, p. 23); others are conferred by international instruments of a universal or quasi-universal character.'

This view, on basic human rights and other rules binding *erga omnes*, is also emphasised in the *Genocide Case* as mentioned in the Judgment. In its Opinion on the reservations to the Genocide Convention the Court confirmed, for the first time, the existence of elementary moral principles that oblige States outside any contractual framework. Even if the Court in the *Barcelona Traction Case* implicitly condemned *aggression* and *genocide* as being unlawful, and respected the rule concerning human rights, including protection against of slavery and racial discrimination, the Court still hesitated to use term *jus cogens*.[202]

In the two paragraphs cited above, the Court thus spoke about rules from which no derogation is permitted, in other words we are speaking about *peremptory rules of international law*,[203] or rules of an obligatory nature, obliging everyone *erga omnes*. This was phrased in the Court's Judgment without mentioning the term *jus cogens*. The Court also clarified the important distinction that has to be made between the obligations of States towards international society and those that have their origin in the area of 'diplomatic protection' or in other contractual situations. Thus, the Court also

---

[202] Because of controversies about the expression and about the contents of the rule, France never ratified the 1969 Vienna Convention on the Law of Treaties. But this does not change the effects that *jus cogens* may have outside such contractual situations.

[203] See, *supra*, in this Part, under B. Intrinsic Rules, III, ii, Compulsory Rules.

emphasised in the *Hostages Case*, that rules concerning diplomatic and consular envoys belong to general international law operating outside any contractual arrangements.[204] Not only are rules on immunity of diplomats and of embassy buildings and relevant personnel, also of those who belong to the consular department, *fundamental rules* of international society but all subjects have a *duty* to assist in the respect for such rules, out of a special obligation of solidarity.[205]

Other tribunals have not had the same hesitation as the International Court of Justice to speak about *jus cogens*. For example, the arbitration tribunal for a dispute concerning the *Maritime Frontier Guinea-Bissau/Senegal*, referred to *jus cogens* as a real hallmark of certain 'legal norms that are binding and that are not susceptible to derogation by any conventional arrangements'.[206]

The Arbitration Commission of the European Conference for Peace in Yugoslavia insisted, it its first Opinion, that States emerging after the dissolution of the Yugoslav Federation should regulate their differences according to the rules of State succession, by recognising that 'imperative norms of general international law (…) impose on all parties to a succession.' In another Opinion[207], the Commission stated that the recognition of States is a discretionary

---

[204] According to the Court, the obligations of the Government of Iran concerned not only contractual obligations established by the Conventions of Vienna of 1961 and 1963 on diplomatic and consular relations: these are also obligations imposed by general international law: *The Hostage Case, United States v Iran* (1980) ICJ *Reports*, 1980, 4, para. 62.

[205] See, *infra*, in Part Three, VI iii a) 5, on Obligation of Solidarity.

[206] '…legal norms that are not susceptible to derogation by conventional means': *The Case Concerning Delimitation of the Maritime Frontier Guinea-Bissau/Senegal*, judgment of 31 July 1989; 35 *AFDI* 1980, 322.

[207] *Opinion* no. 10 of 4th July 1992, see *ibid.*

act 'with the only restraint of respecting imperative rules of general international law.'

The Criminal Tribunal for ex-Yugoslavia (ICTY) stated in the *Furundzija Case* concerning torture that the prohibition of torture is an obligation *erga omnes* and a norm of *jus cogens*.[208]

The European Court of Human Rights also confirmed in the *Al-Adsani Case*, that the prohibition of torture is a *jus cogens* norm and the Court explained the consequences of ignoring the compulsory nature of this rule.[209]

Relying on observations of the behaviour of subjects of the international legal order during the last few decades, we can thus identify, at least, *seven prohibitions*, giving rise to corresponding rights. It is easier to enounce such rules and such rights in a *negative* manner (= the right *not* to be subjected to a specific act) and this could thus be presented as specific rights to *avoid* and be *protected* from and thus enjoy:

> the right *not* be submitted to genocide;[210]
> the right *not* to be submitted to slavery;[211]

---

[208] ICTY, IT-95-17/1-T, (1998). *Cf.* the *Delalić Case*, ICTY, IT-96-21 (2001). Sometimes Courts refer to the latter Case, and to others, without mentioning that the accused was acquitted, a fact that probably reduces the force of the judgment or claims that is reflects any specific principle. *Cf.*, *supra*, Part One, I ii e) 1, on problems following precedents, Part One, I ii c) 3 on Dominance of Anglo-Saxon Ideas on Judge-Made Law.

[209] *Al-Adsani v United Kingdom*, Application 35763/97, ECHR, *Reports*, 1997. At para 30, the Court refers to the *Delalić Case*, cited in the previous note.

[210] ICJ, *Opinion on Reservations to the Convention for the Prevention and Repression of the Crime of Genocide*, (1951), ICJ, *Reports*, 1951, 1, 15; *See*, the Genocide Convention, 1948, 78 *UNTS* 277.

[211] See, *The Case of Aloeboetoe et al.*, before the Inter-American Court of Human Rights, 10 Sept. 1993, *Series* C n° 15.I/A) concerning a treaty declared null and

the right *not* to be submitted to torture;[212]
the right *not* to be submitted to *apartheid*;[213]
the right *not* to be submitted to racial discrimination;[214]
the right *not* be the object of military aggression;[215]
the right *not* be the object of a nuclear attack.[216]

---

void because of a conflict between its terms and norms of *jus cogens superveniens*. This Treaty had been concluded between the Netherlands and a tribe in Surinam in 1762 and provided for the payment of a sum of 10 to 50 Florins for the return of escaped slaves to the Governor, or for their sale as slaves to the Governor. *Cf. supra*, on slavery in the preceding section, and *infra*, in this Part, under B III v. Prohibition of Harm to Individuals.

[212] *Barcelona Traction Case, Belgium v Spain*, Second Phase, *Reports*,(1970), ICJ, 5 Feb. *Reports*, 1970, Judgment, para. 32-34. Consider also the difficulties in defining 'torture' in view of differences in subjective tests: see, for a discussion in detail about the prohibition of torture in the context of attacks of I have called '*genocidal terrorists*', see my article 'Illegal combatants and the Law of War', *George Washington University Journal*, 2006 and *supra* in this Part, B III I on Ethics and Intrinsic Law.

[213] See the *Barcelona Traction Case* (1970), ICJ *Reports*, (1970).

[214] Racial discrimination in international society is clearly not limited to *apartheid* situations but also includes a number of other forms of maltreatment based on race. Most national legal systems now contain prohibitions on various forms of racial discrimination. Yet, there are cases when it is difficult to assess what actually amounts to 'discrimination'.

[215] *The Nicaragua Case*, ICJ, (1986), *Reports*, 1986 para, 180. The International Law Commission has referred to this rule in similar terms saying: 'The law of the Charter concerning the prohibition of force is a conspicuous example of a rule of international law having the character of *jus cogens*', ILC Yearbook, 1966-11, 247.

[216] See, my forceful criticism of the ICJ's *Opinion on the Legality of Nuclear Arms*, (1991) ICJ *Reports* 1991, 1, My criticism was set out in my *Law of War, op. cit.*, but only in its 2nd ed., Cambridge: CUP, 2000, 249-250. There, I severely criticised the failure of the ICJ to fully condemn first use of nuclear weapons; in the 3rd ed. these pages were omitted by a 'technical mistake'.

and it would seem that these prohibitions are coupled with *three positive rights* to be enjoyed by all subjects of the international legal order:

> the right of peoples to dispose of themselves;[217]
> the right of people to have a government elected by a majority of the citizens;[218]
> the right to be protected as a diplomat by privileges of immunity.[219]

These basic rules constitute the minimum *substratum* of rules from which derogations by treaties or other agreements are not admitted. They are thus rules that bind all and that are consequently functioning *erga omnes*. It seems reasonable to expect States and other subjects of international law to support the following of such rules. The International Court of Justice has repeatedly stated that it is even a *duty* of all States to uphold such fundamental rules even if they themselves are not involved in a specific dispute.[220] At any rate, no specific acceptance or consent is required by States or other subjects of international law, for the rules *jus cogens*. This

---

[217] [This right] has been recognised by the United Nations and by the International Court of Justice, see the *The Opinion on Namibia*, ICJ (1971), *Reports*, 1971, 31; *The Opinion on West Sahara Occidental*, ICJ, (1975) *Reports*, 1975, 31, 33; ICJ, *The West Timor Case*, ICJ, (1995), *Recueil*, 1995, 102.

[218] This right is illustrated by the fact that a State does not obtain recognition by other States unless they introduce a democratic system based on majority votes: See, UN General Assembly Resolutions on Rhodesia *e.g.*, 1514 (XV); and on South Africa demanding even 3/4 majority, Resolution 844 (IX). It should be noted that these rules concern recognition of new of re-established States: once a State is established and functioning, it is more difficult to ensure the respect for this rule.

[219] *The Hostages in Teheran Case, (United States v Iran)*, (1980), ICJ, Reports, 1980, 4.

[220] See, in particular, *The Hostages in Teheran Case*, in the previous note.

does not prevent numerous disagreements concerning the exact latitudes of a rule or even of its exact contents.

For example, to apply the rules on discrimination cited above, it is very difficult indeed to establish the limits of acceptability in practice. In this context, it is useful to underline that the rules of *jus cogens* are not immutable or static but, just as the rules of natural law,[221] they are flexible according to the needs of international society. *Slavery* was not illegal a few hundred years ago; aggressive war was not *illegal* before 1945; *apartheid* was not *illegal* before the 1960's when attitudes changed concerning human rights.[222]

The insistence that rules of *jus cogens* exist and play an important role in international society facilitates the development of attitudes concerning the protection of the hypothetical goal: the survival of humanity.

The *maxims* discussed above are clearly some compelling rules but they are of a *technical and formal nature*. The rules of *jus cogens*, on the other hand, have material contents. In this sense these rules can also be distinguished from *formal* general principles. The rules of *jus cogens* are invariably imperative and compelling as the Latin term *cogens* indicates.

The *jus cogens* category does cover the basic maxims and some basic material rules but should perhaps be restricted to prescriptions to which an overwhelming majority of individuals would subscribe without hesitation. But there are some further rules of international law that prohibit harm and that therefore also form part of *intrinsic rules* of the international legal order. These rules are different, in a sense, from those of *jus cogens* as their application

---

[221] In detail, *infra*, Part Three, IV vi on 'Allergy' to Natural Law.
[222] See, my *Law of War*, op. cit., 69 *et seq.*

will invariably involve conditions and modifications depending on actual circumstances. In other words, these rules are not as absolute as the rules of *jus cogens*. Yet, they are *intrinsic* in the international legal system in the sense that they are indispensable to the functioning of the international legal order.

iii. Prohibition of Harm to Groups: Use of Force

By harm to 'groups' we mean harm to groups and collectivities of individuals. Such harm is usually caused by a military attack on another State. Such an attack can be carried out by a State, a group of allied States, or, increasingly in the last decades, by terrorists. This prohibition also covers actions by States against their own citizens.[223]

Modern international law prohibits the use of force in international society. Resort to war is particularly prohibited.[224]

In this respect two alineas of article 2 of the Charter of United Nations clearly set out the most essential prophylactic rules in international society. Article 2(4) states that:

> 'All Members shall refrain in their international relations from the threat or use of force against the territorial integrity or

---

[223] A case in point is the intervention by police in Spain against citizens who had not committed any crime or offence as the legislation stood at the time of the purported referendum in Catalonia, see, *supra*, in Part One, I iii d) and in this Part, *supra*, B III I, under Ethics and Intrinsic Law in the context of self-determination.

[224] See, my *Law of War*, 3rd ed., 2013, passim; Article 2(4) of the United Nations Charter; the Briand Kellogg Pact, 1928, in the vast literature, see Brownlie, *The Use of Force by States*, 1963; Northedge, *The Use of Force in International Relations*, 1974. For analysis of recent practice, of the use of force, see my *Law of War*, *op. cit.*, Ch. I. *Cf.* recent attempts to abolish the death penalty.

political independence of any state, or in any other manner inconsistent with the Purposes of the United Nations.'

and article 2(7) provides that:

'Nothing in this Charter shall authorise the United Nations to intervene in matters which are essentially within the domestic jurisdiction of a State, nor shall it require Members to refer such cases to a settlement procedure under the present Charter; However, this principle shall not prejudice the application of the coercive measures provided for in Chapter VII.'

Intervention,[225] mentioned specifically in article 2(7), is prohibited as a specific act of aggression.[226] Use of force in general is forbidden under article 2(4). But as we shall see, it is intervention that has caused most problems in recent decades.

The prohibitions in article 2(4) and 2(7) do not result from any 'customary law' as, in any event, such a pretended source of these rules would be based on 'negative custom', that is on the logically impossible ground that States and individuals had *refrained* from using force that it then became compulsory to respect this 'non-practice'.[227]

The root of these prophylactic rules is not to be found in the nebulous 'customary law' but in the very basis of international law: the *intrinsic law* that forbids hindering actions towards the

---

[225] *E.g.* Vincent, J., *Non-Intervention and International Order*, Princeton: Princeton Univ. Press, 1974, 281.

[226] The General Assembly saw it fit to 'define' this concept and produced a bland definition that says very little. See, Ferencz, B.B., *Defining International Aggression*, 2 vols, New York: Oceana,1975.

[227] See, *in extenso*, *infra*, Part Three, C IV iii b) on 'negative custom'.

hypothetical goal and endangering the safety of mankind and the survival of humanity.

Good examples of the disasterous result of violating these prophylactic rules, or at least misjudging their contents, are the interventions in Iraq and in Libya in the 1990s and later. The intervention in Iraq in 2003 was particularly tragic. Here, intervention with heavy military presence was held to be justified by the United States and the United Kingdom as 'preventive self-defence', although it soon emerged that there had been no threat of imminent attacks from Saddam Hussein in Iraq.

Similar arguments of pretended 'self-defence' were put forward with regard to the 2011 intervention in Libya, an orderly and stable State, albeit led by the forceful General Gaddafi. But Western Powers were unable here, too, to refrain from military force in this specific situation, These ill-judged interventions led to massive instability in Iraq and in Libya. The quantity of arms sent to anti-government forces in Libya were of such massive scale that many weapons found their way to Mali, south of Libya, and led to instability there as well.

Gradually, the whole Arab world in North Africa, was affected, leading to further serious problems caused by refugees seeking to escape the chaos that ensued. Later, refugees were joined by huge crowds of economic migrants, coming from other parts of Africa, even from Sub-Saharan areas. The European Union provided little assistance and appeared to even have encouraged and facilitated migration from non-war zones.[228]

Even the initial intervention in Syria seemed ill-judged as assistance to the anti-government rebels turned out to go also to

---

[228] See, my *Suicide of Europe*, London: Montesa Jagellonica, 2016.

Al-Qaeda that had heavily infiltrated the fractured rebels. It seemed that several of the Great Powers had set aside the important rule in war situations that it is sometimes wise not to assist either party in a civil strife.[229]

Force by nuclear weapons, and of other weapons of mass destruction, that would endanger large sections of population[230] and of the human environment[231] are clearly incompatible with the hypothetical goal. The same is probably true with regard to any non-discriminatory weapons, for example chemical weapons, that are unable to discriminate between military targets and the civilian population. In this area there are noticeable signs of emerging prohibitions.[232]

A particular aspect of the rule prohibiting force concerns the duty to resolve disputes by peaceful settlement. The modalities of such settlement is subject to the detailed consent of the parties[233] but, under prophylactic rules of international society, parties are nowadays not free to resolve their differences by force.[234] Threat of force is also prohibited and by some elasticity of the rule,[235] it

---

[229] See, my *Law of War*, 3rd ed., 2013, Ch.2.

[230] See, *The Opinion on the Legality of Nuclear Arms*, (1991) ICJ *Reports*, 1991, 1, and my *Law of War, op. cit.*, but only in its 2nd ed., Cambridge: CUP, 2000, 249-250, severely criticising the failure of the ICJ to fully condemn nuclear weapons; in the 3rd ed. these pages were omitted by a 'technical mistake'. The 2017 UN Treaty on Prohibition of Nuclear Weapons is unfortunately rudimentary and lacks a verification regime, *UN Treaty Collection*, 20 Sept. 2017.

[231] See, *infra*, on pollution, in this Section.

[232] See further my *Law of War, op. cit.*, Part II, Restrictions on Weapons.

[233] *Infra*, in this Part Three, C III, Consequential Rules.

[234] *E.g. Nicaragua v United States* (1986), ICJ *Reports* and *The Times* 28th June 1986.

[235] This is expressly mentioned *e.g.* in article 2(4) of the UN Charter.

may be that even 'provocations' are included in the prohibition, at least as a novel development.[236] However, deterrence by means of negotiated levels of nuclear arsenals appears, so far, to be compatible with the prohibition of force.

But validating rules, allowing for self-defence, hollow out the prohibitions of the use of force. Yet, there is a noticeable trend away from 'free' use of force. The burden of proof of justifying factors, for example, for self-defence, now lies heavily on the State that resorts to force; and certain blanket notions like 'humanitarian intervention' are now dubious grounds for the use of force. The most perilous form of intervention has surely proved to be what we have called, a 'patronising' intervention, when Western States claim to know what is 'best' for certain culturally different nations. A particularly worrying development has been the pretended right to interfere to protect civilian population, often used as a pretext for intervention in internal affairs. This practice 'R2P, Right to Protect' appears to be a blatant attempt to by-pass the rule of non-intervention by a new vocabulary.[237]

---

[236] Although 'technically' on the high seas, the naval manoeuvres by United States in the Bay of Syrte, preceding hostilities with Libya may be construed as 'provocative'. Similarly, the presence of Soviet submarines outside Swedish territorial waters may violate the new norm on provocation we allege exists; note that not all USSR submarines have remained outside Swedish territorial waters but U-137, a Soviet submarine, entered into *internal* waters and even into the military protected zone of Karlskrona and was grounded *on* a small island, see, my article on 'Foreign warships and immunity for espionage', *AJIL*, 1984, 76. In this context we should note that also 'threat' of force is illegal under article 2(4) of the Charter of the United Nations.

[237] *Infra*, in this Part, See my article 'New aspects of sovereignty and the right to protect – R2P', published by St. Thomas More Institute, London, 2011, available at http://thomasmoreinstitute.org.uk/papers/1890/. See further my *Law of War*, *op. cit.*, Ch. I and II, iii.

iv. Prohibition of Harm to the Environment

With regard to the environment it should be emphasised that there is an intrinsic duty of States and individuals alike to promote protection of the environment. There are also clear obligations of States and individuals alike not to cause *pollution*, to avoid disposing of non-degradable or toxic products in common areas and not to disperse resources by over-use.

In the 1970s and '80s, there was much talk about 'acid rain' but little attention is now paid to that. In environmental contexts, serious problems may be caused by inventing fashionable catchphrases rather than addressing the substantive problems. So, after 'acid rain', there was much talk about 'global warming' but that expression has lately given way to the much wider notion of 'climate change'. Some claim there is no problem, as any climate change is merely due to normal weather cycles.[238]

There are two major problem areas concerning the human environment: the question of pollution and the question of use of resources.

a) Use of Resources, Climate Change and Pollution

1. Use of Resources

There is a duty of all in international society to preserve the 'common good'. This duty involves avoiding the destruction of

---

[238] http://www.nationalreview.com/article/425232/97-percent-solution-ian-tuttle 2017.

forests without replanting and avoiding over-fishing to allow fish-stocks to replenish.

Apart from duties concerning *using resources* there is also a duty incumbent on all to *preserve resources*; this is probably the only *inter-generational* duty in international law, and one that has only crystallised in the last four decades, since the Stockholm Declaration in 1972.[239]

That Declaration confirmed the right of States and their citizens to use resources in their territories unless they harmed the resources of others. Principle 21 of the Declaration thus stated that:

> 'States have, in accordance with the Charter of the United Nations and the principles of international law, the sovereign right to exploit their own resources pursuant to their own environmental policies, and the responsibility to ensure that activities within their jurisdiction or control do not cause damage to the environment of other States or of areas beyond the limits of national jurisdiction.'

But like much in the environmental debate, we here speak about rules that would apply *anyway* in international law. Unfortunately, much has been exaggerated in the field of discussion about environmental duties that the core of environmental obligations has been obscured: it goes without saying that subjects of the international legal order must all respect to use their own resources as well as those of the common environment in a responsible manner. They must not act in a way that is detrimental to resources of others or to resources common to all in international society.

---

[239] Declaration of the UN Conference on the Human Environment, Stockholm, 1972, see, www.un-documents.net/index.htm.

2. Climate Change

The heart of the environmental problem is clearly to assess what detrimental environmental developments are caused by *human behaviour*. Contributing factors to climate change could be a shift in the pole of the Earth, shifts in the continental plates, volcanic eruptions or due to any other factors that cannot be controlled by humans.

Much of the environmental debate has become emotional and it is now politically incorrect to question whether all global warming is the result of normal cycles and not necessarily caused, or aggravated, by human behaviour. The point is clearly that if it is *not* caused by human behaviour, it would be better to find means to adjust to climatic changes than to forbid certain practices, or insist on modification of cars, aeroplanes, vacuum cleaners and other appliances, to reduce emission of CO_2, allegedly one of the main causes of global warming.[240]

3. Pollution

Harm which consists in causing or spreading pollution is prohibited under international law as evidenced in numerous decisions by courts[241] and in a host of detailed conventions.[242] Particularly

---

[240] The alleged 97% of scientists affirming CO_2 as the main cause of global warming was, in 2015, 43%: *National Review*, Oct. 8, 2015; there also appears to have been a 19 year stand-still in the change of temperatures, *ibid*.

[241] *Trail Smelter Case* (1938) (1941), 3 RIAA 1905; *Lake Lanoux Case* (1957), 12 RIAA 281.

[242] *E.g.* those appertaining to the law of the sea: MARPOL 1973; The London Dumping Convention, 1972, 1976 *UKTS* 43; The Oslo Convention, 1972, 1975

nuclear pollution is so serious that States may be under obligation to apply uniform safety standards to minimise risks of leaks that can affect international society.²⁴³

The primary question to be asked with regard to pollution is who is causing the harm and whom is being harmed. One can distinguish between pollution caused by another State, such as a nuclear leak from a State owned power plant,²⁴⁴ and that caused by individuals, for example, the oil pollution by merchant ships. It may be worth noting that before the fall of communism, all Russian ships were obviously State owned.

Damage or injury by either activity leads to a duty of mitigation and of reparation.²⁴⁵ There is also an incidental duty of warning.²⁴⁶ Serious oil pollution at sea²⁴⁷ has caused considerable damage to coast lines and to the fisheries industry as well as to the general

---

UKTS 119. For those relating to air pollution, see the 1979 Convention on Long Range Transboundary Air Pollution, although with few substantial obligations, 18 *ILM* ; *cf.* Rosencranz, A., 'The ECE Convention of 1979 on Long Range Transboundary Air Pollution, *AJIL*, 1981, 975.

[243] Statement by IAEA 21 May 1986 in connection with the Chernobyl disaster on 26 April 1986, *The Times*, 22 May 1986.

[244] As, for example, the Chernobyl disaster in April 1986.

[245] *Supra*, in this Part, B II, on General Principles.

[246] See, *infra*, in this Part, B III iv b), in the next section, and C I ii b) Duty to Warn.

[247] The *Torre Canyon*, 1967, near Guernsey in the English Channeln see, Quéneudec, J.P., 'L'incidence de *l'Affaire Torre Canyon* sur le droit de la mer', *AFDI*, 1968, 701; *The Showa Maru*, in 1975, in the Malaccca Straights, where moving sand dunes make navigation difficult and unpredictable*; The Amoco Cadiz*, 1973, in the English Channel, 3.1 miles from the coast of Brittany*; The Exxon Valdez*, 1989, off the coast of Alaska; *The Braer*, 1993, off the coast of Scotland causing considerable damage to salmon industry, causing deformities in farmed salmon smolts. International Oil Pollution Compensation Fund under Section 4 of the Merchant Shipping Act 1974 has proved reluctant to refund economic losses, see, *Landcatch v Braer Corporation; Landcatch v International Oil Pollution*

environment. Since the resources of an individual or a shipping company may be limited, his home State, or, in the case of ships, the flag State, should probably assist by further agreement[248] in the uninsured margin,[249] if harm is caused to other groups.[250] It may also be noted that numerous of most serious oil pollution cases at sea have been caused by ships registered under convenience flags, of mainly Panama and Liberia. In such States the norms for seaworthiness may not be as demanding as in other sea-faring States. It would therefore seem reasonable that the flag State would be liable to contribute to reparation of damage caused by oil pollution by ships, as this might lead to improvement of such standards in the convenience countries. For the State is to the individual not, as many claim, a shield, assuming all international rights and duties, but rather the focal point of imputation[251] that should assume certain risks by activities of its subjects even if it is itself without fault.[252]

Pollution is always a question of degree: what is not thought of as pollution from one source may, in combination with further emissions from other sources, cause serious environmental damage.

Compensation Fund, (1999), Scotland, Court of Session, Inner House, Second Division.

[248] See, *infra*, in This Part, under C I, on Promotional Rules.

[249] Shipowners have normally an insurance for such cases but there is an upper limit which oil disasters may well exceed.

[250] See my 'Supertankers och internationella sund', *Festskrift Schmidt*, Stockholm, 1976, 117.

[251] *Supra*, Part One, I iii c).

[252] Such regulation would lead to improvement of ship standards and to a change in the convenience flag system: no States would want to be liable, as flag States, for substandard ships.

In spite of obvious detrimental effects to particularly water and fisheries, it is difficult, in the case of acid rain, to identify exactly the multiple sources. Once it is established that emissions from a certain region, such as the Midlands or the Ruhr district, are responsible for acid rain in Scandinavia, there arises a duty to the British and German governments to promulgate legislation on filters or other devices to reduce the seriousness of pollution.

An enhanced duty exists to prevent nuclear pollution. Although IAEA has no authoritative power to order safety standards, States concerned are under a legal duty under prophylactic rules to adopt as binding the substratum of reasonable IAEA suggestions and recommendations.[253]

b) Prophylactic Rules for Threats to the Environment:
   Duty to Warn

There is, of course, no duty upon States or others to come together to take any specific action regarding the environment without any compelling reason. But such a reason may exist if geographical nearness exposes one State to specific danger due to some activity inside another State.

There may, for example, be a question of a disaster which has crossboundary effects. In the Chernobyl incident in April 1986 it was apparent that neighbouring States, and States much further away, regarded the Soviet Union as having *a duty to warn* anyone concerned about the leak of radioactive material. Such a duty was clearly imposed by other States on the USSR and, to a large extent,

---

[253] *Infra*, in Part Four, VI iii a) 2, on Variability of the Basis of Obligation, Social Necessity.

recognised by the USSR as a duty in law albeit it was argued by the USSR that the disaster was not of such proportions as to warrant any earlier warnings.[254] Clearly, a duty can be seen as safeguarding the wider obligation to cooperate for the hypothetical goal or, at least, not to take or allow action which endangers the goal.

A *duty to warn* was also held to exist by the International Court of Justice in *The Corfu Channel Case*[255]; in that case there was a danger posed by mines that could probably also be construed to constituting an environmental threat.[256]

v. Prohibition of Harm to Individuals

a) Human Rights

Naturally, a State may bind itself to far reaching concessions and privileges of individuals by treaty. Numerous such agreements do provide enhanced protection of individuals,[257] wherever they are. But even outside such agreements,[258] it has become clear that

---

[254] *The Times*, 29 April 1986.

[255] *Corfu Channel Cse* (*United Kingdom v Albania*), 1949, ICJ *Reports*, 1949, 18.

[256] *Cf. infra*, in this Part, under, C I ii b) on duty to warn about closure of ports.

[257] For example, the Genocide Convention 1949 78 *UNTS* 278; the United Nations Covenants on Economic, Social and Cultural Rights and on Political and Civil Rights, 1966; Convention on the Elimination of all Forms of Racial Discrimination, 1971, HR J 1971 213; the European Convention of Human Rights 1950; the Inter-American Convention on Human Rights, 119 *UNTS* 3; Convention on Slavery 1926, 60 *LNTS* 253.

[258] See, for example, protection by the Helsinki Act, which is, technically, not a 'treaty': see, Arangio-Ruiz, G., 'Human rights and non-intervention in the Helsinki Act', 157 *RCADI* 1977 iv 195 at 213; on the Act, see further, Russell, H.S., 'The Helsinki Declaration', 70 *AJIL* 1976 242; Prevost, J.F., 'Observations sur la nature

individuals, to which ever State they belong or are present, must be granted a certain level of humane treatment.²⁵⁹ Such basic human rights are owed to all, especially to a State's own citizens. But we are here only talking about the bare *substratum*, the core of human rights, and not about incidental detailed rights,²⁶⁰ or what we have called 'luxury human rights', like the right to clean air or even the right to work; the international order cannot cater for such good ambitious targets, except by programmatic aspirations.²⁶¹ Individuals have for some time received upgrading treatment in international law, a trend possibly starting by the conclusion of minorities treaties after the First World War.²⁶²

The basic human rights have already been set out in this work in the context of *Ethics and Intrinsic Law*.²⁶³ The whole framework of human rights must be seen in the scenario that shows that now there are fairly clear rules that individuals enjoy certain basic

---

juridique de l'Acte Final de la Conférence sur la Securité et la Coopération en Europe', *AFDI*, 1975, 129; Ghebali, V.Y., 'L'Acte Final de la Conférence sur la Securité et Coopération en Europe', *AFDI*, 1975, 73; Andréani, G., 'La Conférence sur la Securité et Coopération en Europe' in SFDI Colloque, *Regionalism et Universalisme*, Bordeaux 1976, 1977, 114; Buergenthal, T., (ed.), *Human Rights, International Law and the Helsinki Accords*, New Jersey: Allanheld Osmon, 1977.

²⁵⁹ On Human Rights in general, see *e.g.* Hannum, H., (ed.) *Guide to International Human Rights Practice*, Philadelphia: Pennsylvania Univ. Press, 1984; Meron, T., ed.), *Human Rights in international: Legal and Policy Issues*, Oxford: OUP, 1984; Glaser, K., and Possony, S.T., *Victims of Politics, The State of Human Rights*, New York: Columbia Univ. Press, 1979.

²⁶⁰ Alston, P., 'Conjuring up new human rights: A proposal for quality control', *AJIL*, 1984.

²⁶¹ See my *International Law and the Independent State*, op. cit., Ch. 4, and *infra* in Part Three, C II A ii a) and C II A iii d) on Programmatic Declarations.

²⁶² See further, my *Law of War*, op. cit., 271 *et heq.*

²⁶³ See, *supra*, in this Part, B III ii b) on Compulsory rules: *jus cogens*.

rights: they must thus not be subjected to genocide,[264] slavery,[265] *apartheid*,[266] or to other forms of racial discrimination[267] or to torture.[268]

To these rights must be added the *freedom of expression* without which the other basic rights are undermined; the freedom of expression is the only right which ensures that violations of the other basic rights come to light.[269] Ancillary to the right of freedom of expression, there may be a right to leave and return to one's own country, as such freedom of movement sometimes is a pre-condition of revealing deteriorating conditions with regard to human rights in a country.[270]

---

[264] See, the Genocide Convention 1948, *UNTS*, 277, 78 and *supra*, in Part One, I iii d) 17 on Individuals and, in this Part, B III ii Prophylactic Rules and *jus cogens*.

[265] Treaty of London 1841; The General Act of the Congo Conference of Berlin 1885; the General Act of the Anti-Slavery Conference of Brussels 1890, as revised by the Treaty of St. Germain of 19919, 8 *LNTS* 16; Agreement on Suppression of White Slave Traffic, 1904, 1 *LNTS* 1 and 1910, 3 *LNTS* 278; Convention on Suppression of Traffic in Women and Children 1922, 9 *LNTS* 415; League of Nations Slavery Convention 1926, 60 *LNTS* 253; Convention for Suppression of Traffic in Persons and of the Exploitation of Prostitution of Others 1949, 55 *UNTS*.

[266] Since 1952 the problem of apartheid has been regularly monitored and discussed by the General Assembly; see *e.g.* Resolution 37/69 B 1982; for sanctions, see *e.g.* 36/172 N 1981.

[267] See, note above for the 1971 Convention. See, Vierdag, E.W., *The Concept of Discrimination in International Law*, The Hague: Nijhoff, 1973. For UN Resolutions, see, *e.g.*, GA Resolution 36/55 of 1981.

[268] *E.g.* GA Resolution 3452 (XXX) 1974; 32/64 and 32/64 of 1977 and the Torture Convention 1984. See, *supra*, on *jus cogens* in this Part, under B III ii.

[269] This right cannot not be limited by a State, see *infra* in this section under B II ii b) Communications.

[270] See, The European Convention on Human Rights which guarantees such a right, article 4; on this right under other systems, see Council of Europe, *The Right To Leave a Country*, Issue Paper, 2013.

A basic human right is also *the right of property*: like Plato who at the end of his life changed his views on communal property (and on the State's removing children from their parents) so is it clear after the demise of communism, that no society can function unless individuals have the right of property and the right to bring up their children.[271]

Relevant conventions on basic human rights are clearly binding on third parties as the prohibiting rules reflect what is found in *intrinsic law*, that sometimes may go beyond what contractual obligations may provide.[272] Conventions on basic human rights are thus binding on third parties as declaring rules which form part of the main body of general international law.[273] Thus, individuals enjoy certain ensured basic rights whether or not they are nationals of a State and whether or not that State is bound by any treaty on

---

[271] Plato favoured the idea that the State should be the sole owner of property and even take care of children, rather than the parents; *The Republic*, Books V-VII, 462b-c, but he relented later and suggested in *The Laws*, that there could be private property but the State would have to supervise that this did not lead to imbalances, *The Laws*, Book VIII, 888. Note, that Aristotle criticised any view that prohibited private property of individuals or ordered property to be held in common as an individual can only practice charity if they have some private property: *Politics*, VII.9.1329a23–4, 13.1332a32–8. *Cf.* my *Äganderätten*, Stockholm: Jagellonica, 1994. Linked to the notion of property is also the right of privacy: *Osorio v Dole Food Co.*, 665 F. Supp. 2d 1307, 1316-18 (S.D. Fla. 2009). *Cf.* Fourteenth Amendment to the U.S. Constitution and Protocol 1, article 1 of the European Convention of Human Rights.

[272] See, my *Essays on the Law of Treaties*, London: Sweet & Maxwell, 1967, 116 *et seq.* and see the *Genocide Case* (1951) ICJ *Reports* 23 where the International Court emphatically stated that the principles underlying the Genocide Convention form part of rules recognised by civilised States as binding upon all States.

[273] See, with regard to the Genocide Convention my *Essays, op. cit.*, 117, on that 'its' obligation may be 'apparent' as the roots of its obligations are in underlying 'rules' and not in the 'Convention'.

human rights. The proof that this is so may be found, with regard to serious deviations from prophylactic rules, in the practice of the War Crimes Tribunals and in the severe international criticism of a State that limits rights of equality by an *apartheid* system, and further by continuing objections to systems that allow racial discrimination or that curtail the right of freedom of expression.

b) Humanitarian Rules

It is not an entirely novel trend that sets standards for the treatment of individuals. It was individuals, not States, that could feel pain in war and deserved to be protected by a rule that any belligerent must avoid using weapons that cause 'unnecessary suffering'.[274]

c) Protection of Aliens

In times of peace, individuals could always count on good treatment by a State provided they were 'aliens'. This was the main question for regulation in the field of responsibility.[275] But this state of affairs, amply evidenced in its absurdity in the case law of the

---

[274] This has been accepted as a guideline since the 1868 St. Petersburg Declaration and is entrenched in all later relevant treaties, see the Hague Conventions of 1899 and 1907; the Geneva Conventions of 1949 together with the Additional Protocols of 1977; see, in detail, my *Law of War*, op. cit., 271 *et seq.*

[275] See, *e.g.* Borchard, E., 'The 'minimum standard' of the treatment of aliens', *ASIL*, 1939 51 on the practice of decisions of international tribunals; for later developments, see, in detail, the ILC *Reports on State Responsibility*, by Garcia Amador, A/CN.4./96 (1956) and further reports in the ILC, and *e.g.* survey in *Yearbook* 1978 ii 66 *et seq.*

United States – Mexican Claims Commission,[276] is not worthy of representing current rules of general international law: in the domain of human rights *all* individuals enjoy nowadays an improved situation, according to a *minimum standard* that applies to aliens as well as to nationals.[277]

d) Protection of Diplomats: Rules on Immunity

Certain further rights are incidental to the juxtaposition of subjects in international society. If the subjects are the more consolidated entities, such as States or organisations, their envoys will enjoy immunity so that they can carry out their functions unhampered.[278] At least functional immunity is also granted to consuls.[279] As long as all have corresponding rights, established according to symmetric

---

[276] See, Feller, A.H., The Mexican Claims Commission, 1923-1934, New York: Macmillan, 1935; Nielsen, F.K., *International Law as Applied to Reclamations Mainly in Cases Between United States and Mexico*, New York: Byrne, 1933; *cf.* earlier literature on State responsibility in general, *e.g.* Ago, R., Le délit international, 68 *RCADI* 1939; Dumas, J., 'La responsabilité des Etats à raison des crimes et délits commis sur leur territoire au prejudice d'étrangers', 36 *RCADI*, 1931. The practice of the Commission appeared to some to be merely an expression of 'dollar diplomacy': Jessup, P.C., *A Modern World of Nations*, New York: Macmillan, 1956, 96.

[277] See my *International Legal Order, op. cit.*, 281-305, human rights, at 305, on minimum standards.

[278] Vienna Convention on Diplomatic Relations, 1963, 500 *UNTS* 95; Satow, *Guide to Diplomatic Practice*, 4th ed., 1957; Denza, E., *Diplomatic Law*, Oxford: OUP, 4th ed., 2016; Hardy, M.J.L., *Modern Diplomatic Law*, Manchester: Manchester Univ. Press, 1968.

[279] Vienna Convention on Consular Relations, 1963, 57 *AJIL* 995; Lee, L.T., *Vienna Convention on Consular Relations*, 1966; *idem, Consular Law and Practice*, 1961.

reciprocity, States willingly accept the extension of immunity to non-State entities such as international organisations. Immunity is also sometimes thought to attach to non-diplomat individuals, such as international civil servants and journalists, who may be treated as enjoying immunity.[280]

IV. Effect of Violation of Intrinsic Rules

International courts and tribunals have an *ex officio* duty to verify in all cases that the *compulsory maxims* and *compulsory general principles*, set out above,[281] have been respected. If there has been a violation, they have the *duty* not to allow a claim of a Plaintiff and not to allow the legal effect of any judgment that is contrary to these maxims. The same goes for the few compulsory general principles,[282] also described in the preceding sections. With regard to the latter category though, it may be noted that these general principles, albeit compulsory, are of a wider ambit and therefore susceptible to application with some discretion in the individual case.

That serious legal effects ensue in the case of violations of the binding maxims and the binding general principles, both parts of the intrinsic law of international society, is accepted in practice

---

[280] On the immunity of a Soviet employee of the Sugar Council in London and of Western journalists in Poland, see my article on 'Foreign warships and immunity for espionage', *AJIL* 1984 62 n 57.

[281] *Supra*, in this Part, B I and II iv.

[282] *Supra*, in this Part, B II iv.

as demonstrated and confirmed above all in numerous decisions of arbitration tribunals. Here, claims have been refused and legal effect has been denied to judgments that have violated such intrinsic rules without which the international legal system cannot function. It is clear that especially the rule *ex turpi causa non oritur actio* (that no one should be allowed to benefit from his own illegal actions) has led to numerous claims having failed.[283]

National Courts, as well as arbitration tribunals, have also refused to enforce judgments obtained in violation of what in English law is known as '*natural justice*' – violation above all of the maxims *audiatur et altera pars* (both parties must be heard) and *nemo judex in causa sua* (prohibiting bias), in the United States known as part of the rule of '*due process*'.[284]

All courts and tribunals are furthermore under an obligation, like all other subjects of the international legal order, to uphold and protect fundamental rules of international society. The International Court of Justice underlined this duty of all States, and thus implicitly of all subjects of the international legal order, in the *Hostages in Teheran Case*, to show solidarity. All must, in this way, support the respect for one of the most 'fundamental rules' in international law, the one concerning the immunity of diplomats, a rule without which

---

[283] *World Duty Free Company Ltd. v The Republic of Kenya*, ICSID Case No. ARB/00/7, Award Oct. 4, 2006 (bribery); *Kuwait Airways Corp. v Iraqi Airways Co.*, [2002] AC 19, 12, (fraud), available at http://www.publications.parliament.uk/pa/ld200102/ldjudgmt/jd020516/kuwait-1.htm.; *Inceysa Vallisoletana v El Salvador*, ICSID Case No. ARB/03/26, Award, Aug. 2, 2006, (fraud); available at http://www.italaw.com/sites/default/files/case-documents/ita0424_0.pdf.

[284] For example, *Osorio v Dole Food Co.*, 665 F. Supp. 2d 1307, 2009, 1316-18, S.D. Fla. 2009.

international society cannot function.²⁸⁵ A similar plea of solidarity to enhance the respect for fundamental rules of international law was made by the International Court of Justice in the *Namibia Case*.²⁸⁶

All subjects of international law, especially all courts and tribunals, have thus the duty of *solidarity* to uphold and protect all *compelling maxims, compulsory general principles* as well as all binding *prophylactic rules*, forbidding harm. Courts and tribunals have a further duty to verify whether transactions or other actions of subjects of international society have violated such rules and, in their judgments, give appropriate effect to uphold such compulsory rules of the international legal order.

C. Extrinsic Rules

I. Stabilising Rules

Certain rules demand no action on the part of States, organisations or individuals, but are designed to keep a situation 'frozen' by clear assessment of portions of rights and duties. Such rules are particularly frequent in territorial matters but also in other areas where symmetry and reciprocity are more fundamental than in other fields of international law.

---

[285] *Hostages in Teheran Case, (United States v Iran)*, 1980, ICJ *Reports*, 26.
[286] *The Namibia Case, Advisory Opinion*, (1971), ICJ *Reports* 56.

i. Distributive Rules

a) Allocation of National Space

1. General Divisional Rules

Rules on distribution of rights concern, for example, title[287] or delimitation of territory[288] of the water margin[289] or the continental shelf.[290] It is such divisional rules which demarcate the area of territorial competence of each State. Within the area allocated to each State, there is a heavy presumption that local laws override those of other States. However, as we shall see, States cannot, even within this *reserved domain*[291] evade *jus cogens* and other compelling rules of international law. On the other hand, in numerous matters the government within the delimited geographical area is, of course, the *suprema potestas*.[292]

---

[287] *Western Sahara Case* (1975), ICJ *Reports*, 12; *Sovereignty over Frontier Lands*, (1959) ICJ *Reports*, 209.

[288] *Temple of Vihear Case*, (1962), ICJ *Reports*, *223*; *Cf.* Ronzitti, N., 'Les confins en droit international', 1983.

[289] *Gulf of Maine Case*, (1984), ICJ *Reports*, 12.

[290] *Tunisia v Libya* (1982), ICJ *Reports*, 18; *Libya v Malta* (1985), ICJ *Reports*, 13; *Gulf of Maine Case* (1984), ICJ *Reports*, 12; *North Sea Continental Shelf Cases* (1969), ICJ *Reports*, 12; *Anglo-French Continental Shelf Arbitration* (1977).

[291] *Cf. supra*, Part One, I ii c) 2 and I iii a). See, further, my *International Law and the Independent State*, 1994, London: Gower, *passim* and conclusions at 232.

[292] On the efforts to remove suspected terrorists to other areas outside the national geographical space to avoid restricting interrogation pratices, see my article on 'Extraterritorial rendition', *University of North Carolina Journal*.

From such distribution we must distinguish sharing of use[293] and sharing of 'common areas'.[294] Other typical rules of this category with a clear distinction between sharing of the use of the waters and of the waters themselves.

Special rules assess the confinement of airspace that a State may claim.[295] All rules of this type apply on the basis of symmetrical division as understood as a rule which allots 'adequate', and 'equitable' (but not necessarily identical) portions to each party.[296]

Once distributive rules have been established, they exercise a stabilising effect on international society for they assert the division of competence. Yet, this by no means implies that such division is in any way permanent. The rules of distribution are highly dynamic and subject to recurrent change and revision according to adapted views on what is equitable',[297] in the light of current social values. Therefore, the rules on distribution, inherently dynamic, are capable of giving rise to rules on redistribution.[298] But once a second set of rules has been adopted on redistribution (which belong to a

---

[293] *Cf.* Goldie, L.F.E., 'Title and use (and *usufruct*) An ancient distinction too oft forgot', *AJIL* 1985 689.

[294] On a wider notion of *bonum commune*, see Verdross, A.v., *Abendländische Rechtsphilosophie*, Vienna: Spinger, 1963, 268 *et seq.*

[295] For a summary of relevant rules, and on the Karman theory, see my *International Law and the Independent State*, London: Gower, 2nd ed., 1987, 83 *et seq.*

[296] *Cf.* the discussion of 'equitable' principles in the ICJ, see, *Tunisia v Libya* (1982), ICJ *Reports*, 18; *Tunisia v Libya Interpretation Case* (1985), ICJ *Reports*, 12; *Libya v Malta*, (1985), ICJ *Reports*, 13.

[297] See *supra*, under Contingent Maxims, in this Part, B I iii.

[298] See *infra*, in this Part, C II i b), Duty to Share? It is occasionally emphasised that borders cannot be changed 'by force'; but then borders of half of Europe were changed after the First and Second World War.

subsequent type of rules),²⁹⁹ this gives rise to new allocation of competence, by a new, albeit revised, set of distributive rules.

2. The Notion of Prescription

It is not unusual to speak of 'consolidation' in international law.³⁰⁰ But we stretch this further to show that consolidation by behaviour, with territorial connection, amounts to prescription proving title or right of use. The notion of prescription, understood in its broadest sense, is an area where use and custom is relevant. As will be shown later,³⁰¹ unless it has such territorial anchorage, 'customary' law is often merely nothing but a nebulous notion, superfluous and confusing to the theory of international law, as being unfounded in legal and political realities.

Territory, or use thereof, can be acquired by prescription. It is in the context of distributive rules that we should see such a notion. It is, in practice, one of the most important notions in international law for it is this concept that represents genuine 'customary' law.³⁰² It has clear territorial connotations and explains, indeed, many cases decided by the International Court which many assume 'prove' the existence of general 'customary' law.³⁰³

---

[299] *Infra*, in this Part, C II ii c), Further Regimes.
[300] DeVisscher, Ch., *Théories et Réalites en droit international public*, Paris: Pedone, 1953, 244; Johnson, D.H.N.,'Consolidation as a root of title in international law', *Cambridge LR* 1955, 215.
[301] *Infra*, Part Three, C IV iv, The Fallacies of Customary Law.
[302] *Ibid., loc. cit.*
[303] E.g. *The Corfu Channel Case*, (1949) ICJ *Reports*, 18; *Anglo-Norwegian Fisheries Case*, (1951), ICJ *Reports*, 116; *North Sea Continental Shelf Cases*, (1969), ICJ *Reports*, 12; *Tunisia v Libya*, 1982), ICJ *Reports*, 13; *Libya v Malta*,(1985), ICJ

There is a close territorial connection, both in the use and in the right to appropriate certain water sections or portions of the continental shelf[304] and in the case of right of passage over land,[305] through the territorial sea or through international straits.[306]

b) Jurisdiction and Nationality

Rules on distribution define what jurisdictional competence each State may exercise.[307] Other distributive rules govern matters like, for example, nationality and allegiance to a State.[308] The *'allegiance'* that citizens owe to a State, may be construed to be given in return for the *protection* of the State, particularly important when citizens travel to countries where the legal system is uncertain or malfunctioning.

Reports, 12; *Rights of Passage over Indian Territory*, (1960), 6; *Temple of Vihear Case Case*, (1962), ICJ *Reports*, 6; *Sovereignty over Certain Frontier Lands*, (1959), ICJ *Reports*, 209; *The Arbitral Award Made by the King of Spain on 23 December 1906*, (1960), ICJ *Reports*, 192; *cf. The Aegean Sea Continental Shelf Case (Application)* 1976, ICJ *Reports*, 5.

[304] See, the previous note *e.g.* for *The Fisheries Case*, *North Sea Continental Shelf Cases*, and for the *Tunisia Libya* and *Libya Malta Cases*.

[305] See, the same note for *The Rights of Passage Case*.

[306] See, the same note for *The Corfu Channel Case*; *cf.* my article 'International straits and UNCLOS', Anglo-Soviet Symposium, Moscow, 1986 and my 'Supertankers och internationella sund', *Festskrift Schmidt*, 1976.

[307] *Cf.* Mann, F., 'The doctrine of jurisdiction in international law', 111 *RCADI* i 1964 9; *cf. The Lotus Case* (1927), PCIJ Series A, No. 10.

[308] Van Panhuys, H.F., *The Role of Nationality in International Law*, Leyden: Sijthoff, 1959; de Castro, F., La nationalité, la double nationalité et la supra nationalité, 102 *RCADI* 1961 i; Makarov, A.N., *Allegemeine Lehren des Staatsangehörigkeitsrecht*, Stuttgart: Kohlhammer, 1962. Nationality could well be forfeited in case of lack of allegiance *e.g.* by citizens who leave to fight with terrorist armies, like ISIS.

c) Sovereignty and Democracy

Although it is important to have a clear notion of the hallmarks of a State,[309] it must also be remembered that many units devoid of statehood, are still capable of being 'subjects' or 'actors' in the international system.[310]

The root of democracy in modern international law is thus the idea that the State, when acting externally, represents a political society. It is this society which precedes and surpasses the State. Thus,

> 'la maitresse, c'est la liberté et la servante, c'est la personnalité juridique de l'état'.[311]

Sovereignty is thus nothing but a 'functional reality'.[312] And, as the State is nothing but a combination of functions and forces, it only lives if those functions and forces are properly combined. But if that equilibrium ceases to exist

> '...la nation, comme le corps, retourne à la pourriture'.[313]

---

[309] See, *supra*, Part One, I iii d) 1, on hallmarks of States.

[310] See, *supra*, *e.g.* under Part One, I iii d), on Entitled Persons; *cf. infra*, under Part Three, C V iii, on A Model of Formation of Rules.

[311] 'The mistress is 'liberty' and the servant is the legal personality of the State', Hauriout, *Leçons sur le mouvement social*, 1899, 134; *cf.*, *idem*, 'Philosophie du droit et science sociale', *RDP*, 1899, 474.

[312] Carré de Malberg, R., *Philosophie du droit des gens*, Paris: CNRS, 19301, 53.

[313] 'The nation, like the body, returns to dust', Chardon, H., *L'organisation de la démocratie. Les deux forces: le nombre, l'élite*, Paris: Perrin, 1921, 18.

The State thus serves as a focus of imputation for any act which can be referred to its own unit. Some have sought to dispense with the notion of imputation,[314] but it is hardly possible to identify who are the true authors of acts, nor is it possible to assess the value of consent, unless the notion of imputation is retained as a main tool.

An act may be imputed to a non-State unit or actor in international society. But it is States, which as separate 'blocs' form the basic and most solid structure of international society, both in political and in legal terms. It is thus between States that such entrenching rules develop.

ii. Rules on Mutual Contacts

May a State exclude itself from all contact with the other members of international society? In the past, efforts to remain isolated[315] have sometimes met with considerable protests from others. But once a State does take part in international intercourse it must abide by the rules. Thus, if a State wishes to remain outside the 'club', it cannot expect the advantages of membership either. As Manning[316] has put it in Anglo-Saxon terms of games, a question may be phrased as 'Do you wish to play the international law game?' and if so, certain rules must be followed by all 'players'.

---

[314] Brownlie, *Responsibility, op. cit.*, 367.

[315] *Cf.* the situation in China, *e.g.* Eckel, P.E., *The Far East Since 1500*, New York: Harcourt Brace & Co., 1947; Escarra, J., *La Chine et le droit international*, Paris: Pedone, 1931; *cf.* my article on 'The problem of unequal treaties', *ICLQ*, 1966, 1069. But closure of ports must be notified, see *infra*, in this Part, B III iv b), Duty to Warn.

[316] Manning, C.A.W., *The Nature of International Society*, London: Macmillan, reissue for the LSE, 1975.

Certain rules flow from the mere juxtaposition of subjects as soon as these enter into contact with each other.

a) Objective Regimes

There exists a duty to respect the existence of others in international society. Some even consider such duties part of the 'fundamental rights' of States.[317] The theory of fundamental rights has been much criticised[318] as having roots in 'natural law' and, because of such overtones, it is normally rejected by extreme positivists. However, one need not resort to evaluation in terms of 'natural law':[319] one could easily perceive rules concerning a duty to 'respect'[320] a created legal entity, as derived from a *functional social need* to acknowledge entities and situations that factually exist. One must

---

[317] Sibert, M., *Traité de droit international public*, Paris: Cours de droit, 1951, ch. 4; Jellinek, G., *System der subjektiven öffentlichen Rechte*, Tübingen: Mohr Siebeck, 1905; Phillimore, W., *Droits, op. cit.*, 25; Barile, G., *I diritti assuluti dell'ordinamento internazionale*, Milan: Giuffré 1951; Cavaglieri, A., *I diritti fondamentali degli stati nella società internazionale*, Pisa: Filippo Serafino, 1906; Graf, K.B., *Die Grundrechte der Staaten im Völkerrecht*, Basel: Helbing & Lichtenhahn, 1948;

[318] *E.g.* Brierly, J.L., ed. Waldock, H., *Law of Nations*, 6th ed., Oxford: OUP, 1963 49 *et seq.*

[319] On the other hand, there is a dynamic revival of theories of natural law which can no longer be dismissed as anachronistic; on the contrary, many such rules explain more succinctly certain State behaviour. Numerous actions of States that may be pragmatically observed are coherent only if seen in the light of natural law rules, see my *International Law*, 1993, Chapter III.

[320] On equality as an aspect of sovereignty, see my *Independence, op. cit.*, 3 *et seq.* and on unequal treaties, *ibid.*, 195 *et seq.*

concede that the views of the International Law Commission on 'objective regimes'[321] concern precisely such problems.

The fact that a State is 'there', cannot be ignored by others. The decline of the constitutive theories of recognition[322] alone bears witness, that entities may graduate as 'States' once they fulfil certain criteria of statehood,[323] whether or not they have been 'recognised' as 'States' by other States. The criteria of statehood do not entail any obligation on the part of an entity to pursue any particular policy. But there are some new limitations and there is no 'complete' freedom incidental to sovereignty,[324] and a new State may be intensely disliked by others. It is therefore important to remember that, to be a State, an entity does not have to be particularly 'good'.

There is no question that, for example, Rhodesia emerged as a State after UDI: any 'constitutional' problems which allegedly prevented a break with the United Kingdom did not concern international law but pertained to the constitutional law of the United Kingdom, and were unable to affect an objective situation in international society. The successor State, Zimbabwe, has certainly not been perceived as a 'good' State, but blamed for

---

[321] See, 2 ILC *Yearbook* 1960 96

[322] Crawford, J., *The Creation of States in International Law*, Cambridge: CUP, 1979, 10, 131; Chen Ti Chiang, *The International Law of Recognition*, London: Stevens, 1951; Lauterpacht, H., *Recognition, op. cit.*, But see *supra*, in this section, on the role that recognition still plays with regard to diplomatic relations, and further, my *International Law*, 1993, Chapter II.

[323] Crawford, *Creation, op. cit.*, 31; Jessup, P., *A Modern Law of Nations*, ch. 4; Waldock, Sir Humphrey, 106 *RCADI* 1962 ii 138 *et seq.*

[324] See *supra*, in this Part, B III, Prophylactic Rules.

mismanagement and corruption. But this does not detract from its right to statehood.

However, we can discern a difference between an entity which nowadays seeks to emerge as a State – upon which a number of conditions may be imposed, especially with regard to democratic elections[325] – and a State which already exists: a State which is already in existence will not be deprived of its statehood because of deviations from even basic rules of international law. But then, on the other hand, its responsibility will be engaged for any violation of such rules and sanctions may ensue for any unacceptable behaviour.[326]

b) Communications: Right of Transit, Duty to Warn and Right of Contact

When a State enters into contact with other States certain minimum rules on communications become necessary. Such rules concern, for example, the passage of ships through territorial waters. The rules of innocent passage, for example, thus represent specific 'rules of the road'. These are incurred by social necessity and are not 'imposed' by the majority on the minority.[327] The *substance* of the rules concern global communications and all must accept such rules, just as much, on the national scale, even those who do not drive, must respect the rules of the road. However, the Law

---

[325] See, further my *International Law*, 1993, Chapter II.

[326] See *infra*, in this Part, C III, Consequential Rules.

[327] It is thus not the maritime nations legislating for those without a sea-coast; Tunkin misconceives this point, see, 'Coexistence and international law', 95 *RCADI* 1958 1951, 1221; *idem*, 'Remarks on the juridical nature of customary norms', 49 *Calif. LR* 1961 419.

of the Sea and its innocent passage rules may not be immediately relevant[328] to all subjects of international law.[329]

There is probably a general right of 'innocent' passage over land, at least from enclaves and landlocked States. There may have been 'usage' developing such rights[330] but some minimum right, with stringent requirement of 'innocence' – that is to say 'non-military' traffic – is probably always present. A duty to allow passage or transit may follow from another rule, not necessarily entrenched in treaties.[331]

There is also an important *duty to warn* if a State decides to close its ports. Communications between States are naturally governed by rules that are freely adopted by these subjects of the international legal order and States are clearly free to close their ports or, indeed, their airports. But in doing so they probably have a duty to *alert* others. In other words there is a *duty to warn*.[332]

---

[328] *Infra*, Part Three, under I ii, The Doctrine of Legal Relevance.

[329] But landlocked States have a pronounced interest in certain rules, such as those on access, *infra*, in this Part, C II iii c), Further Regimes and C II i b), Duty to Share?

[330] This is one of the few true expressions of 'customary' law, *supra*, in this Part, B II i a) 2, the Notion of Prescription and *infra*, C ii b), The Fallacies of Customary Law.

[331] *Infra*, in this Part, C I ii, Duty to Share. Seidl-Hohenveldern, I., *Völkerrecht*, 3rd ed., 1975 on '*das Recht auf Verkehr*'; Alexandrowicz, Ch., *The Law of Global Communication*, New York: Columbia Univ. Press, 1971; Tabibi, A.H., *Right of Landlocked States to Access to the Sea*, Uppsala: Scandinavian Institute for African Studies, 1973; and *cf.* my Independence, *op. cit.*, 59-75 on transit over land and my article on 'Landlocked States and the Law of the Sea', in *Acta Scandinavia Juris Gentium* 1976. *Contra*, Charpentier, J., 'Le problème des enclaves', SFDI, Colloque 1979, *La frontière*, 1980, 46.

[332] *Cf. supra*, in this Part, B III iv b), duty to warn about environmental disasters,

This rule was illustrated in in *The Nicaragua v United States Case*.³³³ Although not relating to a disaster or any type of danger, it was clear that there is a duty to warn others about the closure of ports.³³⁴ Behaviour of States thus indicate that any State which wishes to close its ports, is under duty to notify others.³³⁵

The duty to warn has its roots in the principle of *foreseeability* which is fundamental to the Rule of Law: only if actors can adapt their behaviour according to clearly known parameters, whether laid down by legal rules or derived from factual situations, can they enjoy what in Europe is called *securité de droit (Rechtssicherkeit, rättssäkerhet)* and which in English law is embodied in the very notion of the Rule of Law.

Rules allowing for contact exist with regard to communication by radio and other means.³³⁶ In the latter case the right to communicate was earlier said to be controlled, or mitigated, by other rules concerning prohibition of propaganda.³³⁷ But the prohibition must always be weighed against the interests to retain the right of freedom of expression, which the State cannot curtail as it has become an entrenched human right.³³⁸ It is highly questionable whether the right to broadcast nowadays has any limits, short of

---

[333] (1986), ICJ *Reports* 1986 and *The Times* 28 June 1986.

[334] *Supra*, in this Part, C I ii, Rules on Mutual Contact.

[335] On the Portendinck incident, see Politis, N., 'Le problème des limitations de la souverainté', *RCADI* i 1926, 96.

[336] *E.g.*, article 31 of the ITU Convention 1865, 56 *BFSP* 1870 294; and ITU Convention 1965 *TIAS* 6267 and my *Law Making, op. cit.*, 223 *et seq*. On limits for transfer, *cf. e.g.* Gotlieb-Dalfeb-Katz, 'Transborder transfer of international information by computers and computer systems', 68 *AJIL* 1974.

[337] Stone, *Control of International Conflict*, 1957, 227.

[338] *Supra*, in this Part, B III v a), Human Rights.

what may agreed to protect young children[339] and the physical limits imposed by wave band rules.[340]

c) Formal Rules on Treaties

Other rules relating to contacts in international society relate to the *form* of treaties. It is convenient for States to adopt uniform rules in this respect, for reasons of social necessity. Here, custom is relevant in so far as practice indicates and identifies other social needs of contact for which procedures are amended. But this does not mean that the rules *constitute* customary law. The rules are adopted by social necessity and any further binding rules must be developed by further agreement.[341] When States establish other units for various purposes, they also endow those units with certain incidental rights related to making contact with other units, in so far as such contacts are made necessary to attain the purposes for which the entities were founded.[342] Such units abide by form and methods of conclusion applying the models of treaties as adopted by States.[343]

---

[339] For example, provisions prohibiting pornography, European Convention on Broadcasting 1989.

[340] Frequencies are allocated by the International Telecommunications Union (ITU), see my *Law Making*, *op. cit.*, Chapter Four.

[341] *Infra*, in this Part, C II i, Promotional Rules.

[342] See my *Law Making*, *op. cit.*, 29 *et seq.* on incidental rights for 'operative acts' and on implied powers in general.

[343] On procedures similar to 'ratification' of agreements by international organisations, see my article on 'Organs of international organisations exercising their treaty making power', *BYIL*, 1962, 421.

II. Supplementing Rules

The substantive entrenching rules described above are supplemented by rules which *either* elaborate the basic rules by 'promotional' rules,[344] adopted by common consent, *or* safeguard the observance of the basic rules by special consequential rules.[345]

i. Promotional Rules

a) Duty to Cooperate?

If we examine the way members of international society behave, we may infer that there does not appear be any general duty to cooperate in international society. States and others remain free to set themselves new targets for contractual[346] action but short of this, or what is incidental to other rules,[347] or what comes under a duty to warn,[348] there do not appear to be any compulsory rules on general cooperation.[349]

Naturally, as numerous international organisations have developed there is now a considerable bulk of rules as to how

---

[344] *Infra*, in this Part, in the following section.
[345] *Infra*, in this Part, C III, Consequential Rules.
[346] See *infra*, in this Part, C II ii c), Further Regimes..
[347] See, *infra*, in this Part, on Duty to Share in the following section.
[348] *Supra*, in the preceding section.
[349] But note that before the demise of communism, certain Soviet writers, traditionally cautious of admitting general obligations, suggested, in what may have been more lip service than a genuinely founded belief, that such a duty to cooperate exists, see Tunkin, G.I., *Law and Force, op. cit.*, 383. As long as such an alleged duty was not formulated, it was hollow and meaningless and could therefore safely be claimed to be 'binding'.

cooperation is conducted by/between such organisations and other actors. But in such an area, rules on cooperation have evolved within an already established framework; outside that type of framework, no general duty to cooperate can be identified.

Certain cooperative action concerns disasters which have already occurred but which demand collective action. Disasters which others cannot ignore may concern draught or famine, as in Ethiopia in the '80s, or an earthquake, as in Mexico in 1985. Mere humanitarian compassion may explain the international response; and the Bandaid private rescue venture in Ethiopia may well illustrate the role of individuals who, disillusioned with the bureaucracy of States and of large organisations, took action themselves.

Another duty to cooperate possibly implies that certain acts, that are necessary to avoid disasters, must be taken. Such preventive action may also include the economic plight of developing countries. Certain measures to this effect are outlined in parts of declarations on the New International Economic Order (NIEO).[350]

b) Duty to Share?

The New International Economic Order, promoted by the United Nations,[351] indicates a further dimension of rules in international society. This novel dimension concerns the redistributive justice

---

[350] GA Resolution 3201 (SVI), 13 ILM 1974 715; *cf.* Resolution on action on the Establishment of NIEO 3202 (SVI), *ibid.*, 720; Resolution on Development and Economic Cooperation 3362 (SVII), 14 *ILM* 1975 1524. See, Hossain K., (ed.), *Legal Aspects of the New International Economic Order*, New York: Nichols, 1980;

[351] See the previous note and, in greater detail, *e.g.* Bedjaoui, M., *Le nouvel ordre économique international*, Paris: UNESCO, 1980.

which attempts to remedy the economic and social plight of developing countries. The trend to now take action to rectify some inequalities,[352] and the fact that States and others behave as if there were substantive rules in this field, may have come about by a mobilisation of effort, much as suggested by one theory. According to this, some degree of inequity must be felt before the major motivating force striving for equity is mobilised.[353]

A dramatic change has now taken place in international society with regard to the treatment of developing countries. Many Resolutions of the General Assembly[354] now assert that natural resources in all countries belong to the members of the territorial State,[355] that international water resources must be shared[356] and that 'all' have a right to the 'common heritage of mankind'.[357]

Such rules are promotional to the welfare of members of international society, but they are binding only in so far as other

---

[352] See *e.g.* Touscouz, J., *Les Nations Unies et le droit international économique*, SFDI, *Colloque de Nice* 1985, 23 *et seq.*

[353] Adams, J., 'Inequity in social exchange' in Berkowitz, L., (ed.), 2 *Advances in Experimental Social Psychology*, New York: Academic Press, 267.

[354] On their legal effect, see extensively, my *International Law*, 1993, Chapter III.

[355] Resolution on Permanent Sovereignty over Natural Resources 1803 (XXVII) 1962; *cf.* Convention on Economic, Social and Cultural Rights, 1966, article 25.

[356] See, *e.g.*, ILA *Yearbook* 1966 486.

[357] See, particularly discussions during the Third UN Conference on the Law of the Sea, GA A/39/504 Add.1 23 October 1984, 69. On 'mankind' rather than 'States' and on the emphasis on the individual, *cf. supra*, under Part One, I ii b), on the Hypothetical Goal and *cf.* Colliard, C.A., in SFDI *Colloque* 1973 189; *cf.* Virally, M., *L'organisation mondiale*, Paris: Colin, 1972, 317; Dupuy, R.J., 'La Convention sur le droit de la mer et le Nouvel Ordre Economique International,' *Impact: Science et Société*, 1983, No.3/4. 335. For a view that 'common heritage of mankind' has little legal meaning and has been abused as a blanket phrase for numerous alleged duties, see my own *International Law*, 1993, Chapter VIII.

States are precluded from appropriating such resources exclusively for themselves. The problem of sharing most acutely concerns resources which do not already belong to a specific State, such as 'common' areas, ocean floor or Outer Space. For States to *share* in these resources, further agreements may be necessary to *assist* some States which lack relevant technological means to benefit from such resources. But other States are not obliged by international law to provide such assistance, unless they assume specific contractual rights to this effect.[358] On the other hand, States which deny their help to less fortunate countries must remember that by withholding assistance, they may contribute to strategically volatile situations which, in turn, may affect their own security or economy.

A State cannot be expected to share *its own* natural resources with anyone without clear and specific consent. On the other hand, there is room for suggesting that common natural resources cannot be appropriated unilaterally by any one State. If such resources are to be shared, it cannot concern title but merely use, and such right of use of resources must be shared equally.[359] Furthermore, *all* States, land-locked as well as seafaring, must have the right to participate.

The 1969 Moratorium Resolution[360] sought to implement the unratified, (at the time of the Resolution, not even finally drafted), Law of the Sea Convention, by claiming that all States

---

[358] See, the Law of the Sea Convention of 1982 which provides for duty to share, for example in the exploitation of the Ocean Floor; because of these far reaching provisions the great sea faring nations chose not ratify the Convention and little was gained by seeking to place the onus of sharing on those who had the right to evade obligations by withdrawing from the Convention.

[359] *Supra*, in this Part, B I iii, on equality as a maxim.

[360] GA Resolution 2574 1969.

and 'physical and juridical' persons, must refrain from all activities of exploitation of the resources of the seabed and ocean floor; moreover, no claim to any part of that area or its resources will be 'recognised'. Yet, such a Resolution cannot have any binding effect *unless* States *agree* on the 'sharing' principles, which at least the great seafaring nations never did, *or* such rules as the Resolution pretend to be binding, already form part of general international law. As indicated above, a general obligation does exist in international law to the effect that no State may *monopolise* resources of the High Seas[361] and that therefore, the Ocean Floor and seabed areas are not open for unilateral appropriation although resources may be available for sharing of use. Thus, a distinction must be retained between sharing resources and allowing certain shared *use* of resources.

c) Programmatic Rules

Certain rules provide for the framework of further action, thus, programmatic rules,[362] a framework within which future implementing measures will be taken. Whether or not this is the result of a possible duty to warn,[363] setting down rules to avoid disasters in the future, or the result of voluntary cooperation by normal promotion for the betterment of conditions, such rules emerge as clearly programmatic.

---

[361] Nor in Outer Space, see my *International Law*, 1993, Chapter VIII.

[362] *Cf. infra*, in Part Three, A ii a), 'Programmatic Declaration for Later Action' and A iii d) on 'Programmatic Declaration for Vague Action'. These two references deal with *acts* that marks the entry into effect of Programmatic Rules.

[363] *Supra*, in this Part, B III iv b), Duty to Warn.

Programmatic rules impose certain concrete but general goals which present themselves as intermediate to the hypothetical goal. The connexity to the hypothetical goal is more pronounced in the field of disarmament. Analysing the contents of recent programmatic resolutions, however, there is clear evidence of linkage of all such resolutions to the hypothetical goal. Yet, the normative contents of programmatic declarations is low and the rules present themselves as agenda rather than as fixed legal obligations.[364]

On the other hand, programmatic rules provide guidelines for further regulation. As they, in some cases, also re-state already emerging law, they are more than mere rules *de lege ferenda*.

ii. Unifying Rules

a) Integration

Cross boundary integration by trade contacts and various types of transactions will have a unifying effect.[365] But the motive and effect of such contacts must not be confused with international rules on such matters. The cause and factual effects of transboundary transactions will always be a much larger sphere that the contents of legal rules on matters of integration.

---

[364] *Infra*, in Part Three, A ii a) and A iii d) on Programmatic Declarations.

[365] Burton, J.W., *Systems, op. cit., passim;* Pescatore, P., *The Law of Integration, Emergence of a New Phenomenon in International Relations Based on the Experience of the European Communities*, Milan, Giuffré; Taylor, P., *The Limits of European Integration*, London: Croom Helm, 1973; Harrison, R.J., *Europe in Question: Theories of Regional International Integration*, London: Allan & Unwin, 1974; de Vree, J.K., *Political Integration*, The Hague: Mouton, 1975.

The root of the term 'integration' is the Latin word *integer* that means 'whole'. Efforts of integration are clearly aiming towards making a 'whole' of some parts: the paramount example is the European Union that is seeking to 'integrate' or 'unite' a number of States. Some of the consequences are not always welcome if integration also means an extinction of national features or traditions and especially if legal structures are replaced by supra-national organs.

b) Institutionalisation of Functions

Integration presupposes common institutions.[366] But the institutional network of international society has other aspects. Certain rules concern the very institutionalisation of functions in international society. Legislative function exists latently in any legal system.[367] International law is, of course, different from other legal systems in so far as it lacks a legislature. But the latent function, exercised in for example treaties between States, is supplemented by an important new type emanating from international organisations. Such organisations may be either inter-governmental or non-governmental and will, by their very existence, contribute to the stabilisation of international society. Within their framework further acts will be taken[368] to promote development of that society. But the fact that these entities exist must be mentioned in this context as

---

[366] *E.g.* Taylor, P., *Integration*, *op. cit.*, in the previous note.
[367] Scelle, G., *Droit*, *op. cit.*, *loc. cit.*
[368] *Infra*, in the next section and on Theory of Acts, in Part Three.

part of the unifying structure of international society. Organisations have a 'managerial' role in international society.[369]

Organisations can be grouped into the very loose type of associations,[370] possibly deprived of personality,[371] and those which form more or less organic 'wholes' with their own structure and functions.[372] Some scholars have studied the organisations with emphasis on an analysis of their 'authoritative structure' and development of bureaucracy.[373] Others have focused more on the problems relating to decision making[374] However, the relevance of organisations in this section of this study is not the subsequent exercise of power which will be considered later[375] but the unifying framework established by the very existence of institutions. Their integrating effect is particularly noticeable in technical matters, by which States become highly inter-dependent, and in the field

---

[369] Pugh, D.S. & Hinings, C.R., (eds.), *Organisational Structure: Extensions and Replications*, Farnborough: Saxon House, 1976; Hickson, D.J. & McMillan, C.J., *Organisations and Nations*, Farnborough: Gower, 1981.

[370] March, J.G., 'The theory of organisational equilibrium' in Etzione, A. & Lehman, E.W., *A Sociological Reader on Complex Organisations*, 3rd ed., 1979, 14.

[371] See *supra*, in Part One, I iii d) 1 and 2, International Organisations.

[372] *Ibid.*, *loc. cit.* and Taylor, P., *Integration*, *op. cit.* and Selznick, P., *Leadership in Administration*, New York: Harper & Row, 1957.

[373] Weber, M., *The Theory of Sociology and Economic Organisations*, 1947; reprinted New York: Free Press, 1997; Perrow, *Complex Organisations*, New York: Random House, 1979; Mayntz, R., *Bürokratische Organisation*, Cologne: Neue Wissenschaftliche Bibliothek, 1968.

[374] See my own *Law Making*, *op. cit.*, *passim*. Cf. Mott, P.E., *Characteristics of Effective Organization*, New York: Harper & Row, 1972; 75; Kuhm, A., & Beam, R.D., *The Logic of Organisation*, San Francisco: Jossey Bass, 1982, 105; Ermacora, F., & Golsong, H., 'Problem der Rechtsetzung durch internationale Organisationen', 10 *Bericht* DGVR, 1971, 1.

[375] *Infra*, in the following section under d).

of customs unions and common markets which tie the economies and production facilities of various States together.

c) Further Regimes

By express agreement States can provide more details on basic rights than those which they incur by social necessity.[376] For example, a vast new area of implementing regulations, expanding basic rules of contact, is found in the 1982 Law of the Sea Convention.[377] This body of final law contains rules on distribution between States,[378] on distributive rules,[379] rules which bear on communications between States,[380] and rules on sharing.[381] Further rules, above the mere *substratum* that follows from social necessity,[382] is added by further consent by promotional rules.

The 1982 Law of the Sea[383] Convention[384] which has not been ratified by the major maritime power, the United States, establishes a 'provisional further regime' to be adopted by States by express agreement. But some claims have already been settled

---

[376] *Supra*, in this Part, B III, Prophylactic Rules.

[377] But note the limited practical importance of this regime, given that the United States has not ratified the Law of the Sea Convention.

[378] *Supra*, in this Part, C II i b), Duty to Share?

[379] *Supra*, in this Part, C I i, Stabilising Rules, Distributive Rules.

[380] *Supra*, in this Part, C I ii, Rules on Mutual Contact.

[381] *Supra*, in this Part, C II i b), Duty to Share?

[382] Note the flexibility of this notion depending on changing values of society, *supra*, in this Part, B III, Prophylactic Rules and *infra*, Part Three, VI ii a) 2, Social Necessity.

[383] There is a vast literature on the Law of the Sea and numerous bibliographies. For the main textbooks see, *e.g.*, O'Connell, D., *The Law of the Sea*, 2 vols.; Oda, *The Law of the Sea in Our Time*, 2 vols., 1986.

[384] 11 *ILM* 1982.

by prescription.[385] The Latin American claims[386] and the Icelandic claims[387] thus appear to have been validated. By now, most States have indicated their clear consent to a 200 mile limit for the EEZ by proclaiming *themselves* such zones.[388]

d) Law Making Rules, Recommendations, Standards and Pre-Standards

By the regulatory power conferred upon them by States, international organisations have a considerable influence on unification of States or groups of States. For example, technical organisations like the UPU, ITU, WHO, WMO, and ICAO have large, well developed law making powers[389] which tie States nearer to each other: it is impossible (and perhaps pointless) for States to break loose from such technical cooperation even though, technically and legally, there always exists a possibility for Member States to denounce their membership. The organisations are not independent or 'superior',[390] for they depend on the initial and previous consent of States, given as *abstract consent*.[391]

---

[385] *Supra*, in this Part, C I i a) 2, The Notion of Prescription.

[386] Szekele, A., *Latin America and the Development of the Law of the Sea*, 2 vols., New York: Oceana, 1976.

[387] *Icelandic Fisheries Case*, (1972), ICJ *Reports*, and my *Independence, op. cit.*, 35.

[388] *Supra*, in this Part, B I iv, Stabilising Maxims.

[389] See in detail, my *Law Making, op. cit., passim*.

[390] Non-technical organisations like the EU cannot invoke any 'supra-nationality' to prevent a State leaving, as Brexit shows: see, *e.g.*, Monaco, R., 'Le comunità sopranazionali nell'ordinamento internazionale', 2 *Scritti in memoria di V.E. Orlando*, 67; Jaenicke, J., 'Die Sicherung des übernationalen Characters der Organe internationaler Organisationen', *ZaöRVR*, 1951, 2. *Cf.* my *Suicide of Europe*, London: Montesa Jagellonica, 2016.

[391] See, for this terminology adopted by me in my *Law Making, op. cit.*, 393: when the States conclude (or adhere to) the basic treaty setting up an organisation in they

Other rules which are not technically binding are often issued by international organisations, NGOs, or national or international bodies and institutes, and may, contain provisional standards, or *pre-standards*, which are often adopted by States to facilitate, for example, cooperation in technical fields. We may here merely think of standards for classification of books,[392] or for hygiene in the treatment of foodstuffs.[393]

Other recommendations may concern practical suggestions for trade patterns, *e.g.* non-reciprocal preference systems introduced by WTO or UNCTAD, that States accept and adopt *in casu*.

A further type of recommendation is aimed at the improved harmonisation of laws or rules in a special region or among members of a specific organisation, again adopted by States and converted from recommendations to obligations by their own consent in the individual case.

From regulatory rules, and from recommendations and provisional standards which by consent *in casu* are converted into regulatory rules, we must distinguish individual decisions by organisations: they are usually only exhortations to refrain from specific action (such as use of force) and, more rarely, exhortations to take measures to remove obstacles to progress in the field of human rights. But such decisions are devoid of law making power although they may be relevant as reminders of prophylactic rules,[394]

---

also agree, in advance, to future rules that the organisation will enact within its mandate, normally laid down in the founding treaty that becomes the 'Constitution' of the organisation.

[392] On IBSN standards, see my *International Law*, 1993, Chapter IV, and my article on 'Legal value of recommendations', *op. cit.*, 15.

[393] See my *International Law*, 1993, *loc. cit.*

[394] *Supra*, in this Part, B III, Prophylactic Rules.

or relevant as programmatic declarations, setting intermediate goals.[395]

iii. Substantive Rules for All Contacts: *lex mercatoria*

International law must provide rules for all types of cooperation between States and between the units they create.[396] Thus, there must also be rules for acts *de jure gestionis* for the exceptional case when agreements between States or other units are not governed by any specific municipal law. There must then also be rules that can be fetched from norm-pools to cover regulation of trade agreements of States and of other subjects.

If States do enter into contact with each other and conclude certain trade transactions, the international legal order must also be able to cater for such behaviour and supply rules for such transactions.

As the International Court of Justice held in the *Serbian Brazilian Loans Case*,[397] contracts concluded by States in their 'private' capacity are either governed by some municipal law or by international rules on the matter. This led some commentators to wonder whether, beside common analogous rules, there is body of '*international private law*' (rather than 'private international law'), *i.e.* a body of rules on private law 'matters', such as trade and loans,

---

[395] *Supra*, in this Part, C II i c), Programmatic Rules and *infra*, Part Three, A ii a) and A iii d).

[396] If such contacts are necessary to attain the objectives for which units were created, *supra*, in this Part, C II i c), Programmatic Rules.

[397] (1929) PCIJ Series A. No. 20 and 21, 41.

but existing as a sub-section of a larger notion of international law.[398]

The rules concern, it seems, acts which are taken *de jure gestionis* by States. It is in this context that material general principles of law,[399] derived from municipal systems, are uplifted to form part of international law[400] and probably supplemented by separate rules to form an independent body of rules. There is evidence in practice that relevant rules in international law exist for transactions that take place between States and that are not subjected to any specific municipal laws.[401]

The main right and freedom of parties to contracts is to chose which ever applicable law they consider appropriate, and this also applies to States. On the other hand, as Lord Denning stressed in the famous *Trendtex Case*, concerning purchase of cement,[402]

> 'If a government ... buys ... boots or cement as a commercial transaction, that government should be subjected to all rules of the market place.'[403]

The *Institut de droit international* considered the matter of applicable law in the case of contracts between States and private

---

[398] See my *Law Making, op. cit.*, 184 *et seq.*
[399] *Supra*, in this Part, B II, General Principles.
[400] Verdross, A.v.,'Les principes généraux du droit dans le système des sources de droit international', *Hommages Guggenheim*, 1968, 521.
[401] See, on this *infra*, in this Part, B II iii on Substantive General Principles.
[402] *Cf. Trendtex Trading Corp v Central Bank of Nigeria* , CA 1977 2 *WLR* 356.
[403] The State would thus not have any right to immunity; the question whether the Central Bank was organically part of the State structure was held less relevant than the business nature of the transaction.

persons,[404] and contracts between international organisations and private persons.[405] Many pointed out that it is difficult to give any precise contents to a *lex mercatoria* governing international contracts.[406] But, depending on how 'public' international law is defined,[407] international contracts could probably be submitted to the rules of 'public' international law.[408]

The problem of contracts between international organisations and private persons is slightly different.[409] Also international organisations can act *de jure privatorum*,[410] not necessarily subjecting their agreements to any municipal law. The rules on these matters must then be located in the international legal system. Such rules on action *de jure gestionis* could also provide substantive rules for application by international enterprises,[411] if they chose 'international law' as the law of their contracts.[412] Contracts between international organisations and private persons have, however, other peculiarities than contracts between States and private persons in so far as they sometimes are more akin to contracts between States and their own nationals.[413]

---

[404] *Report* by van Hecke, G., 57 *Annuaire* 1977 i 192.
[405] *Report* by Valticos, N., *Annuaire* 1977 i 1, 132.
[406] *E.g.*, Batiffol, H., *ibid.*, 212.
[407] Lalive, P., *ibid.*, at 226. See, *supra*, in this Part, A ii, on our view that public and private international law both form part of 'international law'.
[408] *E.g.*, Doehring, K., *ibid.*, 216.
[409] *Report* by Valticos, N., *Annuaire* 1977 i 1, 132.
[410] *Branno v Ministry of War*, ILR 1955 757 and my *Treaty Making, op. cit.*, 55.
[411] *Supra*, Part One, I ii b) 12 and 13, under National Private Bodies and International Companies.
[412] See, *Institut de droit international*, Resolution, article 4, 60 Annuaire, 1983, 106.
[413] Virally, *ibid.*, 189.

Multinationals have also been discussed by the *Institut* in the context of applicable law,[414] but in the case of multinationals, the problem of rules governing their conduct, particularly in developing countries,[415] has over-shadowed the less practical problem of applicable law.[416]

a) 'Filling in' Rules

As we have seen above, certain *formal* general principles form part of the binding *intrinsic law* of international society.[417] But, in arbitrations, (a useful mechanism to resolve international disputes expecially in trade and investment matters), the *substantive* general principles are of great use.

From time to time, courts, and especially arbitration tribunals, have to resort to 'general principles' where there are gaps or *lacunae* in the material rules of substantive international law. But here the term 'general principles' is used in a different sense than the formal and procedural 'general principles' that we have analysed above.

There are thus times when courts 'borrow' substantive rules from various sources and then call these prescriptions 'general principles'. Then, the term implies something else, namely material rules derived from a variety of national systems. Thus, when scholars speak about 'substantive general principles of international law', they mean rules that have been extracted from a *multitude of national legal systems* as the lowest common denominator. It is

---

[414] *Report* by Goldmann, 57 *Annuaire* i 266, 318 and Resolution ii 338.
[415] *Supra*, Part One, I iii d) 14, Multinationals.
[416] *Institut de droit international*, *Annuaire*, 60 1983 ii 338, Resolution.
[417] See, *supra*, in this Part, B II iii.

clear that arbitration tribunals actually do contribute to considerable clarification of rules of international law by resorting to substantive general rules.[418] Such tribunals also highlight situations, when they face unacceptable provisions in a foreign law and rightly see themselves obliged to disregard such material rules.[419]

It is important to stress, in the context of 'filling in' rules, that in a 'normal dispute', parties have very often already chosen the forum and the applicable law in an arbitration clause in a contract. First, of all, as mentioned above, the question of supplementing any chosen legal system only becomes relevant *if there is a dispute* and furthermore, *if the parties do not resolve that dispute amicably.* The question of applying the chosen law *and* of verifying if any 'filling in' rules are needed, only arises if and when a dispute has reached a court or an arbitration tribunal.

Finding the common law, or the appropriate law for a dispute, occasionally requires supplementing what the parties to a transaction have foreseen. Sometimes a tribunal or a court may need further material rules to decide a dispute. When such further substantive rules are sought to decide a dispute, we have a wide

---

[418] Berger, K., 'General principles of law in international commercial arbitration: How to find them – How to apply them, 5 *World Arbitration & Mediation Review* 2011, 97; Derains, Y., 'The application of transnational rules in ICC arbitral awards, 5 *World Arbitration & Mediation Review*, 2011, 173; Friedmann, W., 'The uses of 'general principles' in the development of international law', 57 *AJIL*, 1963, 279; Nolan, M.D.& Sourgens, F.G., 'Issues of proof of general principles of law in international arbitrations', 3 *World Arbitration & Mediation Review*, 2009, 505.

[419] See, Paulsson, J., 'Enclaves of justice' 1, *University of Miami Law Legal Studies Research Paper* No. 2010-29, available at http://papers.ssrn.com/sol3/papers.cfm?abstract_id=1707504. *Idem*, 'Unlawful laws and the authority of international tribunals', 23 *ICSID Foreign Investment Law Journal*, 2008, 215, 221-22.

range of choice of an appropriate legal system.[420] But at some stage we may consider the *common basic rules of the main law systems*.[421] Sometimes an arbitration tribunal or a court, needs to resort to such common rules, as supplementary material to decide a dispute.

Some of the Drafters of article 38 of the PCIJ worried that the Permanent Court may pronounce a *non liquet* (*i.e.* not accepting a Case because of lack of competence) if there were no available legal rules to apply.[422] Yet, a court or tribunal is 'never out of a law': courts, investment and arbitration tribunals will always have the right to resort to any source to access 'filling in' rules[423]; this is an implied right, automatically acquired when the court or tribunal was created.[424] The exercise of such power does not depend on any specific authorisation but is available to all courts and tribunals in order to ensure that justice is made: it is thus an *implied power to supplement applicable law*, given to courts and

---

[420] *Filartiga v Pena-Irala*, 630 F.2d 876, 887 n.20 (2d Cir. 1980); see further also *Hinderlider v La Plata River & Cherry Creek Ditch Co.*, 304 U.S. 92, 110 (1938); U.S. courts variably 'apply Federal law, state law, and international law, as the exigencies of the particular case may demand.'; *The Nereide*, 13 U.S. 388, 423 (1815), stating that 'the Court is bound by the law of nations which is a part of the law of the land'.

[421] Weil, P., 'Principes généraux du droit', *Mélanges Goldman*, Paris: Litec, 1982, 386.

[422] So Hagerup, Representative of Norway, PCIJ, *Procès-verbaux des séances du Comité consultatif des juristes 16 juin – 24 juillet 1920*, 296 et seq.

[423] *Infra*, in this Part, C II iii on 'Filling in Rules' and on '*lex mercatoria*'.

[424] See, *mutatis mutandis*, on the *theory of implied powers* of international organisations, always entitled to all necessary action for the purposes for which the organisations were created: my *Law Making, op. cit.*, Ch. 1.

tribunals in conjunction with their creation and establishment in international society.

Material general principles may then provide *substantive* rules, for example rules on notions not known in all legal systems, such as the concept of *trusts*,[425] in the sense it is understood in English law; a Court may then 'borrow' substantive general rules on such matters from the relevant national system(s).

The Courts of the EU have occasionally 'borrowed' national rules to complete the 'applicable' law in a Case.[426] In the *AM & S Case*[427], before the Court had recourse to general principles concerning *privileged communications* and *confidentiality*, that served to fill gaps in the applicable law.[428]

A court might even deduce a substantive rule by finding that that the same rule exists in a number of jurisdictions: in the *Filartiga Case*,[429] a tribunal in the United States found that torture was forbidden in 55 States in the United States. The Court then decided that there is a 'general principle' forbidding torture.

However, one should watch out for the danger of extracting rules from a great number of national legal systems, as such rules

---

[425] *South-West Africa Case* (*Ethiopia v South Africa, Liberia v South Africa*) ICJ *Reports*, 1950.

[426] This was so even in the very first Community, The European Coal and Steel Community, (*la Communauté Européenne du Charbon et de l'Acier*), see Reuter, P., 'Le recours de la CJCE à des principes généraux de droit', *Mélange Rolin*, Paris: Pedone, 1964, 263; and *Cases 7/56 & 3-7/57, Reports*, 1957, 81.

[427] 2 *CMLR* 1982 264.

[428] *The AM&S Case* (*Europe v The Commission of the European Communities*) (1982), 155/79, *Reports*, 1982, 1575; *Cf.* Janis, M.W., *An Introduction to International Law*, Leiden: Kluwer, 1988, 49.

[429] *The Filartiga Case* (*Filartiga v Pena-Irala*), [1980], 630 F 2d 876 (2d Circ).

might become diluted by compromises and simplifications.[430] The task to pull out similar rules from national systems is obviously easier if we limit ourselves to a few States, possibly with similar socio-economic systems. For example, in Western Europe, before the fall of communism, there was considerable difference in attitudes between States in Western and Eastern Europe. Thus, it was argued in the *British Nationalisation Case*,[431] that the right to receive *adequate*, *prompt* and *effective* compensation in the case of nationalisations was guaranteed to citizens of the then European Communities: such a *rule could be deduced from all the legal systems of Western Europe*.

After the fall of communism, it is indeed clear that compensation in the case of nationalisations is now a general principle of universal application: in other words, the right of private property is now an entrenched human right.[432] Some ex-communist States have even now offered indemnities for nationalisations in 1945.[433]

However, by borrowing rules from national systems, courts must not introduce further obligations than those of which the

---

[430] There is a comparable problem when national courts apply general principles derived from international law: Guggenheim, P., 'Die Anwendung allgemeiner Rechtsprinzipen des Völkerrechts im Landesrecht', in Leibholz, G. & Bracher, K.D., *Die moderne Demokratie und ihr Recht*, Tübingen, (Mohr), 1966, 702.

[431] *The Lithgow Case* (*Sir William Lithgow & Autres v United Kingdom*), (1986), ECHR, Reports, 1986. Astonishingly, the majority of the Court did not accept this proposition about compensation for nationalisation of private property, see the Judgment of 8 July 1986. Furthermore, this Case was not even reported in the *Financial Times*.

[432] See, *infra*, in this Part B III v a). We may disregard other views by the few remaining communist States.

[433] US Dept. of State, https://2001-2009.state.gov/p/eur/rls/or/93062.htm.

parties were aware. To do so could endanger the *Rule of Law* and the security under the law to which all subjects are entitled.

In this work, we set out certain intrinsic rules without which international society cannot function. *Formal* general principles belong to this category. *Substantial*, or *substantive*, or, indeed, *material* general principles are generally not *intrinsic* in the international legal system: such material rules, borrowed from national systems or forming part of international law, are very often optional and parties are usually free to decide on the choice of applicable rules. It is important to stress the difference between the two types of 'general principles', as the terminology of some writers is sometimes confusing in this respect.

b) The Quest for a *lex mercatoria*

There have, in the past, been some attempts to search for an international *lex mercatoria*[434] but the problem seemed earlier to be of limited practical importance. Yet, it is important for international lawyers to consider the conceptual classification of such rules.

Problems arise with increasing frequency as many agreements recently concern what we may call 'culturally different legal systems'.[435] On the other hand, for there to be a concrete problem about the search for the law to be applied to an inter-State contract, there has to be a *dispute*, and, secondly, this *dispute must come*

---

[434] *Cf. supra*, in this Part, B II iii b) and *infra*, in this section; *cf.* Lando, O., 'Lex mercatoria', *ICLQ* 1984 747; Baxter, R., 'International commercial law and international business questions', *ICLQ* 1985 538.

[435] *Cf.* See, Paulson, J., 'Unlawful laws and the authority of international tribunals', 23 ICSID, *Foreign Investment Law Review*, 2008, 215.

before a court or tribunal. And, thirdly, for there to be a problem, the parties must have refrained from choosing (as they are free to do)[436] any specific municipal system for their contract. In discussions about these problems commentators appear not to consider such simple questions about the scenario before a problem becomes concrete.

To use general principles as substantive rules is more common in the case of arbitrations. An arbitration tribunal often has permission by the parties to resort, in the case of need, to supplement substantive rules that correspond to the lowest common denominator of national legal systems. General principles, functioning as substantive rules can thus be used *ad hoc*, from time to time, to furnish the applicable legal rules in a specific dispute.

For almost a century the International Institute for the Unification of Private Law (UNIDROIT) has been modernising, harmonising, and coordinating the rules of private commercial law to formulate uniform law instruments, and numerous treaties have been concluded between States that effectively do the same.[437]

---

[436] As States often do: see Loan Agreement between Malawi and Denmark of 1966 and Mann, F., 'About the proper law of contract between States, *International Studies*, 1973; 241. For other examples, see *idem*, 'Another agreement between States under national law?, *AJIL* 1974 490; *Cf.* Verhoeven, J., 'Traités ou contrats entre Etats? *Sur les conflits de lois en droit des gens*,' *Journal de droit international*, 1984.

[437] See, Hague Conference on Private International Law, Feb. 15-17, 2012, Conclusions and Recommendations on Access to Foreign Law in Civil and Commercial Matters, available at http://www.oas.org/dil/private_international_law.htm. *Cf.* Convention for the Unification of Certain Rules Relating to International Transportation by Air, opened for signature Oct. 12, 1929, 49 Stat. 3000, 137 *LNTS* 11; Protocol to Amend the Convention for the Unification of Certain Rules Relating to International Carriage by Air Signed at Warsaw on 12 October 1929, opened for signature Sept. 28, 1955, 478 *UNTS* 371; Convention, Supplementary to the Warsaw Convention, for the Unification of Certain Rules Relating to International Carriage by Air

There has been an ongoing process of harmonising rules of international commercial law to serve as useful tools in international society. Arbitration procedures are, of course, much assisted by such efforts. The quest to find appropriate substantive rules is always a challenge in such cases, if the parties have not chosen a specific adequate law for the court to apply.

It must be noted though that parties that rely on, for example, the *'Uniform Customs and Practices for Documentary Credit (UCP)'* published by the International Chamber of Commerce, have not, by reference to such an instrument, actually chosen a specific 'law', although they might have been under the impression of having exercised their right of choice of applicable law. In one Case the Court thus refused to enjoin payment on an international letter of credit despite the fact that the contract had been expressly made subject to the *'Uniform Customs and Practices for Documentary Credit (UCP)'*, published by the International Chamber of Commerce, which allowed issuance of an injunction under the given circumstances. The Court held that the UCP was not the law

> 'of a foreign jurisdiction, but rather . . . a compendium of commercial practices published by the International Chamber of Commerce'.

Therefore, a provision in a letter of credit that the UCP governs the transaction" did not 'prevent application of California's Commercial Code.'[438]

Performed by a Person Other than the Contracting Carrier, Sept. 18, 1961, 500 *UNTS*. 31.

[438] *Trans Meridian Trading Inc. v Empresa Nacional de Comercializacion de Insumos*, 829 F.2d 949, 953-54 (9th Cir. 1987).

Arbitration practice shows thus that substantive principles deduced from multiple systems function in quite an efficient way to resolve conflicts, especially when investment problems or other commercial issues are at stake.[439] This does not necessarily mean that such 'borrowed' rules would be *identical* to those in national legal systems.

Nor does the system of borrowing substantive rules suggest that there are *lacunae* in the international legal system because international law is 'less developed' than national law, as is sometimes claimed.[440] International law is a highly sophisticated system with mechanisms for every eventuality. It is a far more flexible and dynamic set of rules than most national legal systems.

III. Consequential Rules

Viewed in relation to a hypothetical goal,[441] certain entrenching,[442] and specifically certain prophylactic[443] rules can be classified as empirically viable. These have been described above, not in any detail but as forming part of a systematic table. Once such

---

[439] *Sapphire International Petroleum v National Iranian Oil Company*, *ILR*, 136; *British Petroleum Company (Libya) v The Government of the Libyan Arab Republic*, (1979), 53 *ILR*, 297; *Saudi-Arabia v Arabian American Oil Company (Aramco)*, (1963), 27 *ILR* 1963, 117; *Texaco-Calasiatic v Libya*, (1977), *JDI*, 1977, 350;

[440] See *supra* in Part One, under I vi, A primitive law?

[441] *Supra*, Part One, I ii b), The Hypothetical Goal.

[442] *Supra*, in this Part, C, Entrenching Rules, comprising Prophylactic and Stabilising Rules.

[443] *Supra*, in this Part, B III, Prophylactic Rules.

entrenching rules exist, subsidiary rules emerge to safeguard the subsistence of the main rules. Respect for the basic rules is guaranteed by the rule of obligation coupled with 'solidarity' rules.[444] Other rules prescribe specific and immediate consequences for violations. These ensuing rules are thus 'consequential'.

i. Correctional Rules

a) Sanctions

1. General Nature

Certain consequential rules have as their purpose to correct misbehaviour implying a violation of a main rule. These are rules on, for example, sanctions. Rules on sanctions concern the *form* and *manner* in which the duty to uphold fundamental rules is crystallised. But sanctions can also concern the violation of lesser rules of international law.

Sanctions cannot be studied without a close reference to the prophylactic rules surveyed earlier.[445] But they present themselves as justifications or exemptions from the prohibitions of the use of force in that category. Therefore, although sanctions imply, in many cases, the *authorised* use of force, these measures are imposed as a reaction to a violation of an antecedent binding rule, for example the one forbidding the use of force. Sanctions are thus measures which

---

[444] *Infra*, Part Three, VI iii a) 5, Solidarity Rules.
[445] *Supra*, in this Part, B III, Prophylactic Rules.

enforce international law.[446] Contrary to municipal law there are no centrally organised sanctions in the international legal system. Yet, the function of sanctions is required in any legal system[447] and there is an effective way of imposing such measures in international law. It must be emphasised that the legal character of international law is not affected by the absence of organised sanctions.[448] The question of the basis of obligation is thus a distinct problem[449] and not necessarily dependent on the presence of sanctions although

---

[446] See, in general, Kunz, J.L., 'Sanctions in international law', *AJIL* 1960 324; Kelsen, H., 'The nature of international law: International delicts and international sanctions, in *Principles of International Law*, ed. Tucker, 1966, 3; Brierly, J.L., 'Sanctions', in *The Basis of Obligation in International Law and Other Papers*, Oxford: OUP, 1958, 201; Brown-John, C.L., *Multilateral Sanctions in International Law*, New York: Praeger, 1975; Coplin, W.D., 'The enforcement of international law: The operation of sanctions', in Lauterpacht, H., *The Function of International Law*, Oxford: OUP, 1966, 19; Kuyper, P.J., *The Implementation of International Sanctions*, The Hague: Sijthoff & Noordhoff, 978; Hsu Mo, 'The sanctions in international law', 35 *Grotius Society Transactions* 1949 3. On economic sanctions, see, MacDonald, R.St.J., 'Economic sanctions in the international system', *CYIL* 1969 61; Barber, J., 'Economic sanctions as a policy instrument', *Int. Aff.* 1979 367; Mersky, R.M., *Transnational Economic Boycotts and Coercion*, New York: Oceana, 1978; Derpa, R.M., *Das Gewaltverbot der Satzung der Vereinigten Nationen und die Anwendung nicht-militärischer Gewalt*, 1979; *cf.* my *Independence, op. cit.*, 158-159; *cf.* my *Finance and Protection of Investments in Developing Countries*, 2nd ed., 1987, 76 *et seq.*

[447] *Cf.* on the necessity of legislative functions, *supra* and Scelle, *Droit, op. cit., loc. cit.*

[448] *Cf.* Kruger, in *Festschrift Spiropoulos*, 1957 p 265 on the normative force of factual situations. *Cf.* Fitzmaurice who states that the foundation of authority of international law resides in the fact that States recognise the system as binding and the legal order does therefore not have to be coupled with sanctions to be binding, see Fitzmaurice, G., 'The foundations of the authority of international law', *MLR*,1956, 1.

[449] See *infra*, Part Three, VI iii a), Variability of the Basis of Obligation.

the presence of such coercive measures are likely to strengthen the basis of obligation whichever we conceive that to be.

2. The Two-Fold Nature of Sanctions

Sanctions in international law may imply measures taken to induce a subject of the international system to cease breaking legal rules of that order, or, to punish the subject for acts in the past. Sanctions can thus be either intervening as primarily corrective measures in the midst of illegal acts taken by a subject to change the flow of events from a certain point, and compel that subject to act lawfully in the future. Sanctions can also intervene *ex post facto* when the acts no longer occur; in this latter case sanctions have a purely punitive function.

It may be added that sanctions in international society rarely have the intended effect of correcting subjects that have violated international rules but often cause major suffering to the poorest in society.

3. The Subjects and Objects of Sanctions

The intervention of sanctions presupposes that an international legal rule has been violated. If such a violation has taken place the international system allows for certain countermeasures to be taken.

The first question that must be answered before sanctions are introduced is thus: What was the offence? Was it an offence? The type of sanction allowed by the legal order will obviously depend on whether a violation actually took place and, if it did, on what type of rule was violated. Furthermore, the subjects and objects affected by international sanctions will again depend on which type of norm was violated.

4. Sanctions and the Use of Force

Certain sanctions may be taken by States but international organisations and even individuals may play a role in the system of sanctions.

Sanctions may sometimes involve the use of 'reprisals',[450] entailing measures that would have violated international law if it were not for the justification as legitimate sanctions. This highlights the intricate relationship between prophylactic and correctional rules: very often there are conflicting statements as to the alleged true 'facts' and it turns on these 'facts' whether the recourse to force is 'legitimate'.

---

[450] On the distinction between reprisals against States and against individuals, see my *Law of War, op. cit.*, 254 *et seq.* On reprisals in general, see Bardeleben, H. v., *Die zwangsweise Durchsetzung im Völkerrecht*: Giese & Strupp, 1930; Colbert, E. S., *Retaliation in International Law*, New York: King's Cross Press, 1948; Haumant, A., *Les repressailles*, Paris: Girard, 1934, Hindmarsh, *Force in Peace*, Cambridge, Mass.: Harvard Univ. Press, 1933; Keller, L.v., *Die nicht-kriegerische militäre Gewaltmassnahme*, Berlin: Vahlen, 1934; Kelsen, 12 ZaöRVR, 1932 481; Le Fur, L., *Des Represailles en temps de guerre*, Paris: Sirey, 1919; Politis, N., 38 *Annuaire de l'Institut*, 1934, 1; Rapisardi-Mirabelli, A., *La ritorsione*, Venice: Ferrari, 1919; Schütze, H.A., *Die Repressalien unter besonderer Berücksichtigung der Kriegsverbrecherprozesse*, Bonn: Rechsvergl. Untersuchungen, 1950; Schumann, E., *Die Repressalien*, Rostock: Hinstorff, 1927; Strupp, ii *Mélanges Mahaim*, 1935 341; Verdross, A., v., *Die völkerrechtliche Kriegshandlung und der Strafanspruch der Staaten*, Vienna: Engelmann, 1920. Reprisals can also imply acts against individuals, Kalshoven, F., *Belligerent Reprisals*, Leyden: Sijthoff, 1971; *cf.* Albrecht, 'War reprisals in the War Crime Tribunals and in the Geneva Convention of 1949', 47 *AJIL* 1953 590.

Other correctional rules concern 'retorsion' which is said to involve lesser measures which themselves do not violate international law (if they are not justified as means of sanction). But if they are of such nature they do not need 'justification' anyway, and the whole category appears somewhat superfluous as a notion. The concept of retorsion postulates, for example, on the part of States, a duty not to be 'unpleasant' to each other; and there is clearly no such duty. Claims as to the existence of such minor details of behaviour will only water down or diminish other 'true' duties of the members of international society.

b) Institutionalised Correction

Sanctions may be imposed through an institutionalised body such as the United Nations. According to the general rules of the Charter all sanctions involving use of force should be channelled through the United Nations: self-defence under article 51 of the Charter is a mere temporary right 'until' the United Nations takes action.[451] The peace keeping operations of the Organisation[452] may be perceived, as its name indicates 'keeping' the peace rather than correcting a wrongdoing and 'restoring' the peace. If one conceives

---

[451] Note the inertia of the UN failing to act swiftly in the Falklands affair, which might have justified United Kingdom to send a Task Force in May 1983; *cf.* condemnation of the rescue operation by the United States in the Iran hostage crisis in 1980 and the condemnation of United States 'self-defence' against Nicaragua in 19834 by the ICJ, *Nicaragua v United States*, ICJ *Reports*, 1986 and *The Times* 28 June 1986.

[452] Higgins, R., *United Nations Peace Keeping, op. cit.*; Cassese, A., *United Nations Peacekeeping*, Alphen aan den Rijn: Sijthoff & Noordhoff, 1978.

the situation in that way, rules on peacekeeping belong to the section on 'stabilising rules' above.[453]

But the action of the United Nations can perhaps more adequately be seen as a correctional measure, although one must be aware of the extreme limited powers that the Organisation has to change, rather than maintain, a *status quo*.

Collective sanctions by States can also be 'endorsed' by the United Nations and thus receive an institution imprint.[454]

ii. Settlement Rules

Rules on methods of settlement, by conciliation, mediation, arbitration or judicial decision appertain to the category of consequential rules. These rules provide for the *framework* of settlement and for the *penalties* (or other measures) that may be imposed on the guilty party. However, the substantive rules that are used in such settlements to ascertain whether or not international law has been violated, are derived from the basic rules set out above,[455] supplemented by any promotional rules applicable between the parties.

---

[453] *Supra*, in this Part, C I, Stabilising Rules.

[454] *Cf.* sanctions against Rhodesia, *e.g.*, GA Resolutions 2024 (XX) 1965; 2151 (XXI) 1966; 2262 (XXII) 1967; 2383 (XXIII) 1968; 2505 (XXIV) 1969; 2652 (XXV) 1970; 2769 (XXVI) 1971; 2945 (XXVII) 1972; 2946 (XXVII) 1972; 3115 (XXVIII) 1973; 3116 (XXVIII) 1973; 3297 (XXIX) 1974; 3298 (XXIX) 1974; 3396 (XXX) 1976; 3397 (XXX) 1976; 31/154 A and B, 1976; 32/116 A and B, 1977; 33/38 A and B 1978 and 34/192 1979; sanctions against South Africa, *e.g.* GA Resolutions 36/172 B and D 1981 on sanctions in general and arms embargo; 37/69 1982 Cf. 31/6 K 1976. 32/105 K 1977, 33/183 O 1978, 34/93 Q 1979, 35/206 Q 1980 on foreign investment.

[455] *Supra*, in this Part, B, Intrinsic Rules.

a) Institutional Judicial Rules

The establishment and management of international courts and tribunals institutionalises the judicial function in international society. Naturally, only a partial institutionalisation has taken place of the judicial function which is latent or inherent in the international legal order.[456] Courts and tribunals will apply their own procedural rules, in many cases developed by analogy to municipal rules of court procedure.[457]

On substantial issues courts and tribunals may pronounce on sharing[458] or demand specific action to be taken. In this area there is an important interaction between acts creating the court or tribunal, acts adhering to its jurisdiction and acts by the court or tribunal itself, producing a decision for the behaviour of the parties. But this decision does not set down principles[459] of general application. International courts and tribunals are not law makers in the international system even if Anglo-Saxon lawyers, by analogy

---

[456] Scelle, *Manuel*, *op. cit.*, *loc. cit.*

[457] See, on the right of intervention, Rules of Procedure of the ICJ article 62; *Libya v Malta*, (1984), ICJ *Reports*, 3; Davì, A., *L'intervento davanti della Corte Internazionale di Giustizia*, Naples: Jovene, 1984; Decaux, E., *L'intervention*, SFDI, Colloque Lyon 1986; but see for hesitation on analogies, Bastid., S., L'intervention devant les juridictions, *Revue politique et parlamentaire*, 1929; on injunctions, Rules of procedure of the ICJ article; *e.g.* the Order in *The Hostage Case* 15th December 1979, ICJ *Reports* 1979 10; Elkind, J;K., *Interim Measures*; The Hague: Nijhoff; 1981. Injunctions may form the main issue and, if granted, dispose of the main issue, see Pescatore, P., Les mésures conservatoires et les référés, SFDI, *Colloque de Lyon*, *La juridiction internationale permanente*, 1986.

[458] On equality, *supra*, in this Part, B I iii, Contingent Maxims and C I ii b), Duty to Share.

[459] On Substantive General Principles see *supra*, in this Part, B II, General Principles and *infra*, C II iii on Rules for All Cooperation: *lex mercatoria*.

with their internal system, often assume this is the case. A judgment or award is only operative between the parties and may, at the most, elucidate to others the law as it was applied in that case.[460]

In recent years the ICJ has reduced its important work as a jurisdictional Court as numerous cases have merely called on the Court to act as a 'surveyor', drawing delimitation lines without applying much substantive law. In so far as questions of delimitation are laid down by the ICJ by equitable principles which by their nature only operate *in casu*, the ICJ has further reduced its role as a guide on generally applicable rules.

b) Rules on Penalties

The correctional rules of international society have serious limitations. Courts and tribunals can only impose consequences to which States have previously agreed. Thus, the jurisdiction of the ICJ depends on previous adherence to the Optional Clause or the express consent to adjudication *in casu*. As a result, only penalties that States see fit to impose on themselves can ensue. They may be ordered to restore a situation, pay reparation[461] or possibly 'apologise'.[462] Individual delinquents before international courts may also incur penalties in accordance with what States consider appropriate.[463]

---

[460] *Cf.* Condorelli, L., 'L'autorité de la décision des juridictions internationales permanentes', SFDI, *Colloque de Lyon*, 1986.
[461] *Chorzow Factory Case* (1928), PCIJ, *Series* A No. 17 33.
[462] E.g. *The I'm Alone*, 3 RIAA 1609;
[463] *Nuremberg Charter*, Principle VI; *Tokyo Charter*, article 5.

PART THREE: OPERATION OF RULES

I. Theory of Acts

If, then, rules exist in the above-mentioned categories in international society, these rules must have come into being in some way. The *intrinsic rules* enter into effect automatically as set out above, as soon as there is a legal system. But all other rules? We submit that they are the result of legal acts of the members of international society. These members must also be able to take acts to manifest their will to bring about revision and change of the rule system.

i. The Notion of a 'Legal Act'

In effect, a 'legal act' in the international legal order could be viewed as

> '*une manifestation de volonté d'un ou plusieurs sujets de droit international à laquelle une norme cet ordre juridique rattache des conséquences correspondantes à la volonté.*'[1]

---

[1] A 'manifestation of will' of one or several subjects of international law to which a norm of this legal order attaches consequences corresponding to (this) will, Bastid, S., *Cours de droit international public*, Paris: Univ. de Paris, 1966-1967, 364.

It is thus an international rule that lends efficacy to the act.[2] But, in turn, the act can give rise to international legal rules: if, for example, an act concerns the conclusion of a treaty establishing a regime or in other ways implies the consent to specific regulation, it is the act that will initialise the operation of these further rules. Other acts, may, in a similar way, enable further rules to emerge within the framework of an organisation to regulate further behaviour.[3]

In the legal language of civil law countries – not necessarily shared by Anglo-Saxon jurisprudential legal vocabulary – one can distinguish between an 'act' (meaning an individual measure designed for a particular case) and a 'regulation' (designed to be susceptible to recurring application). Only the second category is usually able to generate norms and rules.[4] But the term 'act' is not normally interpreted that strictly[5] but thought to cover both types. The concept of an 'act' is thus broad enough to cover both individual decisions and regulations; for a regulation is itself issued by an act. On the other hand, a 'legal act' has often been restricted to those which actually produce rights and obligations[6] and the production of such rights and obligations have been thought to be equivalent to the creation of a norm.[7]

However, we have preferred to interpret the word 'norm' to concern only cases where there is a possibility of recurring

---

[2] Sereni, A.P., 3 *Diritto internazionale*, Milan: Giuffré, 1956-1965, 1293.
[3] See my *Law Making, op. cit., passim*.
[4] See, *supra*, in Part Two, under B I, Rules Principles, Norms and Decisions.
[5] Jacqué, J.P., *Eléments pour une théorie de l'acte juridique en droit international public*, Paris: LGDJ, 1972, 64 *et seq*.
[6] *Ibid.*, 70. Disregard, in this context, the Anglo-Saxon terminology of *'Bills'* and *'Acts'* implying measures of national legislation.
[7] *Ibid., loc. cit.*

application, *i.e.* we understand a 'norm' to be a bracket under which future action can be subsumed. Furthermore, we understand an 'act' that engenders rights and obligations to be a 'legal act'. On the other hand, such an act does not necessarily give rise to a 'norm' but leads possibly only to an *in casu* solution, incapable of future reapplication, except as an enlightening precedent.

Thus, not all acts create norms.[8] But, conversely, all norms in international society are the product and result of legal acts. Such norm-producing legal acts are of various nature, types and character.

Rules in the international legal order are, we suggest, usually produced and activated by the juxtaposition of complex acts or varying type and form in converging patterns. The essence of this mechanism of *interactivism* is that individuals and other subjects of international law may jointly take acts that are internationally *relevant*, and these acts may then be capable of producing norms of behaviour.

ii. The Doctrine of Legal Relevance

A variety of actors contribute to the formation of rules in international society. The role of actors is perceived in the society by their very existence. Although not mentioned in traditional textbooks on international law, multinationals or standardising bodies are important entities in international society.

Numerous 'actors' in international society may be authors of legal acts giving rise to the operation of rules. A host of 'actors'

---

[8] On varying normative effect, *infra*, in this Part, B I iii, Types According to Normativity.

are, as we have demonstrated above, 'legal persons'. A legal person is an entity, as we have seen,[9] that can assume legal rights and duties. Many writers are grappling with difficulty to explain that, on the one hand, certain actors are clearly 'there', but, on the other hand, they are held not to possess international personality. Some writers suggest that non-State entities may be subjects 'for certain purposes only'.[10]

In this work, other suggestions are made, based on what we can observe is actually happening in international society. There are certainly numerous 'actors' that enjoy international legal personality. On the other hand, the impact of their behaviour is not always noticeable in international society. In other words, much of what these actors do, is not done on the international scene.

Expressed in a different way, many acts of the entities described above are not *internationally relevant*: often they are acts taken inside a State's legal system, without any international repercussions. Then the acts do not give rise to any situation where international rules are needed. However, all are potential actors in the international sphere, and they must know what the law provides, so that they can act within its framework and limits.

If an individual resorts to usurpation of power of the democratic order of a State[11] or if he resorts to terrorism[12] or genocide[13] his acts become internationally relevant and he may incur personal responsibility for his acts under international law.

---

[9] *Supra*, Part One, I iii d), Entitled Persons.
[10] Brownlie, *Principles*, *op. cit.*, 65.
[11] *Supra*, on democracy, Part Two, B II i c) 1, Hallmarks of States.
[12] *Supra*, Part Two, B III, Prophylactic Rules.
[13] *Supra*, *ibid*, *loc. cit.*

Conversely, if individuals are victims of outrageous violations of basic human rights or of abuse of the democratic process, their situations become internationally relevant.

Many acts are thus not internationally relevant. This is, in fact, normally the case with individuals, groups, and many companies. On the other hand, large portions of international law are not relevant to such individuals or entities.[14]

We submit that there is a presumption that an act has international relevance if it has transboundary effects[15] or if it emanates as a joint act from actors in different States. Thus, acts by States, international organisations and multinationals may be presumed to be internationally relevant.

But the question of relevance is only pertinent when there is a need to *apply* legal rules. In many cases there is no need to apply such rules, unless there is a dispute between certain parties that comes before a court or a tribunal, or unless there is a question of criminal jurisdiction for violation of the basic rules just mentioned. Thus, what is often overlooked, it is only if a dispute comes before a court or a tribunal that a need arises to exactly identify legal rules, and to consider the applicability of 'international' rules.

The degree of relevance is, however, not static. Until recently, international law was thought not to concern intra-State affairs, that is to say the international legal system had nothing to do with 'internal' State matters. The sphere of *the reserved domain*[16]

---

[14] *Supra*, Part One, I iii d) 1-19.

[15] For example, in the case of national 'movements', *cf.* Beloff, M., *Foreign Policy and the Democratic Process*, Baltimore: John Hopkins Press, 1955, 4.

[16] *Cf. supra*, Part One, I ii c) 2 , I iii b) and Part Two C I i a) on Allocation of National Space, See, further, my *International Law and the Independent State*, 1994, London: Gower, *passim* and conclusions at 232.

precluded even discussions about matters within the territory of a State.[17] But long gone are the days when a State could do whatever it wished in its own territory. The competence of a State is now limited by peremptory rules of international law regarding diplomats, human rights of individuals, duties concerning the environment, and free passage.[18]

After the Second World War, and expecially after the the War Crimes Trials, it became clear that individuals cannot escape liability for certain crimes. Conversely, protection of individuals was enhanced to comprise also basic human rights. The continued expansion in this field is noticeable. Thus, a right to democracy appears to have emerged entitling individuals to self-determination, free elections and certain types of government.

Contents of relevance may thus change. But the rule of relevance is basic to the international legal system.

If taken as a relative, rather than as an exclusive, concept, the State-centric paradigm may still serve a useful purpose by supplying one point of focus in international law. Acts taken by States are often the most important types in international society but these acts are supplemented by numerous acts of groups and individuals. International relevance can sometimes be assessed on the basis of the objectives of groups and individuals. Some acts of groups and individuals are thus internationally relevant; others are not. If such persons have the intention to perform, on an *ad hoc* or

---

[17] See, further, my *The International Legal Order*, op. cit.

[18] My *International Law and the Independent State*, London: Gower, 2nd ed., 1994, sets out these limitations of State power as seen from inside the State: the duties to respect the various intrusions in the illimited sovereignty, otherwise only restricted by specific treaties voluntarily entered into by the State.

on a more lasting level, acts which, in their formation or execution, involve groups or individuals in *other* States, or any other entity outside their own State, it would seem probable that their acts were relevant to the system of international law.

Acts are tainted by the quality of their authors. As we have seen, acts taken by States and by international organisations, are *presumed* to be internationally relevant. They will therefore be of a different type than those of individuals and other entities whose acts may only occasionally be relevant to the international system.

Furthermore, acts may give rise to rules which are of limited importance in so far as they only regulate bilateral behaviour of parties on a contractual basis. Such acts do not give rise to general rules and are incapable of being generally normative except for the relationship of the two parties.[19] Certain such acts, for example, contracts between companies, are thus of reduced international relevance.

But non-State entities and individuals only act in international society within a framework laid down by the more powerful units, the States. It is thus States that still lay down the framework of action of others in international society. States do this, not because of any inherent power, but because they form, as structural units, a convenient form of agglomeration of individuals. It is also States which form convenient centres of imputation for various acts in international society.

States can enact rules binding on all entities and individuals. Non-State entities and individuals can devise rules for mutual

---

[19] *Contra* Baxter, R.R., 'The normative value of bilateral treaties', 129 *RCADI* i. 1970 25 at 87-88.

relationships[20] or for 'adoption' by States,[21] but the basic framework is laid down by rules which, in turn, are created by legal acts of States. These acts are of heterogeneous form and contents.

iii. Graduated Scale of Presumption of Consent

If we think in terms of consent, which is convenient and politically necessary in the case of units like States, we may discern a different need for consent to rules depending on their place in our classification. Thus, there appears to be a lighter burden of proof for consent the nearer a rule is to the top of the chart: for the maxims and, at least for the substratum of prophylactic rules; *no specific consent* is necessary. For stabilising rules on mutual contacts, there is arguably less need for clear consent than in the case of promotional rules or correctional rules.

Consent may thus be presumed by mere participation in international society for certain rules.[22] For example, consent to rules on communication or on formalities of treaties, is also presumed, whereas much clearer consent is needed, for elaboration of promotional rules on cooperation or for rules on judicial settlement.

---

[20] *Infra*, in Part Three, B ii a), Permissive Acts.
[21] *Infra*, in this Part, II B iii d), Acts of Adoption.
[22] *Infra*, in this Part, B i a) 1, Passive Participation.

II. Typology of Acts

Acts vary according to the rule areas described above[23] and then fall into distinctive groups. The establishment of new rules for the rights in the national territorial space, jurisdiction or immunity, the creation of a new international organisation, the establishment of an economic zone, or revised rules for the continental shelf, or rules relating to natural resources or economic development will be brought about by a legal act.

Often, however, acts, and engendered rules, have a twofold nature, being at the same time concerned with distributive rules,[24] as well as with promotional rules[25] in the sense that they give special concession to developing nations or other deprived States. Rules relating to different rules may also be brought into existence in different ways.

It is thus in conjunction with 'norm-pools' largely set out above in the previous Part, that deals with large sections of rules for various needs in international society. Among those rules we have noted the different component of *intrinsic law*, *i.e.*, rules on maxims, general principles and prophylactic rules forbidding harm.

These compulsory rules are coupled with a vast network of *extrinsic* or *optional* rules that subjects of international society may select and adopt as necessary rules for their own action or for mutual relationships. Rules from these extrinsic and optional norm-pools are activated by 'legal acts' as described in this Part. There is a great variety of such acts and some complexity in the

---

[23] *Supra*, in Part Two, C I, Stabilising Rules.
[24] *Supra*, in Part Two, C II a), Distributive Rules.
[25] *Supra*, in Part Two, C II i, Promotional Rules.

way they interact. But we can observe that the general optional rules in international society come into effect or are 'activated' in this manner, rather in the fairly obscure and incomprehensible way by 'custom', as alleged in virtually all traditional textbooks.[26]

A. Types According to Substance

i. Types According to the Envisaged Goal

a) Structural Acts

Acts creating the basic structural rules of international society, such as basic rules of distribution of national space or on contacts such as those on immunity, communications or forms of treaties, creation of international organisations, establishment of economic zones or revised rules for the continental shelf, may be classified as 'structural acts'. In a sense therefore, such structural acts merely create a framework for international contacts, a framework which may be elaborated and implemented by further consensual action.

Other structural acts are those which create correctional rules, which clearly need full consent of participating States. International adjudication and arbitration rules are subject to less change than many other rule areas. But by further acts certain details have been clarified.[27]

---

[26] For criticism of the unsatisfactory theories on customary law, see, *infra*, under IV i – vii.
[27] *E.g.* on right to intervene, see *Libya v Malta*, (1984), ICJ *Reports* 1984, 12.

b) Operative Acts

Certain rule areas concern efforts to attain the hypothetical goal. This is particularly the case with promotional rules on international cooperation. In this work, these acts are called 'operative acts' on the lines of other terminology we have adopted for international organisations.[28] These rules are created by clear consensual acts for which express and not implied consent must be present. Unless States give such consent, ensuing declarations will be devoid of normative effect.

ii. Types According to Immediacy

Certain acts visualise the gradual attainment of targets whereas others are prompted, often by recent dramatic events, to prescribe immediately detailed rules.

a) Programmatic Declarations for Later Action

Acts may declare set goals towards which parties should strive.[29] For example, acts may imply laudable efforts to assist or aid.[30]

---

[28] See my *Law Making*, *op. cit.*, *passim*, where I used the term 'primary acts' for all measures taken to set up the internal workings of an organisations, thus rules on headquarters and staff. Distinct from these are what I call in my work, the 'operative acts' that is to say, the acts that the organisation will have to take to attain the objectives for which it was founded. Such 'operative acts' will necessarily vary from organisation to organisation depending on the goal for the entity was created by the founding Treaty. The 'primary acts', on the other hand, are more or less the same in all organisations, see *op. cit.*

[29] *Supra*, in Part Two, C II ii c, Programmatic Rules.

[30] *Supra*, *loc. cit.*

Such acts establish a framework within which future detailed acts may be taken but, because of their generality, they often contain little legal content. Only in so far as there some such content, do they merit to be considered as legal acts at all.[31] However, they are, because of their present frequency in international society, becoming most important: occasionally they present themselves as *pacta de contrahendo*; sometimes they offer, without such a nature, a useful point of reference for future action.[32] They are, from a practical point of view, becoming increasingly important as *guidelines* for action.[33]

b) Responsive Acts

By responsive acts we mean those that spring up after an event and which immediately cater for the need for new rules. Examples may include new rules on Outer Space.[34] Is it primarily acts like these that writers are unable[35] to explain as 'customary law'[36] as rules

---

[31] *Supra, loc. cit.*

[32] Virally, M., 'La valeur des recommandations des organisations internationales', *AFDI*, 1958,

[33] See, in detail, my *International Law*, 1993, Chapter IV and my article on 'Legal value of Recommendations', *op. cit.*

[34] See, *e.g.* the Outer Space Treaty 1967, 610 *UNTS* 205; The Moon Treaty 1979, UN A/34/664.

[35] But McDougal, Lasswell & Vlasic, '*Law and Public Order in Space*' 1963, 227, claim they have succeeded in explaining both customary prescription and *opinio juris* in new space law.

[36] Further, *infra*, in this Part, IV iv, The Fallacies of Customary Law.

'appear'.[37] Short of resorting to contradictory fictions,[38] the quick emergence of such rules cannot be easily explained as 'customary' rules.

We, on the other hand, adopt the view that by *'responsive acts'*, *i.e.* acts responding to a new event, new rules can be immediately created by an *immediate social need*. The form of such acts would often be that of 'parallel recognition'.[39]

In other cases, responsive acts lead to the immediate conclusion of a treaty. Although embassies had been protected for centuries under general international law, the Vienna Convention on Diplomatic Immunity of 1961[40] placed special emphasis on the protection of embassies. Certain provisions were included in their final form – said the negotiators – as a result of attacks on Belgian embassies,[41] following Lumumba's death in February 1961.[42]

Occasionally rules are codified in a treaty after a specific disaster: the lack of life boats in *The Titanic* that sank in 1912 with a great loss of lives, resulted, through such a responsive act

---

[37] Before the relevant treaties States recognised rules as existing: See, discussion in the General Assembly and GA Resolution 1721 (XVI) on International Cooperation in the Peaceful Uses of Outer Space, 16 UN GAOR, Suppl. No. 17, 6 A/5021.

[38] See, *infra*, under C ii b), The Fallacies of Customary Law.

[39] *Infra*, in this Part, II B iii c), Parallel Acts and e) Acts of Recognition.

[40] Article 20.

[41] For example, the burning and plundering of the Belgian Embassy in Cairo.

[42] Sweden, UD, *Report by the Swedish Delegation, Konferensen i Wien 2 mars 14 april 1961 angående diplomatiska förbindelser och immuniteter, Den svenska delegationens slutrapport*, 1961, 19.

in the *SOLAS* (Safety of Lives at Sea) Convention, providing for a compulsory number of life boats.[43]

iii. Types According to Normativity

a) Individual Acts

Individual acts dispose of an immediate issue and are not norm-creating, for to be so, there must be a rule of 'general' and 'abstract' application. In the case of an individual decision, the effect of the act is confined to the addressee of the act. A decision by a court or tribunal belongs to this category.[44] Constitutions of some international organisations have expressly provided for individual acts, sometimes even called 'individual decisions'[45] and in some cases such decisions are explicitly binding.

b) General Acts

General acts are susceptible to recurring application and are the prototypes of rule-generating acts. To this category we may count acts like law making treaties, or regulations by international organisations.

---

[43] See, the SOLAS Convention 1914; now the 'Consolidated SOLAS Convention with the 1988 Protocols, International Maritime Organisation 2014.

[44] *Cf. supra*, Part Two III ii a) on Institutional Judicial Rules: the effect is limited to *inter partes*.

[45] On the European Coal and Steel Community, see, *e.g.* Reuter, P., *La Communauté Economique du Charbon et de l'Acier*, Paris: LGDJ, 1952.

c) Exhortations

A third category are the exhortations of, for example, the United Nations Security Council. These are technically individual acts but do not merely dispose of an issue between the parties but often constitute reminders of an existing rule system, for the general attention of all the members of the organisations. Although devoid of power to take such binding decisions the General Assembly also often uses the occasion to couple its exhortatory recommendations with reminders of duties, at least obliquely addressed to all members. Resolutions of this type often resemble injunctions in national law in so far as they frequently are negative in form imposing restraint of action ('...refrain from the use of force...refrain from certain practices...'). Often such resolutions freeze a situation by imposing a Stand-Still.[46]

Only rarely are such resolutions formulated in a positive manner to demand specific action.

d) Programmatic Declarations for Vague Action

Programmatic declarations, looking as they do to the future, have been discussed in connection with classification according to immediacy of the acts. But they are also relevant in this section as their normative value, unless enhanced by specific consent to take certain action, is at the low end of the scale of normativity. They are not, like individual decisions, lacking in generality; on

---

[46] *E.g.* Resolution 1962 (XVIII) 1963 on extra atmospheric activities.

the contrary, they are so general in form that it is for that reason they are often devoid of normative contents.

B. Types According to Mode of Consent

i. Types According to Degree of Participation

a) Basic Participation

1. Passive Participation

When States join together in a society, certain basic rules are immediately engendered. These are, for example, the *intrinsic logical rules*, thus the *maxims and the basic formal general principles*, to which is added the *intrinsic social rules*, thus the *basic prophylactic rules* without which international society cannot function.

The rules of these two types are spontaneously[47] created in the international legal order by *logical* necessity and by *social* necessity of minimum contacts. By mere membership of international society and by means of acts of '*passive participation*' in that society basic rules of this category are formed. There is a presumption that such participation implies consent to these rules. Along the *graduated*

---

[47] *Cf.* Ago, R., 'Positive law and international law', *AJIL* 1957 691; *cf.* Nguyen Quoc Dinh & Dallier & Pellet, A., *Droit international public*, 4th ed., Paris: LGDJ, 1990, 296; *cf.* Daillier, P., Forteau, M. & Pellet, A., *Droit international public*, Paris: LGDI, 8th ed. 2009.

scale of presumption of consent,[48] there is thus strong presumption towards the top end of the scale for consent by mere participation for logically and socially necessary rules. Thus, it is here suggested that there is a greater presumption of adherence to the substratum of prophylactic and stabilising rules than to those concerned with elaboration of promotional or correctional rules.

2. Active Participation

As contacts increase between States, further rules on mutual contact are engendered. These rules on further contact, *e.g.* on delimitation of national space, immunity, communications or forms of treaties, are not created by 'custom', as so many suggest, but by immediate social necessity, although custom can entrench the use of such rules.

The rules are thus brought into existence, or 'activated' by legal acts taken by States, *i.e.* by acts that make contact with other units in the world. In this way, States proceed to more '*active participation*' in international society. Once such rules have emerged to operate between certain States, further States that wish to join that 'club', will also have to accept the 'standing rules' by their specific legal acts of active participation.

In other words, States are not obliged or required to take part in international cooperation but if they do, the rules of forms for mutual contact, activated by the first few units that entered into contact, must be followed; or new rules must, by common agreement, be revised/improved/elaborated as certain rules are essential to international intercourse. Similarly, subsequent

---

[48] *Supra*, in this Part, I iii, Graduated Scale of Presumption of Consent.

implementing rules within the framework of socially necessary rules are elaborated by common agreement.

b) Enhanced Participation

Further detailed promotional rules are created by more specific acts of *'enhanced participation'* taken by States. For example, such further legal acts create organisations, decide on increasing sharing or on rules of management of self-punishing correctional rules. For this category, consent is never presumed: it must be clear and unequivocal.

ii. Types According to Degree of State Control

a) Permissive Acts

Acts of States may allow activities of other actors in international society and, more specifically, allow such actors to regulate their mutual relationships in the way they wish. 'Permission' to act is often given by mere tolerance by 'permissive acts' or 'acts of non-restraint' of such activities. States thus 'permit' multinationals, individuals, NGOs or Institutes to act in transboundary situations by not imposing rules of legislation restraining them. Multinationals are all registered in a State, and so are their subsidiary branches and companies as well as units with which they may wish to conclude contracts: it is a fallacy to think that States could not, if they wished, restrain undesirable activities by legislation. Other companies, NGOs, Institutes and individuals are all tied by allegiance of nationality or domicile to specific States and these actors, too, can be restrained in transnational activities.

b) Acts of Delegation

States may, for their convenience, decide to set up an organisation which, in turn, is given power to make regulations or taking binding authoritative[49] decisions. The rule areas emerging have clearly their origin in the *abstract consent* of States[50] given by States in the basic constitution of the organisation, which also conveys implied powers, necessary to attain the objectives for which the organisation was created.[51]

The ensuing rules which an organisation may adopt represent an important part of international law. These rules are thus created by acts of the organisation, on the basis of powers given to it by States in its constitution, under the principle of delegation.

iii. Types According To Form of Expressed Consent: Statement Acts

As opposed to adherence to rules of international law through action by various participation acts, a State may become bound by any rule, or engender any new rule, by virtue of its expressed consent. This category thus concerns statements and declarations of consent. Some such declarations are embodied in contractual acts, others are taken in a unilateral or parallel form.

---

[49] *Infra*, in this Part, II B iii f), Authoritative Acts.
[50] See my *Law Making, op. cit.*, 363 for my theory of *abstract consent*.
[51] *Ibid.*, 25, on the doctrine of implied powers.

a) Contractual Acts

The typical consensual act in international society is the treaty. By bilateral treaties States carry out certain exchange transactions; or they establish a network for future reference, such as in a boundary treaty or in an extradition agreement. Some bilateral regimes may be of great international relevance, such as, for example, a bilateral agreement on arms control or on disarmament between the United States and Russia.

Multilateral treaties establish more commonly important sets of rules for future behaviour. By treaties States (and organisations) can regulate any matters short of those which violate the fundamental principles of international law.[52] But it is also possible that many treaties, for example those that restrict the sovereign power of States in their own territory, are subject to specific rules of '*continuous consent*'[53] and are therefore only operative for as long as States regard them as desirable. It is also possible that there are new rules operating under a treaty that do not have popular consent and in this way individuals, when being part of the 'majority' in a State, may influence the life of a treaty.

'Law making treaties'[54] or what we may call 'treaties on behaviour', establishing framework regimes,[55] operate, but not always, between a large number of parties. These agreements

---

[52] Article of the Vienna Convention on the Law of Treaties and *supra*, Part Two, II B I, Prophylactic Rules, on *jus cogens*.

[53] See my *Independence, op. cit*, 1979, for my theory on *continuous consent*.

[54] See *e.g.* Reglade, 'La nature juridique des traités internationaux et du sens de la distinction des traités lois et des traités contrats,' 31 *RDPSP* 1924 505.

[55] *Supra*, Part Two, C II ii c), Further Regimes and *infra*, in this Part, II C iii a) Framework Acts.

are different from 'treaty-contracts' which concern exchange transactions. The normative contents of law making treaties is enhanced whereas treaty-contracts can only be of reduced international relevance. But both types rest on contractual principles although law making treaties may sometimes be a guise for parallel acts.[56]

b) Promissory Acts

Promissory acts, often taken in a unilateral form,[57] may be coupled with those of other States forming parallel acts, described below. Thus, promissory acts may often be components of parallel acts.

It would seem reasonable to be able to rely on a State's vote in an international organisation on certain matters to ascertain the State's assumption of obligations. Some are quite willing to accept such views, but prefer to explain the binding force of any resolution of an international organisation as either an inter-State agreement,[58] or as a clarification of what 'customary' international law already says,[59] whereas the simplest way may be to say that there exists a possibility of States actually assuming more obligations by a unilateral declaration to that effect. Naturally, a State may not be

---

[56] *Supra*, in this Part, I ii, Doctrine of Legal Relevance, See, *infra*, in the next section on 'parallel acts'.

[57] *Infra*, in this Part, II C i a), Unilateral Acts.

[58] See *infra*, *loc. cit.* and accompanying notes.

[59] E.g., Schacter, O., 'Interpretation of the Charter in the political organs of the United Nations', in Engel & Metall, (eds.), *Law, Structure and the International Legal Order, Essays in Honour of Hans Kelsen*, 1964, 271.

held to any legal obligation by a simple vote in an international organisation.[60]

Even if a State has made its position unequivocally clear by speeches or emphatic statements with regard to the identification of certain overriding common goals[61] to be achieved, like the abatement of pollution, or with regard to the renunciation of future territorial claims to, for example, Antarctica or to the moon or planets in Outer Space, it cannot be claimed that the State has bound itself. Some have sought to suggest that, if other States have acted in reliance on such statements, a State is precluded by *estoppel* from rescinding the allegedly assumed obligations.[62] It is highly dangerous to impute obligations to a State or to any other subject of the international legal order on the basis of pronouncements and statements: unless there is a demonstrated clear contractual undertaking, a State is not bound under international law. Thus, if a treaty is negotiated and signed but subject to ratification, no obligations are incurred before such ratification has taken place.

With this perspective it might seem, at first sight, that the judgment of the International Court of Justice in the *Eastern Greenland Case*[63] was wrong in law: here, the Norwegian Foreign

---

[60] See further *infra*, and, in greater detail, my *International Legal Order*, *op.cit.*, Chapter IV, 212-252, on the irrelevance of voting figures.

[61] Not the hypothetical goal, *supra*, Part One, II ii, but intermediate goals agreed by consent.

[62] See, Martin, A., *L'estoppel en droit international public*, Paris: Pedone, 1979; Bowett, D., 'Estoppel before international tribunals and its relation to acquiescence', 33 *BYIL*, 1957, 176 and *supra*, in Part Two, A II iv, on estoppel in international law.

[63] *Eastern Greenland Case (Norway v Denmark)*, PCIJ, Series A/B, 1933 No. 53, 71.

Minister, Mr Ihlen, had made a pronouncement in the Norwegian Parliament (*Stortinget*) that Norway would have no further claims to Eastern Greenland. Denmark argued in the Court that the '*Ihlen Declaration*' was binding Norway in international law and Norway would therefore be precluded to have any further claims to Eastern Greenland. But the background of the Ihlen Declaration is not always explained. In the 1920s, Norway occupied and claimed as its own parts of Eastern Greenland, a territory previously governed by Denmark. A Danish diplomatic representative asked Norway's Minister of Foreign Affairs about the country's intentions toward Eastern Greenland. The Minister replied that Norway did not intend to contest Danish sovereignty over the whole of Greenland. Denmark later sued Norway in the Permanent Court of International Justice on the ground that Norway violated Danish sovereignty in Eastern Greenland. It was in this context that the *Ihlen Declaration* should be understood.[64]

Rather than perceiving decisions of international organisations as disguised inter-State agreements,[65] and rather than relegating such decisions to mere instances of individual State practice, one could see such resolutions as promissory unilateral declarations, often in parallel acts,[66] by respective Members States. Many municipal systems lend legal and binding force to public unilateral declarations, made in solemn form. However, in the international legal order, the sovereignty of States is paramount and there must be no presumption of obligations unless there is a form of the above mentioned contractual bond.

---

[64] See, *infra*, in this Part under II C i a), on Unilateral Acts.
[65] So Blix, H., *Treaty-Making Power*, *op. cit.*, *loc. cit.*
[66] *Infra*, in the following section, Parallel Acts.

We may further distinguish between decisions of international organisations that are binding by virtue of the Constitutions of that organisation[67] and such decisions that are not binding by virtue of any such Constitutions but only have the 'force' of a recommendation. Yet, even in the last mentioned event a State may 'appear' to be 'bound' by the decision, not by virtue of the decision itself, but by virtue of a reflection of rules of *lex lata*, thus binding for other reasons.

Undoubtedly, a State cannot very well assume obligations under international law without being aware of such additional obligations. On the other hand, this is precisely what the traditionalists argue with regard to customary law where States are often held to have expressed their *opinio juris* although they have not done or said anything specific. Some argue that by sheer acquiescence they are bound by a certain rule.[68] It is equally dangerous to attach any legal importance to the explicit statements a State makes in the General Assembly: the State is there not aware of any potential effects of any legal consequences of its statements. Here too, a State is largely unaware of some surreptitiously slow development of rules to which it is held to have assented by acquiescence.

Naturally, express manifestations of will in an organisation cannot lead to legal obligations unless such legal effects are foreseen by the Constitution of the organisation and the State has given its clear consent. A State may thus only be held to have expressed its willingness to be bound by a unilateral declaration, inside or

---

[67] For a survey, see my *Law Making, op. cit., passim.*
[68] Thirlway, H.V.A., *International Customary Law and Codification*, 1972, The Hague: Nijhoff; D'Amato, A., *The Concept of Custom in International Law*, New York: Cornell Univ. Press, 1971.

outside an international organisation, if there is a clear declaration of intent, related to certain specific objectives and the State has expressed its clear consent to any ensuing legal obligations.

c) Parallel Acts

Certain acts are hallmarked by a certain parallelism: they are taken by actors who stand, as it were, on the same side and not, as in the case of contractual relations, opposite each other. These acts could perhaps be compared to Triepel's category of *Vereinbahrungen*[69] by which States were thought to be able to bring about binding rules.

The fusion of wills in one direction is significant. It is apparently by alleged parallel acts (although the term is not used) that some claim, for example, that States are bound by votes in the General Assembly.[70] Most also claim that numerical figures of voting are relevant.[71] But States cannot become bound without knowing that they are assuming obligations; and when they vote *they do not know the outcome of the final vote*.[72] Therefore, not even unanimity indicates clear State consent. And *consensus*, the new fashionable voting mode,[73] cannot *ipso facto* create legal obligations.[74]

---

[69] Triepel, H., *Völkerrecht und Landesrecht*, Leipzig: C.L. Hirschfeld, 1899.
[70] See, Brownlie, *Principles*, *op. cit.* 14, 697.
[71] *E.g. ibid.*, 15, 697.
[72] See my *International Law*, *op. cit.*, 1993, Chapter IV, for a detailed analysis, and my *International Legal Order*, *op. cit.*, Ch. IV, 212-252.
[73] On consensus, see, Cassan, H., 'Le consensus dans la pratique des Nations Unies', *AFDI* 1974; and, in detail, my *International Law*, *op. cit.*, 1993, Chapter IV.
[74] Bastid, S., 'Observations sur une étape dans le développement progressif et la codification des principes du droit international, *Hommages Guggenheim* 1968, 144.

Consensus is not the same as unanimity[75] and, as mentioned, even unanimity cannot entail legal obligation unless there is clear constitutional basis for acts of organisations having such binding effect.[76]

To be bound by parallel acts, there is thus need for clear consent by the parties. Consent cannot normally be presumed or inferred from action, especially not from the oblique action when potential parties are not aware of the possibility of becoming bound through their behaviour. But consent may have been made clear by promissory acts. Parallel acts are thus merely a combination of promissory acts, although possibly of enhanced importance because of the plurality in number.

With regard to parallel acts, the burden of proof of consent may, it is suggested, be somewhat lighter with regard to details elaborating the substratum of prophylactic[77] and stabilising[78] rules according to the doctrine of graduated scale of presumptions of consent.[79] Using this scale of presumptions, it may be clear that at least certain obligations result from certain parallel acts like the Helsinki Act, a 'Final Act' which writers have had problems

---

[75] Seidl-Hohenveldern, I., 'International economic 'Soft Law'', 167 *RCADI* 1979 ii 185.

[76] See my *Law Making*, *op. cit. passim*, and my *International Law*, 1993, Chapter IV, in detail.

[77] *Supra*, Part Two, B III, Prophylactic Rules.

[78] *Supra*, Part Two, C I, Stabilising Rules.

[79] See further, *supra*, in this Part, I iii, Graduated Scale of Presumption of Consent.

to classify in legal terms[80] or the Joint Declaration in the *Aegean Case*.[81]

d) Acts of Adoption

Most important rules emerge in international society by way of adoption by States of 'provisional standards', 'draft-standards' or 'pre-standards', elaborated by NGOs, pressure groups or laid down in 'recommendations' of international organisations, particularly in Resolutions of the General Assembly[82] or of 'Codes' of behaviour of States,[83] of non-State entities[84] or for the regulation of largely intra-State matters.[85] Also certain other adopted rules concern sharing,[86] convenient technical standards,[87] important safety rules[88] or the necessity of warning.[89]

There may be a duty to adopt prophylactic standards and there are obvious social reasons why common technical standards are agreed to as they facilitate international cooperation. But

---

[80] *E.g.* Skubiszewski, K., 'Der Rechtskarakter der KSZES-Schlussakte', in Bernhardt & Münch & Rudolf, (eds.), 1 *KSZES-Schlussakte*, 1977.

[81] (1978), see para 96, ICJ *Reports* 1978.

[82] See, my *International Legal Order*, *op. cit.*, Chapter IV, 212-252, in detail.

[83] *Ibid.*, and *e.g.* the Charter of Economic Rights and Duties GA Resolution 3281.

[84] *Ibid.*, and *e.g.* UNCTAD Code on Liner Conferences.

[85] See, my *International Legal Order*, *op.cit.*, Chapter I and VII on harmonisation of laws.

[86] *Ibid.*, and *supra*, Part Two, C II i b), Duty to Share? *Cf.* for example, by non-reciprocal preferences in GATT/ WTO or UNCTAD.

[87] See, my *International Legal Order*, *op. cit.*, Chapter IV, and *supra*, Part Two, C II i d), Standards and Pre-Standards.

[88] *Ibid.* on and *supra*, *loc. cit.*, on IAEA rules.

[89] *Supra*, Part Two, C I ii b), The Duty to Warn.

recommendations implying 'sharing' can only apply if States freely agree to such measures.

e) Acts of Recognition

With regard to certain fundamental and basic rules, *i.a.* the *substratum* of prophylactic and stabilising rules, States often appear to 'recognise' the existence of the relevant body of law. This is expressed in a collective convergence of convictions.[90] By this way of 'stating'[91] the law, States accept by acts of recognition certain rules. Some of these coincide with those which become binding upon States by presumption of consent to rules of international society by basic acts of participation.[92] But the sphere of rules to which States readily give consent by acts of recognition is probably narrower than that of rules activated by participation: only the most basic rules are accepted by means of recognition. It is with regard to these rules that one may occasionally speak of the 'legal conscience'.[93]

f) Authoritative Acts

Rare types of authoritative acts can only be found in the regulations and other acts of international organisations (and Courts of law;

---

[90] *Cf.* Barile, G., Structure de l'ordre juridique international, 161 *RCADI*, 1978 iii, 49.

[91] *Cf.* Le Fur, L., *Précis de droit international public*, Paris: Dalloz, 2nd ed., 1934, 11.

[92] *Supra*, in this Part, II B I a), Basic Participation.

[93] *Cf.* Krabbe, H., 'L'idée moderne de l'Etat', *RCADI* 1926 iii 559.

and there only with legal effect *inter partes*) where the contracting parties of the basic treaty/constitution,[94] have given their consent[95] to be so bound by the acts. Thus, also in the case of authoritative acts, States have given their consent albeit in advance, by what I have called '*abstract consent*'[96] to provide a basis of future acts of an organisation or of a court.

Authoritative acts are most common[97] in certain technical organisations, like the WHO, WMO, ICAO as well as in UPU and ITU, and in organisations for economic integration like the European Union. In political organisations the power is rare; but it exists under the Charter of the United Nations.[98]

---

[94] See, in detail, my *Law Making, op. cit.*, 24-25.

[95] *Ibid.*, 216.

[96] *Ibid.*, 322. See, for my theory on '*abstract* consent', my *Law Making, op. cit., loc. cit.* Such consent is given on the part of States when they set up an international organisation by a Treaty that is also designed to be the 'Constitution' of the organisation. This form of consent implies the authorisation *in advance* for all acts that the organisation may have to take. Such authorised acts will always include 'primary rules' on staff, internal procedures, headquarter agreements, etc. Other authorised acts will be the 'operative acts' that the organisation will have to take to attain the objectives for which it was founded. 'Operative acts' will necessarily vary from organisation to organisation depending on the goal for which the entity was created by the founding Treaty, whereas 'primary rules' are fairly similar in most organisations, see my *Law Making, op. cit., passim*.

[97] See in detail, my *Law Making, op. cit.*, 217 *et seq.*

[98] See, article 24-25 and *Advisory Opinion on Namibia*, (1971), ICJ *Reports*, 523, for comments on the authoritative nature of the articles. Decisions do not necessarily have to concern threats to the peace (the main field for authoritative action) to be binding: see Resolutions 457 (1979) and 761 (1979) insisting on release of the diplomatic hostages in Teheran, see *Hostages Case* (1980), ICJ *Reports*, 1980, 26.

C. Types According to Form

i. Types According to the Number of Authors

Acts may be unilateral, emanating from one single subject. It is often a matter of construction whether an act is truly unilateral or part of a bi/multilateral act.

a) Unilateral Acts

Unilateral acts have been neglected by most modern international lawyers who do not normally mention this category in the textbooks. Yet, it is becoming increasingly apparent that it is precisely by means of such acts that subjects of the international society often develop and lay down international legal rules.

Some relegate unilateral acts to the nebulous category of 'State practice', claiming that such acts can never be immediately relevant by themselves but only in conjunction with a number of other acts of 'State practice' indicating some emerging customary law. Others seek to prove that most unilateral acts are not unilateral at all but rather part of consensual transactions. Thus, some seek to explain the binding force of the unilateral undertaking of the *Ihlen Declaration*[99] as part of an 'agreement' between Norway and Denmark.[100] As mentioned above, it was indeed remarkable that the Permanent Court of International Justice found that a statement by the Foreign Minister in the Norwegian Parliament (*stortinget*) would be internationally binding on Norway. The remarkable

---

[99] *Eastern Greenland Case*, (1933) PCIJ Series A/B No.53, 52.
[100] See, *ibid.*, 71-72.

feature here is not the *unilateral* character of the act, but the fact that it was made in *an internal organ* of the State and *not directed* to other entities in international society.

But States and other entities in international society do sometimes assume obligations by unilateral acts. Some examples of prominent unilateral acts of States are, for example, recognition of another State, declaration of war, declaration of capitulation, application for membership in an international organisation, excuses and offers of reparation after violations of international law.

Some writers oppose the idea that international organisations can take binding unilateral decisions vis-à-vis the Member States but, when that happens in practice, they seek to explain such decisions as mutual agreements of States.[101] Yet, my theory about '*abstract consent*,[102] demonstrates that there *is* clear State consent for unilateral acts of organisations. Such consent is given on the part of States when they set up an international organisation by a Treaty that is also designed to be the 'Constitution' of the organisation. This form of consent implies the authorisation *in advance* for all acts that the organisation may have to take. Such authorised acts will always include 'primary rules' on staff, internal procedures, headquarter agreements, etc. Other authorised acts will be the 'operative acts' that the organisation will have to take to attain the objectives for which it was founded. 'Operative acts' will necessarily vary from organisation to organisation depending on

---

[101] Blix, H., *Treaty-Making Power*, H., Stockholm: Norstedt, 1960 293 *et seq.*

[102] See my *Law Making, op. cit., passim* and *cf. supra*, in this in this Part, II B iii f), on Authoritative Acts.

the goal for the entity that was created by the founding Treaty, whereas 'primary rules' are fairly similar in most organisations.[103]

Some writers claim that a State can be bound by *estoppel* but, as explained above,[104] first, this is a concept only known in the Anglo-Saxon legal system and, secondly, unless there is a clear agreement to be bound in law, or the rules concern compulsory *intrinsic rules*, a State remains free to consent or refrain from any undertaking.

With regard to organisations, some have come to accept that the function of such entities is largely pursued by unilateral means but only since overwhelming evidence had been produced by treatises that demonstrated actual practice.[105]

But with regard to States, few attach much importance to unilateral acts of States and most textbooks are still silent on the subject. Yet, it is often by unilateral undertakings that States absorb new rights and duties, especially by taking what we call single promissory acts[106] or joint parallel acts.[107]

b) Bilateral Acts

The most common bilateral act is a treaty between two States. Some bilateral acts set up a *regime*, such as under an extradition treaty or under a double taxation agreement, and thus create a subset of rules. Other bilateral treaties, for example on an individual transaction, are of a more transient form and are therefore 'executory' in the

---

[103] See, in detail, my *Law Making*, *op. cit.* Ch. I.
[104] *Supra*, Part Two, B II, General Principles.
[105] *E.g.* my *Law Making*, *op. cit.*, *passim*.
[106] *Supra*, in this Part, II B iii b), Promissory Acts.
[107] See, my *Law Making*, *op. cit.*, *passim*.

sense that once they have been performed, they are exhausted, no act remains for reiterated application. Apart from hollow and bland agreements, for example, on general cooperation or *friendship*, most bilateral agreements are executory and of short duration.

c) Multilateral Acts

The multilateral treaty is a relatively modern newcomer in international society. This type of treaty has increased in frequency and importance. Most multilateral treaties establish norms for future behaviour although, conceivably, such acts might also deal with a transient transaction.

Multilateral treaties are important instruments for the creation of new rules. Numerous multilateral treaties, however, merely codify rule: not 'customary rules' as is usually claimed but rules which are *already present* in international law and to which States have already adhered by passive or active participation in international society,[108] or by further specific consent.

ii. Types According to Solemnity

Acts may be made in a more or less formal way. In some cases, it may be due to time constraints that an agreement is drafted in general terms, as was the case, for example, with the Rome Treaties of the EU, setting up the European Economic Community and Euratom. The earlier Paris Treaty, setting up the Europan Coal and Steel Community, (CECA or ECSC), was much more detailed. Apart from the question of generality of contents, an important

---

[108] *Supra*, in this Part, II B I a) 2, Active Participation.

issue is the solemnity with which an agreement is concluded. Here, we can perceive informal acts implying acquiescence or presumed consent, as well as consensual acts adopted by what can be called 'long' or 'short' procedures.[109]

a) Functional Acts

Certain acts are taken by mere participation, even by passive participation in international society.[110] Such acts are capable of creating sets of rules. They also imply (perhaps presumed[111]) consent to created rules between others and thus widen a previous sphere of subjects to a rule.

b) Verbal Acts

Promissory acts[112] are frequently in verbal form and may concern specific statements, often recorded at a conference or in an international organisation.

c) Written Acts

Some acts are specifically clothed in written form. This is the normal way of concluding treaties; to qualify as a treaty an instrument must be in such form.[113]

---

[109] *Essay* on the *Law of Treaties, op. cit.*, Ch. II, on 'long' procedures involving ratification of treaties.
[110] *Supra*, in this Part, II B I a) 1, Passive Participation.
[111] *Supra*, in this Part, I iii, Graduated Scale of Presumption of Consent.
[112] *Supra*, in this Part, II B iii b), Promissory Acts.
[113] Vienna Convention on the Law of Treaties, article 2 (1)(a).

d) Elaborate Acts

Some acts, particularly treaties, may be made by a 'long' procedure[114] implying not only written form, but in need of ensuing ratification or approval procedure. Also treaties of organisations can be subjected to this elaborate procedure.[115] But it is to be remarked that the trend is to dispense with precisely such long and elaborate procedures.

Many acts are taken in international organisations to create new rules, without reference to parliamentary consent, and the person taking part in the decision-making procedures of the organisations is invariably someone from a Foreign Ministry, or from a government department. By dispensing with elaborate procedures which, in most States, would have involved a discussion in Parliament, a Government may engineer a shift in the constitutional balance of States, from the legislature to the executive.

The rule of democracy demands that Parliament must be aware that such a development has taken place in case the legislature wishes to preclude such a shift of competence. There is evidence that many Parliaments are not even aware of the problem.

iii. Types According to Durability

a) Framework Acts

Certain acts set up a framework for future action within which further action will be carried out. We are here not concerned with

---

[114] See my *Essays on the Law of Treaties*, 1967, 15 *et seq.*
[115] See my article on 'Treaty-making power of organs of international organisations' *BYIL* 1962, 421.

acts of a programmatic character,[116] that very often lack legal contents, but with acts which, for example, set up an international organisation, or a system of recurring conferences[117] or a 'regime'.[118]

b) Transient Acts

Apart from the framework acts, one can distinguish what we may call transient acts, which concern transactions which are not repeatable. Such acts will correspond to what have been called 'exchange transactions',[119] whereas others may cover *e.g.* the non-recurring acts of international aid, such as setting funds aside for a particular purpose which is immediately attained.

iv. Types According to Frequency

a) Extraordinary Acts

Other acts can be classified according to how often they take place. In such a division of measures we may perceive the revision of the Constitution of an international organisation or of any other treaty as an extraordinary act, for it does not lie within the normal external activity of a State.

---

[116] *Supra*, in this Part, B I ii a) Programmatic Declarations.
[117] Such as under the Helsinki Act, *supra*, in this Part, II iii c) Parallel Acts.
[118] *Supra*, in Part One, I vii, The Notion of Regimes.
[119] Burton, *Systems, op. cit., loc. cit.*

b) Current Acts

The normal day-to-day external acts, on the other hand, present themselves as current acts of high frequency, in line with the general external activities of a State.

III. The Mechanisms of *Interactivism*

Observing how rules emerge in practice in international society, it seems reasonable to suggest, that it is by an intricate but clear process of *interactivism*, that most rules operate in the contemporary international legal order. It has already been explained that maxims, certain formal general principles as well as the other components of the intrinsic law, such as the important prophylactic rules forbidding force, are binding on all independent of any express consent: any member of international society, is *ipso facto*, obliged to respect these *intrinsic rules*.

But when it comes to all other rules of international society the situation is different. These supplementary rules are not compulsory but dispositive or voluntary. They are conveniently thought of as being latent rules in large norm-pools. Specific acts, as the various types described above, bring such norms into effect.

This is the way most rules enter into effect. The image might be expanded to describe the subjects of the international legal order as fishermen that bring out relevant rules, when necessary, from the vast and rich norm-pools where rules can be found for any contingency. This can be described as the way the system of *interactivism* functions: specific acts bring into effect general rules for application to specific situation. This is done by voluntary action and by clear consent that can be expressed in various ways, as described in the graduated scale of consent.

IV. Another Way of Making Rules: Customary Law

i. The Traditional Definition of Customary Law

The rules we see operating in international society come into force through the mechanism of *legal acts*. These rules and these acts are of a great variety, as we have described above. The mechanism of *interactivism*, produces a practical means to apply rules to any situation in international society. Pools of rules are present, as set out at the beginning of this work, and norms from these are activated by specific 'legal acts', sometimes by an intersection of such acts. The majority of writers and courts claim that there is another way – the main way, according to them – of producing the rules of the international system, and that, they say, is by way of custom. Obviously, 'custom' is important in every legal system, but we must not confuse the *mode of formation of rules* with their substantive content, that is, the *substance* of these rules.

We have earlier set out the text of article 38 of the Statute of the International Court of Justice that refers to the various sources of law applied by the Court.[120] Article 38 has given rise to numerous comments, and writers do not agree on the meaning of each of the parts of the text. In particular, section c. has given rise

---

[120] See, *supra*, Part Two, A II on General Principles.

to much dispute as discussed above. Para (1) (b) is still unclear: the phrase 'custom ... as evidence of a general practice accepted as law', indicates that there is a 'custom' before any 'practice'. The source of this right would therefore exist *before* the practice,[121] which raises a great number of problems.

What is customary law? Is it true that this wide range concept encompasses any rule of the international community that is deemed to be effective but is not codified? Should we understand by rules of customary law all the rules that cannot otherwise be localised or explained? Let us therefore examine the criteria required by the majority of writers and courts?

According to the universally accepted conventional theory, customary law is created on the basis of three elements: first, by the practice of *several States*; secondly, this practice must have continued for a *certain period of time*; thirdly, this practice must be accompanied by an expression of *opinio juris*, that is to say, the opinion that such practice establishes legal rules.

ii. Emerging Dissatisfaction with Traditional Customary Law

Most textbooks define 'customary international law' summarily as the 'general and consistent practice of States followed by them from a sense of obligation.'[122] The leading case is *United States v Smith*,

---

[121] See, my *International Legal Order*, op. cit., Ch. III, E ii, 185 *et seq.* & *cf.* i:1 Oppenheim, ed. Jennings, R., & Watts, A., Oxford: OUP, 2008, 2, n. 5.

[122] The United States incorporates this in their constitutional documents, *see* Restatement (Third), *The Foreign Relations Law of the United States* § 102(2) (1987).

a case from 1820.[123] Courts determine the content of customary international law by consulting the doctrine and observing the general practice and/or court decisions. But the *Smith Case* only concerned *piracy*. There, it was held that the crime of piracy is defined by the law of nations with reasonable certainty. The Court said

> 'What the law of nations on this subject is, may be ascertained by consulting the works of jurists, writing professedly on public laws; or by the general usage and practice of nations; or by judicial decisions recognising and enforcing that law. There is scarcely a writer on the law of nations, who does not allude to piracy, as a crime of a settled and determinate nature; and whatever may be the diversity of definitions, in other respects, all writers concur, in holding, that robbery, or forcible depredations upon the sea, *animo furandi*, is piracy. The same doctrine is held by all the great writers on maritime law, in terms that admit of no reasonable doubt. The common law, too, recognises and punishes piracy as an offence, not against its own municipal code, but as an offences against the law of nations (which is part of the common law), as an offence against the universal law of society, a pirate being deemed an enemy of the human race.'

There was a time when the pretended 'customary rules' of the law of nations were few and limited. We can gauge this from the cases where we could identify violations of the law of nations: only some rights were held to be protected in this sense and only few situations could lead to legal consequences in the case of infringements. Such situations thus concerned a very limited sphere in which rules binding on individuals for the benefit of other individuals, overlapped with the rules on State relationships. Blackstone referred

---

[123] *United States v Smith*, M 18 U.S. (5 Wheat.) 153, 160-61, 5 L.Ed. 57 (1820).

to this when he mentioned three specific offences against the law of nations addressed by the criminal law of England: violation of safe conducts, infringement of the rights of ambassadors, and piracy.[124]

If customary rules were limited to these traditional fields, few would have a problem accepting their validity and legal force. But at present it is claimed in court cases and in textbooks, that customary rules actually form the bulk of international law.

Many have noticed the highly unsatisfactory character of 'customary international law' as traditionally defined. Some insist that customary law is, at best, a fluid set of rules, not always easy to identify. The Court in the *Flores Case* complained that:

> 'The determination of what offences violate customary international law ... is no simple task. Customary international law is discerned *from a myriad of decisions made in numerous and varied international and domestic arenas.* Furthermore, the relevant evidence of customary international law is widely dispersed and generally unfamiliar to lawyers and judges. These difficulties are compounded by the fact that customary international law – as the term itself implies – is created by the general customs and practices of nations and therefore does not stem from any single, definitive, readily-identifiable source.'[125]

The Court in *Flores* went on to say that:

> '...in determining what offences violate customary international law, courts must proceed with extraordinary care and restraint. In short, customary international law is composed only of those

---

[124] Blackstone, 4 *Commentaries* 68.
[125] *Flores v Southern Peru Copper Corp.*, 414 F. 3d 233 – Court of Appeals, 2nd Circuit 2003; the original judgment uses the American spelling 'offenses'.

rules that States universally abide by, or accede to, out of a sense of legal obligation and mutual concern.'

All of these characteristics give the body of customary international law a *'soft, indeterminate character.'*[126] That is not a good quality for rules that by some are said to make up the bulk of international law.

Other pronouncements of Courts may be conducive to a certain worry about the ready acceptance of 'customary law': in the *Firestone Case*,[127] concerning child labour in Liberia, the court said that:

> 'The concept of customary international law is disquieting in two respects. First, there is a problem of notice: a custom cannot be identified with the same confidence as a provision in 'a legally authoritative text, such as a statute or a treaty. (Modern common law doesn't present that problem; it is a body of judge-created doctrine, not of amorphous custom.) Second, there is a problem of legitimacy – and for democratic countries it is a problem of democratic legitimacy. Customary international legal duties are imposed by the international community (ideally, though rarely – given the diversity of the world's 194 nations – by consensus), rather than by laws promulgated by the obligee's local community'.

There is a further serious problem, often ignored by writers; In cases cited by writers as supporting the traditional notion of customary

---

[126] Henkin, L., *International Law: Politics and Values*, Leiden: Brill & Nijhoff, 1989 29 and *idem*, *General Course*, *RCADI* 1989. *Cf.* Bradley, C.A., & Gulati, M., 'Withdrawing from international custom,' 120 *Yale L.J.*, 2010, 202, 208-15.

[127] *Flomo v Fiestone National Rubber Co.*, US Court of Appeal, 7th Circ. 11 July 2011, appeal from US District Court for Southern Indiana, 5 Oct. 2010.

rules, the Courts turn out, at a closer analysis, to question the legal force of such rules; Customary rules often appear not to be binding 'by themselves': claims that customary usage constitutes a rule which acts directly upon the thing itself by its own force, and not through the sovereign power was severely criticised and disallowed in the leading case on customary law, the *Brown Case*, where the Court said:

> 'usage is a guide which the sovereign follows or abandons at his will. The rule, like other precepts of morality, of humanity and even of wisdom, is addressed to the judgment of the sovereign; and although it cannot be disregarded by him without obloquy, yet it may be disregarded. The rule is, in its nature, flexible. It is subject to infinite modification. It is not an immutable rule of law, but depends on political considerations which may continually vary.'[128]

In this case, the Appellants sought to argue that

> '… in executing the laws of war, the executive may seize all property which, according to the modern law of nations, is subject to confiscation, although it might require an act of the legislature to justify the condemnation of that property which, according to modern usage, ought not to be confiscated.'[129]

But the Court held that

> 'This argument must assume for its basis the position that modern usage constitutes a rules which acts directly upon the

---

[128] *Brown v The United States*, 8 Cranch, (1814) 110.

[129] *Ibid.*, at 128.

thing itself by its own force, and not through the sovereign power. This position is not allowed.'

Claims that customary usage may establish rules that act through their own force and not through sovereign power was also severely criticised and disallowed in a subsequent case, *The Paqueta Habana*,[130] where Chief Justice Marshall repeated the passage from the *Brown Case*, about 'usage' as a guide.

But if customary rules are not 'quite' binding, what is the use of placing such reliance on such rules in any case before a Court, or in a textbook, trying to persuade judges or students of the 'force' of such unreliable sources of law?

iii. The Absurd Views of Customary Law

a) Whose 'General Practice'?

Let us then ask some pertinent questions. What do we mean by *State* practice? What consequences does this statement have in, for example, the Law of War? Is it not the practice of *soldiers* that is relevant in situations of armed conflict? It is only through rather artificial imputation[131] that this practice can be regarded as 'practice of States'.[132]

The majority of writers and courts ignore any practice – and opinions – on the part of individuals (soldiers, citizens or NGOs)

---

[130] *The Paqueta Habana*, 175 U.S. 677, 700, 20 S Ct. 290, 44 L.Ed 320 (1900) 128; *cf.* Story, J., at 154.
[131] See, *supra*, Part One, I iii d), International Personality and Imputation.
[132] See, my *Law of War, op. cit.*, Ch. 1.

because of the obsession that only States (and inter-governmental organisations) are subjects of international law and that only they can have rights and duties under the international legal system. We have demonstrated above that this is not correct: other entities and even, or even primarily, *individuals* have numerous rights and duties under the international legal system. It is not, as many pretend, States, that grant such rights and duties, but rights are *directly granted* and duties are *directly imposed* on individuals and other entities by international law.

Some authors have at least the merit of coherence, when they consider customary law to be created by States, as they claim that only States are 'subjects'[133] of international law and bearers of international rights and duties. Thus, one writer states that:

> 'Custom derives from the *de facto* adjustment of conflicting claims and interests of the subjects of international law; and it has always been and probably still is one of the most fundamental tenets of international law that *individuals and private corporations are not subjects of international law*. The relationship between a State and an individual cannot be creative of an international custom, even if the individual enjoys the protection of another State.'[134] (italics added)

---

[133] *Ibid.* Ch.1. Note that 'usage' might be relevant: see, by Statement by Chief Justice Marshall stated in *The Schooner Exchange v McFaddon*, that views of, for example, immunity or other restrictions of sovereignty in a States's territory may be 'tested by common usage and by common opinion, growing out of that usage', 11 US Cranch 116, 3 Ed 287 (1812). See, on restrictions of sovereign functions in a State's own territory, my *International Law and the Independent State*, *op. cit.*, *passim. Cf. Rahimtoola v Nizan of Hyderabad*, (1957) 3 WLR 884, 910.

[134] Thirlway, *op. cit., loc. cit.*

and

> 'What may be creative of customary law is the relationship between a State which has acted in a certain way towards an individual and another State to which that individual is linked by a bond recommended by international law as sufficient to entitle the State to press an international claim which, while it may be effectively for the redress of the wrongs of the individual, is in law the redress of the wrongs of the claimant State'. [135]

But this writer is not speaking about customary law, but about *diplomatic protection* by one State, complaining to another State, on behalf of a citizen. The difficulty in logic here is caused by this writer's refusal to accept that individuals are also subjects of international law. There are numerous other situations where customary law is actually formed by individuals, for example in the Law of War.[136]

1. Practice of *All* States?

A further unsubstantiated claim of the 'traditionalists' – those who accept the usual definition of 'customary law' – is that the body of 'customary law' is the produce of 'States', in general. Does this mean that *all* States take part in this process?

When lawyers plead before the International Court of Justice or in the War Crimes Tribunals, and refer, as one of the most relevant elements, to the 'practice' of States, which States are involved? The 'practice' they refer to with examples from case law, concern no doubt the European States, sometimes the United

---

[135] *Ibid., loc.cit.*
[136] See, my *Law of War, op. cit., passim.*

States or – but more rarely – those of South America. But where are the examples of 'practice' from Japanese, Chinese, Russian or even Scandinavian States?

We soon realise that the essential 'practice of States' to which writers and courts refer to 'prove' that rules of customary law exist, stems from an arbitrary selection of sample States. Not only is it an arbitrary selection of States, but it is even clear that the selection is limited to languages known by most writers and by the relevant courts: thus, English, French and, occasionally German or Italian. But not even the official languages of the United Nations are represented: when did we last hear about a Russian, Chinese or even a Spanish case, cited in the International Court of Justice?

The arbitrary selection is further limited to States where court judgments are regularly reported. Therefore, little is heard of judgments in the Scandinavian countries, where usually only decisions of the Supreme Court (and not even all of those) are ever reported.

If 'practice of States', is decisive for defining the contents of a rule of customary law, but is representative only of that a fraction of the countries of the world, how can this 'customary rule' claim universal application?

2. Only Practice of *'Civilised States'*?

Article 38 c. of the ICJ Statute refers to a term that some might find embarrassing in today's world, namely to general principles recognised by 'civilised States'. This must mean, by implication, that there are States, today, that are 'not civilised'? If so, does this mean that some States are not entitled to take part in the formation of 'State practice'?

At the time the term 'civilised peoples'[137] was first used in the Statute of the Permanent Court of Justice,[138] the meaning of this expression was clear: in terms of principles of law, it was understood to mean to mean principles recognised by 'peoples benefiting from European civilisation', as formulated by de Martens.[139]

It should be noted that when the Statute of the International Court of Justice was debated after the Second World War, no one proposed that the term 'civilised nations'[140] should be deleted in the proposed Article 38. It was not until the Lebanese judge Ammoun fiercely criticised this expression in 1969[141] that discussions started whether it is appropriate to retain the adjective 'civilised' in the ICJ Statute. But not much has happened to change the situation.

For many years, and still, most jurists accept that the the practice of States arbitrarily chosen among more or less 'European' States is sufficient to 'prove' the existence of a customary rule.

---

[137] '...civilised peoples', was the expression adopted during the discussions about the Statute of the PCIJ, replaced before the adoption of the final version by 'civilised nations'.

[138] Before the adoption of the Statute of the PCIJ, there was little doubt that international law functioned primarily between 'civilised' States: Bluntschli, J.K., *Das moderne Völkerrecht der civilisierten Staaten* 3rd ed., Nördlingen: C.H. Beck, 1878.

[139] Martens, F.F., *Sovermennoe mezhdunarodnoe pravo ysivilizovannykh narodov*, St. Petersburg: Benke,1883; 5th ed.,1887-1888; reprinted Moscow: Yuridischeskii Kolledzh, 1996; idem, *Traité de droit international*, Paris: Librairie A. Maresco Aîné, 1887. *Cf.* German translation, von Martens, F.F., *Völkerrecht. Das internationale Recht civilisierten Nationen* (trans. C. Bergbohm), Berlin: Weidmannsche Buchhandlung, 1883, 2 vols. & Berlin: Weidmann, 1887. *Cf.* French translation, de Martens, F.F., *Traité de droit international*, Paris: Librairie A. Maresco Aîné, 1887.

[140] Carreau, D., & Marrella, F., *Droit international*, 11th ed., Paris: Pedone, 2012, 326.

[141] *The North Sea Continental Shelf Cases*, (1969) ICJ *Reports*, 1969, 133-136.

On the other hand, the reputation of Martens, earlier severely criticised,[142] has been restored as more of his theses are brought to attention: he links the expression 'civilised' nations to the level of *respect for human rights* in various countries. Not only is his name linked to the famous Martens clause in the 1899 and 1907 Conventions on Land Warfare,[143] but also to a theory that approaches our ideas in this work about *intrinsic* rules in international society. For his respect of history, of the Tsars and for his ideas on innate and intrinsic rules, the protection of human rights and the preeminence of the individual in international society, he was intensely criticised and held unacceptable as an international lawyer in the Soviet Union. After the fall of communism he has be reinstated and his works now appear in new editions in Russia.[144]

3. Practice of *'Numerous States'*?

The *Tadić Case* before the International Criminal Tribunal for the former Yugoslavia (ICTY) shows the absurdity of claims that 'general State practice' establishes 'customary rules'. In this case,

---

[142] Nussbaum launched several attacks on Martens, see, Nussbaum, A., *A Concise History of the Law of Nations*, New York: MacMillan, and *idem*, 22 *Nordisk Tidsskrift for International Ret og Jus Gentium* (1952) 51. Furthermore, scholars in the USSR fiercely discarded Martens and his ideas.

[143] See, in detail, my *Law of War, op. cit.*, and, for example, Meron, T., 'The Martens Clause, Principles of humanity, and dictates of public conscience', 94 *AJIL* (2000), 78.

[144] Martens, *Sovermennoe mezhdunarodnoe pravo ysivilizovannykh narodov*, reprinted Moscow: Yuridischeskii Kolledzh, 1996. For example, Holquist, P., '*The Russian Empire as a 'Civilized State': International Law as Principle and Practice in Imperial Russia*, 1874-1878, Washington: National Council for East European Research, 2004.

the Court of Appeal referred to 'a general practice' that established a 'customary rule'. The Court referred to nine cases, all but two cases were decided over 50 years ago, and *all* came from *German case* law.[145]

It is scandalous to claim that a customary rule of universal application can arise from such limited practice. The worst is that the *Tadić Case* was treated as a precedent by other courts that followed these misconceptions.[146] Even worse is that the ICTY Court relied on the *Tadić Case* in numerous subsequent cases where the interest of justice was often ignored.[147]

b) Also Negative Practice?

We have repeatedly referred to the absurdity of a negative customary rule.[148] Even the refusal to resort to the use of barbaric weapons or to genocide is conceived, surprisingly, as evidence of a 'negative' customary law.[149]

Moreover, the prophylactic rules without which international society can not survive are also referred to as 'customary' rules, even when it is a so-called 'negative' custom,[150] which, from the point of view of logic, becomes absurd.

---

[145] *Prosecutor v Duško Tadić*, Affaire No. IT-94-94 1A. For details and further references see, in my *The Law of War*, *op. cit.*, 200 & note 200, *loc. cit.*

[146] See, in detail, my *The Law of War*, *op. cit.*, *loc. cit. et seq.*

[147] *Ibid.*

[148] See, in detail, my *The Law of War*, *op. cit.*, *loc. cit. et seq.*

[149] For a criticism of this absurd notion, see my *International Legal Order*, *op. cit.*, Ch. III, E ii, 185 *et seq.* and my article on 'Illegal Combatants', *op. cit.* as well as my *Law of War*, *op. cit. loc. cit.*

[150] *Ibid.*, *loc. cit.*

c) Practice for a 'Long Time'?

One element demanded for the traditional definition of 'customary law' is that the 'practice' or the 'usage' must have gone on for some time. When lawyers notice that this is not necessarily so in practice in the real world: rules sometimes spring up when they are needed, especially for rules concerning Outer Space, this is explained as 'immediate' or 'instant' customary law.[151] Some jurists are thus of the opinion that material custom, that is, the recurrence of acts, is not really necessary to the formation of a 'customary' rule. Customary international law can, they say, also be 'instantaneous', they say, an idea which is certainly a contradiction in itself, and merely emphasises the need for new categories.

Others, with some justification, prefer to criticise the notion of 'instantaneous' customary law and demand that:

> 'The codification of the law by treaty is a slow process, even though more rapid in many cases than custom; but it is less likely to be influenced by political considerations than is the voting in international associations, and more likely to involve a studied and deliberate act of choice by each State concerned... Custom, on the other hand, grows slowly though not always as slowly as heretofore but it grows through the actual practice of States and therefore tends to reflect accurately the balance

---

[151] See, Cheng, Bin, 'United Nations Resolutions on Outer Space: 'Instant' international customary law?', Resolutions of the United Nations on Outer Space: Instant customary law?', 5 *Indian Journal of International Law*, 1965 and *idem*, 'Nature and sources of international law' in *International Law: Teaching and Practice* (ed. Cheng), London: Stevens, 1982, 222.

of their conflicting interests and to represent their considered intention.'[152]

Some remark that the required element of practice during a certain *time* for a customary rule to emerge is obviously missing in the case of 'instantaneous' customary law. But few have noticed, or commented on, that even a further element of the traditional definition of customary law is absent in the alleged 'customary' rules concerning Outer Space, that of 'numerous States': the practice in this case at the time of the first suggestion of 'instantaneous' customary law is limited to *one, or possibly two*, States.[153]

d) Whose *opinio juris*?

The third criterion for a 'customary rule' to emerge is that States validate it by their 'opinion' that it constitutes 'law', by their so called '*opinio juris*'. Only the opinion of States?

What about the opinions of individuals? The opinions of soldiers in armed conflicts? Do the opinions of the soldiers count for nothing? We cannot, in war or in other situations, ignore the individuals who are the most important subjects in international society. They are the individuals: the human beings, who make up the States.

Even if we focus on the opinion of States, there are problems. If an 'opinion' is that of a State, of whom, within this State, are we talking? The State has no head, no heart, no personal opinions. But

---

[152] Thirlway, *International Customary Law, op. cit.*, 76.
[153] In 1965 when Bin Cheng wrote the article cited in the note above, there were only two States that were active in Outer States.

the people who govern the State do have these. How, then, can we distinguish and identify these 'opinions'?

Could such opinions be found in statements, discussions and votes in international organisations and other fora, attitudes that would reflect the *opinio juris* of States? It is sometimes claimed that if a vote in the General Assembly is carried by an 'overwhelming majority' this indicates that States accept some 'new' customary rule.[154] But no one, neither a State, nor an individual, can be burdened by obligations unless it is clear beforehand that such duties may follow a vote or a statement. And *when a representative of a State votes in the General Assembly he does not know until afterwards that it became a 'land-slide vote'*.[155]

Little is gained by construing an *opinio juris* where there is no displayed will to be bound by any new rule; to call such a rule 'customary' is also far-fetched and contrived.

It would be better to identify rules by the pattern of pools of norms activated by legal acts as suggested in this work. It is also of primordial importance to take the role of individuals, NGOs and other entities than States, into consideration.

iv. The Fallacies of 'Customary' Law

The 'normativists' may frown at the approach of the proponents of the 'social process' of international law, but on the other hand they have not intervened to make a clear case for themselves.[156]

---

[154] See, for detailed criticism, my *International Legal Order*, op. cit., Ch. IV, vii, 224-250.
[155] *Ibid.* at 235.
[156] *Supra*, Part One, I i a)-c).

The reason is undoubtedly that the 'normativist' approach itself is full of archaic notions, which the adherents themselves should get rid of, in order to clarify the essence of a viable theory.

But then what do these authors offer on their side? They criticise the notion of 'instantaneous' customary law, but criticism is of little worth if not accompanied by proposals for new concepts. Moreover, what must be the task of the international jurist, it seems, is not so much to adopt slavish notions like those of 'customary law' but to examine whether, in reality, the practice of international actors justifies a concept such as the one that the 'traditionalists' define as 'customary law'.

The recent authors of the last century have made us prisoners of an unrealistic legal framework, insisting that the dominant source of international law be retained as customary law, leaving innumerable problems without any valid explanations.

The term 'customary law' is used at present for situations for which there is no corresponding practice and in matters for which no clear legal rules have been adopted by any clear *opinio juris*. It is not even posited as a prerequisite that States have acted within their legal competence: thus even an act of aggression is retained as evidence of a 'practice' of States.

'Customary law' has thus become a sort of 'dustbin' of international law: when it is not known where a rule comes from, it is claimed that 'it is a rule of customary law'.

As the above discussion has shown, the courts of justice now accept the practice of a few States, eight or nine, supposed to be the 'plurality' of States. But here we do not even mention the opinions expressed by governments, but only judicial decisions, and even lower courts. The duration of 'practice' is observed, reduced, or even retracted.

However, writers and advocates pleading in major cases before the International Criminal Court and the War Crimes Tribunals, also place most rules of international law as 'customary' rules. The authors, those who plead before the War Crimes Tribunals, and the courts themselves place *all* rules in the category of customary law, even maxims. As we have shown above,[157] maxims are created automatically in every legal system, and have little to do with 'custom'. This is also the case with certain general principles. Neither maxims nor general principles have anything to do with a 'custom' but are simply rules without which no legal system can function.

Norms and rules do not appear mysteriously in international society by a magic wand: but the way in which the international legal rules are created is better explained by the categories described above, logically arranged and organised, operating in an *interactive system*. This process involves multiple mechanisms, which, as the basis for the resulting obligation, may vary depending on the type of rules in question.[158]

The positivists claim that they accept as law only what is clearly laid down and established as law, for example in treaties and agreements. But they nevertheless accept, without the least hesitation, nebulous customary law with its far-fetched psychological element of the *opinio juris*. Certain authors, it is true, have sought to dispense with the requirement of *opinio juris*.[159] Others attach exaggerated importance to State factual practice but pay too little attention to the difficulty of assessing their *opinio*

---

[157] *Ibid., loc. cit.*

[158] *Supra*, in this Part, B, and *infra*, Part Four II, Variability of the Base of Obligation.

[159] Kopelmanas, L., 'Custom as means of creation of international law', 18 *BYIL*, 1935, 127.

juris and ignore the fact that the State is merely an abstract entity, only useful as a community for its citizens and a focal point for imputation of concrete acts.

It is clear that the textbooks today accept, without hesitation, the notion of customary law by stretching it and adjusting it at will to make it *appear* to correspond to reality, whereas it would be preferable to renounce it by adopting a new vision of how international society works. This work has the ambition to suggest wiser ways of visualising how legal acts, in inter-secting patterns, provide the necessary structure for international society.

As we can see, once there is a satellite in geostationary orbit, or an astronaut is on the moon, a latent rule of international law is 'activated'.[160] From the moment when the threat of nuclear weapons appeared, rules were immediately made available in international law.[161] But it is clear that these rules are by no means created by a 'custom'.

All modern authors of international law exaggerate the role of custom beyond all proportion. There are those who agree with the 'clumsy'[162] instrument of custom, but still continue to emphasise that it is 'the major instrument for the creation of rules

---

[160] See, *supra*, Part Two, III i c) under Prophylactic Rules.

[161] *Ibid.*, *loc.cit.* and my criticism of the ICJ for having failed to condemn the first use of nuclear weapons and and for its failure to lay down clear rules in *Opinion on the Use of Nuclear Weapons in Armed Conflict*, (1996), ICJ *Reports*, 1996, 66, in my *Law of War*, 2nd ed., 249-250 (in the 3rd ed. these two pages were omitted because of a technical error. Note the UN Treaty on Prohibition of Nuclear Weapons, open for signature in September 2017, *UN Treaty Collection*, 20 Sept. 2017.

[162] Friedmann, W., *The Structure of International Law*, New York: Columbia University Press, 1964, 121.

of international law'.¹⁶³ Some even make it an 'indispensable' notion.¹⁶⁴ In Anglo-Saxon doctrine, customary law is generally considered almost as important as treaties, a hypothesis which is difficult to justify in modern international society.¹⁶⁵ One writer even claims that treaties create customary law.¹⁶⁶

But such assertions are not compatible with the essence of law, which is predictability, or foreseeability, an essential notion of any legal system. The same authors who accept, sometimes reluctantly, that international organisations and individuals, may be subjects of international law, announce at the same time, but perhaps in another chapter, that customary law has evolved thanks to the custom and the *opinio juris* of the States. Thus, if we accept the assumption that customary law exists (in one form or another), it becomes essential to establish from whom these rules come. Whose custom is relevant? Who are the authors of these rules? Is it only the States? It seems contradictory and illogical to distinguish two separate domains: one for subjects and the other for actors capable of creating customary law.

We can no longer ignore the practice, behaviour and opinions of individuals. An exclusive State paradigm, the 'State' being understood in absolute terms, has become obsolete in relation to

---

[163] *Ibid.*, *loc. cit.*: 'it is a major instrument of law making'.

[164] Fitzmaurice, G., *Institut de Droit international, 18731973, Livre du centenaire*, 1973.

[165] Bos, M., *Methodology, op. cit.*, 59.

[166] D'Amato, A., *The Concept of Custom in International Law*, Ithaka & London: Cornell University Press, 1971. Such a proposal would violate the principle of *pacta tertiis nec nocent nec prosunt*, according to which those who are not parties to an agreement derive neither any advantage nor any obligations under this agreement as they are 'third parties'.

the needs of today's international society and is no longer adapted to reality.[167]

Most modern authors thus fall into the trap which they themselves created by their rigid ideas on the nature of customary law. On the one hand, they insist, with few exceptions, that only States are subjects of international law and that inter-governmental organisation also have such legal personality. But, on the other hand, they all assert, without a doubt, that customary law is formed by States and by them alone.

These commentators misunderstand that the international legal system is 'law for the people' and not a 'law for States'.[168] The very term 'international' means 'between nations', therefore between 'people', rather than between States. The individual, the human being, is certainly the main subject *par excellence* of international law.

v. 'True' Customary Law

Is customary law ever relevant? The arbitrary and dramatic nature of customary law implies that it is largely an illusion.[169] In most cases, where custom and perception reflect what is 'right', customary law does not fill any gaps that are not already addressed by the *maxims* or by *general principles* of international law, including the

---

[167] See *supra*, Part One, I iii, The Drift Away from the State Paradigm.

[168] *Cf.* Martens, *Sovermennoe mezhdunarodnoe pravo ysivilizovannykh narodov*, reprinted Moscow: Yuridischeskii Kolledzh, 1996, I, 236: The ultimate mission of States and of international agreements is the protection of individuals.

[169] *Cf.* Maine, H., *Ancient Law*, 1861, ed. New York, (E.P.Dutton & Co.), 1931, 31.

concept of *ethics* to the extent that they require 'fair' solutions to any particular dispute.

However, in other cases there is room for the formula usage + practice + *opinio juris* for a clear body of law, involving specific legal rights and obligations. The hesitation in this work to admit a vast field of customary law must therefore be accompanied by a brief indication of the field in which the questions of custom or use are relevant to engender concrete legal rules.

a) A Territorial or Maritime Bond

A special case can be made for customary law in the context of '*prescription*'. Here, there is a territorial or maritime anchorage, for purposes of prescription.[170] And here, there are great possibilities that a 'custom' exists, as proof of the existence of a title deed. In this case, custom is even constitutive.[171] Hence, there has certainly developed a customary right of acquisitive prescription.[172] Customary law has been at issue but in the majority of cases before the International Court of Justice, there has been a *territorial* (or *maritime*) bond, when the Court has relied on 'customary' law.[173]

---

[170] *Supra*, Part Two, C II a) 2., on Prescription.
[171] *Supra, loc. cit.*
[172] *Supra*, Part Two, B II i a) 2, on the notion of acquisitive prescription.
[173] *Fisheries Case* (*United Kingdom v Norway*) (1951), ICJ *Reports*, 1951, 116; *North Sea Continental Shelf Case* (*Federal Republic of Germany v Denmark & the Netherlands*) (1969), ICJ *Reports*, 1969, 3; *Continental Shelf Case* (*Tunisia v Libyan Arab Jamahiriya*) (1982), ICJ *Reports*, 1982, 18; *Libyan Arab Jamahiriya v Malte*, (1984), ICJ *Reports*, 1984, 13.

b) Regional Rules

There are exceptions: when the International Court of Justice referred to customary law for other issues than those concerning territorial delimitations that has kept the Court so busy for the last few decades. In one case[174] the alleged existence of a regional rule on extraterritorial asylum. But, in this case, the Court found no support for the assertion of the existence of a customary rule. It might be preferable to seek the essence of asylum practice in human rights rules, in conjunction with the rules of reciprocity.

c) Diplomatic Rules

There is another area where custom plays a role, but in a different way than what is suggested by the traditional concept of customary law. These cases of customary law concern the inter-State relations of States with regard to persons in diplomatic situations. In such cases, rules, based on reciprocity and caused by social needs, form part of the *intrinsic law*, that is indispensable to the international legal order.

The requirements for the immunity of diplomats are paramount to the functioning of international society[175]: it is even a fundamental principle that all members of international society are obliged to contribute to upholding this rule of *jus cogens*.[176]

---

[174] *The Asylum Case (Colombia v Peru)* (1950), ICJ *Reports*, 1950, 71.

[175] *Hostages in Teheran Case*, ICJ, (1980), ICJ *Reports*, 1980, 4. In this section we speak of diplomats; consuls have a much reduced immunity limited to acts in their official capacity, but many arguments here about diplomats apply *mutatis mutandis* also to consuls.

[176] *Supra*, Part Two, III, iii on the category of *jus cogens*.

d) The Law of War

In the field of the Law of War, custom can be highly relevant as signified even by the expression of its contents as 'the laws and customs' of war. But, again, we are not here speaking of 'customary law' the way this is traditionally understood. *Who* is contributing to the various 'customs', gradually accepted as binding law? Is it the States that wave the white flag to surrender? Is it the States that spare unarmed members of an enemy army when they stretch their arms in the air? Is it the States who rescue drowning enemy sailors at sea?

It is not the States but the *soldiers*, *sailors* and *airmen*, thus members of the armed forces that form rules that become binding through their behaviour. It is a fallacy to consider that this would be any 'customary' law developed by States. Again, we notice the consequences of denying that individuals are direct subjects of the international legal order and how remote such denials are from actual reality.

It is not only States that act in international society. It may be what the textbooks claim but to what avail is that, as a guide to statesmen and courts, if it is mere theory not matched by what happens on the ground.

We should thus not speak of customary 'law'. But it is the customary rules developed by individuals in war that crystallises and displays the *intrinsic* law of international society. Rules that do not form part of the *intrinsic law*, have emerged by the above mentioned mechanism of *interactivism* by selection of rules from a norm-pool for social needs by individuals and/or by other subjects of the international legal order.

vi. The 'Allergy' to Natural Law

At times it becomes evident that writers and Courts use the expression 'customary law' just to signify 'general international law'. Often, the expression has actually become a euphemism of natural law, probably only because it is politically more correct to speak of a 'nebulous' custom than of natural law or even of ethics, common sense or normal respect for the human person.

The dislike, or the 'allergy', that writers and courts of law have for natural law is probably due to misunderstandings. The dominant influence of the philosophers and lawyers of the doctrine called 'Uppsala School',[177] has led to the indoctrination of several generations of students in Scandinavia, forced to learn the monolithic ideas that 'natural law' is based on erroneous religious ideas.[178]

---

[177] Olivecrona, *De la loi*, 43, states that: '*si l'on refuse l'idée superstitieuse d'après laquelle le droit émanerait d'un dieu, la seule autre possibilité qui reste est que le droit est la création des hommes. Et en effet, les règles ont toujours été établies au moyen de la législation ou d'une autre manière par des hommes en chair et en os.*' See, further, *supra*, Part One, II ii and Part, Two, A I iii on the *hypothetical goal* and on *intrinsic law*.

[178] See, *supra*, Part Two, B III ii, on Compulsory Rules: *jus cogens*. Yet, the Swedish nihilists argued that no rule of international law is admitted in the internal system unless it is transposed into national law, see, Hägerström, A., *Stat och rätt, en rättsfilosofisk undersökning*, Uppsala: Almqvist & Wiksell, 1904; *Das Prinzip der Wissenschaft*, Uppsala: Humanistiska vetenskapssamfundets skrifter, 1908. *Cf.* Lundstedt, V., *Superstition or Rationality in Action for Peace*, London: Longman, 1925; *idem*, *Le droit des gens: danger de mort pour les peuples*, Paris: Phalanges, 1937; Olivecrona, K., *Law as Fact*, London: OUP, 1939; *idem*, *De la loi et de l'État. Une contribution de l'école scandinave à la théorie réaliste du droit*, trad. Jonason, P. B.-G., Paris: Dalloz, 2011. These ideas are still prevalent in Sweden

Sometimes when a rule is considered a 'customary rule' by an international court or tribunal, it is often a general reference to equitable principles.[179]

In other situations, when a rule is called a 'customary rule',[180] all that is said is really reduced to the fact that there is some evidence that some 'think' that it is the law, but this is not any proof of a rule. In any case, a tribunal remains free to decide on principles of fairness, surely guided by what others 'think', not necessarily on customary law, but on what is an ethical solution. The notion of morality, so often rejected, precisely by positivists who accept the primordial existence of customary law, seems to fulfill most of the needs of rules that customary law purports to fill.

The 'behaviour' of a State is often used to 'prove' its assent to a rule of international law. But the 'behaviour' of a State may be completely contrary to the rules already established in international law: are the practices of *apartheid* or genocide or a practice of bombarding citizens also part of 'customary law' ? It is indeed in the field of humanitarian law that we realise the false character of customary law, as defined and presented by the 'traditionalists', *i.e.* by the majority of the authors of textbooks.

In humanitarian law, we often find ourselves in the presence of 'negative' custom,[181] and we have remarked on the complications of

---

and disagreement is not allowed: see, the *jus docendi Case*, CEDH, http://www.ioir.se/UHAvalkant.pdf and *I.D. v Sweden*, ECHR no. 22255/93.

[179] *Supra*, Part Two, B I iii, Contingent Maxims.

[180] *Texaco Case*, (1977), *ILM* 1978 1.

[181] See, in detail my ideas on the 'absurd' notions of 'negative custom', in my articles on 'Extraordinary rendition', *University of North Carolina Law Journal*, 2008, 701 *et seq.* and on 'Illegal combatants and the Law of War', *Law Journal of George Washington University*, 2007, 1054 *et seq.*

such a concept.¹⁸² For example, as States have not always prevented genocide, does this mean that States have acquired a right by 'customary law' not to have any obligation to prevent genocide? Or since the States – again, in principle – have not always abstained from torture, is torture now legal as a customary rule?

In a remarkable statement the International Court of Justice held in the *Nicaragua Case*,¹⁸³ that the principle of non-intervention should form 'part and parcel of customary international law' although such a claim would be entirely based on negative custom. Another surprising claim by the ICJ was that the Judges held statements in various international fora as evidence of 'State practice' that would contribute to the formation of customary law. This is a serious side-step from the rule that no one is bound by an undertaking unless they are *aware* of their legal obligations.¹⁸⁴

Is it not more acceptable to suggest that there may be a dominant *opinio juris of States and individuals alike* that certain practices and behaviour are not 'acceptable' because they are incompatible with the ethics of international society? This has nothing to do with 'customary law'. There is no need to look for practice – or rather,

---

[182] See the previous note.

[183] *The Nicaragua Case* (*Nicaragua v United States*, (1986), ICJ *Reports* 1986, 106, para 202. *Cf.* criticism by Charlesworth, H.C.M., 'The Nicaragua Case and customary international law', 11 *Australian Yearbook of International Law*, 1987, 1.

[184] See, in great detail on the false assumption of legal force of votes, recommendations statements and votes, Chapter IV of my *International Legal Order*, London: Gower, 1994, 212-252, setting out reasons why voting in various fora cannot equate 'State practice' or be conducive to formation of 'custom'. *Cf.* my article 'The effect of Resolutions of international organisations', in *Theory of International Law at the Threshold of the 21ˢᵗ Century, Essays in Honour of Krzysztof Skubiszewski*, ed. Makarczyk, J., The Hague: Kluwer, s.d., 381.

practice demonstrates what *should not be done*, and it is therefore a prior practice which is followed by a *condemnation*.

The time has come, therefore, to return to the dominant ideas of doctrine and jurisprudence, from a century ago, that is to say, to the natural law that guides, with a flexible approach, to what is necessary in order that the international legal order operates. We are not talking here of any inflexible natural law, but of a system that adapts itself to current needs.

There was a time when slavery was quite acceptable; generations still alive recall where apartheid was not condemned by all. Then, at some point, the general opinion of the world declared, 'this is no longer acceptable'. But there was no 'practice' and there were no binding declarations or treaties on this subject, at least not in the short term. What was there was, though, was a very clear *opinio juris*, which had not been expressed only by States but also by individuals, NGOs, and by people with charisma and influence, such as Pope John Paul II.

Even the Soviet Union accepted in 1987, by the vote of Foreign Minister Edward Shevarnadze, that the United Nations decisions and rules on human rights prevail over national rules. A lecture in 1989 by the author of this work at the *Gosudarstvo i Pravo Institute* of Moscow, an entity close to the government, also accepted as 'interesting' and 'convincing' my theory on the intrinsic rules of the legal order as they were presented as 'socially necessary norms'.[185]

Instead of inventing an 'agreement' between States, and fictitious customary rules, we should rather be interested in the

---

[185] In another place at that time, and now even in Russia, it could be explained that these thoughts are in line with the thinking of St. Thomas Aquinas.

function of ethics. Ethics, obviously closely related to natural law, is also based on practice, opinion or even custom, in a given society at a given moment, as evidenced by the judgment that certain behaviour patterns are 'morally correct'. But the category of ethical rules is fairly easy to verify once the rules are analysed from the application to a given case.

Everyone is aware of the value of, and gaps in, ethical rules, and each court would be more competent to deal with the rules this way. Why then attribute to them a value of rules of 'customary' law, when it is clear that these rules have an ethical value, such as what is perceived as 'just' at a given moment in the life of international society?

It is quite strange that so many authors still accept the vague and floating contours of the contents of the notion of customary law. Outside the domain of territorial or maritime delimitation claims, there is little need for the recourse to customary practices in modern international law. Customary law has become the carpet under which any unidentified act, or any vague rule, is swept away, often by the conviction that it must necessarily represent valid law.[186]

It is preferable to present fresh and perhaps provocative ideas on the theory of the formation of international law. For it has been too long now, that one author after another, perpetuates the belief in the undisputed category of customary law.

It would be much better to define, crystallise and develop notions of ethics and equity, which are well known in natural law. These notions also have a clear function in international law

---

[186] Some are highly critical to the notion of customary law in its traditional form, see, Jennings, R., in Cheng, Bin., (ed.) *Teaching, op. cit.*, 5 *et seq.*

in their own right and it is incorrect to claim they form part of customary law.

The mechanisms of the acts in a systematic and logical manner presented in this book clearly show how these rules, instead of being customary rules, are rules that are *intrinsic maxims* or *general principles*, *intrinsic prophylactic* or *extrinsic supplementary rules*, adopted by optional participation acts, allocation or other voluntary acts.

vii. The Correct Concept of Intrinsic Law

It has become evident in the international legal order that the positive rules decided by States in major Conferences are not sufficient to guide the behaviour of the innumerable[187] subjects of international society. We no longer speak only of the behaviour of States, the most powerful subjects, but more about *individuals, the most important subjects of the international legal order*.

We must now have rules for the treatment and responsibility of terrorists, for activities of individuals operating drones in space, or for organising expeditions by armies of private mercenaries. There are a multitude of tasks that are not fulfilled by traditional law.

It is, of course, convenient to have recourse to treaties, even drafting and protocols for discussion, to elucidate and amplify the rules of the international legal system. But more and more often, written rules, materialised on paper, are missing. It is in this situation that international lawyers 'invent' rules, which they claim are 'customary' rules.

---

[187] *Supra*, Part One, I ii b).

But instead we should recognise that by accepting the theory of *interactivism*, described above, courts can find useful applicable rules for their guidance without having recourse to invented and pretended 'customary rules.' If we recognise the solid structure of maxims, general principles and other intrinsic rules like the prophylactic rules on prohibition of harm, we need not rely on vague and nebulous customary rules. The prophylactic rules are binding and some form part of *jus cogens*.[188] The main rules of international law are based on *intrinsic* law, and constitute rules without which international society cannot survive. Sometimes there are supplementary rules that are optional but useful when they apply to a particular situation.

Ethical rules form a large part of these rules of natural law. Among the categories of natural law according to St. Thomas, a form of natural law concerns biological behaviour. But the rules of natural law also apply to social relations between men within a community. The natural law according to St. Thomas Aquinas implies a natural inclination to act according to reason.[189]

Due to misunderstandings and misinterpretations of St. Thomas's theory, natural law has been considered by radical positivists as a 'religious' notion and thus rejected by those who reject Christian values. Yet St. Thomas points out that St. Isidore of Seville considers that 'natural law is common to all nations', although he is aware that not everyone follows the Gospel.[190] Natural law therefore applies to all nations and to every individual

---

[188] In detail, *supra*, Part Two, III iii.

[189] St. Thomas Aquinas, *Summa theologica*, Benziger Bros. edition, 1947, Question 94.

[190] *Ibid., loc. cit.*, Ia & IIa-e.

because this right is founded in nature and serves the needs of man in society. These are rules that are there to be useful to man and not to impose unfair obligations.

The other misunderstanding of those who reject natural law is their understanding of its contents. Natural law is not entirely 'immutable' or linked to 'religious' ideas they claim. As far as immutability is concerned, St. Thomas himself explains that there are prohibitions that can be added or excluded from natural law.[191] Indeed, natural law is much easier to explain than customary rules: natural law develops in less artificial ways than the nebulous rules of customary law.

We have preferred to use the term *intrinsic law* in this work to describe the essential maxims, general principles and prophylatic rules without which international society cannot function. These are rules that will enlighten the minds of statesmen and lawyers where the limits go between what is permissible and conducive to peace and stability in international society. Conversely, these are the rules that will alert individuals when rules, decisions or other acts are 'contrary to the conscience and sense of justice of all decent human beings. Then, surely such considerations of sense of 'justice' must override a positive Statute?[192]

---

[191] *Ibid., loc. cit.*, Ia & IIa-e.

[192] Oberlandesgericht Bamberg, Urteil 27, Juli 1949, 5 *Süddeutsche Juristenzeitung*, 1950, 207; the Court overruled a Nazi Statute as being contrary to the sense of justice of normal decent people; see Hart, H.L.A., 'Positivism and separation of law and morals' in Dworkin, R.M., *The Philosophy of Law*, Oxford: OUP, 1977, 17, who however, at 32, considers more important to avoid retrospective operation of a rule than to let sense of justice suffer. This is a remarkable standpoint in view of the fact that the Anglo-Saxon tradition is to be more relaxed on the issue of retrospective legal effect than the civil law systems.

V. Assessment of the Legal Effect of Acts

i. Intersecting Patterns

It may be observed that the categories of acts which we have suggested overlap and converge: an act may thus at the same time be contractual,[193] multilateral,[194] operative,[195] elaborate and responsive.[196] One example of that type of intersection of types is, for example, the Outer Space Treaty[197] which was the result of a framework act,[198] leaving scope for later implementation of a detailed regime.[199] The *Codex alimentarius* of the FAO concerning rules on food standards[200] was created by enhanced participation acts,[201] that were parallel,[202] and operative[203] acts of adoption.[204]

There are thus innumerable intersecting patterns of acts. For an act to have binding normative effect for States, however, *one* constituent element must be a basic participation act (by

---

[193] *Supra*, in this Part, II B iii a), Contractual Acts.
[194] *Supra*, in this Part, II C i c), Multilateral Acts.
[195] *Supra*, in this Part, II A i b), Operative Acts.
[196] *Supra*, in this Part, II A ii b), Contractual Acts.
[197] *Supra, loc. cit.*
[198] *Supra*, in this Part, II C iii a), Framework Acts.
[199] *Supra*, Part Two, C II ii c), Further Regimes.
[200] See my *International Law*. 1993, Chapter IV.
[201] *Supra*, in this Part, II B i b), Enhanced Participation.
[202] *Supra*, in this Part, II B iii, Statement Acts and II B iii c) Parallel Acts.
[203] *Supra*, in this Part, II A i b), Operative Acts.
[204] *Supra*, in this Part, II B iii d), Acts of Adoption.

which States adhere to rules by action) or come from the category of statement acts (by which States adhere to or make rules by express consent): only these categories can engage States in legal obligations. To have normative effect for non-State bodies, it is sufficient that one element from the category concerning State control is present.

It is a danger to security of law and to the respect that all subjects should have for the international legal system if it is claimed that they have obligations of which they are not themselves aware. The limited number of maxims without which no legal system can function, are adequate to ensure security of obligation (by relying on the rule *pacta sunt servanda* for a contractual undertaking) as well as fairness of procedure, and the category of general principles must be conceived restrictively. But all rules, including intrinsic rules, require an element of consent: although in the case of intrinsic rules, and the prohibition of harm, such 'consent' is held to have been given as soon as a subject acts in international society by what we call 'basic participation'.[205]

Rules are thus formed, recognised or activated by legal acts. Yet – *except for the intrinsic rules which are automatically operative and binding* – no obligation ensues *ipso facto* from other rules of international society, or from the acts which form them or which recognise them, *unless* there is an element of consent. But for extension beyond intrinsic rules in the field of humanitarian law and in human rights, consent is *presumed*.[206]

---

[205] *Supra*, in this Part, II B i, ii, iii, Types of Acts According to Mode of Consent.
[206] *Ibid, loc. cit.*

ii. 'Actors,' 'Persons' and 'Creators'

The actors whom we have listed above[207] and the acts which we have classified[208] may, in a certain combinations, produce the rule areas we have described.[209] For this to happen, there are certain conditions. First, the act taken must be internationally relevant.[210] Secondly, the actor must be competent to act. Competence of individuals, groups and entities may be founded on mere tolerance of States. Inter-governmental organisations must enjoy express or implicit competence under its constitutive instrument. States have given their '*abstract consent*' when they set up an organisation for a specific purpose.[211] Such entities thus enact derivative legislation. However, the competence of individuals and other non-State entities to create rule in international society does not depend on the authorisation of States.

But States are the *prime law makers* in so far as it is they consent to promotional rules by express consent and agreements. However, they, too, are bound within a certain framework to accept certain basic rules of social necessity. The rules they make by legal acts,[212] by activating, in this way, further rules from a *pool of voluntary norms*,[213] constitute *prime legislation*.

---

[207] *Supra*, Part One, I iii d), Entitled Persons.
[208] *Supra*, in this Part, II A, B and C, Typology of Acts.
[209] *Supra*, Part Two, A-C.
[210] *Supra*, in this Part, I ii, Doctrine of Legal Relevance.
[211] See my *Law Making*, op. cit, loc. cit.
[212] See *supra*, in this Part, II, Typology of Acts.
[213] See, *supra*, in Part One,

Some, but not all, rules of prime and derivative legislation create rights and duties for others than those who created the rules.

Thus, to be an actor in international society, and to be a person, enjoying rights and duties, is not the same as being a creator of rules. Thus, the non-State actors in international society contribute to the matrix of rules and by making functional rules between themselves,[214] as well as instigating 'provisional regimes', or 'pre-standards', and suggesting sets of rules which the States may, or may not, accept.[215] Furthermore, numerous acts by individuals and groups contribute to pressures that gradually prepare the ground for changing the law. This is also true of the changing values of social necessity by which States have to accept certain basic rules.

iii. A Model of Formation of Rules

We shall examine, in terms of the categories established in this work, the 'typical' example of alleged 'customary law': that of immunity of diplomats. This is commonly agreed to be a cornerstone of international law and developed through custom and usage over centuries.

We agree it is a cornerstone. And we agree that it evolved over centuries. But how did it all come about? Was it really evolving in a bulky mass of State practice, 'viewed' by States as the binding law? Or was it not simply the immediate social need of Rulers, or, later, by States, to communicate with each other, to send a messenger and have him back, unharmed after he had said what

---

[214] *E.g.* contracts between companies.
[215] *Supra*, Part Two, II C ii d), Standards and Pre-Standards.

was necessary to say? As soon as there were units in the world, such as tribes or early 'nations', there arose such a need.

The desire to protect a messenger was expressed, we submit, in an immediate conscious decision, imposed by a social need of communication, reinforced by the important notion of reciprocity.[216] This basic rule thus evolved by an act which was initially bilateral,[217] responsive[218] and parallel,[219] derived from a social need by active participation in international society.[220] It can also be conceived as a framework act,[221] as it was open to later action to improve on the details of the regime.[222] Indeed, later agreements between more nations, especially after the rise of the Nation-States in the 16th century, gradually enhanced and elaborated the rules of diplomatic immunity.

But whereas the initial rule had been imposed by a social need, and finding its basis of obligation in that need, later improvements were clearly consensual arrangements between States to supply details within an already existing regime.

Naturally, this process evolved gradually and slowly; but this does not mean that rules consist of 'customary' law. Custom was relevant in so far as it supplied the matrix which States could, or could not, adopt as binding rules by conscious acts.

---

[216] For a work on various aspects on reciprocity (but not referring to arguments on customary law) see, Decaux, E., *La réciprocité en droit international public*, Paris: LGDJ, 1983.
[217] *Supra*, in this Part, II C i b), Bilateral Acts.
[218] *Supra*, in this Part, II A ii b), Responsive Acts.
[219] *Supra*, in this Part, II iii c), Parallel Acts.
[220] *Supra*, in this Part, II B i a), Basic Participation.
[221] *Supra*, in this Part, II C iii a), Framework Acts.
[222] *Supra*, Part Two, C II ii c), Further Regimes.

Hence, there is a clear cut division between the rules on immunity as a binding set of rules and the *courtoisie*, which the traditionalists, if we may call them that, are uneasy about classifying. Why should rules in that area not be binding too? How can you know that they are not binding by implication of 'customary law'? How do you draw the border line between what States 'think' is binding and what they 'think' are merely good manners? The difference is that, in the case of courtoisie, there are not any *compelling social reasons* why rules on *courtoisie* should be binding. They do not easily fit in with the section of 'intrinsic' or other 'prophylactic' rules set out above. But then they must be part of the 'extrinsic' rules; and for those we can check against the *graduated scale of presumption of consent* that applies to such rules.[223] But there is little support for any obligation for rules on *courtoisie* to be binding. Such rules are not part of the basic tenets of the 'club', but are less important rules of 'etiquette'? You are not causing any 'harm' by not following such rules and there is little point in insisting on reciprocity.

In a similar way we may explain why new members of international society are bound by the maze of rules on international law. It is sometimes argued that these new States or entities have not had occasion to assent or express their consent. But this is to misconstrue the importance of consent. Here, we are concerned with a new member joining a 'club' where the Standing Rules have already been adopted. The new State does not have[224] to send

---

[223] *Supra*, in this Part, I iii, Graduated Scale of Presumption of Consent.
[224] *Supra*, Part Two, C I ii, Rules on Mutual Contact.

diplomats or conclude treaties, but if they do, they must abide by relevant rules.[225]

The State that does not abide by the laws can 'go elsewhere'.[226] If, on the other hand, it wishes to take part in communications, it will have to accept rules as they stand, but this new subject may later be entitled to partake in further elaboration of details of a regime.

iv. The Need for Accurate Terminology

A brief analysis of the bland references to 'customary' law in the *Nicaragua Case*[227] indicates that, in the terms of the present work, the Court was concerned with the application of the *maxims* of equality and of *audiatur est altera pars*,[228] with the alleged violation of *prophylactic rules*,[229] concerning the use of force against another State[230] with alleged use of practices contrary to humanitarian rules,[231] as well as with the duty not to obviate rules on peaceful settlement of disputes.[232] Further arguments concerned entrenching distributive rules on national space,[233] rules on mutual

---

[225] *Cf.* rules on treaties and on communications in general, *supra, loc. cit.*

[226] *Cf. The Dialogues of Plato*, ed. by Jowett, 1953, at 53 b and *The Birds* by Aristophanes, in *Four Plays by Aristophanes*, New York: Plume, 1964.

[227] *Nicaragua v United States*, (1984) ICJ *Reports* 1984 392 and ICJ *Reports* 1986 14.

[228] *Supra*, Part Two, B I iii and v, Contingent Maxims, Consequential Maxims.

[229] *Supra*, Part Two B III, Prophylactic Rules.

[230] *Supra, loc. cit.*

[231] *Supra, loc. cit.*

[232] See, Part Two, III ii, on modalities of Settlement Rules.

[233] See, Part Two, C I i, Distributive Rules.

contacts, involving both the right of communication[234] and the duty of warning.[235] The Court also had to consider the violation of further promotional rules[236] in a specific Treaty of Friendship, Commerce and Navigation of 1956.

What the Court was not concerned with, however, was 'customary' law: what the Court referred to when mentioning 'customary' law were rules which had come into being in international society by quite different mechanisms than custom. Instead, it would have been suitable to speak about 'intrinsic law' – as opposed to treaty law – because 'customary' is only a pleonastic adjective which does not reflect the true nature of relevant norms.

VI. The Obligation of Activated Rules

Rules become binding when they are *activated*. Many rules, even those that are compulsory, are not always in operation: it is factual situations that make them enter into force. Naturally, they are already 'in force' in the technical sense but they are not yet *applied*.

i. Activation of Rules

Rules are activated in various ways: we have demonstrated above the cobweb of rules and acts and how they may interact in specific situations.

---

[234] See, Part Two, C I ii, Rules on Mutual Contacts.
[235] See, Part Two, C I ii b), Duty to Warn.
[236] See, Part Two, C II i, Promotional Rules.

a) Intrinsic Rules

We should emphasise that *intrinsic rules* are activated *automatically* whenever a factual situation involves matters within the realm of any *intrinsic prescription*. A Court has even an *ex officio* duty to invoke such rules before coming to any decision or pronounce any judgment.

b) Rules Triggered by Acts

As we have underlined on several occasions, large parts of international law consist of what are known as *dispositive rules*. These are rules that parties to a dispute are free to adopt or refuse, or for a contract they may wish to conclude. These are thus rules that also States – or any other entity with international personality – might decide to select or discard for mutual relationships, or for agreements or treaties with a third party.

Extrinsic rules are largely facultative and optional but are often selected according to the need of a specific situation. Once such rules have been adopted, and thus have been approved by the clear consent of the parties involved, such rules carry compulsory force between the parties.

ii. Traditional Solution of the Obligation

There is no shortage of offers for a basis of obligation in international law.[237] The consent theory, often perverted for obvious political

---

[237] Schachter lists with ease a 'baker's dozen': Schachter, O., 'Towards a theory of international obligation', 8 *Virginia Law Review*, 1968, 300, to which should be

motives,[238] has often been criticised as assuming too much power of the State to refute any law along Hegelian lines.[239] Other theories rely either on the assumption of a '*Grundnorm*', by a curious inversion of gravity at the apex of the international legal structure,[240] either concerning *pacta sunt servanda* or a primordial rule that States would 'behave as they customarily have behaved'.[241] Both of these fictions introduce unnecessary elements.

The *Grundnorm* of *pacta sunt servanda* – often unchallenged in spite of its absurdity – only engenders further difficulty by its inability to explain the nature of the system. The second fiction, relating to an assumed continuation of behaviour is even stranger. For how can States act in international society by looking back, assessing the behaviour of nearly 200 other States, and finding a common pattern which must be followed in the future? And why should one follow the same pattern as in the past? It could even have been an undesirable or 'bad' pattern.

---

added his own theory. Cf. Brierly, J.L., 'The basis of obligation in international law', *BYIL* 1952; *idem*, 'Le fondement du caractère obligatoire du droit international', 23 *RCADI* 1928 iii.

[238] The USSR often invoked such arguments, see Tunkin, G.I., 'Coexistence and international law', 95 *RCADI* 1958 32.

[239] *Cf.* Verdross, A. v., *Le fondement du droit international*, Leiden & Boston: Brill, 1927, i, 265.

[240] Kelsen, H., *Reine Rechtslehre*, Vienna: Deuticke, 1934, 66, 129; *cf.* Perassi, T., 'Teoria dommatica delle fonti di norme giuridiche', *Rivista*, 1917, 195; Sperduti, G., *La fonte suprema del ordinamento internazionale*, Milan: Giuffré, 1942; *cf. supra*, Part One, II i, The Sources of International Law, for criticism of Kelsen's theories.

[241] Kelsen, H., *General Theory of Law and State*, Cambridge, Mass.,: Harvard Univ. Press, 1946, 369; *cf.* 1 Guggenheim, P., *Lehrbuch* 6.

The theories of social obligation, especially as developed by Scelle,[242] have some convincing elements. Although Scelle adopts a more serious wording than Manning[243] there is some similarity between the social obligation and the assertion of a need to comply by the rules of the 'game'.

The problem of legal obligation has lately been avoided by international lawyers, not surprisingly in view of the fact that they no longer agree about the general area of dispute. For if they are not *ad idem* with regard to what international law 'is', how can they pursue any discussions about its obligation?

iii. A New Theory of Obligation

a) Variabiliy of the Basis of Obligation

So how and why do rules become obligatory? *Intrinsic rules* appear to be binding as they are indispensable to the functioning of international society. The extrinsic rules become binding by being accepted by an an act of the affected persons: normally by clear consent but sometimes by the operation of the myriad of acts as we have described in this work.

However, it seems reasonable to suggest that *the basis of obligation* varies according to the nature of a rule.

---

[242] Scelle, G., *Manuel de droit international public*, Paris: Editions Domat Montcrestien, 1948, 13 et seq.

[243] *Supra*, Part Two, C I ii, Rules on Mutual Contact.

1. Logical Necessity

The maxims we have described above[244] are, as being logically inherent in any legal system, binding by virtue of logical necessity.

2. Social Necessity

Prophylactic rules,[245] such as those concerning prohibition of the use of force, pollution or violations of the most basic Human Rights, are binding by virtue of social necessity. For 'social', as an adjective, refers to 'society' and if the functioning of that 'society' is obviated by violation of such rules, then they must be reinstated by social force or obligation.

Stabilising rules,[246] for example those concerning immunity of diplomats, for example, are created because of social necessity: States cannot enter into contact without relying on such rules being upheld. The reason why such rules exist also explain their binding force. They, too, are binding because of social necessity.

Rules on communications, in their rudimentary form, or formal rules on treaties, are also binding by force of social necessity. They may be further elaborated by agreement but the substratum of rules of contact between States are upheld by social necessity, considerably reinforced by reciprocity.[247]

---

[244] *Supra*, Part Two, B I, Inherent Maxims.
[245] *Supra*, Part Two, B III, Prophylactic Rules.
[246] *Supra*, Part Two, C I, Stabilising Rules.
[247] On reciprocity in general, see Decaux, *La réciprocité, op. cit.* For an analysis of reciprocity with regard to rules of war, see my *Law of War, op. cit.*, 339-352.

Promotional rules,[248] on the other hand, are only very rarely binding because of any social necessity; one exception may be the case where a duty to 'share' is perceived as a functioning rule, a eventuality that cannot be presumed.

3. Consent

The most common basis for obligation in international society is undoubtedly consent. It is also suggested that consent, assessed along a *graduated scale of presumptions* according to the rule in question,[249] or given by separate a declarative act, reinforces the basis of obligation of logical[250] and social necessity.[251] Furthermore, all acts elaborating further these two rules areas, as well as promotional rules, have always their root of obligation in the consent of States. Treaties are clearly based on this principle. So is any commitment to allow the exercise of sovereign functions in another State's territory: in this context 'usage' may be relevant. Consent may, in cases concerning restriction of sovereignty, for example regarding immunity 'be tested by common usage and by common opinion, growing out of that usage'.[252] Individual consent, by *ad hoc* decisions, may be given by responsive acts,[253] in the case of situations for which no rules cater. This happened, for

---

[248] *Supra*, Part Two, C II, Promotional Rules.
[249] See, in this Part, I iii, Graduated Scale of Presumption of Consent.
[250] *Supra*, in the preceding section 1.
[251] *Supra*, in the preceding section 2.
[252] Statement by Chief Justice Marshall stated in *The Schooner Exchange v McFaddon*, that jurisdiction may be restricted or extended by 'consent', 11 US Cranch 116, 3 Ed 287 (1812). *Cf. Rahimtoola v Nizan of Hyderabad*, (1957) 3 WLR 884, 910. On Responsive Acts, see, in this Part, II A ii b).
[253] See, in this Part, II A ii b), Responsive Acts.

example, in the case of Outer Space,[254] where there was a clear adoption by consent of States for a new situation. A treaty was later concluded,[255] which entrenched the consent given.

Most voluntary rule areas thus depend on consent of States. This is certainly the case for promotional rules[256] as well as in the case of correctional rules.[257] In both cases there will be clear social pressures that will be conducive to consent being given.

It is important to emphasise the role of consent in modern international law to combat the trend to attach importance to voting figures in the General Assembly, when a State did not yet know the outcome of the voting pattern, or to presumed acceptance,[258] by 'State practice' under 'customary law'; such arguments will not convince States and statesmen of the binding nature of the system. Rather than accepting such propositions, they might reject the whole network of international law, which, by its vagueness and claims of constructive acceptance of rules by those who did not accept obligations by a simple vote in an organisation, has brought itself into disrepute.

4. Reciprocity

The social necessity is, as mentioned, a forceful ground of obligation in international society. But this ground is considerably reinforced

---

[254] *Supra, loc. cit.*

[255] See, Part Two, C II ii, Further Regimes.

[256] *Supra*, Part Two, C II i, Promotional Rules. But see, hesitation of the type of basis of obligation for one basic area, *supra, loc. cit.*, ii, Duty to Share?

[257] *Supra*, Part Two, C III, Consequential Rules.

[258] See, in great detail, my *International Legal Order, op. cit.*, 212-252, on 'apparent binding force' of Resolutions of the General Assembly.

by reciprocity.[259] A specific aspect of reciprocity is the Golden Rule,[260] as applied in international society, implying that subjects of the international legal order should treat others as they wish to be treated themselves. There is no ground that can be more conducive to obedience and compliance with relevant rules.

5. Solidarity Rules

The most basic substantive prophylactic and stabilising rules are guaranteed by special 'solidarity' rules that reinforce the basis of obligation.

There is ample evidence that members of international society consider themselves bound to uphold certain fundamental rules. One aspect of this duty is the obligation of States and others not to lend assistance to another State or entity affected by sanctions for a violation of international law. Article 2(5) of the United Nations Charter prohibits assistance to States against which enforcement action is taken. Furthermore, Article 10 of the Draft Declaration of Rights and Duties of States of 1949 provides that

> 'Every State has the duty to refrain from giving assistance to any State which is acting in violation of Article 9 (which prohibits threat or use of force) or against which the United Nations is taking preventive or enforcement action' (words in brackets added).

---

[259] See,t Decaux, E., *La reciprocité en droit international public*, Paris: LGDI, 1983.
[260] See, *supra*, in Part One, I ii c) 3, on the origin and universality of the Golden Rule.

The views one takes of international law are often coloured by national allegiance and the self-interest of States.²⁶¹ Hugo Grotius' *De Mare Liberum* (1609) may not have contained the same rules if he had not had a brief for the Dutch Government to prove legal rules to oust the Portugese from competition at sea. Similarly, even general rules of international law, which are clearly acceptable to all sides, are understood or interpreted differently in different national contexts.²⁶²

A comparative approach²⁶³ sometimes mitigates nationalistic views²⁶⁴ and counteracts the tendency to a lopsided perspective. Above all, the more short term targets are sought, the more nationalistic various interpretations become. Thus, the long range objectives, for example, the hypothetical goal,²⁶⁵ promote, by their very distance, a unity among actors in the world.

States depend on the solidarity of other members of international society.²⁶⁶ Vattel pointed out that

> '...toutes les Nations sont interessés à maintenir la foi des traités, à la faire envisager partout comme inviolable et sacrée, elles sont de même en droit de se réunir pour réprimer celui qui temoigne la mépriser, qui s'en joue ouvertement, qui la viole et

---

²⁶¹ See, my *International Law and the Independent State, op. cit.*, Ch. I.

²⁶² For ideology, see, *supra*, Part One, I vi, Universality of the System.

²⁶³ *E.g.* Gutteridge, H.C.,'Comparative law and the League of Nations', in Butler, W.E., *International Law in a Comparative Perspective*, Alphen aan den Rijn: Sijthoof, 1980, 13 *et seq.*

²⁶⁴ *Cf. supra, loc. cit.*

²⁶⁵ *Supra*, Part One, I ii b), The Hypothetical Goal.

²⁶⁶ Suarez, *De legisbus*, I, ch. XIX, No.3, XX, No. 9.

foule aux pieds. C'est un ennemi public qui sappe les fondements du repos des peuples, de leur sureté commune'.[267]

The solidarity of members of international society to uphold rules is enhanced in proportion to the importance of the endangered rule. Thus, a breach of a 'lesser' rule may be a 'delict' whereas a violation of a fundamental rule is a 'crime'. An example of a crime would, for example be the violation of

'an international obligation so essential for the protection of fundamental interests of the international community'.[268]

The significance of the distinction is that in the case of an international crime, a State, which is not directly injured, is entitled to invoke the responsibility entailed by the breach, whereas in the case of an international delict, *i.e.* where there has been a breach of a less fundamental rule of international law, only the directly injured State has the right to submit a claim involving the responsibility of the State committing the wrongful act.

The distinction possibly coincides with the difference between 'ordinary' compelling rules of international law and the nebulous

---

[267] *Jus Gentium*, ii, ch. XV, para. 222. 'All Nations have an interest in upholding the faith of treaties, to make (this faith) seem everywhere as inviolable and sacred, and they also have a right to unite to repress anyone who proves himself to despise (this faith), who violates it and tramples it under his feet. It is a public enemy who usurps the foundations of the tranquility of peoples, and their common safety'.

[268] ILC, State Responsibility, Draft by Ago, R., Special Rapporteur, A/CN.4/291, Add. 2, 14. *Yearbook* 1976 ii 18.

notion of *jus cogens*.²⁶⁹ Virtually all international lawyers agree that *jus cogens* exists²⁷⁰ but considerable controversy reigns as to what substantial rules shall be considered as included under the concept.²⁷¹ One hallmark must be that the upholding of such rules are essential to all members of international society. Thus, *jus cogens* would signify basic rules which are of concern to all States and which

> 'protect interests which are not limited to a particular State or group of States but belong to the community as a whole'.²⁷²

But the last reference to a statement of a Soviet lawyer, adviser to the then Soviet Government, may alert us to the fact that many pronouncements have been made on behalf of States that may not all have lived up to what they claim should be the rule for others.

b) Consequences of Violation of the Most Basic Intrinsic Rules

Basic rules like prohibition of genocide, slave trade and the taking of hostages, probably represent the minimum residue of the concept

---

[269] See the Vienna Convention on Treaties, ILC *Yearbook*, 1958, ii, 52; Virally, M., 'Réflexions sur le *jus cogens*', *AFDI* 1966 5; Gomez Robledo, A., 'Le *jus cogens* international: sa genèse, sa nature, ses fonctions', 172 *RCADI* 1982 9; Suy, E., in Carnegie (ed.), *The Concept of Jus Cogens*, 1967.

[270] This includes the last Soviet writers under communist rules, Tunkin, G.I., *Law and Force in the International Society*, New York: Bowker, 1983, at 143;

[271] See, *supra*, in Part Two, B III ii on *jus cogens*.

[272] Tunkin, G.I., in 2 *Papers and Proceedings*, Conference on International Law, Geneva, 1967, 967.

of *jus cogens*, in the centre of our *intrinsic rules*.[273] The observance of these rules is required by all members of international society. If the rules are violated it is not sufficient to condemn their violation by unilateral acts: it is also necessary to lay down, in anticipation of a breach, the absolute nullity of treaties concluded in disregard of such principles.[274] These rules are so important that their non-observance

> 'may affect the very essence of the legal system'[275]

If taken to imply such basic rules, the contents of *jus cogens* might coincide with the *intrinsic rules* of which the most important ones are the maxims, the basic formal general principles as well the prophylactic rules[276] and the rules of social necessity,[277] sketched above.

These rules can be amplified by treaty or by other voluntary action, but certain basic rights granted do not appear to be susceptible to reduction, at least not those which assure certain basic rights to individuals.

---

[273] *Barcelona Traction Case (Second Phase)*, 1970, ICJ *Reports*, 3 at 32 adding the crime of 'aggression' and 'rules concerning the basic rights of the human persons, including slavery and racial discrimination'. *Cf.* Order of 15th December 1979 in the *Hostages Case*, adding 'inviolability of diplomatic envoys and embassies', see para 38; *cf.* Jimenez de Arechaga, General Course in Public International Law, *RCADI*, 1978 i, 64. On the crime of genocide as part of general International Law, see *The Genocide Case, Advisory Opinion*, (1951), ICJ *Reports*, 23.

[274] Vienna Convention on the Law of Treaties, articles 53 and 64.

[275] Suy, E., 'The concept of *jus cogens* in international law', *Conference on International Law, op. cit.*, 18.

[276] See, Part Two, B III, Prophylactic Rules.

[277] *E.g.* rules on mutual contact, Part Two, B II ii..

For example, duties of a State can be divided into those owed vis-à-vis another State and those owed to international society as a 'whole'. Obligations towards the 'whole' concern, for example, the substratum of the *jus cogens* as indicated in a limited way above.[278] Such obligations can be subsumed under rules which operate *erga omnes*.

A violation of fundamental rules is particularly grave and entails specific consequences not always activated by breaches of lesser rules. For example, a violation of a fundamental rule engages the responsibility of a State in a particular way, excluding any defence of reprisals, self-defence or other justification.[279] 'Any' State is furthermore entitled to protest[280] in the case of a breach of fundamental rules. It is thus

> 'competent to any State or to the body of States, to hinder the wrongdoing from being accomplished or to punish the wrongdoer'.[281]

A violation also activates a duty on the part of members of international society. They must 'recognise' the illegality of the situation which has arisen through such a serious breach.[282] Furthermore, it is thus incumbent on all[283] to refrain from lending support

---

[278] *Supra*, Part Two, B II ii c) Human Rights and *The Barcelona Traction Case (Second Phase)*, 1970, 3 at 32.

[279] *Hostages in Teheran Case* (1980), 26.

[280] *Ibid., loc. cit.*

[281] Hall, W.E. *A Treatise on International Law*, Oxford: OUP, 1890, 467; *cf.* 4th ed.1895.

[282] *Namibia Case*, Advisory Opinion, (1971), 54.

[283] Also on States which are not members of the United Nations *ibid.* 53, 56.

or any form of assistance which may perpetuate or uphold the illegal situation.[284] Relationships entered into with entities that have brought about an illegal situation may be void in so far as others may refuse to recognise the validity of transactions.[285] It is questionable, however, whether legal effects under other systems can be affected. However, recognition of illegality and restraint from lending support (combined with sanctions of non-recognition of certain transactions) does not exhaust the effects of a breach of a fundamental rule. Members of international society may take active measures to rectify any infringements. World opinion exercises here a formidable pressure to uphold what we, in this work, have called *intrinsic international law*.

---

[284] *Ibid., loc. cit.*
[285] *Ibid., loc. cit.*

Conclusions

International law is a system regulating acts and situations which are internationally relevant. The bulk of international law consists of intrinsic, sociologically necessary norms, supplemented by further rules created by legal acts. Not all rules of international law are relevant to all subjects. Technical international organisations, like, for example, the ICAO, have little interest in human rights. The law of diplomacy is not of immediate importance to a multinational company. And the law of the sea is not immediately relevant to belligerents in land-locked States in Africa.

There is a presumption that acts of States are internationally relevant and, conversely there is presumption that acts of individuals are not; but in the latter case the presumption is rebuttable and the test of relevance is elastic, to subsume an ever increasing type of activity of individuals and certain non-State entities under rules of international law.

The bulk of international law consists of *intrinsic rules* without which the international legal system cannot function. Some of the *intrinsic* or *inherent* rules are maxims that are found in all legal systems. The maxims and the essential general principles are of a formal character. The most important intrinsic rule that is substantive with material contents is the rule prohibiting harm, entrenched in the international legal system as a vital and basic *prophylactic* rule. This rule is in fact *the key to harmony and peace in international society*.

Intrinsic rules do not depend on approbation or on custom and it is clear in practice that such rules are widely accepted as binding precepts. When States or other subjects of international law deviate or violate such rules, there are immediate excuses, or condemnation of such behaviour. Naturally, culprits are not always immediately apprehended or punished. But in practice there is ample evidence that, sooner or later, many subjects of international law, dictators, war criminals or terrorists, have to answer for their actions if they have violated the law.

One must distinguish between creators, actors and latent subjects of international law: the creators make the law that supplements the essential *intrinsic rules*; actors act under the system and often contribute by pressure to develop the law; and latent subjects may emerge from their passivity to also take on the role of actors. It is only when actions of individuals or any other actors can be perceived as *internationally relevant* that the 'personality' of an individual or of an entity is *activated*.

Thus, *all*, (entities, individuals...), are bound by international law: they are thus *latent subjects* of the legal order. They are *active subjects* in so far as they all, as individuals and groups, enjoy certain direct rights under international law. All subjects are *potential* actors. But is only when subjects presume to act in any way relevant to the international sphere that they become actors in the international legal order.

The actor must know the law, for if he oversteps it he may become personally liable, at least in the case of outrageous violations of basic rules. But actors may also contribute to international law making by pressure on others to accept new rules. The most powerful units, the States, make most of the rules that supplement the intrinsic law, either by their participation in international intercourse, by their own agreements and treaties or by their clear imprint of consent to *provisional standards*, or *pre-standards*.

Provisional standards, or pre-standards, are usefully elaborated by private entities, by international or inter-governmental bodies and, particularly, by Resolutions of the General Assembly of the United Nations. All actors in international society may contribute to the formulation of provisional standards by their internationally relevant acts. The 'persons' and 'actors', never clearly identified by traditional normativists of international law, sometime contribute to the formation of international rules and thus occasionally act as creators.

To be a 'subject' under any legal system means that you can enjoy direct rights and obligations. Individuals are the main subjects of the international legal system as it is they who make up the States and other collective units. It is they who form national and international companies and structures. It is individuals who fight in wars. Individuals enjoy specific human rights but have also direct responsibility and duties when they act in the international sphere: they bear individual responsibility for their possible crimes but also enjoy specific rights if they come to suffer by maltreatment.

States are the main power structures and the main creators of prime international law. In their case there is thus identity between actors/persons/creators. But, entities other than States contribute to the formation of international rules. Again, the main pressure for new rules comes from individuals. It is they who make up the

NGOs that seek to improve international human rights or secure the protection of the environment. The functional and effective areas of actors/ persons/ creators do thus not fully coincide.

The States may be the prime law makers in international society but there are also important forms of delegated legislation through international organisations. But all competence of such entities, however wide and practically important, can be derived back to the 'abstract consent' given by States in the constitutive instrument. This means that States are always free to leave an organisation even if the constituent treaty provides for 'perpetual' obligations; there may be economic problems in leaving a common market, where economies and production have been integrated, but such problems do not affect the legal right of withdrawal.

The derivative law that emanates from inter-governmental organisations is ultimately dependent on State consent and is formed along State models. Agreements are concluded in similar form as State treaties, and even the institutional structure often resembles legislatures, executives and judiciaries. If inter-governmental organisations in many ways, especially for their existence, depend on States, they can often take acts which bind States without the approval of the State that they represent. This may happen by majority or by 'contracting-out' procedures – implying that Member States are bound unless they protest within a given time.

Furthermore, delegates may, by their actions also affect the constitutional framework of the member States. For it is a delegate from the executive, for example from the Ministry of Foreign Affairs, or from another Ministry or Department, who represents the State in an organisation. But the vote of such a delegate may bind the State in many organisations although the legislature in that

State, which normally would have had a say in such matters, has not been consulted. The delegates to international organisations can thus achieve a constitutional shift in the Member States, from the legislature to the executive.

The States thus create prime international law although there are many subsets of derivative law emanating from organisations and also from other actors. Within the various legal circles thus created, actors may perform transactions and legal persons may enjoy rights and duties; the larger 'permissive' legal framework has no longer its limits set by States. Thus, multinationals, for example, do regulate much of their own affairs and not only in a manner 'allowed' by States.

That States have this ultimate 'power' does not necessarily mean that modern international society is entirely dominated by the State paradigm. The States may have the power, especially the power to revoke consent. But there is a considerable amount of derivative law making by other bodies and, from the practical point of view, the role of the State is sometimes in the background. There is a clear drift away from the exclusive State paradigm. Even if States create prime law, the material contents of new rules is normally found in statements and arguments from other quarters, especially from the ever more important NGOs. And the process of adoption of 'provisional standards' is becoming an ever more important mechanism of rule-making by States.

It is mainly individuals and non-governmental bodies that *prompt* changes and development of international law. In this sense they can even be considered to *make law*: they may develop behaviour patterns that are accepted as useful by other subjects and gradually a new rule emerges. Continuous and persistent protests about *apartheid* may illustrate this point. Or to take another example, insistence on the right of women to vote, did produce new rules on democracy not only in the internal law of States but in international law.

For purposes of taxonomy and classification, a *hypothetical goal* of international society, implying the promotion of the welfare of mankind may be adopted. Rules of international society can then be classified in a hierarchical order according to their immediate linkage to the hypothetical goal.

There is a *graduated scale of presumption of consent* according to the hierarchy of the relevant rule area. According to this scale, there are a few basic areas where there is a lighter onus of proof to establish consent, *i.e.* those where specific rules are necessary for social contact.

Minimum *maxims*, and certain formal general principles, are inherent in any legal order, and are thus also present and recognised in international law; States readily accept that the legal order cannot function without such logical maxims.

Entrenching rules further lay down a relatively stable framework for further action. Of these entrenching rules some norms, the *prophylactic rules*, are of basic importance to the survival of international society: they are the rules prohibiting force in general, as well as the substratum of human and humanitarian rights. Such rules are binding on the State itself, as its disregard for such rules would annihilate the international legal order. For the international society is an agglomeration of individuals, who, for convenience, group themselves into States. Thus, it is the individual and the respect for the individual, which must be at the centre of the basic rules of international law.

International law, being a system of rules for matters of international relevance, focuses increasingly on the protection of the individual although, naturally, many rules, for example those on treaties, operate mainly between States as the larger units.

Other rules 'freeze' a given situation by *stabilising rules*, implying rules for division of national space; others concern the form of mutual contact, such as communications or immunity of diplomats.

Supplementing rules improve on the given framework for cooperation by allowing *promotional rules*, implying voluntary additional rules, enacted by States. Some *unifying rules* will, for example, by institutionalisation, tie States functionally or politically together. Other *programmatic rules* are low in normative contents and imply mainly an agenda for the future, depending on political and economic options. *Consequential rules*, including *correctional* and *settlement rules*, safeguard the observance of the main rules.

States can act *de jure gestionis* and, when they do, or when organisations they have created do, international law will provide rules for contracts which, in exceptional cases, may not be subjected to a municipal law. The substantive provisions of a *lex mercatoria*, consist precisely of the *intrinsic rules*, supplemented by rules of *international private law*, made up by a network of commercial concepts, absorbed *ad hoc* in international law. Similar rules apply also to non-State actors in international society, in court cases and in arbitrations.

Rules of international society are made by a process that may be called *interactivism*: rules are created by *legal acts, which in different patterns and convergence, produce relevant norms*. There is a great variety of combinations of acts of various substance and form.

Intrinsic rules need no consent, apart from participation in international society: maxims, certain formal general principles as well as prophylactic rules prohibiting force, are *automatically binding on every subject of the international legal order.*

Differently expressed, consent to these rules is *presumed*, by the mere *basic participation in international society*: as soon as a State takes part in international society, certain minimum obligations automatically follow. Similar obligations to follow the 'rules of the game' are imposed on all subjects of the international legal order.

But for *further* obligations to ensue for States or others there must be some form of *specific consent*. The *graduated scale of presumed acts of consent* is highly relevant in this context: States must thus, in one way or the other have consented to binding rules. In the case of States, there must be *at least one act of basic participation*, by which States adhere by *consent* to further voluntary rules. This can be done by *action*, in the form of a variety of measures set out above, for example, by acts of *adoption*, or by a *declarative* act (which can concern any type of voluntary rule) and by which a State gives it consent by its *statements.*

States have a legal duty to recognise and obey basic prophylactic rules without which international society cannot survive. Above such duties, States have considerable power to make rules in international law. To have this power, States must themselves be representative units and reflect the will of the majority of the nation. This is the essence of the rules of democracy and of self-determination. There is an incidental right of self-determination implying a right of secession of units or portions of States, or entities under foreign domination. But this right must be exercised with caution to avoid a fragmentation of a State, and in, practice, exercised only where there is a *concerted democratic will* to secede.

The bulk of voluntary, optional, international prime law, which emanates from States, is normally made by consent. The source of obligation of *optional international rules* is thus normally the consent of States. But the basis of obligation of other rules is variable. There are a few basic notions, like the traditional maxims, which are binding by force of *logical necessity*.

Furthermore, prophylactic rules, preventing the self-destruction of international society, are binding because of *social necessity*. A similar source of obligation clarifies the binding nature of rules on mutual contact: if a State enters into contact with others (which it is not obliged to do), it must also follow the rules of form of such contact, for example, respecting rules with regard to the law of treaties, and diplomatic immunity. The binding force of these rules is considerably enhanced by reciprocity. For such rules there is also a reinforcing basis of obligation in the constructive consent assessed along the *graduated scale of presumption of consent*. But rules on cooperation, for example, that we call *promotional rules*, *settlement rules* and also other further detailed rules, implementing the substratum of prophylactic or stabilising rules, are all elaborated by the free consent of States.

For all *optional* rules, the consent of States is normally required in clear unequivocal form. For the rules which are binding by social necessity, on the other hand, there is no need to show such consent. Since States cannot have the right to destroy international society, they are bound to respect certain basic social rules. It is only the bare substratum of prophylactic and entrenching rules that follows from social needs for which consent is either inferred by participating acts or assumed under the scale of graduated presumptions.

The details of the rules in these areas will be elaborated further by further action by agreement and consent by promotional rules.

But in the area of certain basic and rudimentary prohibitions and rights, the power of the State to revoke is also limited: for example, standards of treatment of individuals may only be improved, not decreased. Similarly, since States do not have to enter into contact with each other, they must, if they do make such contact with other States, abide by relevant rules to take part in international society.

Customary law, as traditionally understood, is an unacceptable fiction in modern international law. The concept of 'custom', requiring the practice of a number of State actors, during a certain time and their psychological approval by their *opinio juris*, is a concept which obscures rather than clarifies. It is usually used to explain the existence of any rule but there are absurd claims as to how 'usage' and '*opinio juris*' of other States is to be assessed. In the welter of modern State activities it is practically impossible to ascertain what the 'views' are of States of the 'law' short of what can be ascertained in acts of clear consent. It is also undesirable to use such vague criteria for the existence of a rule as it will only lead to uncertainty of the law and reduce the clarity of the international legal order.

There is one area where 'usage' is relevant and that is the area of prescription; then the 'usage' has territorial or maritime anchorage and may prove right of use title. But only in a few other areas is there room for the nebulous notion of customary law in the international system.

But customary law, allegedly the cornerstone of the system according to an overwhelming majority of writers, does not exist in modern international law except in its limited application in the field of territorial or maritime prescription and in a few other areas. In territorial and maritime cases custom and usage can lead to that a claim of right of use, or of a title, is validated.

It may be stressed that many of the *intrinsic rules*, set out in this work may not have their root or origin in 'custom' but in social necessity. But *details* and *modalities* of such rules have obviously become refined through custom, for example in the field of diplomacy or in certain tactics or practices of war. Elsewhere, the concept of 'customary law' will only perpetuate the confusion as to how rules of international law nowadays come into being. Instead, international law is formed by legal acts, either necessitated by the social structure of the society, for example, by acts of participation acknowledging prophylactic and entrenching rules, or voluntarily taken acts, to improve on the few rudiments that social structures impose by the adoption of further promotional rules.

International law is thus based on the intrinsic rule of *prohibition of harm* to other subjects of the international legal order or to the environment: all rules can be traced to this paramount principle. This basic and inherent rule is essential to secure the hypothetical goal of international society that is the survival of mankind.

The main mechanism that entrenches this is *the Rule of Reciprocity*, often referred to as the *Golden Rule*, known since Antiquity in all societies, that is to say the simple rule of reciprocity that no action should be taken towards others that one would not like to accept towards oneself.

These *intrinsic rules* are supplemented by voluntary rules that States and other subjects accept or adhere to by their freely given consent.

The doctrine of *interactivism* in this work assists in explaining the mechanisms by which norms emerge in international society: *legal acts*, taken by subjects of the international legal order, activate, in turn, sets of rules in *various voluntary norm-pools*.

Rules of international society, that supplement the *intrinsic law*, are thus produced by intersecting patterns and combinations of legal acts and norm-pools where States and others can find rules that may be needed for practical situations and which they then adopt by their clear *consent*.

The core of international law is precisely the *intrinsic rules*, supplemented by later rules adopted by clear consent in declarations, treaties and agreements but not by any nebulous flow of behaviour and custom.

Selective Bibliography

See also, for further classical works, and other references, my *Bibliography of International Law,* New York: Bowker, 1976.

Note: Clarendon Press and Oxford University Press are entered as OUP and Cambridge University Press as CUP.

Abi-Saab, G., 'La coutume dans tous ses états – Le droit international à l'heure de sa codification' in *Etudes en honneur de Roberto Ago*, Milan: Giuffré, 1987, vol 1, 53;
—— *Le développement du droit international, Théorie du droit international public,* Paris: Presses Universitaires de France & Geneva: IHEI, 2013;
Adams, R. M., *Finite and Infinite Goods: A Framework for Ethics*, Oxford: OUP, 1999;
Adorno, T. W., *Trois études sur Hegel*, Paris: Payot, 2003;
Akashi, K., *Cornelius van Bynkershoek: His Role in the History of International Law*, The Hague & Boston: Kluwer, 1998;
Ago, R., *Scienza giuridica e diritto internazionale*, Milan: Giuffré, 1950;
—— 'Science juridique et le droit international', 90 *RCADI*, 1956, 849;
—— 'Positive law and international law', *AJIL,* 1957, 691;
—— 'Diritto positive e diritto internazionale' in *Scritti di diritto internazionale in onore di Tomasso Perassi*, Milan: Giuffrè, 1957;

Ahrens, H., *Naturrecht oder Philosophie des Rechts und des Staates auf dem Grunde des ethische Zusammenhanges von Recht und Kultur*, Vienna: Gerold, 1870;

Akehurst, M., 'Custom as a source of international law', 47 *BYIL*, 1974-75, 1;

Alexandrowicz, C. H., *Studies in the History of the Law of Nations*, The Hague: Nijhoff, 1964;

—— *The Law Making Functions of the Specialised Agencies of the United Nations*, Sydney: Angus & Robertson, 1973;

Alibert, C., *Du droit de se faire justice dans la société international depuis 1945*, Paris: LGDJ, 1983;

Allan, P. & Schmidt, C., *Game Theory and International Relations: Preferences, Information and Empirical Evidence*, Aldershot: Elgar, 1994;

Allard, J., *Dworkin et Kant: réflexions sur le jugement*, Brussels: Editions de l'Université de Bruxelles, 2001;

Allot, P., 'Language, method and nature of international law', 45 *BYIL* 1971, 79;

—— *Eunomia. New Order for a New World*, Oxford: OUP, 1990/ 2001;

—— *The Health of Nations. Society and Law beyond the State*, Cambridge: CUP, 2002;

—— *Towards the International Rule of Law. Essays in Integrated Constitutional Theory*, London: Cameron May, 2005; Alvarez, A., *Exposé des motifs et déclaration des grands principes du droit international moderne*, Paris: Editions internationales, 1936;

Anzilotti, D., *La filosofia del diritto e la sociologia,* Florence: Meozzi, 1892;

—— *La scuola del diritto naturale nella filosofia giuridica contemporeana,* Florence: Lonnier, 1892;

—— *Corso di diritto internazionale*, Padua: Cedam, 4th ed., 1955;

Aquinas, St. Thomas, *Summa theologica,* Rome, 1266-1273; Indiana – polis: Benzinger Bros., 1947; Lander, Wyoming: The Aquinas Institute, 2012;

—— *Contra Gentiles*, Paris & Naples, 1258-1273; New York: Hanover House, 4 vols., 1955; Notre Dame, Ind.: Univ. of Notre Dame Press, 1975;

—— *Contra impugnantes Dei cultum et religionem*, Paris, 1256; London: Sands & C., 1902; Turnhout: Brepols Publishers, 2013;

—— *De aeternitate mundi*, Paris, 1271; Milwaukee: Marquette Univ. Press, 1964;

—— *De principiis naturae*, Paris, 1253, trad. Madiran, J., *Les principes de la réalité naturelle*, Paris: Nouvelles Éditions Latines, 1994;

Arangio-Ruiz, G.,'The normative role of the General Assembly of the United Nations and the Declarations of Principles of Friendly Relations, 137 *RCADI* iii 1972 419;

—— 'Human rights and nonintervention in the Helsinki Act', 157 *RCADI* 1977 iv 195;

—— 'Consuetudine (consuetudine internazionale)' in Spirito, P., (ed), 8 *Enciclopedia Giuridica*, Rome: Istituto della Enciclopedia Italiana, 1988;

Araujo, O., *Las doctrinas internacionalistas de Francisco de Vitoria*, Montevideo: Imp. LJGU, 1948;

Aréchaga, J. E., Pinto, M.C.W., Röling, B.V.A., *et al.*, *International Law and the Grotian Heritage*, The Hague: T.M.C. Asser Institute, 1983;

Aron, R., *Les grandes doctrines de sociologie historique: Montesquieu, Auguste Comte, Karl Marx, Alexis de Tocqueville, les sociologues et la révolution de 1848*, Paris: Centre de documentation universitaire, 1960;

—— *Les étapes de la pensée sociologique: Montesquieu, Comte, Marx, Tocqueville, Durkheim, Pareto, Weber*, Paris: Gallimard, 1967;

—— *Paix et guerre entre les nations*, Paris: Calmann-Lévy, 1962;

—— *Penser la guerre, Clausewitz*, Paris: Gallimard, 1976;

—— *Sur Clausewitz*, Brussels: Editions Complexe, 1987;

Aristotle, *Sur la justice*; *éthique à Nicomaque livre V*, Paris: Flammarion, 2008;

—— *The Politics*, London: Penguin, 1981;

—— *Nicomachean Ethics*, Indianapolis: Hackett Publishing Company, 1984;

—— *Oevres complètes*, Paris: Flammarion, 2014;

Arts, B., Noortmann, M., Reinalda, B., *Non-StateActors in International Relations*, Aldershot: Ashgate, 2001;

Arzinger, R., *Das Selbtsbestimmungsrecht im allgemeinen Völkerrecht*, Berlin: Staatsverlag der DDR, 1966;

Augustine, St., *The City of God*, (*De Civitate Dei*), Trans. Babcock, W., New York: City Press, 2012;

—— *The City of God*, (*De Civitate Dei*), Trans. Walsh, Oxford: Aris & Phillips, 2013;

—— *Cité de Dieu,* vols. I-X, ed. Paris: Sagesses, 1988;

—— *De Libero Arbitrio Voluntatis*, ed. Sparrow, C.M., *On Free Will*, Charlottesville: Virginia Univ., 1947;

—— *De la Libre Volonté,* ed. Vindobonae: Hoelder-Pichler-Tempsky, 1956;

Allard, J., *Dworkin et Kant: réflexions sur le jugement*, Brussels: Editions de l'Université de Bruxelles, 2001;

Asamoah, O., *The Legal Significance of the Declarations of the General Aassembly of the United Nations,* The Hague: Nijhoff, 1966;

d'Aspremont, J., *Formalism and the Sources of International Law: A Theory of the Ascertainment of Legal Rules*, Oxford: OUP, 2011;

Audit, M., *Les conventions transnationales entre personnes publiques*, Paris: LGDJ, 2002;

Austin, J., *Province of Jurisprudence Determined,* London: John Murray, 1832;

—— *Lectures on Jurisprudence or the Philosophy of Positive Law,* London: R. Campbell, 1874;

Banez, D., *De iure et iusticia decisiones*, Salamanca, s. n., 1594;

Barcia Trelles, C., *Francisco de Vitoria et l'école moderne du droit international*, Paris: Hachette, 1928;

—— *Vazquez de Menchaca. Sus teorias internacionales*, Barcelona: Patria, 1940;

Balladore Pallieri, G., *Diritto internazionale pubblico*, Milan: Giuffrè, 1941;

Balossini, C. E., *L'elemento giuridico nelle relazioni internazionali*, Novara: Cattaneo, 1935;

Barnard, F. M., *Herder's Social and Political Thought: From Enlightenment to Nationalism,* Oxford: OUP, 1965;

Balossini, C. E., *L'elemento giuridico nelle relazioni internazionali*, Novara: Cattaneo, 1935;

Barberis, J., 'L'*opinio juris* comme élément constitutif de la coutume d'après la Cour de la Haye', 50 *RivDI* , 1967, 543;

—— 'Réflexions sur la coutume internationale', 36 *AFDI*, 1990, 1;

Bartelson, J., *A Genealogy of Sovereignty*, Cambridge: CUP, 1995;

Basdevant, J., 'Règles générales du droit de la paix', 58 *RCADI* iv, 1936, 335;

—— *Cours de droit international public, 1945-1946*, Paris: Pedone, 1946;

Bastid, S., *Cours de droit international public*, Paris: Cours IEP, *1956-1957; 1966-1967; 1976-1977;*

—— 'Les organisations non-gouvernementales, *Institut de droit international, Rapport,* 43 *Annuaire,* 1950 i 475;

—— *Le droit des gens: Le droit des crises internationals*, Paris: Cours IEP, 1959;

—— 'Observations sur une étape dans le développement et la codification des principes du droit international', *Hommages Guggenheim*, Geneva: Imprimérie de la Tribune, 1968, 144;

—— 'The special significance of the Helsinki Final Act' in Buergenthal, T., (ed.), *Human Rights, International Law and the Helsinki Accords*, New York: Montclair, 1977, 11;

Batiffol, H., *Aspects philosophiques du droit international privé*, Paris: Dalloz, 1956;

Bauchet, P., *Concentration des multinationales et mutation des pouvoirs de l'Etat*, Paris: CNRS Editions, 2003; Baxter, R.R., 'Treaties and custom', 129 *RCADI*, 1970, 25;

Beaulac, S., *The Power of Language in the Making of International Law: The Word Sovereignty in Bodin and Vattel and the Myth of*

Westphalia, Leiden: Brill, 2004; Bederman, D., *International Law in Antiquity*, Cambridge & New York, CUP, 2002;

Bedjaoui, M., *Fonction public internationale et influences nationales,* Paris: Pedone, 1958;

—— *Pour un nouvel ordre économique international*, Paris: UNESCO, 1978;

Behme, T., *Samuel von Pufendorf: Naturrecht und Staat. Eine Analyse und Interpretation seiner Theorie, ihrer Grundlagen und Probleme*, Göttingen: Vandenhoeck & Ruprecht, 1995;

Bauchet, P., *Concentration des multinationales et mutation des pouvoirs de l'Etat*, Paris: CNRS Editions, 2003;

Beck, R. J., Arend, A. C., Vander Lugt, R.D., *et al.*, *International Rules: Approaches from International Law and International Relations*, New York & Oxford: OUP, 1996;

Beigbeder, Y., *Le rôle international des organisations non-gouvernementales*, Brussels: Bruylant, 1992;

Belissa, M., *La cosmopolitique du droit des gens (1713-1795): Fraternité universelle et intérêt national au siècle des Lumières et pendant la Révolution francaise*, Lille: ANRT, Université de Lille, 1996;

Belch, S. F., *Paulus Vladimiri and his Doctrine Concerning International Law and Politics*, The Hague: Mouton, 1965;

Bello, E.G., *African Customary Humanitarian Law*, Geneva: ICRC, 1980;

Ben Achour, Y., *Le rôle des civilisations dans le système international (droit et relations internationales)*, Brussels: Bruylant, 2003;

Bengtson, H., *Die Verträge der griechisch-römischen Welt von 700 bis 338 v. Chr.*, Munich & Berlin: Beck, 1962;

Bentham, J., *Plan for a Universal and Perpetual Peace*, London: Sweet and Maxwell, 1927;

—— *The Works of Jeremy Bentham*, ed. John Bowring, London, 1838-1843: Russell & Russell, New York, 1962;

Berber, F., *Lehrbuch des Völkerrechts*, Munich: C.H. Beck, 1977;

Bergbohm, K. M., *Staatsverträge und Gesetze als Quellen des Völkerrechts*, Dorpat: Mattiessen, 1876;

—— *Völkerrecht: das internationale Recht der civilisierten Nationen, systematisch dargestellt von Friedrich von Martens*, Berlin: Weidmann, 1883-1886;

—— *Jurisprudenz und Rechtsphilosophie; kritische Abhandlungen*, Leipzig: Duncker & Humblot, 1892;

Berljak, M., *Il diritto naturale e il suo rapporto con la divinità in Ugo Grozio*, Rome, Università Gregoriana, 1978.

Bernhardt, R., 'Ungeschriebenes Völkerrecht', *ZaöRVR*, 1976, 5;

Berns, T., *Souveraineté, droit et gouvernementalité: lectures du politique moderne à partir de Bodin*, Paris: Scheer, 2005;

Bernsdorff, J.v., 'Georg Jellinek and the origins of liberal constitutionalism in international law', 4:3 *Göttingen JIL*, 2012, 659;

Bertens, H., *Hugo de Groot en zijn rechtsphilosophie*, Tilburg: Bergmans, 1905;

Besold, C., *Dissertatio politico-juridico de foederum jure*, Strasbourg: Lazarus Zetznerus, 1622;

Bex, J., *Essai sur l'évolution du droit des gens*, Paris: Rivière, 1910;

Biersteker, T. J., *International Law and International Relations: Bridging Theory and Practice*, London: Routledge, 2007;

—— & Weber, C., *State Sovereignty as a Social Construct*, Cambridge: CUP, 1996;

Birkett, J., 'International legal theories evolved at Nuremberg', 32 *International Affairs*, 1947 1;

Black, C. E. & Falk, R. A., *The Future of the International Legal Order*, Princeton: Princeton University Press, 1969;

Bleckmann, A., Völkergewohnheitsrecht trotz widersprüchlicher Praxis?' *ZaöRVR* 1976 374;

—— Zur Feststellung und Auslegung von Völkergewohnheitsrecht, *ZaöRVR* 1977 504;

Bleicher, S., 'The legal significance of recitation of General Assembly Resolutions', *AJIL* 1969 444;

Blumberg, P.I., *The Corporate Challenge to Corporation Law,* New York & Oxford: OUP, 1993;

Bluntschli, J.K., *Psychologische Studien der Staat und Kirche*, Zurich: Beyel, 1844;
—— *Das moderne Völkerrecht der civilizierten Staaten als Rechtsbuch dargestellt,* Nördlingen: Druck & Verlag der Beck'schen Buchhandlung, 1872;
Bobbio, N., et al., *La guerre et ses théories*, Paris: Presses Universitaires de France, 1970;
Bobik, J., *Aquinas on Matter and Form and the Elements* (Notre Dame, Ind.: Univ. of Notre Dame Press, 1998;
Bodin, J., *Six livres de la République*, (1576), Paris: Armand Colin, 1932;
Born, G., *International Commercial Arbitration,* The Hague: Kluwer, 2nd, 2004;
Bögli, H., *Beiträge zur Lehre vom ius gentium der Römer,* Bern: A. Francke, 1913;
Böhme, H.-J., *Politische Rechte des einzelnen in der Naturrechtslehre des 18. Jahrhunderts und in der Staatstheorie des Frühkonstitutionalismus*, Berlin: Duncker & Humblot, 1993;
Boisson de Chazournes, L., and Condorelli, L., 'De la 'responsabilité de protéger': Ou d'une nouvelle parure pour une notion déjà bien établie', 110 *RGDIP*, 2006, 3;
Bolintinanu, A., 'Expression of consent to be bound by treaty in the light of the 1960 Vienna Convention, *AJIL,* 1974, 672;
Bonanate, L., *Elementi di relazioni internazionali principi di analisi e di teoria*, Turin: Giappichelli, 1997;
Borschberg, P., *Hugo Grotius Commentaries in Thesis XI: An Early Treatise on Sovereignty, the Just War, and the Legitimacy of the Dutch Revolt,* Bern: Peter Lang, 1994;
Bos, M., *The Present State of International Law and Other Essays,* 1973;
—— 'Legal archetypes and the normative concept of law', *NILR*, 1976, 7;
—— 'The recognized manifestations of international law: A new theory of sources', *GYIL,* 1977, 9;
—— 'The hierarchy among the recognized manifestations ('Sources') of international law' in *Estudios de derecho internacional, Homenaje al Adolfo Miaja de la Muela,* 1979;

—— 'Will and order in the Nation-State system, Observations on positivism and positive international law', *NILR*, 1982, 3;

—— 'The identification of custom in international law', *GYIL*, 1982, 9;

—— *Methodology of International Law,* Amsterdam: Elsevier, 1984;

Bowett, D., *Self-Defence in International Law*, Manchester: Manchester University Press, 1958;

Boucher, D., *The Limits of Ethics in International Relations. Natural Law, Natural Rights, and Human Rights in Transition*, New York: OUP, 2009;

Bowett, D.W., 'Estoppel before international tribunals and its relation to acquiescence', 33 *BYIL*, 1957, 176;

Brice, G., *The Maritime Law of Salvage*, 5th ed., by Reeder, J., London: Sweet & Maxwell, 2013

Brierly, J.L.,'Le fondement obligatoire du droit international', 23 *RCADI*, 1928 iii 463;

—— *The Basis of Obligation in International Law and Other Papers,* Oxford: OUP, 1958;

Brower, J., 'Matter, Form, and Individuation' in ed. Davies, B., & Stump, E., in *The Oxford Handbook of Aquinas*, Oxford: OUP, 2012, 85.

Buckle, S., , *Natural Law and the Theory of Property: Grotius to Hume*, Oxford, OUP, 1991;

Bulmerincq, A., *Die Systematik des Völkerrechts von Hugo Grotius bis auf die Gegenwart,* Dorpat, 1858;

Bull, H., 'The case for a classical approach' in Knorr & Rosenau, (eds.), *Contending Approaches to International Politics,* Princeton: Princeton University Press, 1969;

—— *The Anarchical Society*, New York: Columbia University Press, 1977;

—— *The Control of the Arms Race, Disarmament and Arms Control in the Missile Age*, London: Weidenfeld & Nicolson, 1961;

—— (ed.), *Intervention in World Politics*, New York: New York University Press, 1984;

Buonafede, A., *Istoria critica del moderno diritto di natura e delle genti*, Perugia: Baduel, 1789;

Burton, J. W., *A Theory of International Relations*, Cambridge: CUP, 1967;

—— *Systems, States, Diplomacy and Rules*, Cambridge: CUP, 1968;
—— *Conflict & Communication: The Use of Controlled Communication in International Relations*, London: Macmillan, 1969;
Bustamente y Sirvén, A. S. d., *Droit international public*, Paris: Recueil Sirey, 1934;
Burckhardt, W., *Die Organisation der Rechtsgemeinschaft*, Basel: Helbing & Lichtenhahn, 1927;
Buzan, B., 'Negotiating by consensus: Developments in Technique at the United Nations Conference on the Law of the Sea', *AJIL* 1981, 324;
—— *People, States, and Fear: The National Security Problem in International Relations*, Brighton: Wheatsheaf Books, 1983;
—— *People, States and Fear: An Agenda for International Security Studies in the Post-Cold War Era*, New York: Harvester Wheatsheaf, 1991;
—— *An Introduction to Strategic Studies: Military Technology and International Relations*, Basingstoke: Macmillan, 1987.
—— 'The logic of regional security in the post-Cold War world', in Hettne, B., *et al.* (eds), *The New Regionalism and the Future of Security and Development, The NewRegionalism*, London: Macmillan, 2000;
—— *From International to World Society: English School Theory and the Social Structure of Globalisation*, Cambridge: CUP, 2004;
Buzzini, G.P., 'La théorie des sources face au droit international général: Reflections sur l'émergence du droit objectif dans l'ordre juridique international', 106 *RGDIP*, 2002, 58.
Byers, M., *Custom, Power and the Power of Rules: International Relations and Customary International Law*, Cambridge: CUP, 1999;
Cahin, G., *La coutume internationale et les organisations internationales: l'incidence de la dimension institutionnelle sur le processus coutumier*, Paris: Pedone, 2001;
Calvo, C., *Recueil complet des traités, conventions, capitulations, armistices et autres actes diplomatiques de tous les Etats del'Amérique*, Paris: A. Durand, 1862;

—— *Le droit international théorique et pratique: précédé d'un exposé historique des progrès de la science du droit des gens*, Paris: Guillaumin, 1887-1896;

—— *Manuel de droit international public et privé*, Paris: A. Rousseau, 1892;

Campbell, T.D., *The Legal Theory of Ethical Positivism*, Aldershot: Dartmouth, 1996;

Cannizzaro, E., & Palchetti, P., eds., *Customary International Law and the Use of Force: A Methodological Approach*, Leiden: Nijhoff 2005;

Cao, H. T. & Fenet, A., *Mutations internationales et évolution des normes*, Paris: Presses universitaires de France, 1994;

Carmola, K., *Private Security Contractors and New Wars: Risk, Law, and Ethics*, London: Routledge, 2010;

Carr, E. H., *International Relations since the Peace Treaties*, London: Macmillan, 1937;

—— *The Twenty Years' Crisis (1919-1939), An Introduction to the Study of International Relations*, London: Macmillan, 1939;

—— *International Relations Between the Two World Wars (1919-1939)*, London: Macmillan, 1947;

Carré de Malberg, R., *Contribution à la théorie de l'état*, Paris: Sirey, 1920;

—— *Philosophie du droit des gens*, Paris: Sirey, 1930-1931;

—— *Contribution à la théorie générale de l'État*, Paris: CNRS Éditions, 1985;

—— *La Loi, expression de la volonté générale*, Paris: Economica, 1984;

Carrillo Salcedo, J.A., 'Consideraciones sobre el fundamento, naturaleza y significado de las operaciones de la Naciones Unidas destinadas al mantenimiento de la paz', 18 *REDI*, 1965 164;

—— *Dignidad frente a Barbarie – Derechos Humanos,* Madrid: Trotta, 2000;

—— *Soberania de los Estados y Derechos Humanos en Derecho Internacional Contemporaneo,* Madrid: Technos, 2001;

—— *El Convenio europeo de derechos humanos*, Madrid: Technos, 2004;

Caron, D.D., Schille, S.W., Cohen Smutny, A., & Triantafilou, E.E., eds., *Practising Virtue: Inside International Arbitration*, Oxford: OUP, 2015;

Cassels, A., *Ideology and International Relations in the Modern World*, London: Routledge, 1996;

Castaneda, J., 'La valeur juridiques des resolutions des Nations Unies', 129 *RCADI* 1970 i 205;

Chaumont, A., *Etude sur la vie et les travaux de Grotius ou le droit naturel et le droit international*, Paris: Durand, 1862;

Chevalley, L., *La déclaration des droits des gens de l'Abbé Grégoire (1793-1795)*, Cairo: P-Barbey, 1912;

Chigara, B., *Legitimacy Deficit in Custom: A Deconstructionist Critique*, Aldershot: Ashgate, 2001;

Chou Nau Chow, *La doctrine du droit international chez Confucius*, Paris: A. Pedone, 1940;

Cicero, *De legibus, (On Laws) & De Republica, (On the Republic)* trans. Fott, D., New York; Cornell Univ. Press, 2014;

Clementinus, P., *De evolutione definitionis iuris gentium. Studium historico--iuridicum de doctrina iuris gentium*, Rome: Università Gregoriana, 1940;

Charney, J.I., 'Universal international law', 87 *AJIL*, 1993, 529;

Cheng, Bin, *General Principles of Law as Applied by International Courts and Tribunals,* Oxford: OUP, 1953;

—— 'United Nations Resolutions on Outer Space: 'Instant' international customary law?' 1965 5 *IJIL*, 1965;

—— 'Custom: The future of general state practice in a divided world' in MacDonald, St.J., & Johnston, (eds.), *The Structure and Process of International Law,* Boston: Nijhoff, 1983;

Chung, D. E., *Transnational Advocates, Norm Advancement, and U.S. Corporate Self-Regulation in China (1993-2003)*, OUP, 2005;

Claret, P., *La personnalité collective des nations: théories anglo-saxonnes et conceptions françaises du caractère national*, Brussels: Bruylant, 1998;

Clark, I., *Legitimacy in international society*, Oxford: OUP, 2005;

Clausewitz, C. v. *Vom Krieg, Hinterlassenes Werk*, Berlin: Dümmler, 1832; English ed., Howard, M. & Paret, P., eds., *On War,* New Jersey: Princeton University Press, 87.
—— *Vom Kriege* 1834; 18th ed., Bonn: Dümmlers Verlag, 1972;
Colbert, E.S., *Retaliation in International Law*, New York: King's Crown Press, 1948;
Coleman, Jules (ed.), *Hart's postscript: Essays on the Postscript to 'The Concept of Law'*, Oxford: OUP, 2001;
Condorelli, L.,'La coutume' in Bedjaoui, M., ed., *Droit international: Bilan et perspectives*, Paris: Pedone 1991, 187;
Connaughton, R., *Military Intervention in the 1990s: A New Logic of War*, London: Routledge, 1992.
Consiglio, E., 'Early Confucian legal thought: A theory of natural law?', *Rivista di filosfia del diritto*, 2/2015, 359;
Constantopoulos, D. S., *Verbindlichkeit und Konstruktion des Positiven Völkerrechts*, Hamburg, Rechts- und Staatswissen-schaftlicher Verlag, 1948;
Contamine, P., *Guerre, Etat et Société à la fin du Moyen-Age*, Paris: Mouton, 1972;
Corbett, P., 'The consent of States and the sources of the law of nations', *BYIL,* 1925, 20;
Cot, J., *La conciliation internationale*, Paris: Pédone, 1968;
Crawford, J.R., *Creation of States in International Law*, 2nd ed. Cambridge: CUP, 2008;
Cronin, B., *Institutions for the Common Good: International Protection Regimes in International Society*, Cambridge: CUP, 2003;
Cropsey, J., *Plato's World: Man's Place in the Cosmos*, Chicago: University of Chicago Press, 1995;
Crowe, M.B., *The Changing Nature of Natural Law*, The Hague: Nijhoof, 1977;
Dahm, G., *Völkerrecht*, Stuttgart: W. Kohlhammer, 3 vols., 1958;
—— *Die Stellung des Menschen im Völkerrecht unserer Zeit*, Tübingen: Mohr Siebeck, 1961;

D'Amato, A.A., 'The neo-positivist concept of international law', *AJIL*, 1965, 321;
—— 'On consensus', *CYIL*, 1970, 104;
—— *The Concept of Custom in International Law*, Ithaka: Cornell University Press, 1971;
Damien, R., *Le conseiller du prince de Machiavel à nos jours: genèse d'une matrice démocratique*, Paris: Presses universitaires de France, 2003;
Damrosch, L.F., Danilenko, G.M., & Mullerson, R. eds., *Beyond Confrontation: International Law for the Post-Cold War Era*, Boulder: Westview, 1995;
Danilenko, G., *Law Making in the International Community*, Dordrecht: Nijhoff, 1993;
Davison, S.A., 'A natural law based environmental ethic', *Ethics and the Environment*, 14: 1-13.
Detter (de Lupis Frankopan), I., *Treaty-Making Power of International Organisations,* D.Phil. thesis, Oxford, 1962;
—— 'Organs of international organisations exercising their treatymaking power', *BYIL* 1962;
—— *Law Making by International Organisations,* Stockholm: Norstedt, 1965;
—— *Essays on the Law of Treaties,* London: Sweet & Maxwell, 1967;
—— *Bibliography of International Law,* New York: Bowker, 1976;
—— 'Problems with unequal treaties', *ICLQ*, 1976;
—— 'Supertankers och internationella sund', *Festskrift Folke Schmidt*, Stockholm: Norstedt, 1976;
—— 'Landlocked States and the Law of the Sea', *Scandinavian Studies in Law*, Stockholm: Norstedt, 1976;
—— 'Foreign warships and immunity for espionage', 78 *AJIL*, 1984, 53;
—— 'International straits and UNCLOS', *Anglo-Soviet Symposium on the Law of the Sea*, Moscow, 1986;
—— 'Ubåtsspionaget och folkrätten', (Submarine espionage and international law), *Svensk Juristtidning,* 1985;

—— 'Ubåtsspionaget: missförstånd på missförstånd', (Submarine espionage: misunderstanding upon misunderstanding), *Svensk Juristtidning,* 1985;

—— 'Treaties of the modern era', *Oxford World Encyclopedia,* Oxford: OUP, 1986;

—— 'The legal value of recommendations of international organisations', *AngloSoviet Symposium on Public International Law*, London, 1986;

—— *International Law and the Independent State,* 2nd ed., London: Gower, 1986;

—— *Finance and Protection of Investments in Developing Countries,* 2nd ed., London: Gower, 1986;

—— 'Legal value of recommendations of international organisations', *University College London Symposium,* 1987;

—— 'International straits and UNCLOS', *Ezegodnik mezdunarodnovo pravo,* Moscow, 1986;

—— 'What is international law and international relations?', *Journal of International Studies,* 1987;

—— 'The human environment: Stockholm and its follow-up', in Taylor & Groom, *Global Issues in the UN Framework,* London and New York, 1989;

—— 'Legal issues of privatisation in Eastern Europe', Expert Report Provided for the UN European Commission, UN publ., & *SIRIL Occasional Papers,* 1990;

—— 'Implementation of environmental conventions', *SIRIL Occasional Papers,* 1990;

—— *International Law and the Independent State*, London: Gower, 1987; 2nd ed., 1992;

—— *Practical EC Law*, Stockholm: Jagellonica, 1993;

—— *The International Right of Property*, Stockholm: Jagellonica, 1993;

—— *International Law*, Stockholm: Juristförlaget, 1993;

—— 'Militarisation of Outer Space, space satellites and jurisdiction', *Rome Space Symposium',* 1993;

—— 'The role of States in international environmental regulation', in *International Environmental Negotiations, Process, Issues*

      and Contexts, Swedish Council for Planning and Coordination of Research, Forskningsrådsnämnden & Swedish Institute of International Affairs, Stockholm, 1993;
—— *The Concept of International Law*, 2nd ed., Stockholm: Norstedt, 1995;
—— *The International Legal Order*, 2nd ed., London: Dartmouth, 1994.
—— 'The effect of resolutions of international organisations', in Makarczyk J. (ed.), *Theory of International Law, Mélanges Krzysztof Skubiszewski*, Dordrecht: Nijhoff, 1996;
—— 'Illegal combatants and the Law of War', 75 *Law Journal of George Washington University*, 2007, 1701;
—— 'Extraordinary rendition and the Law of War', 79 *North Carolina Law Journal*, 2008, 1050;
—— *New Aspects of Sovereignty and the Right to Protect – RP2*, London: St. Thomas More Institute, 2011, available at http://thomasmoreinstitute.org.uk/papers/1890/;
—— *The Law of War*, Cambridge: CUP, 1st ed, 1988, 2nd ed. 2000, Cambridge: CUP; 3rd ed. Aldershot: Ashgate, 2013;
Dickinson, E. d. W., *The Equality of States in International Law*, Cambridge, Mass.: Harvard University
Dickson, J., *Evaluation and Legal Theory*, Oxford: Hart Publishing, 2001;
—— 'Methodology in jurisprudence: A critical survey', *Legal Theory*, 2004, 10 (3), 117;
Dionisio , G., 'Natural law tradition and Confucian culture: Beyond East-West divide' *Filocracia,* 1:1, 2014, 62;
Donnedieu de Vabres, H., *Les principes modernes du droit pénal international*, Paris: Sirey, 1928;
Dos Santos, T., *A teoria da dependencia: balanço e perspectivas*, Rio de Janeiro: Civilização Brasileira, 2000;
Dupuis, C., *Le principe de l'équilibre et le concert européen de la paix de Westphalie à l'acte d'Algésiras*, Paris: Perrin, 1909;
Dupuy, R.-J. 'Coutume sage et coutume sauvage' in *Mélanges offerts à Charles Rousseau: La Communauté Inter-nationale,* Paris: Pedone, 1974, 75;

—— Droit déclaratoire et droit programmatoire: de la coutume sauvage à la `soft law', in *SFDI, Colloque de Toulouse, L'élaboration du droit international,* Paris, 1975, 132;

Dupuy, P.-M., 'Le juge et la règle générale' 93 *RGDIP*, 1989, 569;

Dworkin, R.M., (ed.), *The Philosophy of Law*, Oxford: OUP, 1977;

—— 'Is law a system of rules?', in Dworkin, R.M. (ed.), *The Philosophy of Law*, Oxford: OUP, 1977, 38;

—— *Taking Rights Seriously,* 6th ed., Cambridge, Mass., Harvard University Press, 1979;

—— *Law's Empire*, Cambridge, Mass., Harvard University Press, 1986;

Dyer, H. C., *Moral Order – World Order: The Role of Normative Theory in the Study of International Relations*, Basingstoke: Macmillan, 1997;

Edkins, J., Persram, N., Pin-Fat, V., et al., *Sovereignty and Subjectivity*, Boulder: L. Rienner Publisher, 1999;

Egger, F. V., *Das natürliche öffentliche Recht nach den Lehrsätzen des seligen Freyherrn C.A. von Martini…(und auf das positive europäische Völkerrecht)*, Wien: Geistingers Buchhandlung, 1809-1810;

Elfstrom, G., *International Ethics: a Reference Handbook*, Santa Barbara: ABC-CLIO, 1998;

Falk, R. A., *Law, Morality and War in the Contemporary World*, New York: Pall Mall Publ., 1963;

—— *Legal Order in a Violent World*, Princeton: Princeton University Press, 1968;

—— *The Status of Law in International Society*, Princeton: Princeton University Press, 1970;

Fauchille, P., *Manuel de droit international public (droit des gens),* Paris: A. Rousseau, 1898;

—— *Traité de droit international public*, Paris: Rousseau, 1922;

Fenwick, C. G., *International Law*, New York: Century & Co., 1924;

Ferrari Bravo, L., 'Méthodes de recherche de la coutume internationale dans la pratique des Etats' 192 *RCADI*, 1985, 233;

Fichte, J. G., *et al., La doctrine de l'état, 1813: Leçons sur des contenus variés de philosophie appliquée*, Paris: Vrin, 2006;

Finnis, J., *Natural Law and Natural Rights,* Oxford: OUP, 1980;
—— *Fundamentals of Ethics,* Oxford: OUP, 1983;
Fiore, P., *Nuovo diritto internazionale pubblico secondo i bisogni della civiltà moderna*, Milan: Presso la Casa Editrice e Tipog. degli Autori-Editori, 1865;
Fitzmaurice, G., 'The foundation of the authority of international law', *MLR* 1956;
—— 'The general principles of international law considered from the standpoint of the Rule of Law, 92 *RCADI* 1957 ii 5;
—— 'Some problems regarding the formal sources of international law, in *Symbolae Verzijl,* La Haye: Nijhoff, 1958, 153;
—— '*Vae victis* or woe to the negotiators', 65 *AJIL,* 1971, 370;
—— 'The future of public international law and the international legal system in the circumstances of today in *Institut de Droit International, Livre du Centenaire 18731973*, Basel, 1973, 196;
Forteau, M., *Le droit de la sécurité collective et droit de la responsabilité des États*, Paris: Pedone, 2006;
Fortuin, H., *De natuurrechtelijke grondslagen van de Groot's volkenrecht*, Gravenhage: Nijhoff, 1946;
Fox, H., *The Law of State Immunity*, 3rd ed., Oxford: OUP, 2015;
Franck, T. M., *The Power of Legitimacy Among Nations*, New York: OUP, 1990;
Franke, M. F. N., *Global limits: Immanuel Kant, International Relations, and Critique of World Politics*, Albany: State University of New York Press, 2001;
Friedmann, W. G., *What's Wrong with International Law?* London: Watts, 1941;
—— *The Changing Structure of International Law*, London: Stevens, 1964;
—— *De l'efficacité des institutions internationales*, Paris: A. Colin, 1970;
—— *Legal Theory,* New York: Columbia University Press, 1967;
—— *Law in a Changing Society*, Harmondsworth: Penguin, 1972;
Friedrich, C.-J., *The Philosophy of Law in Historical Perspective*, Chicago: University of Chicago Press, 1958;

Fulbecke, W., *The Pandectes of the Law of Nations*, London, s. n., 1602;

Gall, J., *Hanc collegii politici classis posterioris disputationem septimam, de bello bellique jure,* Tübingen, s. n., 1614;

Gardner, J., 'Legal positivism: 5 ½ myths', 46 *American Journal of Jurisprudence*, 2001, 199;

Garratus, M., *Tractatus de represaliis*, Lyon, s. n., 1549;

Gentili, A., *Hispanicae Advocationis*, Ancona, s. n., 1551;

—— *De iuris interpretibus dialogi*, London: J. Wolf, 1582-1589;

—— *De iniustitia bellica Romanorum actio,* Oxford: J. Barnes, 1590;

Gierke, O. V., Barker, E. & Troeltsch, E., *Natural Law and the Theory of Society (1500-1800)*, Cambridge, CUP, 1934;

Giesen, K.-G. & Pijl, K.v.d., *Global Norms in the Twenty-First Century*, Newcastle: Cambridge Scholars Press, 2005;

Gilbert, A. H., *Machiavelli's Prince and Its Forerunners: 'The Prince' as a Typical Book 'de Regimine Principum'*, Durham, N.C.: Duke University Press, 1938;

Girard, M. & Allan, P., *Les individus dans la politique internationale*, Paris: Economica, 1994;

Glahn, G. V., *Law among Nations*, New York: Macmillan, 1965;

Glaser, S., *Introduction à l'étude du droit international pénal*, Brussels: E. Bruylant, 1954;

Glaser, S., *Infraction internationale, ses éléments constitutifs et ses aspects juridiques; exposé sur la base du droit pénal comparé*, Brussels: E. Bruylant, 1957;

Glaser, S., *L'arme nucléaire à la lumière du droit international*, Paris: Pedone, 1964;

Goebel, J., *The Equality of States. A Study in the History of Law*, New York: Columbia University Press, 1923;

Göhler, H., *Freies Kriegsführungsrecht und Kriegsschuld*, Leipzig: R. Noske, 1931;

Gong, G. W., *The Standard of 'Civilization' in International Society*, Oxford: OUP, 1984;

Goodhart, A. L., *The Nature of International Law*, London: Grotius Society, 1937;

Gorckum, H. de, *De bello justo,* s. l., s. n., 1503;

Goyard-Fabre, S. & Ingber, L., *Des théories du droit naturel*, Caen: Centre de Publications de l'Université de Caen, 1988;

Graven, J., *Les crimes contre l'humanité*, Paris: Sirey, 1950;

Graven, J., *Le difficile progrès du règne de la justice et de la paix internationale par le droit des origines à la Société des Nations*, Paris: Pedone, 1970;

Green, L., *Authority of the State,* Oxford: OUP, 1990;

Grotius, H., *Mare Liberum,* Leiden: L. Elzevir, 1609;

—— *De jure belli ac pacis libri tres: in quibus jus naturae & gentium, item juris publici praecipia explicantur,* Paris: Jacobaea, 1625;

Guerrero, A.A., *Tractatus de bello justo et injusto,* Naples, s. n., 1543;

Guerrero, J. G., *L'ordre international. Hier, aujourd'hui, demain*, Neuchâtel, Editions de la Baconnière, 1945;

Guggenheim, P., *Lehrbuch des Völkerrechts: unter Berücksichtigung der internationalen und schweizerischen Praxis*, Basel: Verlag für Recht und Gesellschaft, 1948; trad. *Traité de droit international public: avec mention de la pratique internationale et suisse*, Geneva: Georg, 1953;

—— *Les principes de droit international public,* Paris, s. n., 1953;

Giuliano, M., *La comunità internazionale e il diritto*, Padua: Cedam, 1950;

Guillaume, G., *Les grandes crises internationales et le droit*, Paris: Seuil, 1994;

Guzman, A.T., 'Saving customary international law', 27*MichJIntlL*, 2005, 115;

Haakonssen, Knud, *Natural Law and Moral Philosophy: From Grotius to the Scottish Enlightenment*, Cambridge: CUP, 1996;

Hackworth, G. H., *Digest of International Law*, Washington, D.C.: Government Printing Office, 1940-44, 8 vols.;

Haggenmacher, P., *Grotius et la doctrine de la guerre juste*, Paris: Presses Universitaires de France, 1983;

—— 'La doctrine du droit coutumier dans la pratique de la Cour Internationale', 90 *RGDIP*, 1986, 5–126.

Hackworth, G. H., *Digest of international law*, Washington: U.S. Govt. Print. Off., 1940;

Hägerström, A., *Aristoteles etiska grundtankar och deras teoretiska förutsättningar*, Uppsala: Akademiska boktryckeriet, E. Berling, 1893;

—— *Till frågan om den objektiva rättens begrepp,* Uppsala: Almqvist & Wiksell, 1917;

—— *Inquiries into the Nature of Law and Morals*, Stockholm: Almqvist & Wiksell, ed. Karl Olivecrona, trans. Broad, 1953;

Haines, C. G., *The Revival of Natural Law Concepts*, Cambridge, Mass.: Harvard University Press, 1930;

Härle, E., *Die allgemeinen Entscheidungsgrundlagen des Ständigen Internationalen Gerichtshofs*, Berlin: F. Vahlen, 1933;

Hart, H.L.A., *The Concept of Law*, Oxford: OUP, 1961; 2nd ed. with a postscript by Raz, J., & Bulloch, P., eds., Oxford: OUP, 1994; 3rd ed. par Green, L., Raz, J. & Bulloch, P., Oxford: OUP, 2012;

—— 'Immorality and treason', in Dworkin, R.M. (ed.), *The Philo-sophy of Law*, Oxford: OUP, 1977, 83;

—— 'Positivism and the separation of law and morals' in Dworkin, R.M., (ed.), *The Philosophy of Law*, Oxford: OUP, 1979;

—— *Essays in Jurisprudence and Philosophy,* Oxford: OUP, 1983;

Hartmann, A. & Heuser, B., *War, Peace and World Orders in European History*, London: Routledge, 2001;

Hatschek, J., *Völkerrecht als System rechtlich bedeutsamer Staatsakte*, Leipzig & Erlangen: Deichert, 1923;

Hatschek, J., *Völkerrecht im Grundriss*, Leipzig: Deichert, 1926;

Hayek, F.A., *The Constitution of Liberty*, Chicago: University of Chicago Press, 1960;

—— *Law, Legislation and Liberty*, 3 vols., (*Rules and Order; The Mirage of Social Justice; The Political Order of a Free People),* Chicago: University of Chicago Press, 1973;

Hegel, G.W.F., *Grundlinien der Philosophie des Rechts oder Naturrecht und Staatswissenschaft im Grundrisse,* Berlin: Gans, 1854; Hamburg: Meiner Verlag, 1955;

―――― *Eigenhändige Randbemerkungen zu seiner Rechtsphilosophie*, aus der Hds. hgg. von Georg Lasson, Leipzig: Meiner, 1930;
―――― *Frühe Studien und Entwürfe: 1787-1800*, bearb. und kommentiert von Gellert, I., Berlin: Akademie Verlag, 1991;
―――― *Werke, vollständige Ausgabe*, Berlin: s. n., 1832-1840;
―――― *Sämtliche Werke*, Stuttgart: Glockner, 1927-1940;
Heller, H., *Die Souveränität. Ein Beitrag zur Theorie des Staats- und Völkerrechts*, Berlin & Leipzig: Walter de Gruyter, 1927; Henckaerts, J.M., 'Study on customary international humanitarian law: A contribution to the understanding and respect for the Rule of Law in armed conflict', 87 *ICRC*, 2005, 175;
Herczegh, G., *General Principles of Law and the International Legal Order*, Budapest: Akadémiai Kiadó, 1969;
Herczeg, I., 'Futurity research in international law', in Haraszati, G., *Questions of International Law,* Budapest: s.n., 1977;
Herder, J.G., *Idéen zur Philosophie der Geschichte der Menschheit,* (1784-1791), Wiesbaden: Fourier, 1985;
―――― *Sämtliche Werke*, ed. Suphan, B., Olms, Hildesheim, 1967;
―――― *Philosophical Writings,* ed. Forster, M.N., Cambridge: CUP, 2002;
Heuser, B., *Penser la stratégie de l'Antiquité à nos jours,* Paris: Picard, 2013;
Heydte, F. A. F. V., *Die Geburtsstunde des souveränen Staates. Ein Beitrag zur Geschichte des Völkerrechts, der allgemeinen Staatslehre und des politischen Denkens*, Regensburg: Habbel, 1952;
Herrero Y Rubio, A., *Nociones de historia del derecho de gentes y de relaciones internacionales*, Valladolid: Martin, 1954;
Hervada, J., *Historia de la ciencia del derecho natural*, Pamplona: Ediciones Universidad de Navarra, 1987;
Higgins, R., *Problems and Process: International Law and How We Use It*, Oxford: OUP, 1994;
Hinsley, F.H., *Power and the Pursuit of Peace: Theory and Practice in the History of Relations between States,* Cambridge: CUP, 1963;
Hobbes, T., *Elements of Law, Natural and Politic,* ed. Oxford: OUP, 2008;
―――― *Leviathan,* ed. Oxford: OUP, 2000;

Hoffmann, S., *Conditions of World Order*, New York: Simon & Schuster, 1970;
—— *Duties Beyond Borders: On the Limits and Possibilities of Ethical International Politics,* Syracuse: Syracuse University Press, 1981;
Hoffmann, G., *Strafrechtliche Verantwortung im Völkerrecht, zum gegenwärtigen Stand des völkerrechtlichen Strafrechts*, Frankfurt am Main: Metzner, 1962;
Hoffmann, S., *The State of War: Essays on the Theory and Practice of International Politics*, New York: Praeger, 1965;
Hoijer, O., *Les traités internationaux*, Paris: Editions internationales, 1928;
Hoijer, R., *A Rational Choice Theory of State-Formation*, Oxford: OUP, 2002;
Holsti, K. J., *The dividing discipline: hegemony and diversity in international theory*, Boston: G. Allen & Unwin, 1987;
—— *Change in the International System: Essays on the Theory and Practice of International Relations*, Aldershot: Elgar, 1991;
—— *Taming the Sovereigns: Institutional Change in International Politics*, Cambridge: CUP, 2004;
Hopkins, J. A. H. & Alexander, M., *Machine-gun Diplomacy*, New York: Lewis Copeland, 1928;
Hosack, J., *On the Rise and Growth of the Law of Nations, as Established by General Usage and by Treaties*, London: Murray, 1882;
Huber, E., *Recht und Rechtsverwirklichung: Probleme der Gesetzgebung und der Rechtsphilosophie*, Basel: Helbing & Lichtenhahn, 1921;
Huber, M., *Die Soziologischen Grundlagen des Völkerrechts,* Berlin: Rothschild, 1928;
—— *Das Internationale Rote Kreuz. Idée und Wirklichkeit*, Zurich: Niehans, 1951;
Huber, R. E., *Nationalstaat und Verfassungsstaat. Studien zur Geschichte der modernen Staatsidee*, Stuttgart: Kohlhammer, 1965;
Hume, D., *An Enquiry Concerning the Principles of Morals,* London: A. Millar, 1751;
—— *A Treatise of Human Nature,* 1739, ed. Selby-Bigge, Oxford: OUP 2014;

Ihmels, J., *Das Naturrecht bei Alberti: die Lehre des Compendium juris naturae*, Leipzig, s. n., 1955.

Ingebritsen, C., *Small States in International Relations*, Seattle & Reykjavik: Univ. of Washington Press/Univ. of Iceland Press, 2006;

International Law Association, *Report*, 'Formation of customary international law', by Mendelson, M.H., 2000;

Isidorus Hispaniensis, St. Isidore of Seville, *The Etymologies of Isidore of Seville*, trans. Barney, S.A., New York, CUP, 2006;

Jackson, R. H., *Quasi-States: Sovereignty, International Relations and the Third World*, Cambridge: CUP, 1990;

Jacqué, J.P., *Eléments pour une théorie de l'acte juridique en droit international public,* Paris: Sirey, 1972;

Jellinek, G., *Die rechtliche Natur der Staatenverträge*, Vienna: Hölder, 1880;

—— *Die Lehre von den Staatenverbindungen*, Vienna: Hölder, 1882;

—— *System der subjektiven öffentlichen Rechte,* Freiburg im Breisgau: Mohr, 1892;

Jenks, C.W., *The Common Law of Mankind*, London: Stevens, 1958;

—— *Law, Freedom, and Welfare*, London: Stevens, 1963;

—— *International Law in a Changing World*, Dobbs Ferry: Oceana, 1963;

—— *Law in the World Community*, London: Longman, 1967;

—— *A New World of Law? A Study of the Creative Imagination in International Law*, Harlow: Longman, 1969;

Jessup, P.C., *Transnational Law,* New Haven: Yale Univ. Press, 1956;

—— *A Modern Law of Nations,* Hamden: Archon Books, 1968;

Jhering, R., *Der Kampf um's Recht*, Berlin: Philo, 1925;

Jimenez de Aréchaga, E., 'Customary international law and the Conference on the Law of the Sea', in Makarczyk, J., ed., *Essays in International Law in Honour of Judge Manfred Lachs*, The Hague: Nijhoff, 1984;

Jouannet, E., *Emer de Vattel et l'émergence doctrinal de droit international classique*, Paris: Pedone, 1998;

Justinian, see Watson.

Kaltenborn, C. V., *Die Vorläufer des Hugo Grotius auf dem Gebiet des ius naturae et gentium sowie der Politik im Reformationszeitalter*, Leipzig: Mayer, 1848;

Kant, I., *Critik der reinen Vernunft,* Riga: Hartneck, 1781; *Kritik der reinen Vernunft*, Hamburg: Meiner, Hamburg, 1998;

—— *Zum ewigen Frieden* (Königsberg: Königliche Preußische Akademie der Wissenschaften, 1795;

—— Project de paix perpétuelle, Essai philosophique, Königsberg: Nicolovius, 1796;

—— Grundlegung der Metaphysik der Sitten, Königsberg: Nicolovius, 1797;

Kello, L., *Foundations for a Positivist Ideational Theory of International Relations*, Oxford: OUP, 2002;

Keohane, R. O., *After Hegemony. Cooperation and Discord in the World Political Economy*, Princeton: Princeton University Press, 1984;

—— *Neorealism and its Critics*, New York: Columbia University Press, 1986;

Kelsen, H., *Hauptprobleme der Staatsrechtslehre entwickelt aus der Lehre vom Rechtssätze*, Tübingen: Mohr Siebeck, 1911;

—— *Das Problem der Souveränität und die Theorie des Völkerrechts, Beitrag zu einer reinen Rechtslehre*, Tübingen: Mohr Siebeck, 1920;

—— *Allgemeine Staatslehre*, Berlin, J. Springer, 1925;

—— *Grundriss einer allgemeinen Theorie des Staates*, Vienna: Rohner, 1926; trad. Laroche, B. & Faure, V., *Théorie générale du droit et de l'Etat, suivi de la doctrine du droit naturel et le positivisme juridique*, Brussels: Bruylant, 1997;

—— *Der soziologische und der juristische Staatsbegriff*, Tübingen: Mohr Siebeck, 1927;

—— *Rechtsgeschichte gegen Rechtsphilosopie: Eine Erwiderung*, Vienna: Springer, 1928;

—— *Reine Rechtslehre*, Leipzig & Vienna: Springer, 1934;

—— 'Théorie du droit international coutumier', 1 *RITD*, 1939, 253;

—— *Law and Peace in International Relations*, Cambridge, Mass., Harvard University Press, 1942;

—— *Peace through law*, Chapel Hill: The Univ. of North Carolina Press, 1944;

—— *La paz por medio del derecho*, Buenos Aires: Losada, 1946;

―― *Principles of International Law*, New York: Rinehart, 1952;

―― *Pure Theory of Law*, Berkeley: University of California Press, 1967;

―― *What is justice?: justice, law, and politics in the mirror of science: collected essays*, Berkeley: University of California Press, 1971;

―― *Essays in legal and moral philosophy*, Dordrecht: Reidel, 1973;

―― *Allgemeine Theorie der Normen*, ed. Ringhofer, K. & Walter, R., Vienna: Mainz Verlag, 1979;

―― *Auseinandersetzungen zur reinen Rechtslehre: kritische Bemerkungen zu Georges Scelle und Michel Virally*, Vienna & New York, J. Springer, 1987;

Keohane, R. O. & Nye, J. S., *Transnational Relations and World Politics*, Cambridge, Mass.: Harvard Univ. Press, 1972;

Kern, E., *Moderner Staat und Staatsbegriff*, Hamburg: Rechts- und Staatswissenschaftlicher Verlag, 1949;

Kervégan, J.-F., *Hegel, Carl Schmitt: le politique entre spéculation et positivité*, Paris: Presses Universitaires de France, 1992;

Kimmenich, O., *Völkerrecht im Atomzeitalter: Der Atomsperrvertrag und seine Folgen*, Freiburg: Rombach, 1965;

Kipp, H., *Völkerordnung und Völkerrecht im Mittelalter*, Cologne: Deutsche Glocke, 1950;

Kirgis, F.L., 'Custom on a sliding scale', 81 *AJIL*, 1987, 146;

Kitto, H.D.F., *Greek Tragedy, A Literary Study*, London: Methuen, 1984;

Klecatsky, H. R., Marcic, R., et al., *Die Wiener rechtstheoretische Schule*, Vienna & Frankfurt & Zurich: Europa-Verlag, 1968;

Kleist, P., *Die völkerrechtliche Anerkennung Sowjet Russlands*, Königsberg & Berlin, Ost-Europa-Verlag, 1934;

Klineberg, O., *The Human Dimension in International Relations*, New York: Holt Rinehart & Winston, 1964;

Knorr, K. E., *The Power of Nations: The Political Economy of International Relations*, New York: Basic Books, 1975;

Korowin, E. A. & Robinson, J., Kraus, H., *Das Völkerrecht der Übergangszeit*, Berlin: W. Rothschild, 1929;

Korowicz, M.S., *La souveraineté des états et l'avenir du droit international*, Paris: A. Pedone, 1945;

Koskenniemi, M., *From Apology to Utopia, The Structure of International Legal Argument,* 1989; with an epilogue of the author, Cambridge: CUP, 2005;

—— *The Gentle Civilizer of Nations: The Rise and Fall of International Law (1870-1960)*, Cambridge/New York: CUP, 2005;

Kossoy, E., *Living with guerrilla: guerrilla as a legal problem and a political fact*, Geneva: Droz, 1976;

Kosters, J., *Les fondements du droit des gens: contribution à la théorie générale du droit des gens*, Leiden: Brill, 1925;

Krabbe, H., 'L'idée moderne de l'Etat', *RCADI* 1926 iii 559;

Krasner, S. D., *International Regimes*, Ithaca: Cornell University Press, 1983;

Kraus, H., *Gedanken über Staatsethos im internationalen Verkehr,* Berlin: Deutsche Verlagsgesellschaft, 1925;

Kreijen, G., *State Failure, Sovereignty and Effectiveness*, The Hague: Nijhoff, 2004;

Krippendorff, E., *Internationale Beziehungen*, Cologne: Kiepenheuer & Witsch, 1973;

Krieger, L., *The Politics of Discretion. Pufendorf and the `Acceptance of Natural Law*, Chicago: University of Chicago Press, 1965;

Krüger, H., *Völkerrecht, Gewohnheitsrecht, Naturrecht. Referate zweier Seminare über die Problematik des Gewohnheitsrechts und seine Bedeutung als Völkerrechtsquelle*, Hamburg: Universität Hamburg, 1967;

Kunz, J. L., *Völkerrechtswissenschaft und reine Rechtslehre*, Leipzig & Vienna: Deuticke, 1923;

—— *The Changing Law of Nations: Essays on International Law*, Ohio: State University Press, 1968;

—— 'The nature of customary international law', *AJIL*, 1953, 662;

La Brière, Y. de, *Le droit de la guerre juste,* Paris: Pedone, 1938;

Lachance, L., *Le droit les droits de l'homme*, Paris: Presses Universitaires de France, 1959;

Lacharrière, G., *La politique juridique extérieure*, Paris: Economica, 1983;

Lachs, M., 'Some reflections on substance and form in international law', in Friedmann, W., & Al., eds., *Transnational Law in a Changing Society, Essays in Honor of Philip C. Jessup,* New York: Columbia University Press, 1972, 99;

—— *The Teacher in International Law*, The Hague: Nijhoff, 1982;

Landheer, B., *On the Sociology of International law and International Society*, The Hague: Nijhoff, 1966;

Lapradelle, A. G. d., *Maîtres et doctrines du droit des gens*, Paris: Editions internationales, 2nd ed., 1950;

Lardy, P., *La Force obligatoire du droit international en droit interne*, Paris: LGDJ, 1966;

Lasson, A., *System der Rechtsphilosophie*, Berlin: Guttentag, 1882;

Laski, H. J., *A Grammar of Politics*, London: G. Allen & Unwin, 1967;

Lauterpacht, H., *Private Law Sources and Analogies of International Law*, London & New York: Longman, Green & Co., 1927;

—— *The Nature of International Law and General Jurisprudence*, London: Fisher Unwin, 1932;

—— *An International Bill of the Rights of Man*, New York, Columbia University Press, 1945;

—— *Kelsen's Pure Science of Law*, Oxford: OUP, 1933;

—— *Recognition in International Law*, Cambridge, CUP, 1948;

—— *International Law and Human Rights*, London, Stevens, 1950;

—— *The Law of War on Land*, London: *H.M.S.O.*, 1958;

—— *The Function of Law in the International Community*, Hamden: Archon Books, 1966;

—— *International Law: The Collected Papers of Hersch Lauterpacht*, Cambridge: CUP, 1970;

—— & Waldock, C.H.M., *et al.*, *The Basis of Obligation in International Law and Other Papers*, Oxford: OUP, 1958;

Lawrence, T. J., *A handbook of public international law*, London: Macmillan, 1920;

Leeuwen Boomkamp, M. V., Panhuys, H. F. v., *et al.*, *International Society in Search of a Transnational Legal Order*, Leiden: Sijthoff, 1976;

Le Fur, L., *Guerre juste et juste paix*, Paris: Pedone, 1920;

―― *Necessité d'un droit international pour coordonner les diverses activités nationales*, Lyon: Chronique sociale, 1924;
―― *Nationalisme et internationalisme au regard de la morale et du droit naturel*, Paris: Chronique sociale, 1926;
―― *Le Saint-Siège et le droit des gens*, Paris: Sirey, 1930;
―― *Les grands problèmes du droit*, Paris: Sirey, 1937;
―― *La guerre d'Espagne et le droit,* Paris: Les Editions Internationales, 1938;
―― *Précis de droit international public*, Paris: Dalloz, 1939;
―― *Eléments de droit international public*, Paris: Dalloz, 1941;
Ledermann, L., *Les précurseurs de l'organisation internationale*, Neuchâtel: La Baconnière, 1945;
Leger, J. S., *The 'Etiamsi Daremus' of Hugo Grotius. A Study in the Origins on International Law*, Rome: Università Gregoriana, 1962;
Leiter, B., *Naturalising Jurisprudence: Essays on American Legal Realism and Naturalism in Legal Philosophy*, Oxford: OUP, 2007;
Lepard, B.D., *Customary Law, A New Theory with Practical Applications*, Cambridge: CUP, 2012;
Leske, F., *Die Rechtsverfolgung im internationalen Verkehr: Die Beschlagnahme, Liquidation und Freigabe deutschen Vermögens im Auslande, unter Benutzung amtlichen Materials*, Berlin: Heymann, 1923;
Lindley, M. F., *The Acquisition and Government of Backward and Practice Relating to Colonial Expansion*, London: Longmans, 1926;
Lingens, K.-H., *Internationale Schiedsgerichtsbarkeit und Jus Publicum Europaeum*, Berlin: Duncker & Humblot, 1988;
Linklater, A., *Men and Citizens in the Theory of International Relations*, London: Macmillan, 1982;
Lisska, A., *Aquinas's Theory of Natural Law: An Analytic Reconstruction*, Oxford: OUP, 1996;
Livet, G., *Guerre et paix de Machiavel à Hobbes*, Paris: Colin, 1972;
Lissitzyn, O. J., *International Law Today and Tomorrow*, Dobbs Ferry: Oceana, 1965;
Liszt, F. V., *Das Völkerrecht systematisch dargestellt*, Berlin: Häring, 1902;

―― *Vom Staatenbund zur Völkerrechtsgemeinschaft: ein Beitrag zur Neuorientierung der Staatspolitik und des Völkerrechts*, Munich: Müller, 1918;

―― & Gidel, G. C., et al., *Le droit international*, Paris: Pedone, 1927;

Little, R. & Williams, J., *The anarchical society in a globalised world*, Basingstoke: Palgrave Macmillan, 2006;

Locke, J., *Essays on the Law of Nature*, von Leyden, W., ed., Oxford: OUP, 1988.

Lucas, D.W., *The Greek Tragic Poets,* London: Cohen & West, 1950;

Lundstedt, A. V., *Die Unwissenschaftlichkeit der Rechtswissenschaft*, Berlin: Rothschild, 1932;

―― *Le droit des gens: danger de mort pour les peuples,* Brussels: de la Phalange, 1937;

Luard, E., *The Balance of Power. The System of International Relations (1648-1815)*, New York: St. Martin's Press, 1992;

Machiavelli, N., *Il Principe*, (1513), (publ.1532), Rome: Salerno, 2006;

Makarczyk, J., (ed.), *Études de droit international en l'honneur du Juge Manfred Lachs*, The Hague & Boston: Nijhoff, 1984;

Mandaraka-Sheppard, A., *Modern Admiralty Law*, London: Cavendish Publishing 2006;

―― *Modern Maritime Law and Risk Management*, 2 vols., London: Routledge, 3rd ed., 2013;

Manning, C.A.W., *The Nature of International Society,* New York: John Wiley, 1962;

Manz, J. J., *Emer de Vattel: Versuch einer Würdigung. Unter besonderer Berücksichtigung seiner Auffassung von der individuellen Freiheit und der souveränen Gleichheit*, Zurich: Schulthess, 1971;

Martens, F.F. de, *Sovermennoe mezhdunarodnoe pravo ysivilizovannykh narodov*, St. Petersburg: Benke, 1883; 5th ed., 1887-1888; reprinted Moscow: Yuridischeskii Kolledzh, 1996;

―― *Traité de droit international*, Paris: Librairie Maresco, 1887;

―― *Völkerrecht. Das internationale Recht civilisierten Nationen* (trans. Bergbohm, C.), Berlin: Weidmannsche Buchhandlung, 1883, 2 vols. & Berlin: Weidmann, 1887;

—— *Traité de droit international*, Paris: Librairie Maresco Ainé, 1887;

—— *La paix et la guerre*, Paris: A. Rousseau, 1901;

Masters, R. D., *Machiavelli, Leonardo, and the Science of Power*, Notre Dame: University of Notre Dame Press, 1996;

Maurach, R. & Meissner, B., *Völkerrecht in Ost und West*, Stuttgart: Kohlhammer, 1967;

MacCormick, N., 'A moralistic case for a-moralistic law?', 20 *Valparaiso University Law Review*, (1), 1, 1985;

Mälksoo, L., 'Theory in Russia: A civilizational perspective; Or can individuals be subjects of international law?' in Orford, A., Hoffman, R.& Clark, M., *The Oxford Handbook of the Theory of International Law*, Oxford: OUP, 2016, 237;

Marmor, A., *Interpretation and Legal Theory*, Oxford: OUP, 1992; 2nd ed., Oxford: Hart Publishing, 2005;

—— *Positive Law & Objective Values*, Oxford: OUP, 2001;

—— *Philosophy of Law*, Princeton: Princeton Univ. Press, 2011;

—— 'Farewell to conceptual analysis (in jurisprudence)', in Waluchow & Sciaraffa, eds., *Philosophical Foundations of the Nature of Law*, Oxford: OUP, 2013, 209;

Mayall, J., *The Community of States: A Study in International Political Theory*, London: Routledge, 2017;

McCarthy, L. J., *Justice, the State and International Relations*, Basingstoke: Macmillan, 1997;

McDougal, M. S., 'International law, power and policy, A contemporary conception', 82 *RCADI* 1953 i 137;

—— *Studies in World Public Order*, New Haven: Yale University Press, 1960;

—— & Feliciano, F. P., *Law and Minimum World Public Order: The Legal Regulation and International Coercion*, New Haven: Yale University Press, 1961;

—— & Lasswell, H.D., & Reisman W.M., 'Theories about international law: Prologue to a configurative jurisprudence', 8 *Virginia JIL* 1967 188;

—— Reisman, W.M., *International Law in a Contemporary Perspective, The Public Order of the World Community,* New York: Foundation Press, 1981;

McWhinney, E., *International Law and World Revolution*, Leiden: Sijthoff, 1967;

Meijers, H., 'How is international law made? The stages and growth of international law and the use of its customary rules', *NYIL,* 1978 3;

Ménissier, T., *Machiavel, la politique et l'histoire: enjeux philosophiques*, Paris: Presses universitaires de France, 2001;

Merle, M., *Le droit de la nature et des gens*, Bordeaux: Brethe de la Gressaye, 1967;

Meron, T., *Human Rights and Humanitarian Norms as Customary Law*, Oxford: OUP, 1989;

—— 'Revival of customary humanitarian law', 99 *AJIL* 2005, 817;

Mesnard, P., *L'essor de la philosophie politique au XVIe siècle*, Paris: Boivin & cie., 1936;

—— *Oeuvres philosophiques de Jean Bodin*, Paris, Presses Universitaires de France, 1951;

Midgley, E. B. F., *The Natural Law Tradition and the Theory of International Relations*, London: Paul Elek, 1975;

Mirkine-Guetzévitch, B., *Droit constitutionnel international*, Paris: Sirey, 1933;

—— *Les constitutions européennes,* Paris: Presses Universitaires de France, 1951;

Mitchell, J. M., *International cultural relations*, London & Boston: Allen & Unwin, 1986;

Mitteis, H., *Die Rechtsidée in der Geschichte*, Weimar: Böhlaus, 1957;

Modelski, G., *Principles of World Politics*, New York: Free Press, 1972;

Monaco, R., 'Observations sur la hiérarchie des sources du droit international', *Festschrift Mosler,* Berlin: Springer, 1983, 599;

Moore, M., 'Hart's concluding unscientific postscript", 4 *Legal Theory*, 1998, 301;

Murphy, L., 'The political question of the concept of law,' in Coleman, J., (ed.), *Hart's postscript: Essays on the Postscript to 'The Concept of Law'*, Oxford: OUP, 371;

Murphy, M.C., *Natural Law and Practical Rationality*, New York: CUP, 2001;

Montijn, A. M. M., *Un principe nouveau de droit international public*, The Hague: Librairie Belinfante, 1919;

Morabia, A., Le Ğihâd dans l'Islam mediéval, Le 'Combat Sacré'des origines au XIIème siecle*, Paris: Albin Michel, Coll. Bibliothèque de l'Evolution de l'Humanité, 2013;*

Morelli, G., *Nozioni di diritto internazionale*, Padua: Cedam, 7th ed., 1967;

Morgenstern, F., *Legal Problems of International Organisations*, Cambridge: Grotius Society, 1986;

Morgenthau, H., *Die internationale Rechtspflege: ihr Wesen und ihre Grenzen*, Leipzig: R. Noske, 1929;

Morgenthau, H. J., *Politics among Nations: The Struggle for Power and Peace*, New York: A. Knopf, 1959;

—— 'Positivism, functionalism and international law', 34 *AJIL* 1040, 260;

Moskov, A., *La garantie internationale en droit des minorités*, Brussels: E. Bruylant, 1936;

Mosler, H., *Die Intervention im Völkerrecht*, Berlin: Junker & Dünnhaupt, 1937;

—— *The International Society as a Legal Community*, Leiden: Sijthoff, 1974;

Moye, M., *Le droit des gens moderne.* Paris: Sirey, 1920;

Müller-Schmid, P. P., *Begründung der Menschenrechte*, Stuttgart: Steiner Verlag, 1986;

Münch, I. V., 'Zur Objektivität in der Völkerrechtswissenschaft', 9 *AVR*, 161-1962, 1;

—— *Staatsrecht-Völkerrecht-Europarecht: Festschrift für Hans-Jürgen Schlochauer*, Berlin & New York: de Gruyter, 1981;

Nageswar Rao, V., '*Jus cogens* and the Vienna Convention on the Law of Treaties', 14 *Indian JIL* 1974 362;

Nardin, T. & Mapel, D., *Traditions of International Ethics*, Cambridge: CUP, 1992;

Nawaz, M., 'Other sources of international law: Are juridical decisions of the International Court of Justice a source of international law?', *Indian JIL* 1978 526;

Nguyen, Q. D., *Cours de droit international public (1971-1972)*, Paris: Les cours de droit, 1972;

—— *Droit international public*, Paris: LGDJ, 1975;

—— & Daillier, P., & Pellet, A., *Droit international public*, Paris: LGDJ, 1987;

—— & Daillier, P., & Pellet, A., & Forteau, M., *Droit international public*, Paris: LGDJ, 9th ed., 2009;

Niemeyer, T., *Rechtspolitische Grundlegung der Völkerrechtswissenschaft*, Kiel: Verlag des Institutes für Internationales Recht, 1923;

Niemeyer, T., *Völkerrecht*, Berlin & Leipzig: de Gruyter, 1923;

—— *Völkerrechtliche Kollektivverträge*, Kiel, Verlag des Institutes für Internationales Recht, 1924;

Nijman, J. E., *The Concept of International Legal Personality: An Inquiry into the History and Theory of International Law*, The Hague: T.M.C. Asser Press, 2004;

Nippold, O., *Der völkerrechtliche Vertrag: seine Stellung im Rechtssystem und seine Bedeutung für das internationale Recht*, Bern: Wyss, 1894;

—— *Das Geltungsgebiet des Völkerrechts in Theorie und Praxis*, Breslau, s. n., 1908;

—— *Vorfragen des Völkerrechts*, Tübingen, s. n., 1913;

—— *Die Gestaltung des Völkerrechts nach dem Weltkriege*, Zurich: Füßli, 1917;

Nörgaard, C. A., *The Position of the Individual in International Law*, Copenhagen: Munksgaard, 1962;

Nozick, R., *Anarchie, état et utopie*, Paris: Presses Universitaires de France, 1988;

Numan, O. W. S., *Cornelius van Bynkershoek, zijn leven en zijne geschriften*, Leiden: J. Hazenberg, 1869;

Nussbaum, A., *A Concise History of the Law of Nations*, New York: MacMillan, 1954;

Nys, E., *Notes pour servir à l'histoire littéraire & dogmatique du droit international en Angleterre*, Brussels: Muquardt, 1888;

―― *Les Théories politiques et le droit international en France jusqu'au XVIIIe siècle*, Paris: Thorin, 1891;

―― *Les origines du droit international public*, Paris: Thorin, 1894;

―― *Le droit international devant l'histoire*, Brussels: Bureau de la Revue, 1894;

―― *Le droit international, les principes, les théories, les faits*, Brussels: A. Castaigne, 1904;

―― *Le droit de la nature et le droit des gens au XVIIe siècle*, Brussels: M. Weissenbruch, 1914;

O'Connell, D. P., *International law*, London: Stevens, 1965; Oderberg, D.S. & Chappell, T., (eds.), *Human Values: New Essays on Ethics and Natural Law*, New York: Palgrave, 2004;

Oertzen, P. V., *Die soziale Funktion des staatsrechtlichen Positivismus*, Frankfurt: Suhrkamp, 1974;

Oestreich, G., *Geist und Gestalt des frühmodernen Staates*, Berlin: Duncker & Humblot, 1969;

Okeke, C. N., *Controversial Subjects of Contemporary International Law: An Examination of the New Entities of International Law and their Treaty-Making Capacity*, Rotterdam: Rotterdam University Press, 1974;

Olivecrona, K., *Law as Facts*, Copenhagen, Munksgaard, 1939;

Oppenheim, H. B., *System des Völkerrechts*, Frankfurt am Main: Literarische Anstalt, 1845;

Oppenheim, L., *International Law: A Treatise*, London: Longmans & Green, 1905; ed. 1955;

―― *Die Zukunft des Völkerrechts*, Leipzig: Engelmann, 1911;

Ottenwälder, P., *Zur Naturrechtslehre des Hugo Grotius*, Tübingen: Mohr, 1950;

Painter, S., *French Chivalry: Chivalric Ideas and Practices in Medieval France*, Ithaca, New York: Great Seal Books, 1965;

Palladini, F. & Hartung, G. (éds.), *Samuel Pufendorf und die europäische Frühaufklärung*, Berlin: Akademie Verlag, 1996;

Paradisi, B., *Il problema storico del diritto internazionale*, Florence: Sansoni, 1944;

Parry, C., *The Sources and Evidences of International Law*, Manchester: Manchester University Press, 1965;

Partsch, K. J., *Die Anwendung des Völkerrechts im innerstaatlichen Recht: Überprüfung der Transformationslehre: Bericht*, Karlsruhe: C. F. Müller, 1964;

Patel, S. R., *Recognition in the Law of Nations*, Bombay: N. M. Tripathi, 1959;

Pathak, R., 'The general theory of the sources of contemporary international law', 19 *Indian JIL* 1979 483;

Paulsson, J., 'Enclaves of justice' 1, *University of Miami Law Legal Studies Research Paper* No. 2010-29, available at http://papers.ssrn.com/sol3/papers.cfm?abstract_id=1707504;

—— 'Unlawful laws and the authority of international tribunals', 23 *ICSID Foreign Investment Law Journal*, 215, 221-22 (2008).

Pella, V. V., *La répression de la piraterie*, Paris: Hachette, 1928;

Pellet, A., *Recherche sur les principes généraux de droit international*, diss., Brussels: Bruylant, 1974;

—— 'The normative dilemma: Will and consent in international law making', 12 *AustYBIL*, 1988– 89, 22;

—— 'Article 38' in Zimmermann, A., Tomuschat, C., & Oellers-Frahm, K., (eds), *The Statute of the International Court of Justice, A Commentary*, Oxford: OUP, 2006, 677;

Perassi, T., 'Teoria dommatica delle fonti di norme giuridiche', *RivDI* 1917 193;

Perret, R. L., *De la faute et du devoir en droit international; fondement de la responsabilité*, Zurich: Polygraphischer Verlag, 1962;

Perry, S., 'Hart's methodological positivism', in Coleman, J., ed., *Hart's postscript: Essays on the Postscript to 'The Concept of Law'*, Oxford: OUP, 2001, 311;

—— 'Interpretation and methodology in legal theory', in Marmor, A., *Interpretation and Legal Theory*, Oxford: OUP, 1995, 97;

Pescatore, P., 'Les aspects fontionnels de la Communauté Economique Européenne, notemment les sources du droit' in *Aspects juridiques du Marche Commun,* ed., Université de Liège, Liège: Faculté de Droit 1958;

—— *Le droit d'intégration* , Leiden: Sijthoff, 1972;

—— *The Law of Integration, Emergence of a New Phenomenon in International Relations Based on the Experience of the European Communities,* Leiden: Sijthoff, 1974;

Pfluger, J., *Die einseitige Rechtsgeschäfte im Völkerrecht,* Zurich: Schulthess, 1936;

Phillipson, C., *The International Law and Customs of Ancient Greece and Rome*, London: Macmillan, 1911;

Pillet, A., *Les fondateurs du droit international: F. de Vitoria, A. Gentilis, F. Suarez, Grotius, Zouch, Pufendorf, Bynkershoek, Wolf, Watter, de Martens – leurs oeuvres, leurs doctrines*, Paris: V. Giard & E. Brière, 1904;

Pillinini, G., *Storia del principio di equilibrio*, Venice: Libreria Universitaria Editrice, 1973;

Philonenko, A., *Métaphysique et politique chez Kant et Fichte*, Paris: Vrin, 1997;

Piotte, J.–M., *Les grands penseurs du monde occidental: l'éthique et la politique de Platon à nos jours*, Saint-Laurent: Fides, 1997;

Plato, *The Republic*, ed. Bloom, A., London: Basic Books, 1991;

Platon, *La République,* ed. Paris: Flammarion, 1982;

Pocock, J. G. A., *Le moment machiavélien: la pensée politique florentine et la tradition républicaine atlantique*, Paris: Presses Universitaires de France, 1997;

Polin, R., *Politique et philosophie chez Thomas Hobbes*, Paris: Presses Universitaires de France, 1953;

Politis, N., 'Le problème des limitations de la souveraineté et la théorie de l'abus de droit dans des rapports internationaux,' 6 *RCADI* 1924 ii 5;

Popcock, J.G.A., *Politics, Language, and Time: Essays on Political Thought and History,* London: Allen Lane, 2007;

Porter, J., *Nature as Reason: A Thomistic Theory of the Natural Law*, Grand Rapids: Eerdmans, 2005;

Postema, Gerald, *Bentham and the Common Law Tradition*, Oxford: OUP, 1989;

Pound, R., 'Philosophical theory and international law', *Bibliotheca Visseriana*, 1923, 21;

―― '*Law and Morals*, Chapel Hill: Milford, 1924;

Prevost, 'Observations sur la nature juridique de l'Acte Final de la Conférence sur la Securité et la Coopération en Europe', *AFDI* 1975 129;

Proudhon, P.–J., *La guerre et la paix: recherches sur le principe et la constitution du droit des gens*, Paris: Hetzel, 1861;

Puchala, D. J., *Theory and History in International Relations*, New York: Routledge, 2003;

Pufendorf, S. V., *Einleitung zu der Historie der vornehmsten Reiche und Staaten in Europa,* Frankfurt: Knochen, 1683; trans. *Introduction à l'histoire des principaux états, tels qu'ils sont aujourd'hui dans l'Europe,* Utrecht: J. Ribbius, 1685;

―― *Le droit de la nature et des gens*, Basel, Thourneisen, 1732, trans. Barbeyrac, J., 4th ed., 2 vols., Caen: Centre de Philosophie Politique et Juridique de l'Université de Caen, 1987;

―― *De jure naturae et gentium*, 2 vols., F. Böhling, ed., in Series: *Samuel Pufendorf, Gesammelte Werke*, Schmidt-Biggemann, eds., 4 Vols., Berlin: Akademie Verlag, 1998; Berlin: Gruyter, 2005;

―― *Les devoirs de l'homme et du citoyen tels qu'ils lui sont préscrits par la loi naturelle*, trans. Barbeyrac, J., Hildesheim: Georg Olms & Amsterdam: Coup & Kuyper, 1734-35;

―― *Elementorum jurisprudentiae universalis libri duo*, 2 vols., Buffalo, NY: William S. Hein & Oxford: OUP, 1931;

―― & Bruzen de La Martinière, A. A. & Grace, Th. F. de, *Introduction à l'histoire moderne, générale et politique; commencée par le baron de Pufendorff, augm. par M. Bruzen de la Martinière*, Paris: Merigot, 1753-1759;

Pursiainen, C., *Russian Foreign Policy and International Relations Theory*, Aldershot: Ashgate, 2000;

Quester, G. H., *Offense and Defense in the International System*, New York: Wiley, 1977;

Radbruch, G., *Rechtsphilosophie*, Basel: Verlag für Recht und Gesellschaft, 4th ed., 1950;

Rae, H., *State Identities and the Homogenisation of Peoples*, Cambridge: CUP, 2002;

Ralston, J. H. & Marquis, H., *Le droit international de la démocratie*, Paris: M. Giard, 1923;

Ramel, F. & Cumin, D., *Philosophie des relations internationales*, Paris: Presses de sciences politiques, 2002;

Randelzhofer, A., *Völkerrechtliche Aspekte des Heiligen Römischen Reiches nach 1648*, Berlin: Duncker & Humblot, 1967;

Rawls, J., *A Theory of Justice*, Cambridge, Mass.: Harvard University Press, 1971;

—— & Freeman, S. R., *Lectures on the History of Political Philosophy*, Cambridge, Mass.: Harvard University Press, 2007;

Raz, J., *The Concept of a Legal System: An Introduction to the Theory of the Legal System,* Oxford: OUP, 1980;

—— 'Legal principles and the limits of law', in Cohen, M., ed., *Ronald Dworkin and Contemporary Jurisprudence*, Totowa, NJ: Rowman & Allanheld, 1984;

—— *The Authority of Law*, Oxford: OUP, 1979;

—— *Ethics In The Public Domain*, Oxford: OUP, 1994;

—— *Authority of Law,* Oxford: OUP, 2002;

—— 'Can there be a theory of law?', in Golding & Edmundson, eds., *The Blackwell Guide to the Philosophy of Law and Legal Theory*, Oxford: Blackwell, 2004;

Redfern & Hunter on Arbitration, Oxford: OUP, 6th ed., 2015;

Redlich, M. D. A. V., *International Law as a Substitute for Diplomacy*, Chicago: Independent Publishing Co., 1929;

Redslob, R., *Histoire des grandes principes du droit des gens depuis l'antiquité jusqu'à la veille de la grande guerre*, Paris: Rousseau, 1923;

—— *Les principes du droit des gens moderne*, Paris: Rousseau, 1937;

—— *Traité de droit des gens: l'évolution historique, les institutions positives, les idées de justice, le droit nouveau*, Paris: Sirey, 1950;

Reed, L., Paulson, J., & Blackaby, N., *Guide to ICSID Arbitration*, The Hague: Kluwer, 2004;

Reeves, J. S., *La communauté internationale*, Paris: Hachette, 1925;

Regala, R., *World Peace through Diplomacy and Law*, Dobbs Ferry: Central Book Supply, Oceana, 1964;

Regout, R., *La doctrine de la guerre juste, de Saint Augustin à nos jours d'après les théologiens et les canonistes catholiques*, Paris: Pedone, 1935;

Reibstein, E., *Die Anfänge des neueren Natur- und Völkerrechts. Studien zu den 'Controversiae Illustres' des Fernandus Vasquius*, Bern: Haupt, 1949;

Reisman, W.M., 'The cult of custom in the late 20th Century', 1987, 17 *CalWIntlLJ*, 1987, 133;

—— & Willard, A., *International Incidents: The Law that Counts in World Politics*, Princeton: Princeton University Press, 1988;

Reuter, P., *Institutions internationales*, Paris: Presses Universitaires de France, 1955;

—— *Droit international public*, Paris: Presses Universitaires de France, 1958;

—— *Droit international public*, Paris: Presses Universitaires de France, 4th ed., 1973;

—— & Combacau, J., *Institutions et relations internationales*, Paris, Presses Universitaires de France, 1985;

Richer d'Aube, F., *Essai sur les principes du droit et de la morale*, Paris: B. Brunet, 1743;

Roberts, A.E., 'Traditional and modern approaches to customary law: A reconciliation', 95 *AJIL* 2001, 757;

Robinson, J., *International Law and Organization. General Sources of Information*, Leiden: Sijthoff, 1967;

Robledo, A. G., *Fundadores del derecho internacional: Vitoria, Gentili, Suarez, Grocio*, México: Universidad Nacional Autónoma de México, 1989;

Röd, W., *Geometrischer Geist und Naturrecht. Methodengeschichtliche Untersuchungen zur Staatsphilosophie im 17. und 18. Jahrhundert*, Munich: Verlag der Bayrischen Akademie der Wissenschaften, 1970;

Rhonheimer, M., *Natural Law and Practical Reason: A Thomist View of Moral Autonomy*, New York: Fordham University Press, 2000;

Robé, J.-P., Lyon-Caen, A. & Vernac, S., *Multinationals and the Constitutionalization of the World Power System*, Oxford & New York: Routledge, 2016;

Romano, S. *Corso di diritto internazionale*, Padua: Cedam, 1933;

Rommen, H. A., *Die Staatslehre des Franz Suarez*, München–Gladbach: Volkvereinsverlag, 1926;

―― *Die ewige Wiederkehr des Naturrechts*, Leipzig: Hegner, 1936;

Rosecrance, R. N., *International Relations: Peace or War?* New York: McGraw-Hill, 1973;

Rosen, S., *The logic of international relations*, Cambridge: Winthrop Publishers, 1977;

Rosenne, S., *Practice and Methods of International Law*, London & New York: Oceana, 1984;

Ross, A., *Teorie der Rechtsquellen. Ein Beitrag zur Teorie des positiven Rechts auf Grundlagen dogmenhistorischer Untersuchungen*, Uppsala & Leipzig: Franz Deuticke, 1929;

―― *Kritik der sogenannten praktishen Erkenntnis. Zugleich Prolegomena zu einer Kritik der Rechtswissenschaft,* Copenhagen, 1933;

―― *Virkelighed og gyldighed i retslaeren. En kritik af den teoretiske retsvidenskabs grundbegreper,* Copenhagen: Levin & Munksgaard, 1934;

―― *Lehrbuch des Völkerrechts*, Stuttgart: W. Kohlhammer, 1951;

―― *On Law and Justice*, London: Stevens, 1958;

Roth, G., *Governmental Illegitimacy in International Law*, Oxford: OUP, 1999;

Rotondi, G., *Leges Publicae Populi Romani*, Hildesheim: G. Olms, 1952;

Rousseau, C. E., *Droit international public*, Paris: Dalloz, 1970;

Rousseau, J.–J., *Discours sur l'origine et les fondements de l'inégalité parmi les hommes*, Amsterdam: J. F. Jolly, 1754;

—— *Discours sur l'économie politique*, Genève: E. du Villard, 1758;

—— *Du contrat social, ou principes du droit politique*, Amsterdam: M. M. Rey, 1762;

—— *Jugement sur la paix perpétuelle*, Paris: Cazin, 1782;

—— & Launay, M., *Oeuvres complètes*, Paris: Editions du Seuil, 1967;

Rozakis, C., 'Treaties and third States: A study in the reinforcement of the consensual standards in international law', *ZaöVR*, 1975, 1;

—— *The Concept of Jus cogens in the Law of Treaties,* Amsterdam: North Holland, 1976;

Runciman, D., *Pluralism and the Personality of the State*, Cambridge: CUP, 1997;

Russel, F., *The Just War in the Middle Ages*, Cambridge: CUP, 1975;

Ruyssen, T., *Les sources doctrinales de l'internationalisme*, Paris: Presses Universitaires de France, 1954;

Sahovic, M., 'Rapports entre facteurs matériels et facteurs formels dans la formation du droit international', 199 *RCADI*, 1986, 171;

Sanchez Davila, T. d. J. D., *De procuranda salute omnium gentium*, Anvers, s. n., 1613;

Santarem, P., *Tractatus de assecurationibus et sponsionibus mercatorum,* Cologne, s. n., 1599;

Santarem, P., *Tractatus de mercatura*, Lyon, S. Bartolomaei, 1556;

Sassoferrato, B. de, *Commentaria tractatus represaliarum*, s. l., s. n., 1589;

Sauer, W., *System des Völkerrechts, eine lehrbuchmässige Darstellung*, Bonn: L. Röhrscheid, 1952;

Sauer, E. F., *Grundlehre des Völkerrechts*, Köln: B. Pick, 1948;

Savigny, F. K. V., *The History of the Roman Law during the Middle Ages*, Edinburgh: A. Black, 1829; trans. Guenoux, C., *Histoire du droit romain au moyen age*, Paris: Charles Hingray, 1839;

—— *Introduction générale à l'histoire du droit*, Paris: Meisnier, 1829;

—— *System der heutigen römischen Recht*, Berlin: Veit & Comp., 1840-1849; trans. Guenoux, C., *Traité de droit romain*, 8 vol., Paris: Didot Frères, 1855;

Scelle, G., *Zouch (1590-1660)*, Paris: Giard & Brière, 1903;

—— *Précis de droit des gens, principes et systématique*, Paris: Sirey, 1932;

—— *Théorie juridique de la révision des traités*, Paris: Sirey, 1936;

—— *Manuel de droit international public*, Paris: Domat–Montchrestien, 1948;

—— *Cours de droit international public*, Paris: s. n., 1948;

—— 'Le phenomène juridique du dédoublement fonctionnel', in Schätzel, W., and Schlochauer, H., (eds.), *Festschrift Hans Wehberg,* Frankfurt: Klostermann, 1956, 324;

Schachter, O., 'The relation of law, politics and action in the United Nations', 109 *RCADI* 1963 ii 165;

—— 'Towards a theory of international obligation', 8 *Virginia JIL* 1967, 300;

—— 'The twilight existence of nonbinding international agreements', *AJIL* 1977 296;

—— 'Entangled treaty and custom' in Dinstein, Y., ed., *International Law at a Time of Perplexity: Essays in Honor of Shabtai Rosenne*, Dordrecht: Nijhoff, 1989, 717;

Schaefer, F., *Der völkerrechtliche und der Völkerbundgedanke bei Thomas von Aquin und Immanuel Kant*, Essen: Centraldruck, 1932;

Schätzel, W., *Internationales Recht: gesammelte Schriften und Vorlesungen*, Bonn: L. Röthscheid, 1959;

Schauer, Fredrick, 'Positivism as Pariah', in *The Autonomy of Law: Essays on Legal Positivism*, ed. George, R.P., Oxford: OUP, 1996;

Schaumann, W., *Die Gleichheit der Staaten*, Vienna: Springer, 1957;

Scheuner, U., *Die völkerrechtlichen Grundlagen der Weltwirtschaft in der Gegenwart*, Tübingen: Mohr Siebeck, 1954;

—— 'Conflict of treaty provisions with a peremptory norm of general international law and its consequences', *ZaöRVR*, 1967 520;

―――― & Tomuschat, C., *Schriften zum Völkerrecht*, Berlin: Duncker & Humblot, 1984;

Schiffer, W., *Die Lehre vom Primat des Völkerrechts in der neueren Literatur*, Leipzig & Wien: F.Deuticke, 1937;

―――― *The Legal Community of Mankind*, New York: Columbia Univ. Press, 1954;

Schifter, R. & Taitte, W. L., *Morality and Expediency in International and Corporate Relations*, Dallas: Univ. of TexasPress, 1992;

Schindler, D. & Huber M., *Recht, Staat, Völkergemeinschaft: ausgewählte Schriften und Fragmente aus dem Nachlass*, Zurich: Schulthess, 1948;

Schlochauer, H.-J., *Die Idée des ewigen Friedens*, Bonn: L. Röhrscheid, 1953;

Schopper, A. L., *Disputatio politica de bello*, Altdorfi, s. n., 1621;

Schilling, O., *Das Völkerrecht nach Thomas von Aquino*, s. l., s.n, 1919;

Schmitt, C., *Die Diktatur: Von Anfänge des modernen Souveränitätsgedanken bis zum proletarischen Klassenkampf*, 1921, 7th ed. Berlin: Duncker & Humboldt, 1994;

―――― *Politische Theologie. Vier Kapitel zur Lehre von der Souveränität*, Berlin: Duncker &Humboldt, 1922;

―――― *Die geistesgeschichtliche Lage des heutigen Parlamentarismus*, Berlin: Duncker & Humboldt, 1923;

―――― *Tyrannei der Werte*, 3rd ed., Berlin: Duncker & Humboldt, 2010;

―――― *Der Begriff des Politischen*, Berlin: Duncker & Humboldt, 1932; trad. *La notion du politique*, Paris: Calman-Lévy, 1972 & Flammarion, 1992;

―――― *Legalität und Legitimität*, Berlin: Duncker & Humblot, 1932; trans. *Legalité ligitimé*, Paris: LGDJ, 1936;

―――― *Der Nomos der Erde im Völkerrecht des jus publicum Europaeum*, Cologne: Greven, 1950; trans. *The Nomos of the Earth in the International Law of the Jus Publicum Europaeum*, 1950, London: Telos Press, 2003;

―――― *Die Lage der europäischen Rechtswissenschaft*, Tübingen: Internationaler Universitätsverlag, 1950;

Schrader, H., 'Custom and general principles as sources of international law in American federal courts', 82 *ColLR,* 1982, 751;

Schweisfurth, T. (ed.), *et al.*, *Völkerrechtstheorie*, Berlin: Berlin Verlag, 1972;

—— 'Zur Frage der Rechtsnatur, Verbindlichkeit und völkerrechtlichen Relevanz der KSZESchlussakte, *ZaöRVR* 1976 681;

Scott, A., *The Image of the State and the Expansion of the International System*, Oxford: OUP, 2006;

Seckinelgin, H. & Shinoda, H., *Ethics and International Relations*, Basingstoke: Palgrave, 2001;

Séfériades, S., 'Aperçu sur la coutume juridique internationale et notemment sur son fondement', 34 *RGDIP*, 1936, 129;

Seidl-Hohenfeldern, I., 'International Economic Law', 198 *RCADI,* 1986, iii, 9;

Seiple, R. A. & Hoover, D., *Religion and Security: The New Nexus in international relations*, Lanham: Rowman & Littlefield, 2004;

Selden, J., *The duello or single combat,* London: I. Helme, 1610;

—— *Mare clausum seu de dominio maris libri duo*, London, W. Stanesbeius, 1635;

Senarclens, P. d., *Mondialisation, souveraineté et théories des relations internationales*, Paris: A. Colin, 1998;

Senn, F., *De la justice et du droit: explication de la définition traditionelle de la justice, suivie d'une étude sur la distinction du ius naturale et du ius gentium*, Paris: Sirey, 1927;

Sepúlveda, J. G. d., *De justis belli causis ad amplissimum & doctissimum praesulem*, Rome: V. Doricum & L. Brixienses, 1550;

Sereni, A. P., *Diritto internazionale*, Milan: Giuffrè, 1958;

Shapiro, S., *Legality*, Cambridge, Mass.: Harvard University Press, 2011;

Sibert, M., *Traité de droit international public: le droit de la paix,* Paris: Librairie Dalloz, 1951;

Sibert, M., *Cours de droit international public*, Paris, s. n., 1952;

Sicault, J., 'Du caractère obligatoire des engagements unilatéraux en droit international public', 83 *RGDIP*, 1979, 633;

Singer, M. R., *Weak States in a World of Powers: The Dynamics of International Relationships*, New York: Free Press, 1972;

Siorat, L., *Le problème des lacunes en droit international: contribution à l'étude des sources du droit et de la fonction judiciaire*, Paris, LGDJ, 1958;

Sjolander, C. T. & Cox, W. S., *Beyond Positivism: Critical Reflections on International Relations*, Boulder & London: Rienner Publisher, 1994;

Skalweit, S., *Der "moderne Staat". Ein historischer Begriff und seine Problematik*, Opladen: Westdeutscher Verlag, 1975;

Skubiszewski, K., 'Enactment of law by international organisations', *BYIL*, 19656, 198;

—— 'A new source of the law of nations: Resolutions of international organisations', *Hommages Guggenheim,* Geneva: Imprimérie de la Tribune 1968;

—— 'Resolutions of international organisations and municipal law, *Polish YIL* 19689 80;

—— 'Der Rechtskarakter der KSZESchlussakte in Bernhardt, R., Münch, I., and Rudolf, W., eds., *KSZESchlussakte,* Baden-Baden, 1977;

—— 'Elements of custom and the Hague Court', 31 *ZaöRVR*, 1971, 810;

Sloan, P., 'The binding force of a `Recommendation' of the General Assembly of the United Nations, *BYIL* 1948 1;

Soder, J., *Die Idee der Völkerrechtsgemeinschaft. Francisco de Vitoria und die philosophischen Grundlagen des Völkerrechts*, Frankfurt am Main: A. Metzner, 1955;

—— *Francisco Suarez und das Völkerrecht. Grundgedanken zu Staat, Recht und internationalen Beziehungen*, Frankfurt am Main: Metzner, 1973;

Sohn, L.B., 'The development of the Charter of the United Nations: The present state', in Bos, M., ed., *The Present State of International Law and Other Essays,* Deventer, 1973;

Sophocles, *Three Tragedies, Antigone, Oedipus the King, Electra*, Oxford, 1982;

Soras, A. d., *Morale internationale*, Paris: A. Fayard, 1961;

Sørensen, G., *Changes in Statehood: The Transformation of International Relations*, Basingstoke: Palgrave, 2001;

Sørensen, M., *Les sources du droit international*, Copenhagen: Munksgaard, 1946;

Soto, Dominici (Domingo de Soto), *De Iustitia & De Jure*, Salamanca: Apud Phillipum Nutium, 1556;

Spiropoulos, J., *Traité théorique et pratique du droit international public*, Paris, LGDJ, 1933;

Stavropoulos, N., 'Obligations and the legal point of view', in *The Routledge Companion to Philosophy of Law*, ed. Marmor A., London: Routledge, 2012;

Staub, H., *Völkerrechtliche Lehren Vattels – im Lichte der naturrechtlichen Doktrin; Ein Beitrag zur Gründungsgeschichte des Völkerrechts*, Berlin: F. Vahlen, 1922;

Stone, J., *Legal Controls of International Conflicts*, New York: Rinehart, 1954;

—— *Legal Control of International Conflict*, 2nd ed., New York: Stevens, 1973;

—— *Aggression and World Order; A Critique of United Nations Theories of Aggression*, London: Stevens, 1958;

—— *Social Dimensions of Law and Justice*, London: Stevens, 1966;

—— *Of Law and Nations: Between Power Politics and Human Hopes*, Buffalo: W. S. Hein, 1974;

Stracca, B., *De Mercatura seu mercatore tractatus,* Venice: s.n., 1553;

Striker, G. 'Origins of the concept of natural law' in *Proceedings of the Boston Area Colloquium in Ancient Philosophy*, 2: 79-94, 1986;

Strange, S., *The Retreat of the State: The Diffusion of Power in the World Economy*, New York: CUP, 1996;

Strauss, L., *Droit naturel et histoire*, Paris: Plon, 1954;

Strebel, H., 'Quellen des Völkerrechts als Rechtsordnung', *ZaöRVR*, 1976, 301;

Strupp, K., *Theorie und Praxis des Völkerrechts, ein Grundriss zum akademischen Gebrauch und zum Selbstudium*, Berlin: O. Liebmann, 1925;

—— *Eléments du droit international public: universel, européen et américain*, Paris: Editions internationales, 1930;

Sur, S., *L'interprétation en droit international public*, Paris: LGDJ, 1974;

Sutch, P., *Ethics, Justice, and International Relations: Constructing an International Community*, London, Routledge, 2001;

Strayer, J. R., *Die mittelalterlichen Grundlagen des modernen Staates*, Köln & Wien: Böhlau, 1975;

Stumpf, C. A., *The Grotian Theology of International Law: Hugo Grotius and the Moral Foundations of International Relations*, Berlin & New York: de Gruyter, 2006;

Suárez, F., *De legibus, ac deo legislatore*, Coimbra, s. n. 1612;

—— *De triplici virtute theologica, Fide, Spe et Charitate,* pars III, Coimbra, s. n., 1621;

Sumner Maine, H., *Ancient law, its Connection with the Early History of Society and its Relations to Modern Ideas,* London: J. Murray, 1905;

Sun Tzu, *The Art of War*, trans. Griffith, S.B., New York: OUP, 1971;

Sunga, L.S., *Individual Responsibility in International Law for Serious Human Rights Violations*, Dordrecht: Nijhoff, 1992;

Suy, E., *Les actes juridiques unilatéraux en droit international public*, Paris: R. Pichon, 1962;

—— 'The meaning of consensus in multilateral diplomacy', in Akkerman, R. et Al., (eds.), *Liber Röling*, Leiden: Sijthoff, 1977, 247;

Swanson, J.A., *The Public and Private in Aristotle's Politics*, Ithaka: Cornell University Press, 1992;

Tachi, S., *La souveraineté et l'indépendance de l'Etat et les questions intérieures en droit international*, Paris: Les Editions Internationales, 1930;

Tammes, A., 'Decisions of international organs as a source of international law', 94 *RCADI* 1958 ii 265.

Tedeschi, P., *Recherches sur la formation et le développement de l'obligation en droit international public*, Paris: Lavergne, 1939;

Teson, E., *Humanitarian Intervention*, New York: Pantheon, 1988;

Thierry, H., *Droit et relations internationales: traités, résolutions, jurisprudence*, Paris: Montchrestien, 1984;

Thirlway, H. W. A., *International Customary law and Codification; an Examination of the Continuing Role of Custom in the Present Period of Codification of International Law*, Leiden: Sijthoff, 1972;

Thomas, J., & Gerhard, K. (eds), *Private Military and Security Companies: Chances, Problems, Pitfalls and Prospects*, Wiesbaden: VS Verlag für Sozialwissenschaften, 2007;

Thomas, A.V., & Thomas, A.J., *Non-Intervention*, Dallas: Southern Methodist Univ. Press, 1956;

Thomas, W., *The Ethics of Destruction: Norms and Force in International Relations*, Ithaca & London: Cornell Univ. Press, 2001;

Thorneycroft, E., *Personal Responsibility and the Law of Nations*, The Hague: Nijhoff, 1961;

Tito Lomas, F., *La filosofia politica y juridical de Francisco de Vitoria*, Córdoba: Publicaciones del Monte de Piedad y Caja de Ahorros de Cordoba, Cajasur, 1993;

Tomuschat, C., 'Die Charta der wirtschaftlichen Rechten und Pflichten der Staaten; zur Gestaltungskraft von Deklarationen der UNGeneralversammlung', *ZaöRVR* 1976, 444;

—— & Thouvenin, J-M. (éds), *The Fundamental Rules of the International Legal Order: Jus Cogens and Obligations Erga omnes*, Leiden: Nijhoff, 2006;

Tooke, J.D., *Just War in Aquinas and Grotius*, London: SPCK, 1965;

Triepel, H., *Völkerrecht und Landesrecht*, Leipzig: Hirschfeld, 1899;

—— & Brunet, R., *Droit international et droit interne*, Paris: Pedone, 1920;

Truyol y Serra, A., *Los principios del derecho publico en Francisco de Vitoria*, Madrid: Cultura Hispánica, 1946;

—— *Histoire du droit international public*, Paris: Economica, 1995;

Tuck, R., *Natural Rights Theories: Their Origins and Development*, Cambridge: CUP, 1979;

—— *The Rights of War and Peace: Political Thought and the International Order from Grotius to Kant,* Oxford, OUP, 1999;

Tunkin/Tounkine, G.I., *Droit international public: problèmes théoriques*, Paris: Pedone, 1965;

―― *Contemporary International Law,* Moscow: s.p., 1969;
―― *Theory of international law*, London: G. Allen & Unwin, 1974;
―― *Sila i pravo mezhdunarodnoe sisteme*, Moscow: s.p., 1983;
―― 'Politics, law and force in the inter-State system', *RCADI,* VII, 1989, 219;
Ulpian, *Libri ad edictum, In Justinian Digest*, see Watson;
Vallat, F., *International law and the practitioner*, Manchester: Manchester Univ. Press, 1966;
Valls, A., *Ethics in International Affairs: Theories and Cases*, Lanham: Rowman & Littlefield, 2000;
Valticos, N., 'Contrats entre des Etats et des personnes privées', *Institut de Droit international, Rapport, Annuaire* 1977 i 1, 132;
VanHoof, G., *Rethinking the Sources of International Law,* London: Kluwer, 1984;
Van Ittersum, M. J., *Profit and Principle: Hugo Grotius, Natural Rights Theories and the Rise of Dutch Power in the East Indies (1595-1615)*, Leiden & Boston: Brill, 2006;
Vanderpol, A., *Le droit de la guerre d'après les théologiens et canonistes du Moyen-Age*, Paris: Tralin, 1911;
―― *La guerre devant Christianisme*, Paris: Tralin, 1911;
Vasquez, J. A., 'The post-positivist debate: Reconstructing scientific inquiry and international relations theory after enlightenment's fall', in Booth, K. & Smith, S., eds., *International Relations Theory Today*, 217-240, Cambridge: Polity, 1995;
Vattel, E. de, *Le droit des gens, ou, Principes de la loi naturelle appliqués à la conduite & aux affaires des nations & des souverains*, Leiden: Aux dépenses de la Compagnie, 1758;
Vellas, P., *Droit international public. Institutions internationales, méthodologie, historique, sources, sujets de la société internationale, organisations internationales*, Paris: LGDJ, 1967;
Verdoodt, A., *Naissance et signification de la déclaration universelle des droits de l'homme*, Louvain: Société d'études morales, sociales et juridiques, 1964;

Verdross, A. V., *Die Einheit des rechtlichen Weltbildes auf Grundlage der Völkerrechtsverfassung*, Tübingen: Mohr Siebeck, 1923;
—— *Die Verfassung der Völkerrechtsgemeinschaft*, Vienna: Springer, 1926;
—— *Völkerrecht*, Berlin: J. Springer, 1937;
—— *Abendländische Rechtsphilosophie. Ihre Grundlagen und Hauptprobleme in geschichtlicher Schau*, Vienna: Springer, 1958;
—— '*Jus dispositivum* and *jus cogens* in international law', *AJIL* 1966 55;
—— 'Kann die Generalversammlung der Vereinten Nationen das Völkerrecht weiterbilden?' *ZaöRVR* 1966, 690;
—— *Die Quellen des universellen Völkerrechts*, Freiburg im Breisgau: Rombach, 1973;
—— & Simma, B., *Universelles Völkerrecht: Theorie und Praxis*, Berlin: Duncker Humblot, 1984;
Verhoeven, J. & Seidl-Hohenveldern, I., *Droit international*, Paris: Pedone, 1981;
Verwey, W., *The Establishment of a New International Economic Order and the Realization of the Right to Development and Welfare,* Geneva: s.p., 1980;
Verzijl, J. H. W., Heere, W.P., *et al.*, *International Law in Historical Perspective*, Leiden: Sijthoff, 1968;
Visscher, C. d., *Le droit international des communications: Cours professé à l'Institut des Hautes Etudes Internationales de Paris (1921 et 1923)*, Paris: Librairie Moderne A. Buyens, 1924;
—— *Théories et réalités en droit international public*, Paris: Pedone, 1953;
—— *Les effectivités du droit international public*, Paris: Pedone, 1967;
Villiger, M.E., *Customary International Law and Treaties: Manual on the Theory and Practice of the Interrelation of Sources*, The Hague: Kluwer, 2nd ed., 1997;
Vincent, R.J., *Non-Intervention and International Order*, Princeton: Princeton University Press, 1974;
—— *Human Rights and International Relations*, Cambridge: CUP, 1986;

Virally, M., 'La valeur juridiques des recommendations des organisations internationales', *AFDI,* 1956 66;

—— 'The sources of international law' in Sørensen, M., ed., *Manual of Public International Law*, London: Macmillan, 1968, 116;

Vismara, F., 'La prova di una pratica generale accettata come dirittonella prassi della Corte internazionale di giustizia', *Comunità Internazionale.*, 2000, 439;

Visvanatha, S. V., *International Law in ancient India*, London: Longmans, Green and Co., 1925;

Vitanyi, B., 'Les positions doctrinales concernant le sens de la notion de principles généraux de droit reconnus par les nations civilisées', 86 *RGDIP*, 1982, 46;

Voigt, M., *Das jus naturale, aequum et bonum und jus gentium der Römer*, Leipzig: Voight & Günther, 1856-1875;

Waldron, J., *Theories of Rights*, Oxford/New York: OUP, 1984;

—— 'Normative (or Ethical) Positivism', in Coleman, J., ed., *Hart's postscript: Essays on the Postscript to 'The Concept of Law'*, Oxford: OUP, 2001, 410;

Waluchow, W., *Inclusive Legal Positivism*, Oxford: OUP, 1994;

—— & Sciaraffa (éds.), *Philosophical Foundations of the Nature of Law*, Oxford: OUP, 2013;

Walz, G. A., *Wesen des Völkerrechts und Kritik der Völkerrechtsleugner*, Stuttgart: W. Kohlhammer, 1930;

Waltz, K. N., *Man, the State, and War; a theoretical analysis*, New York: Columbia University Press, 1959;

Walzer, M., *Just and Unjust Wars*, London: Allen Lane, 1978;

—— *Guerres justes et injustes*: *Argumentation morale avec exemples historiques*, Paris: Gallimard, 2006;

Watson, A., *Diplomacy: The Dialogue between States*, London: Methuen, 1982;

—— ed., *The Digest of Justinian*, Philadelphia: Univ. of Pennsylvania Press, 1985;

Watts, A., 'The International Court and the continuing customary international law of treaties' in Ando, N., ed., *Liber Amicorum Judge Shigeru Oda*, The Hague: Kluwer, 2002, 251;

Weber, C., *Simulating Sovereignty: Intervention, the State, and Symbolic Exchange*, Cambridge & New York: CUP, 1995;

Weber, A., *Die Krise des modernen Staatsgedankens in Europa*, Stuttgart: Deutsche Verlagsanstalt, 1925;

Weber, M., *Gesammelte politische Schriften*, ed. Winkelmann, Munich: Drei Masken Verlag, 1921;

—— 'The nature of social action' in Runciman, W.G., *Weber: Selections in Translation*, Cambridge: CUP, 1991;

Weckmann, L., *El pensamiento politico medieval y los origenes del derecho internacional*, México: Fondo de Cultura Económica, 1993;

Weil, P., 'Towards relative normativity in international law?', 77 *AJIL*, 1983, 413;

Weinrib, E.J., *The Idea of Private Law*, Oxford: OUP, 2013;

Weis, P., *Nationality and statelessness in international law*, London: Stevens, 1956;

Weiss, L., *States in the Global Economy: Bringing Domestic Institutions Back In*, Cambridge: CUP, 2003;

Wendt, A., 'Anarchy is what States make of it: The social construction of power politics', 46 *International Organisation*, 1992, 391;

—— 'The State as a person in international theory', 30 *Review of International Studies*, 2004, 289;

—— & Friedheim, D., 'Hierarchy under anarchy', 49 *International Organization*, 1995, 689;

Wengler, W., *Der Begriff des Politischen im internationalen Recht*, Tübingen: Mohr Siebeck, 1956;

—— *Völkerrecht*, Berlin: J. Springer, 1964;

—— 'Rechtsvertrag, Konsensus und Absichtserklärung im Völkerrecht', 31 *JZ* 1976, 193;

—— 'Public international law, Paradoxes of a legal order', 158 *RCADI*, 1977 v 13;

Westlake, J., *Chapters on the Principles of Internatonal Law,* Cambridge: CUP, 1894;

—— *International Law*, Cambridge: CUP, 1910;

Wheaton, H., *Elements of International Law.* London: Fellowes, 1836;

Whiteman, M. M., *Digest of international law*, Washington: Department of State Publications, 1963;

Widman, L., *De represaliis*, s. l., s. n., 1631;

Wigandus, J. D., *De amnistia,* Jena, s. n., 1571;

Wilde, J. d. & Wiberg, H., *Organized Anarchy in Europe: The Role of States and Intergovernmental Organizations*, London: Tauris Academic Studies, 1996;

Wolfke, K., *Great and Small Powers in International Law from 1814 to 1920:* Wrocław: Zakład Narodowy im. Ossolińskich, 1961;

Wright, H. F., *Medieval Internationalism: The Contribution of the Medieval Church to International Law and Peace,* London: Williams & Norgate, 1930;

—— *Catholic Founders of Modern International Law*, Washington: Catholic Univ. of America, 1934;

Wolfke, K., *Custom in Present International Law*, Dordrecht: Nijhoff, 2nd ed., 1993;

Xenakis, S., *International Norm Diffusion and the Development of Greek Policy Against Organised Crime (1989-2001)*, Oxford, OUP, 2006;

Yasseen, M., 'Réflexions sur la détermination du *jus cogens*', in Société française de droit international, Colloque, *L'élaboration du droit international public,* Paris: Pedone, 1974, 204;

Ying Shih Yü, 'Democracy, human rights and Confucian culture,' in *The Fifth Huang Hsing Foundation Hsueh Chun-tu Distinguished Lecture in Asian Studies*, Asian Studies Centre, St. Antony's College, University of Oxford, 2000;

Zamora, S., 'Voting in international economic organisations', *AJIL* 1980, 566;

Zemanek, K., *Das Vertragsrecht der internationaler Organisationen,* Vienna: Mohr Siebeck, 1957;

Ziegler, K.-H., 'Biblische Grundlagen des europäischen Völkerrechts', 86 *Zeitschrift der Savigny-Stiftung für Rechtsgeschichte: Kanonistische Abteilung*, Nr. 1, 2000;

Zimmer, G., *Gewaltsame territoriale Veränderungen und ihre völkerrechtliche Legitimation*, Berlin: Duncker & Humblot, 1971;

Zivier, E. R., *Die Nichtanerkennung im modernen Völkerrecht. Probleme staatlicher Willensäusserung*, Berlin: Berlin Verlag, 1967;

Zotiades, G. B., *International ius cogens: A Contribution to the Study of the Nature of International Law Norms*, Thessaloniki & Athens: P. Sallolas Brothers, 1968;

Zurbuchen, S., 1991, *Naturrecht und natürliche Religion. Zur Geschichte des Toleranzproblems von Samuel Pufendorf bis Jean-Jacques Rousseau*, Würzburg: Königshausen & Neumann, 1991.

Index

A

actors 16-18, 20, 29, 31, 34, 53-55, 57, 66-68, 71, 77, 87, 90-91, 98, 100, 103, 107-109, 116-117, 137-145, 169, 172, 178, 207-208, 212, 217, 224, 238, 258, 264, 267, 299-301, 314, 321, 350, 353, 368-369, 381, 388-391, 393, 396
    and creators 368, 388-90
    and persons 368, 389-390
    and subjects 17, 54, 57, 258, 353

acts
    acts of adoption 217, 304, 323, 366, 394
    acts of delegation 315
    acts of recognition 309, 324
    authoritative acts 315, 324-325, 327
    bilateral acts 328, 370
    contractual acts 315-316, 366
    current acts 333
    definition of a legal act 297-299
    extraordinary acts 332
    framework acts 147, 316, 331-333, 366, 370
    functional acts 330
    general acts 310
    individual acts 310-312
    intersecting patterns of acts 366
    multilateral acts 329, 366
    operative acts 124, 265, 307, 325, 327, 366
    parallel acts 309, 317, 319, 321-323, 328, 332, 366, 370
    permissive acts 304, 314
    promissory acts 317, 322, 328, 330
    responsive acts 308-309, 370, 378

statement acts 315, 366-367
structural acts 306
theory of 'acts' 217, 272, 297
transient acts 332
written acts 330
verbal acts 330
types 306-333
typology of acts 305, 368
    according to participation 312-314, 324
    according to form 326-329
    according to form of consent 315-325
    according to immediacy 307-310
    according to normativity 310-312
    according to number of authors 326-329
    according to solemnity 329-331
    according to State consent 312-326
    according to State control 314-315
    according to substance 306-312
aliens 157, 249-251
    protection of 249-250
assertions, competing 27-53
assessment of the legal effect of acts 366-373

Aquinas 37, 49, 56, 60, 186, 215, 361, 363
aggression 211, 213, 227-228, 231, 235, 250
allegiance 95, 128, 257, 314, 381
Anzilotti 28
Anglo-Saxon 32-33, 44-45, 55, 170, 259, 295, 298, 353
    dominance 71-73
    Judges 32, 55, 199, 230
    system 45, 67, 71-73, 75, 161-163, 199, 207, 328, 365
Antigone 35
apartheid 49, 90, 92, 102-103, 120, 129, 133, 144, 218, 220, 231, 233, 247, 249, 359, 361, 392
apportionment 288, 294, 306, 393
arbitration 118, 148, 154, 162, 168-169, 181, 188, 192, 194, 207, 209, 229, 252, 254, 280-282, 286-287
Aristophanes 50, 372
Aristotle 36-37, 215, 248
audiatur et altera pars 185, 190, 193, 252
Austin 43, 44, 48-49, 136
Australia 45, 72, 92, 360

B

Bacon 42
Bâle-Mulhouse Airport 113

bias 43, 146, 190, 193, 200, 252
belligerents 133, 387
blocking statutes 175
borders 120, 255, 421
Brierly 40-41, 81, 260, 290, 375
British North Borneo
    Company 109
British Petroleum 114, 288
British South African
    Company 109
broadcasts 264-265

C
Canada 45, 72, 92
Catalonia 95-96
Christian
    doctrine of natural law 65,
        63
    writers 37
Christianity 63
civilised
    States and PCIJ/ICJ 85, 248,
        343
classes 28, 98-100, 152
classification of rules 152-153
climate change 144, 239, 241
codes of behavior 323
codification 320-321, 347
community 30-31, 54, 59, 82, 116,
    135-136, 154, 166, 226-227,
    283, 310, 329, 335, 338, 352,
    354, 382-383
        or society? 135-136

comity 124, 151, 153, 158, 163,
    170-175, 177, 179, 189,
        definitione 122, 158
        and Acts of State 175-177
        and extraterritoriality 172,
            174, 178-180
        and jurisdiction 158,
            172-175
        and municipal law 171
        and public policy 175-177
        and refusal to hear cases 175
        and public policy 175-177
        as a link between public
            and private
            international law 177-180
Comte 42-43
conciliation 294
conflict of laws 142, 156, 158-160,
    162, 164, 171-173, 175
common areas
    non-appropriation 209
Commonwealth 60
    British 45, 92-94
    of Dominica 92
communications 99, 111, 183,
    247, 262-263, 274, 283, 306,
    313, 372, 393
        duty to warn 197, 242,
            244-245, 259, 262-264,
            266, 270, 323, 373
Confucius 35, 37-39, 56, 66
    Analects of 38
consent 74, 80, 168, 180-182, 207,
    213, 232, 237, 259, 266, 269,

274-276, 278, 296, 298, 304,
    307, 311-316, 318, 320-322,
    324-325, 327, 329-331,
    333-334, 367-368, 371, 373,
    376, 378-379, 390-392, 394-398
    abstract consent 74, 275,
        315, 325, 327, 368, 390
    continuous consent 316
    form of consent 147
consequential rules 148, 169, 183,
    237, 262, 266, 288-289, 294,
    379, 393
consuls 250, 256
contacts 265, 271, 277, 304, 306,
    312-313, 373
    rules on mutual
        contacts 259, 373
continuous consent see: consent
constitutive document 30, 83-84,
    261, 355, 368, 390
customary law
    another way of producing
        'rules' 334-366
    fallacies of 349-354
    true version of 354-358
convenience 147, 171, 243, 315,
    392
core problem,
    of international law 27-145
correction
    and penalties 289- 292
Courts 17-19, 30, 32, 45, 71-73,
    117-120, 141, 148, 153, 161,
    163, 167, 169, 173-178, 181,
    189, 191-192, 194, 196, 200,
    202, 204, 206, 209-210, 214,
    224-226, 230, 241, 252-253,
    272, 280, 282-284, 295-296,
    324, 334-340, 343, 346,
    350-351, 357-358, 364
Croatia 92, 98, 223
Cyprus 84-85
    Constitution of Northern
        Cyprus 85-87

D

Danzig 84, 91, 101, 141
de jure gestionis 116, 277-279,
    393
de jure imperii
de jure privatorum 124, 279
delegation 141
    delegated legislation 315
democracy 92, 94-95, 102, 300,
    302, 331, 392, 394
    and sovereignty 128,
        258-259
Denmark 52, 286, 318-319, 326,
    355
diplomatic law 64, 250
diplomats 157, 163, 170, 173, 176,
    214, 229, 252, 302, 356, 369,
    372, 377, 393
    immunity of 58, 80, 250-251
    privileges 110, 129
    protection of 250-251

disputes 148, 162, 192, 198, 223, 237, 280, 372
distributive rules 254-258
diversity
    of material rules 181, 183-184
doctrine of international relevance 76, 153
dominance of Anglo-Saxon ideas 32, 71-73, 230
dualism 167
due process 190, 193, 252
duty 39, 64, 103, 126, 132, 147, 171, 209, 214, 226, 229, 232, 239, 240, 242, 244, 251, 253, 260, 289, 293, 323, 372, 374, 380, 385, 394
    to cooperate 266-267
    to share? 255, 259, 267-270, 274, 295, 323, 378, 379
    to warn 197, 242, 244-245, 262-265, 270, 323, 373

E

East India Companies 109-110
ECOSOC 88-89
entrenching rules 259, 266, 288-289, 392, 395, 397
environment 23, 58, 90, 133, 144, 237, 239-241, 243-245, 302, 390, 397,
    and acid rain 239, 244
    and climate change 144, 239, 241
    and pollution 58, 173, 188, 237, 239, 241-243, 377
    and prophylactic rules 244-245
    and resources 239-240
    harm to 259
    protection of 90, 239, 390
    threats to 244-245
environmental protection 239-244
Epictetus 63
Equality 171, 188, 189, 203, 249, 260, 269, 295, 372
equitable use of water 240, 268
equity 112, 268, 362
erga omnes 51, 182, 199-200, 211, 225, 227-228, 230, 232, 385
estoppel 207, 318, 328
exhortations of restraint 311
ethical standards 212
ethics 36, 38, 47, 56, 60, 64-66, 192, 205, 212-213, 216, 218, 231, 234, 246, 355, 358, 360, 362
    and intrinsic law 212
ex aequo et bono 189, 198
European Central Inland Transport 113
European Space Agency (ESA) 113, 124
Eurochémie 114
Eurofima 114

F

force
   prohibition of 234-238
formation of rules 53, 70, 258, 299, 334, 370
foreseeability 31, 33, 264
forum shopping 161, 175
flags of convenience 243
framework 28-29, 48, 57, 109, 111, 128, 147, 150, 154, 228, 246, 267, 270, 272-273, 294, 298, 300, 303-304, 306, 308, 314, 316, 331-332, 350, 366, 368, 370, 390-391, 392-393
   law as 53-54
France 49, 71, 81, 93, 106, 113, 142, 143, 153, 225, 228
freedom of expression 96, 247, 249, 264

G

General Assembly 73, 151, 199, 209, 232, 235, 247, 268, 309, 311, 320-321, 323, 349, 379, 389
general practice 198, 335-336, 340
   for a long time 347-348
   meaning 340-342
   of 'all States'? 342-343
   of 'civilised States' 343-345
   of 'numerous States' 345-346
general principles 22, 57, 75, 85, 148, 166, 176, 180-181, 188-189, 195-210
   formal 181, 202-210
   nature of 196-200
   maxims and 181, 200-201
   substantive 201-202
genocide 18, 133, 188, 197, 211-212, 218, 227-228, 230, 245, 247-248, 300, 346, 359-360, 383-384
   and *jus cogens* 60
Germany 71, 81, 86, 113, 129, 153, 206, 355
global warming 144, 239, 241
Golden Rule
   and reciprocity 22, 65-66, 380, 397
good faith 206-207
Gotland 105
graduated scale of presumption of consent 304, 313, 322, 330, 334, 371, 378, 392, 394-395
Gratian 65
groups
   harm to 234-239
Guadeloupe 93
Guidelines 33, 117-118, 163, 216, 271, 308

H

harm 184-185, 188, 208-211, 253, 305, 371
   prohibition of 25, 57-62, 66, 182, 210-211, 213-214,

231, 233-245, 364, 367, 388, 397
Hegel 58
Hobbes 39, 58, 65
Holy See 84
human rights 18, 58, 68, 79, 88, 95, 101, 116-117, 119-122, 126, 129-133, 138, 140, 144, 165-169, 172-173, 176-177, 193, 204, 213, 215, 219-221, 224, 228, 230, 233, 245-350, 264, 276, 301-303, 345, 356, 361, 367, 377, 385, 387, 389-390
   collective 95, 97
   individual 129, 131, 156, 165, 250, 302
humanitarian rules 58, 213, 249, 372
hypothetical goal 62, 152, 184, 210, 214, 217, 223, 233, 236-237, 245, 268, 271, 288, 307, 318, 358, 378, 381, 392, 397

I
ICC, see International Criminal Court
ICJ, see International Court of Justice
ICTY 76, 130, 230, 345-346
identification of relevant law 73-76

identification of rules 144
immunity 80, 130, 157, 163, 238, 251, 305-306, 313, 378
   diplomatic immunity 58, 80, 170, 176, 214, 229, 252, 309, 356, 369-370, 377, 393, 395
   privileges of immunity 110, 232
   rules on 250-251, 371
   State immunity 172-173, 278, 341
imputation 78, 80, 100, 105, 116, 128, 208-209, 243, 259, 303, 340, 352
   international personality 79
   and imputation 79-80, 340
independence 84-85, 91-94, 96-97, 134, 221-223, 235, 260, 263, 275, 290, 316
India 45, 72
individuals
   as subjects 125-133
   prohibition of harm to 245
INMARSAT 18, 69, 124
insurgents 133
Institutes 18, 78, 107, 156, 272, 276, 314, 341, 354, 368, 390
inter-governmental
   organisations 18-19, 22, 29, 68-70, 72, 81, 86-87, 90-91, 108, 124, 129, 132, 141, 142, 154-155, 196-197, 200, 204, 208, 212, 214, 223, 230-231,

237, 248, 253, 255-257, 264,
275, 283, 293, 295-296, 306,
323, 325, 352, 372, 384
integration 115, 136, 183, 271,
272-273, 325
institutionalization 295, 393
   of functions 272
internal decisions 62
internal law 131, 144, 157, 160,
165-170, 179, 195, 392
international companies 88, 107,
112-115, 121-122, 229, 389
international law 16-23, 27-34,
40, 43-44, 46, 48-49, 52-53,
56, 58-59, 62, 64, 67-75,
77-90, 92-93, 95, 98-105,
108, 110-112, 114-121,
124-166, 168-171, 175-181,
186, 188-190, 195-200, 202,
205-212, 214-215, 217-219,
224-235, 240-241, 246-248,
250, 252-263, 268-270, 272,
276-286, 288-294, 297,
299-303, 308-309, 312,
315-322, 327, 329, 335-342,
344-345, 347, 349-354,
358-360, 362-364, 366, 369,
371, 374-376, 379-389,
391-394, 396-398
   criteria of 143-145
   and internal law 157, 160,
165-170, 392
International Chamber of
Commerce 118, 287

International Court of Justice
(ICJ) 64, 73, 75, 85-86,
94, 140, 148, 179, 189-190,
198-199, 209
International Criminal Court
(ICC) 75, 117, 281, 351
international legal
personality 77-79, 107, 116,
126, 128, 300
International Maritime
Organisation (IMO) 69, 310
International Mosul Company 113
international Orders 105-107
international society 16-18, 20-23,
27, 29, 31, 34, 48-50, 53-59,
61-64, 66-70, 73-75, 77, 80,
85-88, 91-93, 95, 97, 100,
102-103, 106-108, 110-111,
123-125, 127-129, 132,
135-140, 144-147, 150-151,
154, 159, 166, 169-170,
178, 180-184, 186, 189,
195, 203, 207-208, 210-212,
214, 216-218, 223-224, 226,
228-229, 231, 333-234, 237,
239-240, 242, 250-253, 255,
259-261, 265-268, 272-273,
280, 283-285, 287, 291, 293,
295-297, 299-300, 302-306,
308, 312-314, 316, 323-324,
326-327, 329-330, 333-334,
345-346, 348, 351-354,
356-357, 360, 362-365,

367-371, 373, 375-376,
378-386, 388-398
interpretative resolutions
intervention 36, 58, 61-62, 133,
167, 222-223, 234-236, 238,
245, 291, 295
intrinsic
    intrinsic law 57, 363
        definition 57
        and *jus cogens* 224
        and natural law 363-366
    intrinsic rules 180-253, 383,
387-388, 397
Isocrates 63
Italy 71, 113, 153, 206

J

Jellinek 28, 44, 260
joint ventures 121, 123
judicial rules 295-296, 310
judge-made law 31-32, 45, 55,
71-73, 199, 295
jurisdiction 72, 118-119, 155,
157-158, 162-165, 172,
174-175, 183, 192-193, 235,
240, 257, 283,
    and nationality 257-258
jus cogens 62, 64, 73, 78, 117,
141, 168, 180, 182, 199,
224-234, 246-247, 254, 316,
356, 358, 364, 383-385
    and genocide see: genocide

and prophylactic
    rules 224-234
and slavery 228
jus gentium 36-37, 39, 41, 126,
165, 345, 382
jus positum 44
jus quia jussum 44
just war 59-61
    requisites 60-61
    and Aquinas 60-61
justice 30, 43, 52, 76, 136, 177,
190, 193, 205, 210, 216-217,
252, 267, 281, 282, 346, 350,
365

K

Kant 40, 54, 65
Kelsen 27-28, 43-44, 82, 185-187,
190, 290, 292, 317, 375
Kiobel Case 120
Kong Zi 38
Kurds 96-97, 222

L

land-slide votes 349
latent subjects 388
Lateran Treaty 84
law making 31-32, 74-75, 87, 108,
124, 133, 137, 143-144, 149,
151, 164, 210, 264-265, 273,
275-276, 278, 282, 298, 307,

310, 315-317, 320, 322, 325, 327-328, 353, 368, 389, 391
legal personality 31, 77, 79, 86-87, 98, 100, 104-105, 107, 116, 126, 128, 258, 300, 354
Leibniz 40
lex mercatoria 124, 164, 181, 202, 209, 277, 279, 282, 285, 295, 393
lex posterior 188
lex specialis 188
li
    and honour 38
    concept of 38, 39
liberation movements 29, 103-104
logical necessity 195, 217, 312, 377, 395
Lun Yu 38

M

Majorities 92, 102-103
Manning 4, 135, 259, 376
marine pollution 242-243
Martens 126, 128, 132, 344-345, 354
Marx 215
maxims 18, 21-22, 41, 57, 169, 180-181, 197, 200-202, 205, 209, 212, 225, 233, 251-253, 304-305, 312, 333, 351, 354, 363-364, 367, 372, 377, 384, 387, 392, 394-395
    compulsory 163, 251
    conditional 187-188
    consequential 177, 190-194, 372
    contingent 188-189, 255, 295, 359, 372
    essential 57, 202, 365
    inherent 185, 377
    origin of 195
    stabilising 189-190, 275
McDougal 31-32, 70, 129, 308
Mill, John Stuart 65-66
minimum standards of human rights 250
minorities 91-92, 101, 102-103, 133, 246
MNCs, see multinationals
Modalities 34, 55, 237, 372, 397
monists
    versus dualists 27
multinationals 18, 29, 67, 114-119, 121, 123, 160, 280, 299, 301, 314, 391
municipal law 27-28, 89, 107, 118, 123-124, 137-138, 143, 149, 165, 167, 171, 277-279, 290, 393

N

nationality 143, 162-164, 206, 257, 314
national law 28, 101, 108, 118, 123-124, 130-132, 141-143,

156, 162, 167-168, 215, 286, 288, 311, 358
   criteria of 142-143
national private bodies 109-112, 279
national public bodies 108-109
nations 19, 28, 40, 52, 59, 81, 85, 110, 114, 119, 137, 146, 148-149, 165, 170-171, 179, 196, 198, 207, 209, 222-223, 238, 250, 260-262, 269-270, 273, 282, 305, 336-339, 344-345, 354, 364, 370, 382
Nation-State 64, 97, 370
natural justice 190, 193, 252
natural law 30-31, 34-42, 44, 46-52, 55-56, 64-66, 130, 135-136, 186-188, 193, 205, 207, 370, 382
   allergy to 358-363
   correct concept of 363-365
ne bis in idem 193
negative practice 346
nemo judex in causa sua 185, 190, 193, 200, 252
New Haven,
   School of 29-32, 34, 68, 108, 163
new theory 16-17, 19, 21-22, 34, 53, 70, 376
New Zealand 45, 72
NGOs 67-68, 87-90, 107, 166, 276, 314, 323, 340, 349, 361, 390-391

nihilists 47, 215, 358
non-governmental
   organisations 87-91, 108, 128
non-recognition 386
non-State actors 53, 67, 116, 369, 393
Norway 52, 167, 282, 318-319, 326, 355
Nuclear 49, 90, 111, 144, 223-224, 231, 237-238, 242, 244, 352
   nuclear attack 231
   nuclear pollution 242, 244
   nuclear weapons 144, 223-224, 231, 237, 352
      illegality of use 106, 237, 237
nullum crimen 187, 202-203

O

obligation 373-383
   Consent 378-379
   logical necessity 377
   reciprocity: The Golden Rule
   social necessity 377-378
   variability of the basis of
      obligation 51, 244, 376-383
   traditional
      solutions 374-376
opinio juris 334-335, 348-349
   meaning 335
   whose? 348-349, 213
ordre public 205

organisations
> international 73, 85-88, 103, 107-108, 112, 123-125, 144-146, 148, 154, 164, 168, 199, 210, 251, 265-266, 272-273, 275-276, 279, 282, 292, 301, 303, 306-307, 310, 319-320, 322-324, 327, 331, 349, 353, 360, 387, 390-391
> inter-governmental see: inter-governmental organisations
> non-governmental see: non-governmental organisations

operative rules 130, 366-367

P

Pacta sunt servanda 44, 185-187, 189, 367, 375
Palestine 104
parallel declarations 321
par in parem 189
participation
> active participation 313-315, 329, 370
> basic participation 312-314, 324, 366-367, 370, 394
> enhanced participation 314, 366
> passive participation 304, 312-313, 330

peaceful settlement 237, 372
penalties 294, 296
> rules on 296

peremptory norms 64, 78, 168, 199, 225, 227-228, 302
personality 18-19, 22, 31, 58, 67-70, 76-79, 81, 86-89, 91, 98, 100-101, 104-108, 111-112, 115-117, 121, 123-130, 132, 134, 223, 258, 273, 300, 340, 354, 374, 388
> personality and imputation 79-80, 100, 105, 128, 340

pirates 67, 134
> and terrorists 67, 134

Pittacus 63
Plato 35-36, 46, 63, 215, 248, 372
PLO 103-104
Poland 251
Pollution 58, 144, 173, 188, 237, 239, 241-244, 318, 377
pools of norms 21, 398
ports
> closure 236, 259, 263-264
> duty to warn 236, 259, 263-264

positivism 42-46, 49, 51, 136, 186, 190, 365
positivists 34, 45-49, 51-52, 186, 212, 260, 351, 359, 364
> extreme positivists 260

precedents 32, 71, 75, 230
prescription 17, 21, 121, 213, 233, 256, 263, 275, 280, 308, 355, 374, 396-397
preferences 276, 323
pre-standards 108, 275-276, 323, 369, 389
primary rules 325, 327-328
private companies 110, 123-125
private international law 155, 177, 153-164, 177-180, 277, 279, 286
programmatic declarations 226, 271, 277, 307-308, 310, 332
prohibition of force 231, 238
prohibition of harm see: harm
promotional rules 242, 265-271, 274, 294, 304-305, 307, 314, 368, 373, 378-379, 393, 395-397
property
    right of 208, 248, 284
prophylactic rules 22, 55, 76, 165, 168, 181-184, 199, 253, 261, 274, 276, 288-289, 300, 304-305, 312, 316, 322, 333, 346, 352, 364, 371-372, 377, 384, 392, 394-395
    and ethics 212-224
    and harm to groups 234-239
    and harm to the environment 244-245
proportionality 204

protection 60, 90, 101, 106, 121, 128, 132, 170-171, 175-176, 211-212, 214, 227-228, 233, 239, 245, 249-250, 257, 290, 302, 309, 341-342, 345, 354, 382, 390, 393
    of the hypothetical goal 185, 214
public and private law 153-165, 277-279
public policy 175
Pufendorf 39

Q
Qui dixit 191, 194

R
reciprocity (see also Golden Rule) 22, 171, 174, 251, 253, 356, 370-371, 377, 379-380, 395, 397
    as basis of obligation 174, 379-390
    rule of 22, 57, 62-66, 356, 397
recognition 324
recommendations 275
Red Cross 18, 69, 89-90, 134
Relevance 22, 76, 124, 153, 155, 161, 168, 263, 273, 299, 301-303, 316-318, 368, 387, 393

international 49, 153, 155, 161, 168, 301-303, 316-317, 393
    doctrine of 76, 153
regimes 83, 91, 103, 141, 145-148, 171, 256, 260-261, 263, 266, 316, 332, 369
    meaning 145-148
    further regimes 263, 266, 274, 316, 366, 370, 379
Reisman 30-31, 129
referendum 95-97, 222, 234
Reformation 42
relativism 44, 47
reprisals 292, 385
res judicata 193, 200
res communis 209
reserved domain 57, 62, 78, 144, 168, 172, 176, 254, 301
resources 58, 122, 139, 169, 208, 239-240, 243, 268-270, 305
    and the environment 58, 239-240, 243
    use of 239, 269-270
responsibility 78-80, 103, 105, 204, 208-209, 240, 249-250, 259, 262, 300, 363, 382, 385, 389
retroactivity 203
right of property 140, 176-177, 248, 284
    private property 140, 176, 248, 284
Right to Protect (R2P) 238

Rule of law 75, 203, 265, 285, 339
rules
    and decisions 182-183
    and norms 182-183
    and principles 182-183
    'filling-in' rules 209, 280-282
    formal rules 162, 181, 197, 201, 225, 265, 277
    of law
    operative rules see: *operative rules*
    primary rules see: *primary rules*
    substantive rules 21, 110, 118, 124, 158, 162, 177, 181, 197, 200, 202, 210, 268, 277, 279-280, 283, 286-288, 294

S

sanctions 48, 50, 103, 119, 121, 136, 155, 169, 187, 248, 262, 289-294, 379, 386
    and use of force 292-292
    objects of 291-292
    subjects of 291-292
    two-fold nature of 291
Scelle 28, 44, 125, 127, 150, 272, 290, 295, 376
Scotland 97, 242-243
self-defence 58-59, 236, 238, 293

self-determination 91-96, 102, 221-222, 234, 302, 394
Seneca 63
Sextus Pythagorean 63
share 91, 162, 189, 222, 255, 263, 266-270, 274, 295, 298, 323, 378-379
    duty to share 255, 263, 266-267, 269, 274, 295, 323, 379
shipowners
    liability of 243
Shevardnadze 131, 361
sic utere 188
social classes 28, 98-100
social necessity 217, 244, 262, 265, 274, 312-313, 368-369, 377-379, 384, 395, 397
society 16-18, 20-23, 27-31, 34, 48-50, 53-59, 61-64, 66-70, 73-77, 80, 85-88, 91-93, 95, 97, 99-100, 102-103, 106-108, 110-111, 123-125, 127-129, 132, 135-140, 144-147, 150-151, 154, 159, 166, 169-170, 178, 180-184, 186, 189, 193, 195, 203, 207-208, 210-212, 214, 216-218, 223-224, 226, 228-229, 231, 233-234, 237, 239-240, 242, 248, 250-253, 255, 258-261, 265-268, 272-274, 283, 285, 287, 290-291, 293, 295-297, 299-300, 302-306, 308, 312-314, 316, 323, 326-327, 329-330, 333-335, 336, 345-346, 348, 351, 352-353
    or community 135-136
Socrates 62
slavery 212, 218-219, 230-231, 233, 245
    and *jus cogens* 232-233
    Anti-Slavery Convention 219
sociologically necessary norms 56, 66, 387
society 135
    or community? 135
solidarity 389
    as basis of obligation 214, 229, 380
    notion of 389
    solidarity, plea of 253
source of law 75, 149-151
    hierarchy 149
    meaning 149-151
    supplementary 75
sovereignty 28, 44, 98-100, 102, 105-106
    and democracy 258-259
South Africa 49, 92, 102-103, 120, 129, 144, 220, 232, 283, 294
Spiropoulos 125, 290
St. Augustine 37, 60-61
St. Thomas, see Aquinas
stabilising rules 55, 253, 274, 288, 294, 304-305, 313, 322, 324, 377, 380, 393, 395

standards 108, 132, 212, 218, 242-244, 249-250, 275-276, 323, 366, 389, 391, 396
   pre-standards 108, 275-276, 323, 369, 389
   provisional standards 276, 323, 389, 391
States 16-22, 29-32, 34, 39-41, 45-50, 53, 55-58, 61-63, 67-72, 74, 76-77, 86, 90-92, 97-99, 102, 104, 107-112, 114, 116, 119-120, 122, 125, 128-129, 131-133, 135, 138-139, 141-143, 145-149, 154-156, 160-161, 164-180, 183, 189-190, 193-195, 198, 201, 204, 209, 222, 213-217, 221-224, 226-228, 232, 325-240, 242-244, 248-254, 258-270, 272-279, 283-184, 286, 290, 292-294, 296, 300-307, 309, 311-321, 323-325, 327-329, 331, 335-336, 338-345, 347-350, 353-354, 356-358, 360-361, 338-345, 347-350, 353-354, 356-358, 360-361, 363, 365-367, 374-375, 377-381, 383, 385, 387-398
   Equality 171, 189, 203, 249, 260, 372
   hallmarks of State 83-85, 258, 300
   sovereignty 44, 98-99, 128, 171-173, 176, 189, 319, 341

State-paradigm 77, 145, 353-354, 391
   drift away from 77
statute theory and personal law 161-162
Suárez 39, 381
subjects
   of international law 17
subsidiarity 204
suprema potestas 254
Sweden 52, 114, 159, 167, 215-216, 309, 358-359
Syria 62, 97, 236

T

Telos 36-37, 43
terminology 16, 30, 136, 147, 154, 275, 285, 298, 307, 372
   need of accurate 372-373
territorial bond 355-356
terrorism 164, 169, 300
terrorists 18, 90, 165, 169, 231, 234, 254, 363, 388
   and pirates 67, 134
Thales 63
torture 133-134, 220-221, 230, 247, 283, 360
   Torture Convention 221, 247
traditionalists 29, 87, 320, 342, 350, 359, 371
transit 173, 176, 262-263
treaties

formal rules on 265-266
Trieste 84, 105, 147
Turkey 84-85, 97, 194, 218

U
Unifying rules 271-377
unilateral acts 149, 317, 319,
   326-327
    declarations
Universities 16, 71, 107, 109, 160,
   216
UN Covenants on Human
   Rights 119
United Kingdom 20, 59, 73, 97,
   110, 113, 200, 206, 220, 230,
   236, 245, 261, 284, 293, 355
United States 19, 30, 32, 45,
   64, 72, 119-120, 122, 129,
   138, 142-143, 166, 171, 176,
   178-179, 190, 193, 201, 214,
   229, 232, 236-238, 250,
   252-253, 264, 274, 283, 293,
   316, 335-336, 339, 360, 372
    Alien Tort Statute 119

V
Verdross 27, 148, 196, 209, 215,
   255, 278, 292, 375
Versailles
   Treaty of 84, 101
Vessels 243
   and piracy 134

W
Wales 97
Wang-Yang 39
War 18, 39, 49, 55, 59-62, 68,
   76, 89-90, 94-96, 101-106,
   124-130, 132-134, 136, 138,
   165, 167, 188, 217-130,
   132-134, 136, 138, 165, 167,
   188, 218, 220, 223, 225, 231,
   233-238, 246, 249, 255, 279,
   292, 302, 327, 339-340, 342,
   344-346, 348, 351-353, 357,
   359, 377, 388-389, 397
   Law of War 49, 55, 59, 61,
      89-90, 95-96, 102, 104,
      106, 130, 134, 165, 167,
      188, 218, 220, 223, 225,
      231, 233-234, 237-238,
      246, 249, 292, 340, 342,
      345-346, 353, 357, 359,
      377
   war crimes 130, 132, 167,
      188, 249, 302, 342, 351
   war crimes tribunals 130,
      167, 249, 342, 351
   war criminals 18, 67-68,
      127, 130, 133, 165, 388
warn
   duty to 244-245, 262-265
   closure of ports see: ports
   environmental
      danger 244-245